SUBTLE SEXISM

Nijole V. Benokraitis

SUBTLE SEXISM

Current Practice and Prospects for Change

SAGE Publications
International Educational and Professional Publisher
Thousand Oaks London New Delhi

For information address:

SAGE Publications, Inc.
2455 Teller Road
Thousand Oaks, California 91320
E-mail: order@sagepub.com

SAGE Publications Ltd.
6 Bonhill Street
London EC2A 4PU
United Kingdom

SAGE Publications India Pvt. Ltd.
M-32 Market
Greater Kailash I
New Delhi 110 048 India

Printed in the United States of America

Library of Congress Cataloging-in-Publication Data

Main entry under title:

Subtle sexism : current practices and prospects for change / Nijole
V. Benokraitis, editor.
p.. cm.
Includes bibliographical references and index.
ISBN 0-7619-0385-2 cloth: acid-free paper).—ISBN
0-7619-0386-0 (pbk. : acid-free paper)
1. Sexism. 2. Sexual harassment of women. I. Benokraitis,
Nijole V. (Nijole Vaicaitis)
HQ1237.S83 1997
305.3—dc20 96-35662

97 98 99 00 01 02 03 10 9 8 7 6 5 4 3 2 1

Acquiring Editors:	Peter Labella, Alex Schwartz
Editorial Assistants:	Frances Borghi, Jessica Crawford
Production Editor:	Michèle Lingre
Production Assistant:	Denise Santoyo
Typesetter/Designer:	Danielle Dillahunt
Indexer:	Teri Greenberg
Cover Designer:	Lesa Valdez
Print Buyer:	Anna Chin

Contents

Preface

Much of the openly blatant sexism in this country has decreased because of federal and state laws against overt discrimination. As one of my friends, a nurse with 25 years' experience, recently observed: "It's nice to go to work and know that most of the [male] patients won't be grabbing your breasts every time you bend over or pinching your butt every time you turn your back." This doesn't mean that all blatant sexism has disappeared, however. In fact, and as Chapter 1 shows, such large corporations as Mitsubishi have spent millions of dollars fighting sexual harassment charges rather than the harassment itself.

Subtle sexism, which is just below the surface and is often not noticed because it is accepted as "normal" and customary, has replaced much of the blatant sex discrimination of the past. Some subtle sexism is still disguised as "tradition." Many people were very angry, for example, when the Supreme Court ruled in June 1996 that Virginia Military Institute's exclusion of women was unconstitutional and instructed the Institute to accept women or lose its state funding. Many alumni and others decried the decision as violating a "venerable tradition." Writing for the majority opinion in *United*

States v. Virginia (1996), however, Justice Ruth Bader Ginsburg emphasized that it is illegal for the government to impose "artificial constraints on an individual's opportunity" and to "create or perpetuate the legal, social, and economic inferiority of women" (116 S. Ct. 2264, 135 L.Ed.2d 735). Much subtle sex discrimination that perpetuates and reinforces women's inferiority continues, is pervasive, and constitutes one of the most serious problems facing U.S. society today.

The purpose of this reader, then, is to sensitize readers to the widespread prevalence of subtle sexism and to suggest how such practices can be changed. Part One, "The Continuing Significance of Sexism," shows that sex discrimination, including subtle sexism, is robust and thriving. This section summarizes the various types of sex discrimination (blatant, subtle, covert) that women still encounter on a daily basis and explores subtle processes in our everyday interactions. Part Two, "Subtle Sexism in Organizational Settings," focuses on subtle sexism that is both intentional and unintentional. This section begins with a chapter on "good natured" but stereotypical perceptions of Latinas that limit their opportunities in the workplace and shows how both intentional and unintentional subtle sexism excludes women from engineering, discourages many men from seeking jobs in child care professions, and diminishes morale and productivity in the military. Part Three, "Subtle Sexism as Social Control," examines how subtle sexism, innocent and normal though it may seem, reinforces and encourages stereotypes about women's and men's roles. This section begins with an examination of how black women, especially, are controlled and treated as outsiders by both white and black men and women. Other chapters show how women are manipulated or exploited (sometimes unintentionally and sometimes purposely) by family therapists, the courts, and corrections systems. Some of the practices may not be maliciously motivated; however, the results are discriminatory and demeaning. In Part Four, "How to Change Subtle Sexism Practices," the contributors offer suggestions—based on their own or others' experiences—on changing subtle sexism practices. These recommendations range from individual to societal levels. Although many of the earlier chapters also incorporate change-oriented analyses, Part Four is devoted, exclusively, to this issue.

The contributors and I have prepared this reader specifically for students. Every chapter is eminently readable and accessible to both undergraduate and graduate students regardless of discipline. *Subtle Sexism: Current Practices and Prospects for Change* does not presume that students (or faculty) are already familiar with the literature and research on either sex discrimination in general or subtle sexism in particular. We tried to ensure that each chapter is as "student friendly" as possible. The conceptual and methodological approaches are traditional, but there is as little academic jargon as possible. Where the contributors have used sophisticated statistical analyses, they present the results in an engaging and readable manner.

This reader can be used in courses in social work, women's studies, gender roles, political science, public administration, marriage and the family, business administration, communications, criminal justice, social problems, and human resources because the chapters address topics that are germane to all of these disciplines. We hope that *Subtle Sexism: Current Practices and Prospects for Change* will be a catalyst for stimulating class discussions and will encourage students (and faculty) to view gender inequality through wider lenses.

Acknowledgments

I am grateful to the following subscribers on WMST-L, Women's Studies List (Joan Korenman, moderator/list owner), for providing examples of subtle sexism that are cited in Chapter 1 and some of the section introductions: Mary Beth Ahlum, Nebraska Wesleyan University; Barrie Bondurant, Randolph-Macon Women's College; Margaret Duncombe, Colorado College; Tina Eager, Mid-Kent College of Higher and Further Education (United Kingdom); Tracey Hurd, Brown University; Nancy Howard, Central Washington University; Lisa Jadwin, St. John Fisher College; Barbara Rodman, University of North Texas; and Leah Ulansey, Johns Hopkins University. At the University of Baltimore, Regina Bento, Sue Briggs, and Lynn Collins offered valuable suggestions on drafts of the first chapter. In addition, scarcely a week goes by without finding something about sex discrimination in my mailbox from Sue.

The College of Liberal Arts at the University of Baltimore granted a sabbatical leave that facilitated the preparation of the manuscript. I am grateful to Amy Womaski and Sanjoo Modi for their research help and to Linda Fair, secretary in the Division of Criminology, Criminal Justice, and Social Policy, for her administrative assistance. Finally, I thank J. Alex Schwartz, acquisitions editor, and his staff at Sage for their encouragement throughout this project. Jessica Crawford, editorial assistant, and Lisa Bright, promotion manager, were always efficient and responsive. I am especially grateful to Michèle Lingre, production editor, and Kate Peterson, copy editor, for their unflappable and intelligent handling of the myriad tasks involved in producing this book.

We are eager to hear reactions from students and faculty about this collection of readings. You can contact individual authors or write me at the following address:

Nijole Benokraitis
Division of Criminology, Criminal Justice, and Social Policy
University of Baltimore
1420 N. Charles Street
Baltimore, MD 21201
Voicemail: 410-837-5294
Fax: 410-592-6006
E-mail: nbenokraitis@ubmail.ubalt.edu

PART

I

The Continuing Significance of Sexism

As a new Ph.D., I recently went on a job interview where . . . the dean got very irate and belittling when she asked what salary I expected. She basically told me I was uninformed on current salaries for her type of institution and I didn't have the experience to merit the salary. This was in conjunction with her raised voice, fists slamming on the table and her demanding that I answer simplistic questions (e.g., "Have you ever heard of the *Chronicle of Higher Education*?"). I knew of a man who had just interviewed for the position. He had graduated from my institution at the same time as me, was the same age, and had equal or less experience than me. He had named a similar [salary] figure and she had told him simply that "it shouldn't be a problem."

(E-mail correspondence, 1996)

As this new job candidate discovered, sexist behavior is not a relic of the "old days," as a number of my students believe. Neither, as this section illustrates, is there any evidence that sexism is likely to decrease very much after the turn of the century. *Sexism,* or discrimination against people based on their biological sex, usually refers to the economic exploitation and social domination of women by men. As the example of the job-hunting Ph.D. shows, however, women can also engage in sexist behavior.

Part One begins with a broad overview of several types of discrimination that vary along a continuum. In "Sex Discrimination in the 21st Century," Nijole V. Benokraitis shows that many women are often targets of several types of sexism—blatant, subtle, and covert. After describing the several types of inequality, she focuses, specifically, on subtle sexism. Often, as she notes, the several types of discrimination can overlap. As the newly minted Ph.D. example reveals, a "raised voice" and "fists slamming on the table" send such overt messages as "I'm more powerful than you," "I have more authority than you do," or "You're inferior to me." There is nothing subtle here. When, however, the male candidate is more acceptable than his female counterpart (even though they both have similar academic backgrounds and demographic characteristics), then something else is going on. The "something else" may not necessarily be subtle sexism, of course. It may be personality, personal hygiene, an arrogant attitude, or the dean was just having a bad day.

In many cases, however, our sex plays a critical role in how we are evaluated and treated. As Beth Bonniwell Haslett and Susan Lipman show in "Micro Inequities: Up Close and Personal," most of the women attorneys they surveyed experienced micro inequities, "the small, minor ways in which people are treated differently and thus disadvantaged." Each micro inequity, in and of itself, is so small that one is tempted to ignore the "slight." As these slights accumulate, however, they attack one's autonomy and public dignity and subsequently complicate interpersonal relationships and career development. Women with M.D. or Ph.D. degrees, for example, often experience a diminution of their credentials:

> What I frequently encounter as a faculty member is that my students address me as "Miss" or "Mrs." while the institutional norm at my small school—and the title they use for male professors—is "Dr." My colleagues and I view this as a way students show us that we're not equal in status and expertise to our equally-educated male colleagues. (E-mail correspondence, 1996)

What this faculty member (and other similarly situated female professionals) is complaining about is *not* that she is called "Miss" or "Mrs." but that the *continuous* and *differential* usage of titles is an everyday example that reflects and reinforces many women's lower status and authority.

Such slights are especially problematic because they are so common. As Judith E. Owen Blakemore, Jo Young Switzer, Judith A. DiIorio, and David L. Fairchild show in their chapter "Exploring the Campus Climate for Women Faculty," providing a less respectful and less supportive environment for female faculty than for male faculty may result in women's lower morale, greater sense of isolation, and lowered productivity. Differential gender expectations outside the campus can exacerbate professional barriers as well. Blakemore and her associates found, for example, that over two thirds of the women faculty they interviewed (compared to 45% of the men) said that parenting and household responsibilities decreased the ability to travel to conferences or pursue other professional activities.

Professional women are not the only ones who experience subtly "chilly" receptions. In Chapter 4, "Who's Laughing? Hillary Rodham Clinton in Political Humor," Ann Marshall examines how the most accomplished and influential women in politics, such as First Lady Hillary Rodham Clinton, are devalued and demeaned through jokes. Most jokes are generally straightforward and fun, enliven everyday interactions, and can fill uncomfortable conversation gaps during cocktail parties. Hostile humor, however, is considerably more subtle because it is aggressive and attacks any group that is seen as marginal, inferior, or threatening. And as Chapter 4 demonstrates, the more successful and nontraditional the woman is in terms of gender role expectations, the more hostile the humor in assaulting her personality, intellectual capabilities, family roles, and sexuality.

Chapter

1

Sex Discrimination in the 21st Century

Nijole V. Benokraitis

In the mid-1990s, white men make up 33% of the U.S. population. They comprise 85% of tenured professors, 85% of partners in law firms, 80% of the U.S. House of Representatives, 90% of the U.S. Senate, 95% of Fortune 500 CEOs (chief executive officers), 97% of school superintendents, 99.9% of athletic team owners, and 100% of all U.S. presidents ("Affirmative Action," 1996). In contrast, women still earn only 75% of what men earn; two thirds of all part-timers and nearly 60% of all temporary workers are women. A greater proportion of women today work in low-paid, part-time secretarial and support positions than 20 years ago. Also, nearly 90% of the jobs created in the year 2000 will be traditionally female jobs in the service sector with median weekly wages below the poverty level (Harris, 1995; *Women and work,* 1990).

What's wrong with this picture? Nothing, according to some observers. As many news articles announce cheerily every few weeks or so, American women have come a long way in the past 20 years. One journalist noted, for example, that "it has been more than a generation since employers could automatically fire women who married or became pregnant, day care has become more widely available, and the differences between male and female career choices are narrowing" (Wallich, 1996, p. 31). Another writer concluded that "it is not clear that discrimination plays a role today" because in 1994 women accounted for 43% of the lower-level managerial workers. According to this writer, many of these women will rise to top-level jobs as they gain in years and experience due to the "relentless march of demographic change" (Russell, 1995).

The message, then, is that most women are doing very well. And those who aren't just aren't trying hard enough. Even well-intentioned liberals, including some feminists, often portray the successes and failures of women as the consequence of freely made personal choices (see Park, 1996). Such assumptions ignore the fact that many women have few options because sexism is embedded in our structures, norms, policies, and day-to-day cultural practices.

This does not mean that men are immune to sex discrimination. According to the Equal Employment Opportunity Commission (EEOC), the federal body charged with enforcing civil rights acts as they pertain to employment, of the more than 10,000 reverse-discrimination cases filed between 1987 and 1994, 10% had merit ("Affirmative Action," 1996). This figure is minuscule, however, compared to EEOC's backlog of 98,000 cases of discrimination against women (Cohen, 1996). In fact, a vast literature shows that sex discrimination in the United States (as well as other countries) is overwhelmingly a "women's problem." Being a woman is frequently a better predictor of inequality than such variables as age, religion, intelligence, achievements, or socioeconomic status. Quite to the contrary, being a man may neutralize or override racial, age, sexual orientation, or religious discrimination. At many points in their lives, almost all women will be treated unequally simply because they are women and regardless of other characteristics. The rest of this chapter provides some working definitions and examples of sex discrimination, describes how subtle sex discrimination works in everyday life, suggests how women sometimes contribute to sexism, and concludes with a discussion of some possible solutions for sex inequality.

TABLE 1.1 Sex Discrimination Typology

	Characteristics		
Type of Discrimination	*Visibility*	*Intent*	*Remedies?*
Blatant	High	Usually intentional	Always
Subtle	Varies	Intentional and unintentional	Often
Covert	Very low	Intentional	Rarely

Types of Sex Discrimination: Definitions and Illustrations

In this chapter, *sex discrimination* refers to the unequal and harmful treatment of people because of their sex (i.e., biological differences between males and females, which include hormones, chromosomes, and anatomical characteristics). Although most of this chapter (and the rest of the book) focuses on subtle sex discrimination, discrimination varies along a continuum in terms of visibility, intent, and remedies (see Table 1.1). Although the different types of sex discrimination—blatant, subtle, and covert—often overlap or occur simultaneously in everyday life, they are presented separately here for greater analytical clarity.

Blatant Sex Discrimination

Blatant sex discrimination refers to the unequal and harmful treatment of women that is intentional, quite visible, and can be easily documented. Examples of blatant sex discrimination include sexual harassment, sexist language and jokes, physical violence (rape, incest, wife abuse), and other forms of obviously unequal treatment in the family, employment, education, politics, religion, law, and other areas (see Chapters 8, 10, and 12).

Consider a few examples. Nationally, as you saw earlier, women earn about 75 cents to a man's dollar. Interestingly, even in such occupations as secretarial work, in 1993 the mere 2% of male secretaries had median weekly earnings of $399 compared to $385 for 98% of the female secretaries! (U.S. Department of Labor, 1994). Although, according to a *Working Woman* magazine survey, the pay gap for women narrowed significantly in 1995 in some jobs, such as computer analysts, it widened in others. For instance,

TABLE 1.2 University Professors' Salaries, by Rank and Sex: 1995-1996

Rank	*Men ($)*	*Women ($)*
Professor	66,740	58,990
Associate professor	49,390	46,030
Assistant professor	41,250	38,630
Instructor	31,550	30,340
Lecturer	35,720	32,090
All ranks	43,890	35,840

SOURCE: Adapted from American Association of University Professors survey, cited in "Average salaries for full-time," Chronicle of Higher Education, April 12, 1996, p. A18.

female bank tellers, brokers, and other financial service representatives made 55% of what their male counterparts earned, *down* from 66% in 1994. Women health managers at hospitals earned about $30,212 compared to $44,200 for men, or 68% of men's salaries. That was a *decrease* from 1994, when women in those positions earned 79% of men's wages ("Women's Earnings," 1996).

One of the assumptions has always been that once women had access to education, salary inequities would decrease. Not so. In 1992, for example (and the last year for which data are available), women who had a bachelor's degree or more earned less than their male counterparts with only some college ($31,378 and $31,413, respectively) (U.S. Bureau of the Census, 1993).

In many cases, as experience and seniority increase, salary gaps between men and women also increase. As Table 1.2 shows, male faculty fare better than female faculty at all ranks and the salary gap *increases* as the rank increases. In many sectors, in fact, these gaps persist or increase despite similarities in specialization, experience, and other factors. For example, many workplaces now employ women chemists. Nonetheless, only about 1 in 14 women in chemical companies have managerial positions compared to one in five men. In addition, women chemists earn only 88% of what men earn, even after controlling for age, experience, and degree (Amato, 1992). In a nationwide survey of physicians under 45 years of age with 2 to 9 years of practice experience, Baker (1996) found that the mean hourly earnings of male physicians were $56, and those of female physicians were $49. After adjustment for a number of characteristics (such as specialty, practice setting, educational variables, experience, personal characteristics, characteristics of the community, and experience with malpractice claims), men with 10 or more years of experience earned 17% more per hour than their female colleagues. In the internal medicine subspecialties and emergency medicine, men earned 26% more than women.

Sexual harassment is another example of blatant sex discrimination. Although it is not clear whether sexual harassment is more visible because it has increased or because people are more likely to report it today than in the past, harassment is a widespread problem for many women.

In 1991, Frances K. Conley, a professor of neurosurgery at the prestigious Stanford Medical School, announced that she would resign because of "pervasive and debilitating" sexual harassment in her department. She agreed to stay on when a faculty member she had singled out for criticism was removed from his job as acting chairman of the neurosurgery department. Disparaging comments about women persisted, however:

> Dr. Conley believes that the school's male leadership "has to die off" before gender equity can be achieved. "The crotch grabbing and breast grabbing is out," she says, "but there are still demeaning comments." One of her male colleagues, she says, recently referred to an overweight nurse as a "moo cow." (Gose, 1995, p. A49)

Students, too, report daily encounters with sexual harassment. For example, a flyer distributed at Yale Law School rated five women students as the campus's top "Total Packages" and described them in sexual terms (Torry, 1995). Although such blatant discrimination may seem harmless to unreflective men, many women feel intimidated and humiliated. Occasionally, young men persist in sexual harassment even when they recognize that it demeans women:

> Yes, guys, including myself, do comment and joke about girls from time to time. But from a male standpoint, it's perfectly harmless. A girl will walk down the hallway and a guy will say, "Yeah, baby, come on over here and let me see [a part of the body]." The male is just having fun, but the female finds it offensive. When it gets more graphic and sexually explicit, even to me it seems offensive. If a girl came up to me and started saying some of that stuff, it would make me uncomfortable. (17-year-old high school student, cited in Minton, 1996, p. 6)

Besides individual sexual harassment, many companies and corporations have either ignored or accepted such behavior throughout their organizations. In 1996, the EEOC brought a lawsuit against the U.S. subsidiary of Mitsubishi in Normal, Illinois. EEOC and 28 women alleged that massive and pervasive sexual harassment at the plant affected as many as 500 women. According to one woman, the men would gather around her, touching her breasts and reaching between her legs to touch her crotch. The men drew pictures of her engaged in sexual activities, labeled with their name, and placed them on the cars as they moved through the assembly line, weaving through dozens of workers. One night a male co-worker exposed himself to her. In at least one case, a male employee put his air gun between a woman's legs and pulled the trigger. Some men openly admitted the harassment because they felt that "there was nothing wrong with it." (I've wondered whether the town's name is ironic or reflects many of the residents' view of sexual harassment.)

Although they couldn't prove it, the Normal police department suspected that a male employee who had been rebuffed by a female co-worker at Mitsubishi raped, sodomized, and then stabbed her 12-year-old daughter to death. During its 15-month investigation at the Mitsubishi plant, EEOC investigators traveled in groups of three or four for protection because they feared physical violence. Instead of remedying the sexual harassment practices, Mitsubishi provided the travel and gave a full day's pay to the 2,500 employees who protested the EEOC allegation outside the agency's office in Chicago. Because many of the jobs at Mitsubishi pay annual wages as high as $100,000, including overtime, in a community where the median household income is $32,000, a number of women employees dismissed the sexual harassment charges as "no big deal." Others accused the women who brought the charges against Mitsubishi as "traitors" (Grimsley, Swoboda, & Brown, 1996).

One of the most extreme cases of sexual harassment involves forcible sex offenses (including rape). Between 1993 and 1994 a survey of 831 college and university campuses showed that forcible sex offenses increased by 12.2% (892 to 1,001). During the same time period, in contrast, the Federal Bureau of Investigation reported that violent crimes—murder, forcible-sex offenses, robbery, and aggravated assault—had decreased (Lively, 1996). Because rape cases—including those on campuses—are highly underreported, this form of sexual harassment is probably much more severe than available statistics indicate.

Subtle Sex Discrimination

Subtle sex discrimination refers to the unequal and harmful treatment of women that is typically less visible and obvious than blatant sex discrimination. It is often not noticed because most people have internalized subtle sexist behavior as "normal," "natural," or "acceptable." Subtle sex discrimination can be relatively innocent or manipulative, intentional or unintentional, well meaning or malicious. Subtle sex discrimination is difficult to document because many people do not perceive it as serious or harmful. In addition, subtle sex discrimination is often more complex than it appears: What is discrimination to many women may not seem discriminatory to many men or even women. For example, one journalist hailed a study conducted for Avon Products, Inc. as "debunking" recent reports that women at top employment levels are unhappy and unable to balance their personal and professional lives: "The survey of 250 women business owners and 222 female Fortune 500 company executives found that 98% were satisfied with their career choices and 80% reported a healthy balance between their work and personal lives" (Lofton, 1995, p. E4).

Thus, everything seems just great. Yet the first large-scale survey of senior women executives conducted by Catalyst, a New York-based research organization that advocates the advancement of women in business, found that the female executives said they were successful because they exceeded male performance expectations by "sacrificing sleep and personal time in favor of midnight faxes and difficult assignments." Many reported rising each day at 4 a.m. to do paperwork and spend some time with their husbands and children before heading into work. In effect, then, many of the women made considerable sacrifices that men typically don't make to be successful. A majority of the women said that the second most important factor in their success was adjusting their personal style so it would not threaten male executives. Said one respondent: "Don't be attractive. Don't be too smart. Don't be assertive. Pretend you're not a woman. Don't be single. Don't be a mom. Don't be a divorcee." Some said they had learned to play golf, and others have learned to follow sports to make at-work small talk easier (Grimsley, 1996, p. C4). Isn't this a form of subtle sex inequality?

Consider another example—our public monuments. As far as I know, death is not an unexpected result in war. Being killed by a presumed loved one, on the other hand, is not expected. No matter where you live, tour your city's or town's museums and monuments. Who is commemorated? Men who kill each other in senseless fights over occupying a hill, forcing their religion on others, or expanding their boundaries. Who is ignored? Women who are killed by men (and often in similar numbers as those in war) because they are devalued, dehumanized, and denigrated. Isn't spending billions of dollars on war shrines for men but ignoring most of the women who are killed in domestic violence an example of subtle sexism?

Covert Sex Discrimination

Covert sex discrimination refers to the unequal and harmful treatment of women that is hidden, purposeful, and often, maliciously motivated. This form of sex discrimination refers to male behavior that consciously attempts to ensure women's failure—especially in educational and employment situations. Although there are many varieties of covert sex discrimination (see Benokraitis & Feagin, 1995), two of the most common are manipulation and sabotage. Both can be equally effective in keeping women "in their place."

In many cases, manipulative strategies give women undesirable jobs under the guise of equal treatment. Consider the following example provided by a female MTA bus driver:

> Some of us [women] have more seniority than men but our schedules are changed more often, we get the undesirable routes, and the buses we're assigned are in the worst possible working order. When we go to the union meetings to complain, there is always a male driver who complains that women are "too soft for the job" and reminds us that we can't expect any "special treatment." (Author's files)

In other cases, a woman who does not play a properly submissive role may be reminded to do so. At Yale University, for example, women law students have reported getting anonymous notes (presumably from men) in their mailboxes telling them that they talked too much in class (Torry, 1995). Such threats may intimidate women who are labeled as "trouble-makers."

An even more effective form of covert discrimination is sabotage. Through intentional sabotage, male employers and employees undermine or undercut a woman's position. Although sabotage can be contrived and carried out by one person, it often involves covert agreement between two or more people. Sabotage is difficult to prove but easy to deny. It typically comes down to "my word against yours" because effective saboteurs don't leave paper trails.

Sabotage is most common in traditionally male-dominated jobs where men may react negatively to women who are "invading" male territory. According to Connie Fletcher's (1995) study of police officers, for example, police still live and die under an inflexible code that dictates their every move. "The code" is simple: "You don't rat and you don't complain. A cop is supposed to be strong no matter what—suck it up—and never to admit or complain about weakness in himself/herself or in other cops" (p. 234). According to Fletcher, the toll for the code is especially high on women in policing because they are expected to adapt to a male world and take whatever the males hand out without complaint. If a woman challenges the code, she can be sabotaged by her colleagues to the point of risking her life. Consider the following example of a woman police officer who reported a physical attack by a male supervisor:

> They [the Police Officers Association] took out an ad in our newspaper asking for donations for *his* legal bills. They didn't give *her* an attorney. They didn't give her anything. They didn't even give her the time of day.
>
> She started experiencing harassment on the job. She was being covered on the air, which means you're trying to talk on the air and if somebody keys their mike, nobody can hear you. And you can't tell who's doing it—it could be anybody that has a radio. So she's saying, "I'm making a car stop" or "Some guy's running from me," and no one can hear where she is because she's covered. . . . No one was showing up when she needed assistance. So she figured they were gonna get her killed. (Fletcher, 1995, p. 237)

One of the most recent and potentially deadly forms of sabotage is "roofies." The drug, Rohypnol, is described as a sedative 10 times more powerful than Valium. According to pharmacologists, Rohypnol, the brand name for Flunitrazepam, is used in other countries to treat anxiety and insomnia and to sedate surgery patients. On the street, users call the small white pills roofies and "Roche." The substance has also been referred to as "the date rape drug" and "the Quaalude of the '90s." Patients on the drug appear drunk. When it is combined with alcohol, the effects can be deadly. Sedation occurs 15 to 30 minutes after ingestion and lasts about 8 hours. If an overdose occurs, the results can be fatal. An added problem of Rohypnol is that it causes amnesia for most of the sedation period, especially during a patient's first consumption. That makes prosecution of abuse cases difficult:

Because rape victims do not remember what happened, apprehending and prosecuting the saboteur is practically impossible.

How Subtle Sex Discrimination Works

Having discussed the three major types of discrimination—blatant, subtle, and covert—we now turn to a more detailed look at nine types of subtle sex discrimination: condescending chivalry, supportive discouragement, friendly harassment, subjective objectification, radiant devaluation, liberated sexism, benevolent exploitation, considerate domination, and collegial exclusion. These categories deliberately use oxymorons (figures of speech that combine incongruous terms) to emphasize the sexist behavior that seems friendly at face value but has pernicious consequences. Remember, also, that what seems subtle to people who have not experienced these forms of discrimination may seem pretty blatant to people, especially women, who encounter these forms of inequality on a daily basis. Because of space limitations, the discussion is illustrative rather than exhaustive (for a more comprehensive analysis, see Benokraitis & Feagin, 1995, pp. 82-121).

Condescending Chivalry

Condescending chivalry refers to superficially courteous behavior that is protective and paternalistic, but treats women as subordinates. Sometimes, the chivalry is well intentioned because it "protects" women from criticism. For example, "a male boss will haul a guy aside and just kick ass if the [male] subordinate performs badly in front of a client" but may not say anything to a female subordinate (Fraker, 1984). Not providing such criticism may seem benevolent in the short term but will handicap an employee's performance in the long run.

According to Gherardi (1995), courtesy systems are not as innocent as they appear because "hierarchical rituals interweave with chivalric ones" in organizations. The courtesy system is the prime arena for conveying relative rank: deciding who decides, who leads and who follows, who speaks and who listens, and who has the power to position the other. It is relatively "simpler" for men to be in a "one-up position" in which they provide care and consideration for female subordinates. This care and consideration also reflect women's inequality:

> The political nature of gender rituals is highlighted by interactions among colleagues belonging to a peer group, or when the authority structure is at odds with gender lines. The fact that the bookshops are stocked with handbooks on "What to Do When the Boss Is a Woman," or similar, signals that there is or could be a problem of authority/obedience, or at least an embarrassing contradiction. How can a man handle the courtesy system and activate the protector/protected frame when the relative ranks are in his disfavor, and when he risks resembling more a butler than a knight in shining armor? (Gherardi, 1995, pp. 133-134)

Thus, chivalrous behavior can signal status inequality. According to some researchers, outmoded attitudes—on the parts of both men and women—are preventing many qualified women from breaking into top jobs as school superintendents. Unlike their male counterparts, female candidates still get such questions from school board members as "How would your husband feel about your moving?" "Can you deal with a district where the administrators are mostly men?" "Can you handle tough discipline problems?" According to researchers, the oppressive chivalry continues after being hired. Female school superintendents often face greater scrutiny, for example, when it comes to such "masculine" tasks as finances and maintenance issues (see Nakashima, 1996).

Supportive Discouragement

Supportive discouragement refers to a form of subtle sex discrimination where women received mixed messages about their abilities, intelligence, or accomplishments. One form of supportive discouragement involves encouraging women to succeed in general but not rewarding their actual achievements because the latter may not reflect traditionally male interests:

> Having served on several search committees, I'm aware of how often feminist (or even woman-topic) dissertations are dismissed as "jargony," "trendy," etc. . . . I'm not really sure if feminism is still seen as a "fly-by-night" sort of discipline, but the accusation is a difficult one to argue because the people who make it will assure you until they're blue in the face (or you are) that they would love to hire a woman, are not opposed to feminism, etc. etc. But it's only "this" dissertation, you see, they are opposed to. . . . I think there's an awful lot of that "I'm-sure-glad-you're-not-one-of-those-(bra-burners/Marxists/marching-in-the-streeters/take your pick)" rhetoric floating around on the part of senior faculty members with a lot of power over

promotion and tenure decisions. This is a signal that one must tone down one's own voice or risk punishment. Women's publications in women's studies or feminist journals are often dismissed as "minor pub" while men who publish in small presses/journals are heralded as having made it to a "small-but-elite/prestigious" one. (E-mail correspondence, 1996)

Another form of supportive discouragement encourages women to be ambitious and successful but places numerous obstacles in their paths that either limit or derail the progress. Consider the following example from a colleague in the United Kingdom:

One of the largest departments in our College is the Access department which offers part-time courses for people with no formal qualifications who wish to enter higher education or return to work. I would say that about 70% of these students are female and intend to go into teaching or similar work. The College refuses to implement a crèche or other day-care on the basis that it would be too expensive; staffing would cost almost nothing as the College runs courses for Nursery Nurses, childcare workers, etc. This despite the fact that of the people who are offered places on the Access course and turn it down, 80% give lack of child care as the main reason. Of this 80%, 92% are women. The courses are also run in some of the worst accommodations on site—"temporary" buildings which have been there for about 20 years and which are in a terrible state. The Chemistry department (not many women here) has, however, had at least three major renovations in the last 10 years. It certainly makes clear to the many women on the Access course the opinion the College management has of their relative importance. (E-mail correspondence, 1996)

Friendly Harassment

Friendly harassment refers to sexually oriented behavior that, at face value, looks harmless or even playful. If it creates discomfort, embarrassment, or humiliation, however, it is a form of subtle discrimination. According to some female students at the Stanford Medical School, for example, it is in such traditionally male-taught courses as those in surgery and internal medicine that many women encounter the most offensive sexual jokes. A fourth-year student said that many of her days "are spent fending off stupid little comments," many of them sexual, from male residents and doctors. She hesitated to complain, however, because good evaluations from professors are essential to get a good residency (Gose, 1995).

When women don't laugh at "stupid little jokes," moreover, they are often accused of not having a sense of humor:

> In response to a question from a friend of mine (a female graduate student) regarding how to comport herself at a job interview, a male faculty adviser responds, "Just flirt!" When I recount the incident to a male friend (junior faculty in another field at another institution), he responds: "Maybe it was a joke. Lighten up!" The primary sexism of the first remark gets echoed in the secondary sexism of the second remark, which trivializes the offense and the indignation ["no sense of humor"]. (E-mail correspondence, 1996)

Humor and jokes serve a number of functions: They reinforce group solidarity; define the defiant/outsider group; educate; save face; ingratiate; express caring for others; provide a safety valve for discussing taboo topics; maintain status inequality; silence or embarrass people; and provide tension release, hostility, and anger toward any group that is seen as marginal, inferior, or threatening. A single joke can serve several of these functions.

Although women's humor can be a powerful tool for changing stereotypes about females, much of men's sexual humor expresses male dominance over women, negates their personhood, and tries to silence women: "There are whole categories of jokes about women for which there are no male parallels: prostitute jokes, mother-in-law jokes, dumb blonde jokes, woman driver jokes, Jewish mother jokes" (Crawford, 1995, p. 138). Women often don't laugh at many of these jokes not because they don't have a sense of humor, but because the "jokes" are hostile, aggressive, and demeaning (see Chapter 4).

Subjective Objectification

Subjective objectification refers to a form of subtle sex discrimination that treats women as children, possessions, or sex objects. Women are often punished like children—their "allowances" may be taken away, they may be forbidden to associate with their friends, their physical mobility may be limited, they may be given curfews, or they may be threatened with punishment similar to that of children. Consider the following experience reported by a female faculty member at a large university:

> One of the senior male faculty was very unhappy about the woman faculty member we had just hired. She challenged him during departmental meet-

> ings and disagreed with him in public. As we talked, he got more and more angry about her behavior. Finally, he exploded, "What that young lady needs is a good spanking!"

When was the last time you heard anyone threaten to spank an adult male who disagreed with something?

Our culture is continuously bombarded with images of women as little more than sexual body parts. The Media Action Alliance, which publishes the *Action Agenda* newsletter, is constantly filled with examples of posters, ads, videos, and other media materials that glorify violence against women and exploitation of women's bodies. It has been estimated that the average teenager sees between 1,900 and 2,400 sex-related messages per year on television alone (Brown, Childers, & Waszik, 1990). Many of the images, including those in films targeted at adolescents, treat women's bodies as trophies: Boys compete to be the first to "score," to achieve the most sexual conquests, and to "make it" with the sexiest teenage girls (see Whatley, 1994).

A frightening result of such competition can include rape and other sexual assaults on women. Consider the "Spur Posse" case in California. In 1993, eight members of a suburban high school, many of them top athletes at the school, created a clique called the "Spur Posse." Their primary goal was to "score" with as many girls as possible. They kept track of the girls with whom they had intercourse, and some bragged that their individual tallies ran into the 60s. In at least seven cases, girls from 10 to 16 years old said they had been raped. Some of the parents condoned their sons' behavior. One father, in fact, boasted to reporters that the assaults were not rape but indicators of his son's virility and sexual prowess (Seligmann, 1993).

This bizarre perception of women as possessions and trophies follows many boys into adulthood. According to Brooks (1995), what he refers to as "the Centerfold Syndrome" represents "one of the most malignant forces in contemporary relationships between men and women." One of the elements of the centerfold syndrome is objectification:

> Women become objects as men become objectifiers. As the culture has granted men the right and privilege of looking at women, women have been expected to accept the role of stimulators of men's visual interest, with their bodies becoming objects that can be lined up, compared, and rated. . . . Objective physical aspects are critical: size, shape, and harmony of body parts are more important than a woman's human qualities. . . . Men talk of

> their attraction to women in dehumanizing terms based on the body part of their obsession—"I'm a leg man," or "I'm an ass man." (pp. 3-4)

Brooks notes that one of the most harmful effects of such objectification is that real women become more complicated, less appealing, and even ugly: "Stretch marks, varicose veins, sagging breasts, and cellulite-marked legs, common phenomena for real female bodies, may be viewed as repugnant by men who see women as objects" (p. 5). As a result, centerfold syndrome men may be sexually and emotionally inexpressive with the most important women in their lives.

Radiant Devaluation

Although women are less likely to be openly maligned or insulted than in the past, they are devalued more subtly but just as effectively. Often, the devaluation is done in glowing terms:

> A psychologist, one of the most popular instructors in her college, said she would get good teaching evaluations from her male chair but that the positive review would be couched in sex-stereotypical rather than professional terms—she was described as being "mama-ish" and as having a "charming" approach to teaching. Being "mama-ish" and "charming" are *not* the criteria used by tenure and promotion committees. (Benokraitis & Feagin, 1995, p. 102)

On a much broader scale, some scholars contend that the most recent devaluations have focused on antifeminist intellectual harassment through the use of "vilification and distortion or even violence to repress certain areas of research and forms of inquiry" (Clark, Garner, Higonnet, & Katrak, 1996, p. x). Attacks on feminists and feminist scholarship are nothing new. What has changed, however, is that much of the "newest wave of antifeminism cloaks itself in the vestments of feminism: the new antifeminists are women who, claiming to be feminists themselves, now maintain they are rescuing the women's movement from those who have led it astray" (Ginsberg & Lennox, 1996, p. 170). Many of these devaluators often have impressive academic credentials, are articulate, have been supported by conservative corporate foundations, and have found a receptive audience in the mainstream media and many publishing companies, which see antifeminism as a "hot commodity" because it is so profitable. Blaming feminism for such (real or imagined) ailments as the deterioration of relationships between the sexes and the presumed dissolution of the family, and especially when the criticism comes from well-educated self-proclaimed feminists, sells a lot of books.

Liberated Sexism

Liberated sexism refers to the process that, at face value, appears to be treating women and men equally but that, in practice, increases men's freedom while placing greater burdens on women. One of the best examples of liberated sexism is work overloads both within the home and at the job site. Since the 1970s, increasing numbers of women have found themselves with two jobs—one inside and one outside the home. Ironically, women working these "double days" are often referred to as "liberated women." But liberated from what?

Shared parenting reflects more rhetoric than reality. In a national study, Bianchi (1990) found that more than 60% of divorced fathers either did not visit their children or did not visit them and had no telephone or mail contact with them over a 1-year period. Employed mothers with preschool-age children spend 24 hours more a week in child care activities than do their husbands. Because the husband's job typically takes priority over his wife's (his salary is usually much higher), nearly 9 out of 10 mothers care for their children when they are sick, compared to only 1 out of 10 working fathers (DeStefano & Colasanto, 1990). Although in one survey 56% of male employees said they were interested in flexible work schedules that would allow them more family time, in reality fewer than 1% take advantage of the unpaid paternity leaves that some 30% of companies offer today. The Family and Medical Leave Act, which was signed into law by President Clinton in 1993, allows workers of employers with 50 or more employers to take up to 12 weeks of unpaid leave following the birth or adoption of a child. Most men fear the career repercussions of taking paternity leaves or cannot afford unpaid leaves financially, however (see Sommer, 1994).

Benevolent Exploitation

Benevolent exploitation refers to taking advantage of people because it's "good for them," because they care about or respect us, or because we persuade them that the work is critical to the organization.

A very effective form of benevolent exploitation is to teach women to be dutiful and loyal to men in leadership or supervisory roles because such sponsorship will "eventually pay off." Many women spend lifetimes being research assistants, invisible coauthors, and even invisible authors—believing that their sponsor will one day recognize the contributions publicly. During their highly publicized divorce proceedings several years ago, Mrs. Spock claimed that she should have been a coauthor of Dr. Spock's best-selling books on baby care because she did much of the research and writing.

A recent national faculty survey sponsored by the National Center for Education Statistics showed that a third of the country's new, full-time faculty—compared to their senior colleagues—are much more likely to be women, somewhat more likely to be members of minority groups, and less likely to hold tenure-track jobs (see Magner, 1996). As more and more institutions move into the "publish or perish" mode, the gender gap in publishing rates between the "old" and "new" faculty will probably increase. These differences in research productivity can be explained by women's structural position in the university: Women, as a group, carry heavier teaching loads, bear greater responsibility for undergraduate education, and have more service commitments. Women also have less access to graduate teaching assistants, travel funds, research monies, laboratory equipment, and release time for research (Park, 1996; see also Chapter 6). New women faculty are an especially cheap source of labor (remember the discussion of faculty salaries?) in doing the (often) necessary but typically unrewarded service and committee work that department chairs or administrators may assign because the work is tedious or time-consuming. As one E-mail colleague noted: "Women are often assigned to committees which are considered less critical to the university's mission. Ironically, they are often committees which involve large amounts of time!" (see also Chapters 3 and 14).

Considerate Domination

Men often occupy preeminent positions and control important decision-making functions (see Chapter 5). Men's dominance is built into our language, laws, and customs in both formal and informal ways. The dominance is accepted because it has been internalized and is often portrayed as "collegial," authoritative, or mutually beneficial.

Most of us take for granted that the expert and dominant cast of characters in the media are men. The media routinely ignore women or present them as second-class citizens. A recent survey of the front-page stories of 20 national and local newspapers found that although women make up 52% of the population, they show up just 13% of the time in the prime news spots. Even the stories about breast implants quoted men more often than women. Two thirds of the bylines on front pages were male, and three quarters of the opinions on op-ed pages were by men. Fewer than a third of the photographs on front pages featured women. Because the old "women's sections" are now more unisex and focus on both men and women, news about and by women has lost space even in these lifestyle sections (Goodman, 1992; see also Overholser, 1996).

Television news is not much better. In a study of the content of evening news programs on CBS, NBC, and ABC, Rakow and Kranich (1991) found that women as on-camera sources of information were used in less than 15% of the cases. When women did speak, they were usually passive reactors to public events as housewife or wife of the man in the news rather than participants or experts. Even in critical analyses of issues that affect more women than men, women may not appear on the screen. For example, a lengthy story on CBS on welfare reform did not use any women or feminist sources.

Much of the domination is accepted by many women either because they share intimate relationships with the men who dominate them or because men insist that "I know what's best:"

> Five out of the eight members of the Curriculum Committee wanted to change the name from Women's Studies to Women's and Gender Studies. The Women's Studies Committee, of course, had already discussed this issue and decided we wanted to stick to Women's Studies. It was infuriating that faculty members who knew nothing about Women's Studies were willing to change the name of our major! What was their rationale? They wanted to attract a wide variety of students to the major, namely men, and felt the inclusion of "gender" in the title would be more palatable to our male students. Now, doesn't that just take the cake? When have they ever been concerned about the lack of female students in physics or chemistry? (E-mail correspondence, 1996)

In this case, the faculty recognized the "we're-doing-this-for-the-greater-good" brand of domination and stood their ground. Typically, however, many women live up to widely accepted gender expectations that women should be altruistic, self-sacrificing, docile, cooperative, and "obedient."

Collegial Exclusion

One of the most familiar forms of subtle sexism is collegial exclusion whereby women are made to feel invisible or unimportant through physical, social, or professional isolation. When Hall and Sandler's pamphlet *The Classroom Climate: A Chilly One for Women?* was published in 1982, it was an instant success. Among other reasons, Sandler and Hall articulated the feelings that many women had experienced in higher education of being ignored, not having female role models, or being excluded from classroom discussions and activities. Since then, many studies have documented women's exclusion from classroom discourse, textbooks, and other academic activities (see, e.g., Gabriel & Smithson, 1990; Ginorio, 1995; Krupnick, 1985; Lewis, 1990; Maher & Tetreault, 1994; Peterson & Kroner, 1992; Sandler & Hall, 1986).

Although there has been greater awareness of exclusion, it is not evident that there has been change since 1982. At Stanford Medical School, for example, "The male body has been used as the standard, and the women's body has been seen as a variation on that theme," says a third-year female student. Several women once heard a professor dismiss the clitoris with five words: "like the penis, just shorter" (Gose, 1995, p. A50). At Yale and American University law schools, female students' complaints are strikingly similar to those that Hall and Sandler described in 1982: Women feel their speech is stifled in class; professors respond more positively to comments by men, even if a woman voiced the same idea first; male students, even friends, ignore women's comments on legal issues and talk around them; male students and faculty devalue women's opinions; and men don't hear what women say (Torry, 1995).

When I asked the subscribers of the Women's Studies E-mail discussion list if they or someone they knew had ever experienced subtle sexism, many of the responses (from both the United States and Europe) described collegial exclusion. Here are a few examples:

> Just got back from a national conference and heard a female college president relate her experiences at meetings with other college presidents in the state. She was the only female present at the meetings and found that her suggestions/insights were ignored by her male colleagues. However, when the same suggestions later came from one of them, they were acknowledged. She finally took to writing her suggestions on the chalkboard. They couldn't be ignored that way—or at least not for long.

> There was a series of women-only staff development meetings set up by one of the more senior women (there are few) but the "only" time that could be found for this was on Monday at 6:00 p.m. Other staff development meetings are held at lunchtime with time off for anybody who wants to go.

> Women often feel they're isolated. . . . Many women begin with great promise but are demoralized and cut off from support. . . . I'm referring to women who are cut off from support in ways it's hard to explain . . . often the only women in their departments . . . although some are in departments with other untenured women but the Old White Guys have the power. [The women] often are lacking a real (feminist) community.

So far, we've examined some forms of subtle sexism that many women experience on a daily basis (see also Chapter 2). It is just as crucial to recognize that discriminatory patterns may vary greatly because of the differences that exist among women. Is inequality greater among some groups of women than others?

The Snowball Effects of Sex Discrimination

Although recognizing the various forms of sexism—blatant, subtle, and covert—is important, discrimination is much more complex. Inequality is structural in the sense that it is built into our institutions. It is also systemic in the sense that groups with power and privilege can dominate and control those who are less privileged or less powerful. None of these relationships is innate or predestined. Instead, they are *socially constructed* and shape people's lives and experiences. During the past decade or so, discussions of discrimination have increasingly emphasized how institutions themselves are constructed through race, class, and gender relations. Thus, students are often reminded to examine the intersections of race, class, and gender. Such exhortations are problematic, however.

Age, marital status, and parenting are as critical in discussions of discrimination as race, class, and gender. Because sexual orientation is included under "gender" in many analyses, sexuality is getting more attention in much of the research than it did in the past. Ignoring age, marital status, and parenting, however, ignores critical variables that constrict many women's lives. When I was doing the research for a marriage and family textbook (Benokraitis, 1996), for example, I was frustrated by the lack of research on such topics as women's dating and employment experiences after the age of 40.

Because all women grow and change along the life cycle, young, middle-aged, and older women have very different needs (Harris, 1995). What happens to a woman—both physically and emotionally—is still a large unknown in medicine. The first large-scale study of women's experiences at midlife was initiated only in 1996. In this study, launched by the National Institute of Aging, teams of researchers and physicians at several university hospital will examine, for the first time, the biological, emotional, environmental, and behavioral changes that alter a woman's risk factors for disease as she ages (Roan, 1996).

The combination of sexism and age discrimination, which Carpenter (1996) calls "sexagism," can be especially debilitating for lesbians who are seen as "unnatural" in terms of both their age and their sexuality. Don't such women experience considerably more discrimination because of the "snowball" effects of gender, age, and sexual orientation than their younger, heterosexual counterparts? The discrimination may be compounded even further if an aging lesbian's research on women's issues is evaluated as "lacking academic merit" because research on women is devalued by her colleagues (see Gaard, 1996).

Consider, also, Romero's (1992) study of Chicana domestic workers. Most of the women Romero interviewed felt stigmatized by being private household workers because of the low status, low pay, demeaning treatment by employers, or being identified as "just a cleaning lady." Married mothers, however, experienced the additional stress of caring for their own husbands and children after work. Once again, don't such analyses suggest that ethnicity, social class, marital status, and parenting have severe snowball effects that should be included in studies of sex discrimination?

Even in professional occupations, such as medicine, female physicians often "choose" specializations and practices that are lower-paying but that allow them to meet their family responsibilities (Baker, 1996). Black female physicians who treat patients in poor communities may be turned down or dropped from health maintenance organizations because their patients tend to be sicker and cost more. As one black physician stated, "They [health maintenance organizations] want doctors who have the low-cost patients. . . . I see it as discrimination" (Sugg, 1995, p. A6). Thus, having a family or being altruistic penalizes women in even the most respected and highest-paying occupations.

Women's Role in Sex Discrimination

In Petaluma, California, eighth-grader Tawnya Brawdy had to run a gauntlet of boys gathered outside her school who would begin mooing as she approached. According to Tawnya, the harassment went on before school, during classes, between classes, and during lunch, but her (female) teacher told her she would just have to put up with it. (The U.S. Department of Education found that the schools had failed to protect her. Tawnya's mother sued her district for "emotional distress" and collected $20,000 in an out-of-court settlement; Adler & Rosenburg, 1992).

According to some high school students, both students and teachers accept sexism. Girls often giggle at sexist comments or tell a female friend to "chill out" if she complains about guys who make obscene comments about females (Minton, 1996). In fact, according to a 16-year-old female high school student, it is not uncommon for both female students and teachers to accept sexist comments as normal:

> At my school, when boys put girls down or make sexist remarks, some of the girls even laugh. And whenever I say anything, everyone tells me not to take things so seriously. Girls who stick up for themselves are called "femi-nazis" by the boys. When we were having a class discussion, even one of the supposedly "cool" liberal female teachers laughed at the guys' attitudes. That hurts. (Minton, 1996, p. 6)

Acceptance of sexism, especially by female high school teachers, is dismaying. Such reactions are not surprising, however, because women are divided among themselves over sex discrimination issues. Harris (1995) shows, for example, that some of the backsliding on sex discrimination issues can be attributed to women:

> Sixty-three percent of American women do not consider themselves feminists, 54 percent say the women's movement had no effect on their lives, and 50 percent say it does not reflect the views of most women. Former supporters of the National Organization for Women question whether the organization can be effective if its leader is an acknowledged bisexual, and a "new breed" of feminists attack "radical" feminists for being anti-male and for portraying women as victims, rather than as victors in the struggle for equality.
>
> In Texas, it was male legislators, not female ones, who allied with a female state senator to pass laws requiring insurance companies to pay for

> mammography as well as chest x-rays. It was a woman who led the National Federation of Independent Businesses' opposition to the unpaid Family and Medical Leave Act. Even success is problematic: in two states, qualified women running against one another for the U.S. Senate split feminists and the vote. Despite the fact that women increasingly own companies, their companies are not always supportive of women; the *Wall Street Journal* reports that women-owned companies can be "positively antediluvian when it comes to hiring or promoting women into management." (Harris, 1995, pp. 161-162)

One of the reasons some women dismiss the women's movement is that they feel that sex discrimination is no longer a problem, or a minor one. A recent national survey reported, for example, that when women were asked the reasons why the next generation of women are expected to have fewer job opportunities, only 4% said that "there is still discrimination." The top reasons included a bad economy (33%), that the younger generation is lazy and too fun-loving (17%), and that education is not as good or accessible as in the past (12%) (Families & Work Institute, 1995). Those women (and men) who believe that sex discrimination is even more robust than in the past, however, can pursue a number of remedies.

Prospects for Change

Although many women are victims of sex discrimination, both men and women can be effective in generating social change. In terms of subtle sexism, the first step is to recognize it. The next step is to talk about and expose it at every opportunity (see, e.g., Chapters 13 and 15).

Another possibility is to form alliances between women (and men) who have common interests in promoting job or networking opportunities. Recently, for example, a group of women in Washington, D.C., established Leadership America, Inc. Each year the group selects about 100 women to participate in a series of three 4-day session on key policy issues. Once selected, each woman must pay a tuition fee of $3,180, which covers her activities with the group for the year and "grooms" women who want to be appointed to boards of corporations and nonprofit organizations (Salerno, 1996).

Because such memberships are pricey, many of us can organize alliances and network much more informally. For example, the American Council on Education/National Identification Program (ACE/NIP) has spent the past 20 years helping women advance to leadership positions in higher education. Its ultimate goal is "crafting an educational, social and political climate in which the voices of women in all their diversity and richness are valued in setting the public agenda." ACE/NIP is open to all women and sponsors a variety of conferences and workshops on administrative and teaching-related topics.

More locally, at the University of Baltimore, a handful of women faculty, administrators, and staff initiated an informal networking breakfast. The group further broke up into smaller clusters, which started a reading group and an investment club. I do not know how the reading group is doing, but our investment club has already made some money. Besides that, we have met women in other departments and disciplines—across the liberal arts, law, and business schools—who have become resources both within and outside the investment club.

I should note an interesting aside. One of our investment club members, after reviewing this chapter, mentioned that the breakfast meetings, however well intentioned, were subtly exclusionary. She pointed out that attending the meetings was always impossible because "I had to get the kids off to school in the morning." This reinforces my earlier argument that excluding such variables as marital status and having children limits our analyses of subtle sexism.

Many women have become entrepreneurs. One of every four American workers is employed by a business owned by a woman, and women own more than one third of all businesses in the nation. In addition, the number of women-owned enterprises with more than 100 employees grew twice as fast as all other companies between 1991 and 1994. According to U.S. Census Bureau figures, women's share of total nonfarm businesses has reached almost 35% (Mallory, 1996).

Some women who were "downsized" (i.e., laid off) started consulting firms:

> In 1991 I was employed as a Systems Analyst, permanent employee, at a large corporation. I was responsible for a major portion of the software design for a bar code inventory application, and the programming efforts of several programmers. . . . Before I inherited the project, one team had already failed to design and implement it.
>
> Although I was the only female on the project, after enduring the usual "female hazing," I eventually gained the technical respect of my team of programmers.

Sixty to eighty hour weeks were common, both for me and my team of programmers. After about six weeks, the project was almost complete. At that point the Vice President of the company called me into his office and said: "Kathleen, the company is having some financial problems. We have to do some downsizing. We are going to have to lay you off. We are making a big mistake but you will be all right. Your husband has a good job."

After making some discrete inquiries, I discovered the REAL story. My replacement was a man who was a personal friend of the project manager. He was hired at a MUCH HIGHER salary than I was earning, and he was a technical lightweight. After I left the company, my replacement's first act was to deliver the application I designed to the customer UNCHANGED. It was enthusiastically accepted by the customer, and credit for its development and creation was given to my replacement.

So the downsizing story was nothing more than camouflage for sexist discrimination. I wonder how many women reading this have been fed the downsizing line when sexist discrimination was the REAL reason for their layoff?

I was emotionally devastated. After several days of feeling sorry for myself, anger set in. Then I wanted to GET EVEN. I had previously worked as a consultant, and discovered that women consultants are not subjected to as much macho/sexist BS as regular women employees. So I looked for a consulting job and found one in a few days.

As a regular employee I earned $50,000 per year on the old job. As a consultant, I earned $40 per hour and all the paid overtime I wanted. One year after leaving those jerks with their petty macho games, I was earning almost twice what they were paying me.

Living well REALLY IS the best revenge! (E-mail correspondence, 1996)

In other cases, women have initiated lawsuits to remedy sex discrimination. Lawsuits are lengthy (some take up to 12 years to resolve) and can take a financial and emotional toll on the plaintiff (see Monaghan, 1996). On the other hand, many women have won in the courts. One of the most successful cases involved Lucky Stores, Inc., a grocery store chain with 180 branches throughout northern California. In 1984, one employee filed a complaint with EEOC after being a checker for more than a dozen years even though she had applied for a more responsible and better-paying position. The complaint brought her to the attention of a law firm that persuaded two other dissatisfied women from other Lucky Stores to agree to a class action suit (a legal proceeding brought by one or more persons but representing the interests of a larger group). Although Lucky's attorneys argued that women were not promoted because they were not interested in senior-level jobs, the plaintiffs' attorneys had evidence that store managers did not post openings for management-track jobs, did not offer women training for higher-level positions, and expressed prejudicial ideas about women in training sessions. And in the case I described earlier, many of the 800 female workers at the plant could recover damages of up to $300,000 each if Mitsubishi is found guilty of fostering an atmosphere that condoned sexual harassment (Cohen, 1996).

The most encompassing solutions to sex discrimination, both blatant and subtle, should come from organizations and national policies (see Chapters 5 and 16). Most organizations by describing themselves as "equal employment opportunity employers" show their awareness of sex discrimination as illegal. Unless, however, both the federal government and businesses start hiring women at top levels beyond token positions, little will change:

> It seems likely that if the chairmen of IBM, Hewlett-Packard, Unisys, and Digital Equipment were to provide firm signals both within their firms and to suppliers that bias . . . will no longer be tolerated, the reverberations would be felt throughout the electronics and office technology industries, if not societywide. Firms can accomplish a great deal by appointing women as line vice-presidents in powerful areas such as production and marketing and instructing them that bias will not be . . . tolerated. (Larwood, Szwajkowski, & Rose, 1988, p. 284)

Nothing is as easy as it looks and everything takes longer than we expect. Nonetheless, sex discrimination can be at least decreased, and very rapidly, through individual, collective, and organizational action.

References

Adler, J., & Rosenburg, D. (1992, October 9). Must boys always be boys? *Newsweek*, p. 77.

Affirmative action: Beyond the glass ceiling and the sticky floor. (1996). *Issues Quarterly*, *1*(4).

Amato, I. (1992). Profile of a field. Chemistry; Women have extra hoops to jump through. *Science, 13,* 1372-1373.

Average salaries for full-time faculty members, 1995-6. [Boxed text]. (1996, April 12). *Chronicle of Higher Education*, p. A18.

Baker, L. C. (1996). Differences in earning between male and female physicians. *New England Journal of Medicine, 334,* 960-964.

Benokraitis, N. V. (1996). *Marriages and families: Changes, choices, and constraints.* Englewood Cliffs, NJ: Prentice Hall.

Benokraitis, N. V., & Feagin, J. R. (1995). *Modern sexism: Blatant, subtle, and covert discrimination.* Englewood Cliffs, NJ: Prentice Hall.

Bianchi, S. (1990). America's children: Mixed prospects. *Population Bulletin, 45,* 3-41.

Brooks, G. R. (1995). *The centerfold syndrome: How men can overcome objectification and achieve intimacy with women.* San Francisco: Jossey-Bass.

Brown, J. D., Childers, K. W., & Waszik, C. S. (1990). Television and adolescent sexuality. *Journal of Adolescent Health Care, 11,* 62-70.

Carpenter, M. W. (1996). Female grotesques in academia: Ageism, antifeminism, and feminists on the faculty. In V. Clark, S. N. Garner, M. Higonnet, & K. H. Katrak (Eds.), *Antifeminism in the academy* (pp. 141-168). New York: Routledge.

Clark, V., Garner, S. N., Higonnet, M., & Katrak, K. H. (Eds.). (1996). *Antifeminism in the academy.* New York: Routledge.

Cohen, W. (1996, April 22). Big trouble on the assembly line. *U.S. News & World Report,* p. 63.

Crawford. M. (1995). *Talking difference: On gender and language.* Thousand Oaks, CA: Sage.

DeStefano, L., & Colasanto, D. (1990, February). Unlike 1975, today most Americans think men have it better. *Gallup Poll Monthly,* pp. 25-36.

Families & Work Institute. (1995). *Women: The new providers.* New York: Author.

Fletcher, C. (1995). *Breaking & entering: Women cops talk about life in the ultimate men's club.* New York: HarperCollins.

Fraker, S. (1984, April 16). Why top jobs elude female executives. *Fortune,* p. 46.

Gaard, G. (1996). Anti-lesbian intellectual harassment in the academy. In V. Clark, S. N. Garner, M. Higonnet, & K. H. Katrak (Eds.), *Antifeminism in the academy* (pp. 115-140). New York: Routledge.

Gabriel, S., & Smithson, I. (Eds.). (1990). *Gender in the classroom: Power and pedagogy.* Urbana and Chicago: University of Illinois Press.

Gherardi, S. (1995). *Gender, symbolism, and organizational cultures.* Thousand Oaks, CA: Sage.

Ginorio, A. B. (1995). *Warming the climate for women in academic science.* Washington, DC: Association of American Colleges and Universities.

Ginsberg, E., & Lennox, S. (1996). Antifeminism in scholarship and publishing. In V. Clark, S. N. Garner, M. Higonnet, & K. H. Katrak (Eds.), *Antifeminism in the academy* (pp. 169-200). New York: Routledge.

Goodman, E. (1992, April 7). A woman's place is in the paper. *Baltimore Sun,* p. 15A.

Gose, B. (1995, November 3). Women's place in medicine. *Chronicle of Higher Education,* pp. A49-A50.

Grimsley, K. D. (1996, February 28). From the top: The women's view. *Washington Post,* pp. C1, C4.

Grimsley, K. D., Swoboda, F., & Brown, W. (1996, April 29). Fear on the line at Mitsubishi. *Washington Post,* pp. A1, A8-A9.

Hall, R. M., & Sandler, B. R. (1982). *The classroom climate: A chilly one for women?* Washington, DC: Association of American Colleges.

Harris, A. M. (1995). *Broken patterns: Professional women and the quest for a new feminine identity.* Detroit, MI: Wayne State University Press.

Krupnick, C. (1985, May). Women and men in the classroom, inequality and its remedies. *On Teaching and Learning,* pp. 18-25.

Larwood, L., Szwajkowski, E., & Rose, S. (1988). When discrimination makes "sense": The rational bias theory. In B. A. Gutek, A. H. Stromberg, & L. Larwood (Eds.), *Women and work: An annual review* (Vol. 3, pp. 265-288). Newbury Park, CA: Sage.

Lewis, M. (1990). Interrupting patriarchy: Politics, resistance, and transformation in the feminist classroom. *Harvard Educational Review, 60,* 472.

Lively, K. (1996, April 26). Drug arrests rise again. *Chronicle of Higher Education,* pp. A37, A48.

Lofton, D. (1995, November 26). Women executives content, survey finds. *Baltimore Sun,* p. E4.

Magner, D. K. (1996, February 2). The new generation. *Chronicle of Higher Education,* p. A17.

Maher, F. A., & Tetreault, M. K. T. (1994). *The feminist classroom.* New York: Basic Books.

Mallory, M. (1996, February 19). From the ground up. *U.S. News & World Report,* pp. 68-72.

Minton, L. (1996, November 6). Sexism in high school: Readers say girls go along and teachers allow it. *Parade Magazine,* p. 6.

Monaghan, P. (1996, February 23). A coach fears her gender-bias suit is costing her jobs. *Chronicle of Higher Education,* p. A43.

Nakashima, E. (1996, April 21). When it comes to top school jobs, women learn it's tough to get ahead. *Washington Post,* pp. B1, B5.

Overholser, G. (1996, April 21). Front page story: Women. *Washington Post,* p. C6.

Park, S. M. (1996). Research, teaching, and service: Why shouldn't women's work count? *Journal of Higher Education, 67,* 46-84.

Peterson, S. B., & Kroner, T. (1992). Gender biases in textbooks for introductory psychology and human development. *Psychology of Women Quarterly, 16,* 17-36.

Rakow, L. F., & Kranich, K. (1991). Woman as sign in television news. *Journal of Communication, 41,* 8-23.

Roan, S. (1996, April 2). Studying women at midlife. *Washington Post,* pp. E1, E8.

Romero, M. (1992). *Maid in the U.S.A.* New York: Routledge.

Russell, C. (1995, November). Glass ceilings can break. *American Demographics,* p. 8.

Salerno, H. (1996). Where women in leadership inspire each other to greater heights. *Washington Post,* p. C1.

Sandler, B. R., & Hall, R. M. (1986). *The campus climate revisited: Chilly for women faculty, administrators, and graduate students.* Washington, DC: Association of American Colleges, Project on the Status and Education of Women.

Seligmann, J. (1993, April 12). A town's divided loyalties. *Newsweek,* p. 29.

Sommer, M. (1994, June 28). Welcome cribside, Dad. *Christian Science Monitor,* p. 19.

Sugg, D. K. (1995, November 8). Black doctors feel chill at HMOs. *Baltimore Sun,* pp. A1, A6.

Torry, S. (1995, November 20). Voice of concern grows louder on gender bias issue [Business supplement]. *Washington Post,* p. 7.

U.S. Bureau of the Census. (1993). *Money income of households, families, and persons in the U.S.* (Current population reports, Series P-60, No. 184). Washington, DC: Government Printing Office.

U.S. Department of Labor. (1994). *Employment and earnings.* Bureau of Labor Statistics. Washington, DC: Government Printing Office.

Wallich, P. (1996, March). Having it all. *Scientific American,* p. 31.

Whatley, M. H. (1994). Keeping adolescents in the picture: Construction of adolescent sexuality in textbook images and popular films. In J. M. Irvine (Ed.), *Sexual cultures and the construction of adolescent identities* (pp. 183-205). Philadelphia: Temple University Press.

Women and work: Workforce 2000 trends. (1990). Washington, DC: Wider Opportunities for Women.

Women's earnings still trail men's, magazine survey finds. (1996, January 16). *Washington Post,* p. 4C.

Chapter

2

Micro Inequities: Up Close and Personal

Beth Bonniwell Haslett
Susan Lipman

Although we may not consciously acknowledge or believe in stereotypes, nevertheless, stereotypes form part of our implicit knowledge:

> These implicit stereotypes provide the meanings that guide our conscious attention, construct our interpretations and fill in gaps in the actual evidence. Because we "see" what we expect to see, the stereotypes create perceptual bias and sex discrimination in how men and women are treated in face-to-face interaction at work, and in organizational evaluations, including those involving recruitment, hiring, performance, salary, and advancement decisions. (Haslett, Geis, & Carter, 1992, p. 54)

These stereotypes are combined into schemas or structured knowledge about events or people that are subsequently used to interpret ongoing behavior and action. Our gender schema for women might include the expectations for nurturant, supportive, emotional behavior, whereas our schema for men might reflect expectations for aggressive, instrumental, and direct behavior (Deaux, 1976; Feldman-Summers & Kiesler, 1974; Williams & Best, 1982). Stereotypes and schemas both describe and prescribe preferred characteristics; that is, they act descriptively as well as prescriptively. Men and women behave in certain ways, and those are the ways in which they *should* behave.

Ordinarily, over the general population, stereotypes and biases should "average out" or cancel each other out, so more objective, neutral judgments can be reached. However, some stereotypes reflect a cultural consensus in which the expectations all are in the same directions.

Even though we consciously disavow stereotypes, consensual stereotypes form part of the implicit knowledge we use in evaluating others and interpreting ongoing behavior (Basow, 1986). Such implicit perceptual bias causes us to infer that men are competent and possess power and that women are less competent and are subordinate in power and status. Such inferences are "visibly" present in society with women and minorities systematically underrepresented at the higher levels of politics, education, government, and industry. Keep in mind, however, that this perceptual bias is unconscious—it operates in what we perceive and how we evaluate the data we obtain.

A number of studies have documented this implicit gender perceptual bias in laboratory studies. For example, essays attributed to male authors were rated as superior to the same essays when attributed to women. Given identical applications concerning acceptability, service, and longevity, men were more likely to be hired (Gutek & Stevens, 1979). And of course, the "glass ceiling," where the number of women decreases as occupational rank increases, is still alive and well (Morrison, White, Van Velsor, & The Center for Creative Leadership, 1987). Finally, judgments of performance and leadership reveal that given "objectively equivalent competency," men are rated consistently higher than equally competent women (Dobbins, 1985). Nonverbal feedback given to women's leadership contained more expressions of disapproval than the same contributions by men (Butler & Geis, 1990).

It is important to note that almost everyone shares consensual, unconscious perceptual biases against women—thus, most people discriminate against women. For example, men may discriminate against women through overt discrimination such as sexual harassment. Women may discriminate against other women through their reluctance to support other women. And women may discriminate against themselves through limiting their own aspirations or an unwillingness to take risks (Powell, 1993).

Overt, Covert, and Subtle Discrimination

Although unconscious perceptual biases affect judgments about women and their capabilities, it is also important to recognize that other forms of differential treatment still exist.

Benokraitis and Feagin (1995) have outlined several different types of modern sexism: overt, covert, and subtle discrimination. They argue that discrimination exists on multiple levels, including individual, organizational, institutional, and cultural discrimination.

Overt discrimination is unequal, harmful, visible discrimination, for example, rape, abuse, or other physical violence against women. Subtle discrimination is internalized sexist behavior that is customary or natural, for example, "believing that women are *really* not as good, capable, competent and intelligent as men" (Benokraitis & Feagin, 1995, p. 41). Covert sex discrimination is harmful treatment that is hidden, intentionally malicious behavior, for example, giving a woman an extraordinarily demanding task, without needed resources, and then blaming her for not being able to complete it. As they note, the harm of overt discrimination may be mild to very severe; the harm from subtle discrimination severe and from covert discrimination, severe to very severe. In addition, it is easiest to remedy overt discrimination; one could probably remedy subtle discrimination but rarely remedy covert sexism. They point out that as overt, visible discrimination was challenged in the 1960s and 1970s, it became replaced by subtle and covert discrimination.

Rowe (1990) has looked at micro inequities and describes them as the "tiny, damaging characteristics of an environment . . . [that] affect a person not indigenous to that environment" (p. 189). Micro inequities, she suggests, comprise the principal scaffolding for segregation. Their effects exclude people and render them less confident and productive. These micro inequities include the practices of subtle discrimination described by Benokraitis and Feagin. The unique dimension Rowe adds to the discussion is the effects of micro inequities on the target individual and a concern for responding to such micro inequities.

Each micro inequity, in and of itself, is so small that one is tempted to ignore it. Isolated instances of hostile humor, subtle sexual innuendo, exclusion via chivalry, and so forth are minor; however, in the aggregate, micro inequities create a climate of widespread exclusion and subtle hostility. Rowe notes that it is especially difficult to respond to micro inequities because they are irrational, intermittent, subtle, and infinitely varied. Each instance must be evaluated as to the speaker's intent and motivation, which consumes the target's time and energy. Responding is problematic because one's anger may be misplaced or displaced. For example, you might "explode" at the next instance of a micro inequity. To not respond, however, is to allow worse damage, to extend the damage, and to lead to self-fulfilling prophecies regarding the target individual's competence and status. Being excluded from a work team, for instance, may prevent one from being considered for further challenging assignments. Over time, the target individual is demonstrably less competent because she has been denied opportunities to develop her skills. Thus, the initial micro inequity—the perception of not being "good enough"—leads to behaviors that in fact contributed to her declining status when compared to her peers.

Responding to micro inequities involves *face* issues or issues of socially situated identities (Tracy, 1990). In instances of micro inequities, what is at stake is one's public social identity: Targets of micro inequities have their negative face attacked. Negative face refers to one's desire to be unimpeded or autonomous. Micro inequities limit the target's behaviors, especially their ability to respond, because individually each micro inequity is so small and perceived as trivial. Positive face refers to the appreciation or respect accorded an individual. Positive face is also attacked because it is being challenged. Hostile humor, for example, attacks one's positive face (dignity) through chiding or joking about one's competence. If the target responds by stating that the comment was offensive, the target's negative face may be challenged by replies such as "you're too sensitive." Micro inequities may be difficult to respond to because they attack the target on multiple face issues; both positive and negative face may be under attack, as in the case of hostile humor. Tracy notes that face threats are also a function of the social distance, relative power, and degree of mutual interdependence between the interactants. In organizational settings, for example, status and position play into considerations about the degree of face threats. Interestingly, Tracy suggests that conflict may be a face-saving strategy: I will attack you before you attack me, as in hostile humor, and make it difficult for you to challenge me.

Thus far, we have seen a pattern of nonconscious bias and discrimination against those who are different. More overt discrimination has been supplanted by subtle and covert discrimination. Micro inequities are particularly ubiquitous because in each instance the harm seems too small to bother with. In the aggregate, however, they constitute a serious barrier to productivity, advancement, and inclusion. Micro inequities are particularly difficult to respond to because of the face issues involved as well as the seeming "smallness" of each single instance.

The present study is an attempt to understand more fully how micro inequities operate by examining their presence in the legal profession. A group of women lawyers attending a continuing education conference was asked to fill out a survey concerning micro inequities. The legal profession, with its adversarial climate and highly educated practitioners, was thought to provide an excellent test of micro inequities and the targets' ability to respond to them.

Three research questions were posed: (a) What is the nature of micro inequities attorneys confront in their practice? (b) What impact do micro inequities have on their interactions and professional activities? and (c) How do attorneys respond to micro inequities?

Before we turn to these questions, and their results, we need to survey briefly the legal profession and assess the discriminatory practices that characterize this profession. Several recent major studies recount the nature of legal practice in the United States.

The Legal Profession: A Review of Gender Issues

The final report of the Ninth Circuit Gender Bias Task Force was published in May 1994. The purpose of the task force was to assess the effects of gender in federal courts. Such studies have been done in 30 states and essentially found that the court system, designed to protect the civil and criminal rights of citizens, was itself flawed by gender inequities. As in many of our social institutions, gender bias and issues are largely "unseen." This report will be examined closely for gender issues that are reported; similar findings have been found in other federal circuits and in state judiciaries. The Ninth Circuit Report (on California) itself cites several other reports: "There is overwhelming evidence . . . that the negative impact of gender bias operates much more frequently and seriously against women" (also see

Schafran & Wilker, 1986). In Connecticut, the report concluded that "women are treated differently from men in the justice system and, because of it, many suffer from unfairness, embarrassment, emotional pain, professional deprivation and economic hardship" (Connecticut Task Force on Gender, Justice, and the Courts, 1991). In 1989, the Washington State Task Force on Gender and Justice in the Courts concluded that "gender discrimination exists and can negatively impact judicial decision making and affect the outcome of litigation."

The 3,409 respondents of the Ninth Circuit federal practitioners were 84% male and 16% female; 6% were persons of color and 25% of the latter were female. In an overview of the findings, the report concluded:

> There are sharp disagreements about the influence of gender on appointments, hiring, and promotion practices. Generally, men believe that both judicial appointments and the hiring and promotion decisions made within law firms are merit-based. In contrast, although women agree that experience and expertise are taken into account by those who make appointments, hiring and promotion decisions, women believe that other factors also play an important role.
>
> Women judges and women lawyers attribute male-domination of the judiciary in large part to the exclusion of women from the networks that influence judicial appointments. Woman lawyers attribute the small number of women appointed to the bench and various committees to the exclusion of women from formal and informal selection processes. A large proportion of women lawyers believe that men have a better chance than women to be promoted to law firm partnerships and to equivalent positions in public law organizations. Women of color are most likely to believe that gender affects hiring, promotion and case assignment. Conversely, white-Anglo men are most likely to believe that men and women are treated equally in those decisions. Women lawyers, more frequently than their male counterparts, report occasions on which women were passed over for promotion and for important case assignments in favor of men with equal qualifications. Taken together, these data suggest that the women and men of the Ninth Circuit inhabit different worlds, one characterized by feelings of exclusion and the other by feelings of acceptance. (Ninth Circuit Court Gender Bias Task Force, 1994, pp. 786-787; hereafter cited as "Final Report," 1994)

What are the factors giving rise to such different perceptions of inequality? One factor is that the "numerical dominance of males in key positions in the Ninth Circuit bench and bar hierarchy sends a message of exclusion and subordination to many female practitioners" ("Final Report," 1994, p. 790). Male lawyers and judges perceived this as a function of males' greater experience, women's not being a part of the selection network, and women's lack of holding the right professional positions. In contrast, female judges and lawyers believed that the most important factors in explaining the male-dominated judiciary were women's lack of participation in selecting and appointing individuals to various positions, appointers not being comfortable with women, women's not holding positions that prepared them for advancement, and women's lack of visibility ("Final Report," 1994, p. 792). Being outside the "loop of influence and position" clearly hinders women.

Both female and male respondents in private practice believed that men had a better chance of being promoted to partner. Women perceived women as having been passed over for promotion far more frequently than did men. However, a majority believed that both men and women had an equal chance of being hired. Although entry-level positions may have evened out, as they have in some occupations, clearly the glass-ceiling effects limit further advancement. Similar findings held for promotion policies for lawyers within public practice.

Significant barriers to advancement are enacted in daily interaction. A common assumption is that litigators should follow a "male" style, and therefore, this serves to limit women's opportunities in litigation cases. Others note that women are "weeded out": "A large law firm is a very male-dominated place and it's hard for women to survive" ("Final Report," 1994, p. 800). Women frequently do not get appointed to committees; as a result, promotion is difficult because women lack the prerequisite committee participation. If a judge is uncomfortable with female attorneys, this may be used as a rationale against assigning women difficult, challenging cases. Many women believe that they have lost important cases to men because of gender bias. Similar findings exist across both public and private practice.

> These exchanges (between judges and attorneys; among judges, litigants and witnesses; among attorneys, litigants and witnesses; and among attorneys) . . . [are] the "stuff" of professional life—what lawyers *do* is talk to judges, other attorneys, clients, and other laypersons. Moreover, *how* judges talk to attorneys and how attorneys talk among themselves may send important messages to the attorneys' colleagues and to their clients—and may ultimately convey messages about the attorney's own professional worth. Similarly, the manner in which judges and attorneys interact with criminal and civil parties and with witnesses and jurors conveys messages about the

> judicial system's assessment of the validity and worth of the claims of litigants and of their contribution, as witnesses and participants, to the judicial process. ("Final Report," 1994, p. 809)

Interactional differences thus play an important role in the work that attorneys do. Female judges and lawyers believe that they are addressed more informally and receive more inappropriate comments (i.e., on dress and appearance) than males. Female attorneys believe this treatment draws "special attention to their gender or otherwise set[s] them apart from their male colleagues and courtroom opponents" ("Final Report," 1994, p. 813). Respondents noted that male judges seemed unable to handle adversarial conflict between female attorneys (e.g., admonishing them not to get hysterical or to calm down) and letting similar behavior by male attorneys pass without comment. Female respondents believed that judges did not view their behavior as just arguing their cases as any attorney would. Similarly, there are judges who seem to assume that female attorneys are "emotional" when they are simply presenting their cases forcefully. Women also perceived judges to cut them off, to be stricter with them than men, and to make more disparaging and demeaning remarks to them as compared to their male counterparts. Although the adversarial process involves negative interactions, as one attorney noted, "Uncivil behavior occurs with uncivil attorneys, and uncivil attorneys are more uncivil to members of the opposite sex it seems" ("Final Report," 1994, p. 819). Some female attorneys believe that the demeaning remarks by opposing counsel are designed to make them feel uncomfortable and used to persuade others that women are not in control of the situation ("Final Report," 1994, p. 819). One written comment by a courtroom deputy who watches court proceedings and does not participate noted that "in my experience it seems that if there is an opportunity to make asides or direct derogatory statements about opposing female counsel in the courtroom, male counsel are more likely to take advantage of the opportunity" ("Final Report," 1994, p. 819). Both female and male judges observed male counsel cutting off or ignoring female attorneys, and female attorneys reported negative interactions in conversations outside the judges' presence (e.g., in negotiations between attorneys in out-of-court settlements).

In conclusion, the Ninth Circuit study found that overt discriminatory behaviors appear to be relatively rare. However, interactional patterns characterized as a "type of patronizing, trivializing conduct by men attorneys and judges to women attorneys—and male clients' lesser confidence in women lawyers" was clearly evident:

> The research data are replete with descriptions of gender-biased treatment from lawyers' colleagues, supervisors, professional adversaries, and clients. Some of that behavior consists of verbal efforts to diminish a woman in her professional work. In addition, while some women may not be the recipients of unwanted sexual advances, the majority of women respondents were. More than 60 percent of the women report unwanted sexual advances and other forms of sexual harassment from those with whom they are in professional contact.
>
> Lawyers report that gender often influences courtroom procedures, evaluation of witnesses, substantive law, and jurisprudential assumptions. Because much of the behavior is subtle and a good deal of court processes occur informally (from pretrial management, discovery, and alternative dispute resolution, on the civil side, to prosecutorial discretion, the work of pretrial services, and probation on the criminal side), many of the effects of gender are difficult to ascertain and document. But, by the consistency of reporting, certain patterns emerge. ("Final Report," 1994, p. 955)

These findings are from the Ninth Circuit report, but keep in mind that state reports have uncovered the same types of problems, including a recent study (1995) done in the state from which the lawyer sample was drawn for our study.

In brief, there is clear-cut evidence that subtle discrimination and micro inequities have a significant presence in the legal profession. The difficulty of dealing with these issues is also readily apparent. The present survey, which focuses in part on the effect of micro inequities and how individuals cope with them, provides more understanding of these problems.

Research Design and Data Collection

We administered our survey at a conference for women lawyers in March 1995. Thirty-one of the 36 participants responded to the survey. The micro inequities section was part of a larger survey on career issues, interpersonal relations in organizations, and organizational climate.

In terms of demographic characteristics, 26 of the respondents were Caucasian and 5 were women of color. Roughly one third of the participants were under 35 years of age; another third were aged 36 to 45, and the remaining third was over 45 years of age. Twenty-five of the lawyers were married and half had children. A wide range of working conditions was represented in this sample: 4 of the respondents have their own practice; 3

were in the state court system, and the remaining 24 were in law firms. These firms range in size from 1 to 15 members (44%); 16 to 50 members (33%), and over 50 members (23%). A variety of legal areas were represented: family law, domestic and civil litigation, bankruptcy, personal injury, employment and labor law, criminal law, estate planning and probate, tax law, land use planning, and commercial litigation. Twelve of the lawyers had worked for 5 years or less, whereas the remaining 19 worked from 6 to 15 years. Most firms were entirely Caucasian, or predominantly Caucasian. One firm had a minority membership of 20%. The great majority of law firms also had a preponderance of men as members, with most firms having a four to one ratio between men and women. Two firms were entirely female; another firm had 20% men and 80% women.

The survey contained questions about career issues, interpersonal relationships in the workplace, and organizational climate. Questions asked about the effect of micro inequities on the job, their frequency, their personal effect on the respondents, and how the respondents coped with micro inequities.

Results

Because participants could provide more than one answer in replying to a question, the percentages reflect the proportion of the total number of responses to that question rather than the number of respondents answering a question.

Seventy-one percent of the respondents have experienced micro inequities (significant at the $p < .01$ level). Of those experiencing micro inequities, 20% had *rarely* experienced micro inequities, 50% experienced them *sometimes,* and 20% had experienced them either *often* to *all the time.*

The micro inequities included a lack of opportunity (19%), productivity (12%), limits on advancement (17%), performance (15%), and limited promotion opportunities (10%). Other influences (27%) included not being allowed to take initiative, being "out of the loop" of information, having work delayed, being given unimportant work, and not being given any autonomy.

Participants reacted to micro inequities with frustration (35%), stress (23%), anger (17%), withdrawal (12%), ignoring or repressing it (6%), depression (4%), and open hostility (3%). Status relationships, whether with a superior or a peer, appeared to play a role in whether a micro inequity was discussed and its subsequent effect on the relationship. Only one fourth of

TABLE 2.1 Most Harmful, Disruptive Micro Inequities

Exclusion[a]
Being ignored/overlooked[a]
Lack of opportunities[a]
Lack of information[a]
Differential treatment[a]
Sexual innuendo/disrespectful language[a]
Lack of advancement[a]
Isolation[a]
Hostile humor
Lack of autonomy
Hostile working environment
Limited perceptions of one's capabilities[a]

a. Indicates that it was mentioned by several respondents. In order of their effect, exclusion was most frequently mentioned, followed by being ignored, and then lack of opportunity, lack of information, and experiencing different treatment.

respondents said anything about micro inequities perpetrated by a superior (significant at the $p < .01$ level). Of the respondents who discussed it with their supervisors, 16% perceived *less tension* in their relationship, 16% experienced *no change,* and 25% reported *more tension.* Of those experiencing micro inequities with peers, all discussed it with peers. All reported that the relationships were more distant and reported *no change in tension* or *more tension* in the relationship.

Two open-ended questions asked about the most disturbing micro inequities and their effect on the respondent's job. Table 2.1 lists the most disturbing micro inequities. Exclusion, isolation, and being ignored were listed as major negative effects. In addition, respondents reported being treated differently and experiencing a lack of opportunity and information. The competitive environment, large amounts of work, and hostile work environment were also cited as problems.

Discussion

Micro inequities were a significant issue for 71% of the respondents in our study. It is quite possible that many instances of micro inequities were not reported because many people are unfamiliar with the concept and might see micro inequities as normal or customary.

The biggest effect of micro inequities appears to be interpersonal in nature, influencing the target's psychological state and the relationship between the target and the perpetrator of the micro inequities. The most common response to a micro inequity was frustration, followed by stress and then anger. These are all negative emotions, and they increase the difficulty of maintaining effective workplace relationships and a productive workplace climate. In fact, these respondents believed that micro inequities constituted a major source of stress on the job. This additional stress goes well beyond the "alienation" of the modern organization (Rowe, 1990) and adds an additional layer of complexity in interpersonal relationships and workplace conditions.

Open-ended comments from the survey reflect the range of these concerns. One woman commented that the work environment was not supportive because of "isolation and [a] male dominated atmosphere" and "being excluded or [the] information network and informal communication." Such informal connections are major ways in which interpersonal relationships evolve, client contacts developed (e.g., for the purpose of rainmaking or bringing in accounts for the firm) and information is shared. Women noted the penalties from being "out of the loop." One respondent noted, for example, that because she was not given much time or support for developing client relationships, her professional contributions were being limited. Personal connections have always played an important role in professional development and accomplishments. This is likely to be even more crucial in times of economic constraint.

Another respondent commented that micro inequities were a major problem in her work and work relationships and believed that micro inequities lead people into "thinking that [women] may not be able to do things on our own." As noted earlier, this expectation is a type of self-fulfilling prophecy: Treating individuals as incompetent may encourage incompetent behaviors because the opportunity for development and learning never occurs (Haslett et al., 1992).

In addition, such treatment may be internalized and women may begin to question themselves. Women tend to internalize failure (Haslett et al., 1992). Unless women realize that micro inequities reflect systemic subtle bias, they are likely to blame themselves and question their competency. One attorney commented that experiencing micro inequities "makes me feel less able to present myself as an attorney." Another respondent sensed some micro inequities "when you deal with people over the phone (women more likely to be treated casually, called by first name) or in confrontational settings with other attorneys (not necessarily in court)." Yet another attorney noted that the most important consequence of micro inequities was the "seriousness [with] which I'm taken" and being treated in an unprofessional ("being treated like 'staff' ") or inappropriate manner ("not having my time valued by my superiors"). This presents a more difficult interactional setting to negotiate, where face issues as well as the task itself must be negotiated.

Many respondents noted difficulties with sexual innuendoes, a lack of respect, and inappropriate comments (e.g., about clothing or personal dress) not only from peers and superiors within their firm but also from judges, other lawyers, and clients. One respondent reported that she noticed "differences in the perception of male and female litigants in the courtroom by judges. Some male judges don't really seem to listen to or understand women." Women are being treated as women rather than as professionals. As noted earlier, the Ninth Circuit study in California noted a wide array of sexist treatment (some of which were micro inequities) within the legal system. Thus, a multitude of interpersonal relationships appears to be affected by micro inequities.

For women of color, the consequences of micro inequities multiply, incorporating both ethnic and gender identities. As one respondent noted, "The Spanish background pigeonholed my skills to the Latin American client." Other offensive micro inequities involve "joking around about my Spanish clients and their 'relationship' to me (or we all look alike). I laugh it off; my peers know my skills." Although this respondent reacted to a demeaning comment by laughing it off, as part of a larger network of relationships, including clients, such instances nevertheless place interactants in an awkward setting at best, and in a "one-down" position. Another attorney noted "being boxed in (i.e., only being considered for 'minority' issues or being advised to market minority groups instead of other established business marketing groups)." She experienced "well intentioned, but negative sexist/ethnic comments" and "having my color always seen, but seldom having my person seen." Not surprisingly, micro inequities appear more severe when ethnic identity and gender intersect (Fulbright, 1985).

Part of Rowe's (1990) discussion of the complexity and difficulty with micro inequities concerns how difficult it is to respond to micro inequities. The attorneys in this survey found this to be the case as well. Only one fourth of the attorneys challenged a micro inequity, and only a few discussed a micro inequity with a superior who had engaged in such behavior. One attorney reported that she responded to a micro inequity "by leaving the office and not sleeping all weekend . . . never confronting the partner directly—telling my other superior about the incident—who already knew from the perpetrator." She reported that there was no change in the relationship but that "I avoided him." Another reported responding with "open hostility (I try to keep this to a minimum)." Avoidance and hostility create even more stress and are likely to escalate the level of tension. Other professional relationships may also be affected by the aversion or hostility. Another attorney reported an instance of "providing information then being dismissed. Another partner gets the credit. Did nothing. Swallowed it." To advance, one must be competent but also visibly competent: not receiving credit for one's work renders your contribution invisible, and thus your value is not recognized or rewarded.

Another attorney remarked that she told another partner about a micro inequity, but he took no action. She has subsequently ignored other instances of micro inequities. Part of the problem, of course, is that having one partner address the micro inequity places his relationship with the perpetrator in jeopardy. It is not surprising that micro inequities go unnoticed, or if noticed, not corrected. Being a whistle-blower has negative connotations interpersonally and organizationally (Stewart, 1987). Of those responding overtly, most reported no change in the relationship or more tension in the relationship. This, too, is part of the frustration and damage of micro inequities: Even when they are reported, no action is taken, or even worse, the targets are punished for reporting the situation.

If responding overtly appears not to lead to improved relationships, then there is not much point perhaps in addressing the issue. A number of attorneys reported repressing or ignoring micro inequities. As one attorney noted, "You ignore your pain and disappointment and deal with that aspect of the behavior or comment which could *in some conceivable manner* be viewed as positive (i.e., you repress)." The face issues to be negotiated here are paradoxical—for example, putting the best possible "face" on circumstances that should not occur. For most men, such issues may not come up and therefore might be hard to understand. The ultimate sanction, of course, may be loss of employment. As one attorney related, "My previous employers (two different firms) had serious problems. My most recent employer was particularly egregious. The senior partners treated female staff very poorly and expected me to do the same. I believe I would have been summarily fired if I had freely spoken my mind." Even though one may directly experience micro inequities, their presence creates a hostile work environment.

More attorneys confront peers rather than superiors. Even in those cases, respondents note little change in the relationship and, at times, an increase in tension. One attorney reported using tactics of "logic and humor" to address micro inequities and reported a lessening of tension in the relationship. Another reported trying to "argue with them in a friendly manner—got nowhere—maintain a distant cynical relationship" and reported that there was no obvious change in the relationship. Some have chosen not to confront directly, but to work to make changes. One attorney, for example, did not directly question inadequate training opportunities, but volunteered to work on the committee that would determine the organization's policy.

Generally, the practices of exclusion and of being ignored were listed as the most serious patterns of micro inequities. Exclusion results in women being denied opportunities and information crucial for their professional success. Lack of opportunity and information results in women being less able to compete, regardless of ability, because they are denied learning opportunities. This reaffirms the perceived lack of confidence in women that underlies micro inequities. In brief, we have the self-fulfilling prophecy of micro inequities perpetuating limited opportunities for women. Subsequently, women are at a competitive disadvantage with male peers, which, in turn, perpetuates the unconscious bias against women. It comes to, as one attorney noted, "being treated differently from men—[experiencing] more harassment and intimidation by men, [and having] less opportunities than men."

Being ignored is an even more direct micro inequity because even when you do comment, you are invisible. One attorney noted that because "my size, voice, and appearance is not threatening . . . I've been pushed aside when the situation is more 'serious.' " The male values that govern most of our social and political institutions render women invisible as a class of people; male values and perceived desirable qualities provide the standard against which others are judged. Underrepresented groups are not visibly a part of the system and are noted as exceptions, however unconscious that judgment might be. One respondent referred to this as "the systematic code of fear and intimidation that underpins control of the definition of success—so that one is constantly having the ladder knocked out from under her."

Language

It is worth noting that the language used by respondents vividly depicts their reactions to micro inequities. People who engage in micro inequities were often referred to as "perpetrators" as in a perpetrator of a crime. The reference is a fairly pointed, professional one in which I suspect all the metaphorical illusions were intentionally signaled. The lack of a supportive climate is referenced as "having the ladder knocked out from under her." Others referred to being "pigeonholed" or otherwise limited and constrained. The difficulty in responding to micro inequities is graphically depicted in terms such as "swallowing it" and "repressing it."

Micro Inequities: Dilemmas in Responding

When we combine an analysis of micro inequities with the face needs of individuals in interaction, we begin to see the complexities of responding to micro inequities. Micro inequities can attack one's autonomy (negative face) or one's public dignity (positive face); these attacks can be either direct or indirect. A direct micro inequity attacking one's public dignity would be, for example, an insult, whereas an indirect attack would be exemplified by a remark, such as a compliment on one's dress. In ordinary interaction, a compliment may be a very nice comment. In a professional business context, however, such comments mark an irrelevant characteristic to one's competency (and may undermine one's position by drawing attention to nonrelevant aspects). One attorney noted that a judge complimented her on her suit and she, in turn, complimented his attire as well—the point was well taken and the judge made no remarks after this exchange.

Micro inequities that question one's autonomy are more subtle. An example of a direct attack on one's autonomy (negative face) would be a senior partner who denies a female associate an opportunity to participate on a difficult case and thus is limiting her professional activities and development. An indirect attack on one's autonomy would be exclusion from the informal network of information and thus being limited through lack of information.

Generally, micro inequities attacking one's dignity are easier to identify and to respond to because "disrespect" is widely disavowed in our culture and people judge disrespectful individuals negatively (e.g., as rude, disruptive, prejudiced). Limiting another's ability to act is harder to identify because, in some contexts, such limits seem appropriate and reasonable, such as a parent setting rules for teens or a supervisor setting standards for employees. In a similar fashion, direct micro inequities seem easier to respond to than indirect micro inequities. Direct micro inequities are overt and thus can be responded to. In some cases, like an indirect limit on someone's autonomy, a micro inequity may not be recognized because one is unaware of its occurrence.

The Paradox of Response

One can respond fairly easily to an insult, for example, by humor, asking for an apology, or offering an insult in return. However, an indirect micro inequity that challenges one's public dignity—like an inappropriate compliment—is more problematic. If one comments on it, then one may get replies like "You're too sensitive" or "What's wrong with that? Can't I even give a compliment anymore?" A well-intentioned male colleague might be bewildered by a less-than-positive response to a compliment, and that is part of the dilemma of responding to micro inequities. Responding to micro inequities requires the recipient to make split-second judgments about the speaker's intentions and how much it might "cost" one in terms of both personal and professional relationships and the stress one experiences in dealing with these situations. The stress of responding has not been given sufficient attention either in the research literature or in practice, especially its aggregate nature, in which micro inequities build up and may cause an overreaction to a particular incident (no one sees the seven other micro inequities that may have preceded this "final straw"). Whereas a man might overreact to a situation, typically men do not receive as many negative sanctions for such behavior, because that is "acceptable" male behavior to some extent, even in professional settings. In contrast, similar behavior by women is evaluated negatively because it violates implicit assumptions about how women should behave.

An additional burden is also the guilt one may experience if one does not respond to the micro inequities. Not responding, as one attorney put it, means joining the "silent conspiracy" that allows micro inequities to flourish. However, to address every micro inequity one experiences may allow no time or energy for anything else, which contributes to low productivity and high stress.

Responding to an indirect attack on one's autonomy, as in the case of exclusion from an informal network of information, is even more problematic because it operates on systemic hidden bias as well as personal liking. As Kanter (1977) noted in her classic analysis of gender in organizations, managers like, promote, and reward others like themselves. That is, we like others who are like us—the principle of homogeneity. Homogeneity seems to control networks of informal information and opportunity in organizations. Because most senior-level lawyers are males, they are more likely, following principles of homogeneity, to share information with other males. Personal affiliations—likes and dislikes—also operate to control informal information networks. Male professional relationships do not raise questions of personal liking and attractiveness as do cross-sex relationships. Even if a relationship between a male and a female colleague is entirely professional and platonic, some questions may be raised nevertheless about their relationship. Although these questions should not determine one's friendships at work, it is nevertheless an issue that needs to be addressed. As more men and women work together, however, such issues should become less problematic.

The difficulty of responding to micro inequities is a large part of why micro inequities are so complex. As the lawyers in this survey discovered, responding to micro inequities is difficult and there appears to be little payoff for speaking out. However, to not respond is to become a tacit accomplice; hence, the "double-bind" or "damned-if-you-do, damned-if-you-don't" problem. Being aware of this paradox, however, will allow women and minorities to develop strategies that will change these interaction patterns. Not everyone will respond in the same way, but they will develop strategies comfortable for them.

Women's Unique Experience of Micro Inequities

One final point about women's experiencing of micro inequities is their *aggregate* burden. That is, taken individually, each instance of an innuendo or hostile humor may strike one as being minor and not worth "calling someone on it"; however, the daily, cumulative burden of continuously experiencing such micro inequities is significant. Mary Rowe's earlier formulation of micro inequities likens them to the rings of Saturn. Up close, the rings of Saturn are minute particles of dust or ice. However, taken as a whole, they form impenetrable rings or barriers. Over time, as respondents have indicated, micro inequities contribute significantly to stress, frustration, and anger—and constitute a formidable barrier to performance, productivity, and advancement. Such burdens are part of one's daily life and each encounter presents paradoxical demands that must be dealt with immediately.

Everyone experiences micro inequities. However, some underrepresented groups, such as women and minorities, experience no relief. White men encounter micro inequities at some times. Women and other underrepresented groups experience them across the board because they are judged against standards that are based predominantly on male values. Thus, although everyone experiences micro inequities, the sheer burden of them creates a dual reality and burden for women, both personally and professionally. And responses to micro inequities are especially problematic because one can always be accused of being too sensitive. Dube-Simard's (1983) three conditions for problematic intergroup (male vs. female) interaction have been fulfilled by micro inequities: There are clear social differences, these differences threaten self-identity and professional identity, and there is a striking sense of social injustice. Thus, micro inequities make negotiating interpersonal relationships and career development more difficult and complex.

Future research needs to assess more of the effects of micro inequities and assess strategies that may cope with these circumstances. In particular, the simultaneous, paradoxical interactional demands of micro inequities require closer scrutiny. It looms as an increasingly critical issue, both socially and professionally, as our world becomes increasingly global and diverse. Subtle discrimination and micro inequities are not in *anyone's* best interests because we need the talents of all to resolve problems.

References

Basow, S. (1986). *Gender stereotypes: Traditions and alternatives.* Belmont, CA:Brooks/Cole.

Benokraitis, N. V., & Feagin, J. R. (1995). *Modern sexism: Blatant, subtle, and covert discrimination.* Englewood Cliffs, NJ: Prentice Hall.

Butler, D., & Geis, F. (1990). Nonverbal affect responses to male and female leaders: Implications for leadership evaluation. *Journal of Personality and Social Psychology, 58,* 48-59.

Connecticut Task Force on Gender, Justice, and the Courts. (1991). *Report of the Connecticut Task Force on Gender, Justice, and the Courts* (Vol. 12). Hartford, CT: State Government.

Deaux, K. (1976). *The behavior of women and men.* Belmont, CA: Brooks/Cole.

Dobbins, G. (1985). Effects of gender on leader's responses to poor performers—An attributional interpretation. *Journal of the Academy of Management, 28,* 587-598.

Dube-Simard, L. (1983). Genesis of social categorization, threat to identity, and perceptions of social injustice: Their role in intergroup communication. *Journal of Language and Social Psychology, 2,* 183-206.

Feldman-Summers, S., & Kiesler, S. (1974). Those who are number two try harder: The effect of sex on attributions of causality. *Journal of Personality and Social Psychology, 8,* 846-855.

Fulbright, K. (1985). The myth of the double-advantage: Black female managers. *Review of Black Political Economy, 14,* 33-45.

Gutek, B., & Stevens, D. (1979). Differential responses of males and females to work situations which evoke sex role stereotypes. *Journal of Vocational Behavior, 14,* 23-32.

Haslett, B., Geis, F., & Carter, M. (1992). *The organizational woman: Power and paradox.* Norwood, NJ: Ablex.

Kanter, R. (1977). *Men and women of the corporation.* New York: Basic Books.

Morrison, A., White, R., Van Velsor, E., & The Center for Creative Leadership. (1987). *Breaking the glass ceiling: Can women reach the top of America's largest corporations?* Reading, MA: Addison-Wesley.

Ninth Circuit Gender Bias Task Force. (1994, May). Final report. *Southern California Law Review, 67,* 727-1106.

Powell, G. (1993). *Women and men in management.* Newbury Park, CA: Sage.

Rowe, M. (1990). Barriers to equality: The power of subtle discrimination to maintain unequal opportunity. *Employee Responsibilities and Rights Journal, 3,* 153-163.

Schafran, L., & Wilker, N. (1986). *Operating a task force on gender bias in the courts: A manual for action.* Hartford, CT: State Government.

Stewart, L. (1987). Breaking the rules in organizations: Women as whistle blowers. In L. Stewart & S. Ting-Toomey (Eds.), *Communication, gender, and sex roles in diverse interaction contexts* (pp. 135-144). Norwood, NJ: Ablex.

Tracy, K. (1990). The many faces of face work. In H. Giles & P. Robinson (Eds.), *Handbook of language and social psychology* (pp. 206-226). New York: John Wiley.

Washington State Task Force on Gender and Justice in the Courts. (1989). [Report].

Williams, J., & Best, D. (1982). *Measuring sex stereotypes: A thirty nation study.* Beverly Hills, CA: Sage.

Chapter

3

Exploring the Campus Climate for Women Faculty

Judith E. Owen Blakemore
Jo Young Switzer
Judith A. DiLorio
David L. Fairchild

Over the past decade, a number of studies have identified a set of problems for women in academia. Generally, these problems have come to be labeled as the "chilly climate" for women (Balogh & Kite, 1991; Flam, 1991; Sandler, 1991; Sandler & Hall, 1986; Sandler, Silverberg, & Hall, 1996; Swoboda, 1990). Researchers have reported that the university environment is substantially less supportive for women faculty than it is for men. Specifically, women are clustered at the lowest faculty ranks, receive lower salaries, are more likely to occupy temporary or part-time positions, and advance in rank or are tenured less frequently or more slowly (Angel, 1988; Caplan, 1993; Chamberlain, 1988; Fox, 1981, 1991; Sandler & Hall, 1986; Swoboda, 1990; Zuckerman, 1991).

Researchers have also reported that women generally find their daily interactions in academia less hospitable than do men (Aisenberg & Harrington, 1988; Balogh & Kite, 1991; Caplan, 1993; The Chilly Collective, 1995; McKinney, 1990; Sandler, 1991). In a recent review of this research, Paula Caplan (1993) has characterized the difficulties women face as being due to "the maleness of the environment." She reports such problems as the devaluation of women and their work, sexist jokes and comments, sexual harassment, and exclusion from the institution's social networks. In addition, several researchers have reported that students are more demanding of women faculty and may give them poorer evaluations, particularly if the faculty violate gender norms (Basow, 1995; Basow & Silberg, 1987; Fandt & Stevens, 1991; Kierstad, D'Agostino, & Dill, 1988; McIntyre, 1995; Unger, 1979).

In summary, then, academia appears to be a less hospitable environment for women faculty than for men faculty. Many of these studies, however, have used anonymous questionnaires in their surveys. Although surveys are well-established and valuable research tools, interviews are more powerful techniques for exploring individuals' own views of reality because they offer people more opportunity to explain or elaborate on their answers (Fine, 1992; Reinharz, 1992). We chose, therefore, to conduct in-depth interviews of university faculty members.

The present study was triggered by an institutional commitment to examine the campus climate for women faculty. We posed the question: Are there differences in how men and women faculty members describe their day-to-day lives in the university? Our interest was both theoretical and practical. In addition to examining the experiences of both men and women, we wanted to use the information to recommend changes so that the university could better support faculty in their work.

Method

We interviewed 62 of the tenured or tenure-track full-time faculty in the School of Arts and Sciences at a regional commuter campus of a state university. This sample included all of the 42 women (40 white, 2 East Asian) and a representative sample of 20 male (19 white, 1 East Asian) faculty members from all departments.[1] Of those interviewed, 40% of the men and 52% of the women were tenured.

The interview team consisted of six tenured Arts and Sciences faculty members, four women and two men, who had been appointed by the dean to the school's Task Force on Women Faculty. The interviewers included faculty members from psychology, sociology, communication, mathematics, literature, and philosophy. Each interviewed same-gender respondents outside of his or her department. Interviews ranged from approximately 40 minutes to over 2 hours in length. A typical interview lasted about 1 hour.

As soon as possible after the interview, the interviewer produced a typewritten transcript of the interview. These transcripts were later compiled into two lengthy summary documents, one consisting of the responses of tenured faculty and the other consisting of the responses of untenured faculty, each separated by gender. On all transcripts, respondents were identified by code numbers only.

Most of the questions we asked were open ended. They explored such issues as rank; expectations about teaching, research, and service; and interactions with students and colleagues. The primary focus was on the faculty members' perceptions of their daily environments, and in particular, the climate for women. More specifically, we constructed a 51-item structured questionnaire based on previous studies on this topic. We pretested and modified the questionnaire and refined the interview process after interviewing faculty who were not part of the identified pool. The questions varied slightly for tenured and untenured faculty members regarding the promotion and tenure process. Table 3.1 presents examples of the questionnaire items.

Results

Although the data were examined both qualitatively and quantitatively, we focus here primarily on the qualitative responses. Each interviewer read the individual transcripts and the summary documents and noted themes across the responses. When asked, "All things considered, are you satisfied here?" the majority of the faculty (86% of the tenured women; 79% of the untenured women; 100% of the tenured men; 92% of the untenured men) answered affirmatively. Women expressed less satisfaction than men in a number of areas, however, ranging from salary to demeaning remarks based on gender.

TABLE 3.1 Interview Categories and Sample Questions

Category	*Sample Questions*
Teaching	How do your students address you in class? How do they address you in private conversation? Is this what you want to be called?
Tenure/promotion	Do people in your department discuss tenure/promotion with each other? Are you part of those discussions?
Research	Do you have the resources you need to do your research and scholarship? Do you feel that these resources are equitable compared to other faculty in your department?
Service	How does your service load compare to that of others in your department?
Social issues	Do you have a sense of belonging in your department? Are you invited to colleagues' homes, athletic events, poker, social events, etc., in a way comparable to that of your colleagues in your department?
Family issues	Are people in your department sensitive to personal and family issues? Do you feel conflicting demands between personal, family, and university obligations?
Harassment	Have you ever experienced any of the following behaviors from students, faculty, or staff: Undue sexual attention? Verbal sexual advances? Repeated unwanted social invitations? Physical advances of a sexual nature? Sexual bribery? Unwelcome sexual jokes or teasing?

NOTE: The entire set of interview questions may be obtained from Elaine Blakemore, Department of Psychological Sciences, Indiana–Purdue University, Fort Wayne, IN 46815.

Salary and Rank

There were 42 tenured or tenure-track women faculty in the School of Arts and Sciences, approximately 29% of the 147 full-time faculty. Women faculty were concentrated at the lowest faculty ranks in the school: 82% of the instructors, 35% of the assistant professors, 25% of the associate professors, and 4% of the professors were women. Within rank, without controlling for years in rank, salary levels were roughly comparable. For example, at the assistant professor rank the average salary for women faculty was $30,825 compared to $30,477 for men faculty.

Department Climate

We found large differences among respondents in the extent to which they perceived their departments to be supportive. Some departments were seen as very supportive, some as largely indifferent, and others as extremely unsupportive. Although this range of responses characterized both men and women, the most egregious descriptions of unsupportive departments were provided by women. In supportive environments, respondents said such things as "I feel like I have friends here," or "People are friendly, colleagues act collegially." In not-so-supportive environments, respondents felt that "a few are supportive, the rest are indifferent." One female faculty member noted, for example, that "I certainly have found the climate chilly here. I have received no professional or emotional support as a new faculty member. My department and especially my chair have given me almost no support."

In addition, faculty members believed that the department chair played an important role in defining the climate. For example:

> Several years back we had a chair appointed who was insensitive to issues of gender and who favors an "old-boy" style of interaction. At the same time we had another faculty member hired who likes the male-male stuff (sexual joking, "boy talk"). The climate of the department changed dramatically. Within our chair's office there was a suggestive poster and there was joking that was offensive and exclusive. My chair didn't address me by name. This felt very bad. The colleagues I relied on for support never called this for what it was. They never said, "Stop." I didn't have much respect for my colleagues during this time. In all my evaluations of my chair I mentioned his sexism. I signed these evaluations; they were not anonymous. I think [name of female colleague] did the same thing. No administrator ever bothered to talk to me about the issue. It would have helped to have someone talk about it.

> Two years ago there was a bad situation in my department. Fortunately the new chair made it clear that such behavior [sexist jokes] was unacceptable. The chair has immense power in such situations. The chair determines much of the atmosphere in a department.

Some chairs were consistently mentioned as helpful and supportive by our respondents. These chairs were seen as taking clear steps to help faculty deal with difficult students and colleagues and to assist them as they progressed toward tenure and promotion. Other senior faculty were also seen as important in providing support and assistance to both female and male untenured faculty.

Teaching

Generally, we found few differences in the responses of men and women faculty to questions about teaching, but some patterns appeared. Women, and especially tenured women, were more dissatisfied than their male counterparts with the way students addressed them. The majority of the women who were unhappy with their form of address held Ph.D.s and were frequently called "Mrs." or "Miss" instead of "Dr." or "Professor." Women also reported that students expected more nurturing from them than from their male colleagues:

> They [students] expect women to be softer—sometimes they expect me to be "Mommy." It pisses me off that they don't expect men to cut them a break. This diminishes as the students get more senior.

> Students expect more mothering. They're put off by high expectations.

> Now I have a male graduate student who expects me to do his grunt work. He expects me to make his [chemical] solutions and wash his dishes. When I leave my glassware in the sink to clean up later, he piles his on top of mine and expects me to clean his, too.

Women faculty also reported more comments about appearance on student course evaluations:

> I get comments on evaluations that seem immature, such as "She ought to comb her hair differently," or "She ought to dress differently." . . . Their comments about hair and dress suggest that they're not thinking of me first as a teacher. They look first at whether I fit the female stereotype. Teaching seems second to that.

The majority of faculty members of both genders reported that students generally treated them with respect and consideration. Several women, however, reported problem behaviors from a few students, most of whom were male and often from such traditionally male-dominated disciplines as engineering and business.

Research

Women were much less likely (36%) than their male counterparts (75%) to say that the environment at the university allowed them to pursue scholarly activities. The impediments that women faculty cited included a lack of money and other resources, inadequate library facilities, few graduate students, and most important, not enough time.

The majority (74% of women and 85% of men) said that research was discussed among departmental colleagues. Fewer women (57%) than men (80%), however, reported being included in such discussions. Women were also more likely than men (38% and 10%, respectively) to believe that research resources were distributed inequitably. Finally, half of the women (compared to 25% of the men) felt that their colleagues did not value their research.

Service

We asked our respondents about their committee service and their perceptions of service. We also obtained the previous year's committee loads for all faculty in the School of Arts and Sciences. The records showed that tenured women had the heaviest service loads: They served on approximately eight committees, compared to five committees for tenured men and an average of three committees for untenured men and women. When examining the service load of all faculty members, it was clear that a group of senior faculty, more males than females, did not contribute much to the service work of the university. Women, especially, reported working harder because they took committee work more seriously:

> I care and some of my colleagues don't. We have some worthless full professors with respect to service. They don't carry their weight. They get big [salary] increments, though, because they do research.

> It is a fair service load, but I am troubled by the fact that I carry a heavier load because some colleagues don't carry their share of the load.

In addition to examining the actual service loads, we also asked people about their satisfaction with service. Women were less satisfied with their loads, but said it was difficult to do less. Some of the faculty, both men and women, indicated that they felt a strong obligation to do the work that needed to be done. Nonetheless, these faculty members were resentful of the fact that the work was not shared more equitably, and that service was minimally rewarded in salary increases or promotion and tenure decisions.

Promotion and Tenure

Respondents were asked if promotion and tenure (P&T) were discussed in their department and, if so, whether they were included in the discussion. The majority of the women (88%) but 100% of men indicated that P&T was discussed to some extent. Similarly, most people (79% of women but 100% of men) also indicated that they were included in such discussions. There was also great variability in the extent of women's involvement in P&T discussions. For example, some untenured women reported limited participation, whereas others did not:

> Very seldom. Very seldom am I part of those discussions.

> I don't know what their [P&T] standards are. I don't have a clear idea.

> Yes [we talk about P&T], often at lunch, more formally through the mentoring committees. [Mentoring committees had been developed in a handful of departments to assist untenured faculty. They usually consist of about three tenured faculty who visit classes and give advice about teaching, research, service, and university life.]

The respondents were also asked whether they thought they would be supported for promotion (and tenure, where applicable) by their departments. The untenured women seemed to be less certain that their departments would support them for tenure/promotion. About 80% of the untenured men answered with certainty that they thought their departments would support them. In contrast, only half of the untenured women thought they could count on such support. Instead, they indicated that the support was dependent on how well they performed. For example, women said such things as "If I do the job, they will," "As long as I remain competent and publish scholarship," or "It depends on my case."

To conclude, women were somewhat less likely than men to be part of informal departmental promotion and tenure discussions. They were also less likely to feel confident of their department's support in the promotion and tenure evaluation process.

Tenure-Track Instructors: A Female Ghetto

Within the past few years, several tenure-track instructor positions had been established at this institution. The majority of these positions were in the writing program in the English Department and in the precalculus program in mathematics. All of these tenure-track faculty members had master's degrees and taught a four-course load rather than the three-course load with the 25% reduction for research characteristic of other tenure-track faculty at the institution. The average annual salaries of instructors was about $21,000 for instructors, compared to about $31,500 for assistant professors and $38,500 for associate professors. Of the 10 instructor positions that were tenure-track at the time of the interviews, 8 were held by women. Several people thought that these positions would always be female-dominated: "It is a worthwhile observation that the instructors are primarily female. There's a good reason. Most men wouldn't take a job with this amount of work and this kind of pay."

Because women instructors accounted for 40% of the untenured women in the school, conditions that affected the instructors were considered to be an important part of the overall climate for women in the school. Some of these conditions were rather different from those affecting other faculty, however. As a group, the instructors reported that they felt somewhat alienated from the other faculty:

> There's not a lot of discussion between the "real" faculty and us. There's definitely a separation.

> The other lecturers are [supportive]—we're all supportive of each other. I don't have much interaction with many of the professors.

> There is definitely an attitude that some people in the department aren't comfortable with these positions. Their view is that instructors must publish pedagogical research which is perceived as less demanding, less time-consuming to produce, less important than other kinds of research.

Social and Professional Relationships

We asked our respondents if they felt supported by their colleagues, if they felt a sense of belonging in their departments and at the university, and if they had been able to establish a satisfactory social network in their departments and at the university. Untenured women (45%) were less likely to report that they felt supported by their colleagues than were untenured men (75%). Additionally, women reported less of a sense of belonging in their departments (62% of women vs. 85% of men), and at the university (67% of women vs. 95% of men). A sense of feeling like an outsider was especially characteristic of untenured women, only 55% of whom indicated a sense of belonging at the university.

Women were also less satisfied with their social and professional relationships at the university. Among the tenured faculty, 50% of the women compared to 100% of the men reported that they were satisfied. Overall, 50% of the women were satisfied compared to 80% of the men.

Women's Studies

We didn't ask our respondents any direct questions about the Women's Studies Program. When they described how they met people and established a social network outside their departments, however, several women mentioned that they did so through Women's Studies programs and meetings, saying such things as "There would be nothing if not for Women's Studies," "On committees and through Women's Studies," "Primarily through Women's Studies and committees," and "Yes, mainly though Women's Studies."

However, some respondents indicated that this was a double-edged sword because they sometimes encountered disrespect toward Women's Studies from their colleagues: "If I have a conflict between [the department] and Women's Studies, people roll their eyes. They [male departmental colleagues] think it's a waste of time that I'm involved with Women's Studies."

Family and Job Conflicts

We asked our respondents questions about spouses, children, and colleagues' sensitivity to personal and family issues. There were several issues here of particular relevance to women faculty.

Although the majority of respondents, both men and women, indicated that colleagues were sensitive to personal and family issues, women were less likely to do so (81%) than men (100%). The majority of both men and women, however, thought that scheduled activities met family needs, that chairs and colleagues were sensitive to the needs of parents with young children, and that few colleagues ever made negative comments about family responsibilities interfering with faculty members' professional commitments.

When asked whether they felt conflicting demands between family and work responsibilities, many respondents answered affirmatively (68% of women, 45% of men). It is striking that over two thirds of the women felt that family conflicts were important barriers to their professional careers, but what was especially noticeable was the intensity of the qualitative responses. Frequently, a mother of relatively young children would burst out laughing when asked this question. These responses suggested that women with children and family responsibilities found the conflicting demands to be a great burden. Here are some of the women's responses:

> Of course [I have family and job conflicts]! All of us do.

> Yes. There are not words to describe how conflicting the demands are.

> *Yes.* Every moment of every day.

Interestingly, however, most women did not see these conflicts as the university's problem or as being discriminatory:

> I haven't really experienced any personal problems that I would say are related to gender. The only thing that differs between me and my male colleagues is the burden of children. But this is a social problem and not the fault of the university.

> The only thing that I can say—I now believe that regardless of how people treat me there is a big disadvantage to being a woman in my (or any) profession. No one else is contributing to that disadvantage. Because I am a mother of small children there are definitely disadvantages.

Several women indicated that earlier conflicts decreased as their children grew older. Additional family-related conflicts included an inability to travel to conferences and restrictions on sabbatical travel:

> It makes a difference going to conferences for women with children. You can't afford too much babysitting. Professional growth is a problem, going to conferences, going away. The decision is made not to go. Then there's

not too much to put into the [promotion or tenure] case for conferences out of state—because of the children.

It's not so difficult for a husband to say to his wife to go on sabbatical for a year. Most wives seem to have a job they can take a leave from, or are not employed outside the home. That's a problem when you start pursuing grants or visiting fellowships. It's very different for a wife to say that to a husband. I'm not sure how to handle this.

One of the reasons for family and job conflicts is the difficulty in finding someone to care for young children. Of those for whom the issue was relevant, 64% of the women and 70% of the men indicated that they had been able to find adequate child care. Several men and women, however, were disappointed by the university's recent withdrawal from a child care consortium in which it had participated for several years: "It is a big problem that we withdrew from [the consortium]. The teachers are wonderful! Great teachers! This was a way the university could say it was woman-friendly. It can't say that anymore."

We also asked about marital partners' job situations. Women faculty, particularly untenured women, were considerably more likely to say they would leave the university to follow a spouse who got a job elsewhere. That is, 82% of untenured married women and 41% of tenured married women compared to only 17% of untenured and 29% of tenured married men said they would give up their current job if their spouses accepted employment offers elsewhere.

Sexual Harassment

We asked our respondents if they had experienced behaviors (such as sexual attention, verbal sexual advances, sexual bribery, unwelcome sexual jokes or teasing) from students, faculty, or staff at the university. To address the individuals' own perceptions of harassment, we also asked directly if they had been sexually harassed. The majority of our respondents answered no to most of these questions. Women were more likely (50%) than men (11%) to report having experienced unwelcome jokes or teasing of a sexual nature. However, most of the reactions to these jokes were mild. Few of our respondents were particularly upset by them. Instead they dismissed such jokes as being crude or in bad taste rather than sexual harassment.

When questioned specifically about having experienced sexual harassment, women (33%) reported harassment more frequently than men (18%). The most glaring instances of sexual harassment occurred some years ago, however:

> A few days before he was to make a decision on my tenure case, my immediate supervisor made physical advances to me at an out-of-town conference we were attending. Later, [a colleague] told me he tried the same thing with her, only in his office, while working on her tenure evaluation.

Many of the women faculty reported that the situation had improved very much in recent years. Virtually none of our respondents, male or female, reported any episodes of unwanted sexual advances, verbal or physical, from colleagues in recent years. There were a few reported instances of such behavior from students, but these episodes were infrequent and were directed at both male and female faculty:

> Yes, from a handful of students. One guy took my class three times by flunking it on purpose. He kept telling me he was in love with me.

> Once I had a female student who invited me to her apartment for dinner several times. After several refusals, she stopped asking.

Demeaning Remarks Based on Gender

When asked whether they had heard demeaning or unprofessional remarks made about someone because of gender, about half of both the male and female faculty said that they had heard such comments. Most of the time these remarks were made about women, although occasionally they were reported to have been about men. These remarks were generally seen as infrequent and as having decreased in recent years. They were very rarely reported to have been made about the respondent herself. As infrequent as they were, they nevertheless created a chilly climate for women:

> Yes. Only once about me, when I was called emotional.

> In a department meeting one woman faculty member got quite outspoken and a male colleague meowed.

> One day when he learned I had published a book, he looked at me and said: "You? You've written a book?"

> This semester, according to information I was given by a student who was in my class and another class that met in the same room immediately after mine, the professor in the next class picked up the large piece of sidewalk chalk I use for my lectures, raised it up and remarked: "Obviously a case of penis envy." I found that demeaning.

Some of our respondents indicated that their colleagues considered women's issues in general to be "fair game" for unprofessional putdowns:

> I'd like to raise the matter of "gender harassment." When a couple of my colleagues are bothered about matters pertaining to women, they frequently approach me with their concerns, with remarks such as "All these feminists. . . ." Thus, my being a feminist causes these unpleasant, though often trivial, discussions about once every few weeks.

Responses to Gender-Related Problems

Many of our female respondents indicated that they had never been discriminated against and thought that they were treated fairly at the university. In a few cases, however, women faculty reported being treated very poorly. Such problems usually concerned lack of support from the department and especially the chairs. For example, one respondent reported virtually total isolation and a complete lack of support in her department. Another had her office space taken away by the chair and was unable to convince her chair to allow her to teach upper division courses in her specialty. In some instances, the women attempted to get help from outside their departments in resolving these issues. These requests for assistance failed. Our respondents felt frustrated in dealing with the Affirmative Action Office and with the Dean's office. One of our respondents made this suggestion:

> There should be a better way for women to have support when dealing with problems like this. We need someone to talk to in confidence. Perhaps a support group for instance. I shouldn't have to look so hard for help. I finally went to the Chancellor, and I don't think it should go that far. I wonder if women who raise these issues get labeled as trouble.

Discussion

In the present study, the women faculty and a sample of men faculty in the School of Arts and Sciences at a regional campus of a state university were interviewed about their perceptions of their workplace. In general, faculty of both sexes were satisfied with the conditions of the working environment. A number of conditions, however, appeared to be less satisfactory for women than for men.

Consistent with previous research, the women faculty in this institution were concentrated at the lowest ranks. In fact, the university may have established a new "female ghetto" in creating several tenure-track instructor positions with lower pay and higher teaching loads. In spite of the difficulties experienced by the instructors, it should be pointed out that there was strong support for the belief that these positions were a great improvement over the even lower status and pay of part-time faculty.

Previous researchers (Sandler & Hall, 1986; Swoboda, 1990) have reported that women are often isolated from the networks of the institution. Our findings supported that pattern. The women in this study were less likely than men to say that they felt a sense of belonging in their departments and at the university or that they had established satisfactory social networks. Untenured women were also somewhat less certain than untenured men that their colleagues would support them in the tenure process. When asked whether they were part of departmental discussions about research, teaching, and promotion, many more women than men said they were not.

Although women reported less of a sense of belonging in their departments, there were large differences in this perception across departments. Previous research (Swoboda, 1990) shows that there are supportive and nonsupportive departments for women and minorities. Our research supports such findings. Supportive departments make all faculty an integral part of the departments' activities and help their junior faculty in the progression toward promotion and tenure, both formally (e.g., through mentoring committees) and informally.

Our findings were also consistent with earlier descriptions (Caplan, 1993) of the academic environment as less supportive of female faculty. Although our female respondents reported few recent instances of overt sexual advances, they reported experiencing more unpleasant or demeaning sexual jokes, derogatory comments about women, and less support for their research from colleagues. They also reported that students showed women faculty less respect, such as addressing them as "Mrs." rather than "Dr." or

"Professor," and that students expected more lenient and nurturing treatment from women professors.

We also found that tenured women had higher service loads than men and that women were unhappy with those loads. Women were more likely than their male counterparts to say that the university environment did not allow them to do the scholarship they wanted to do. Often, also, women faculty reported distressing conflicts between the needs of their children or families and their roles as faculty members. Finally, the women who reported serious gender-related concerns found they had no responsive place on campus to assist them with these problems.

In conclusion, then, even though we found that the majority of faculty were quite satisfied with their experiences in academia, women had a less supportive climate than did men. Our findings mirror those of several other researchers over several years. How can we understand the dynamic of this state of affairs? Caplan (1993) referred to the university environment as male—as not suited to the special life circumstances of women. We agree with that characterization. University faculty have enormous demands on their time, and demands that often do not fit a typical 9 to 5, 40-hour week schedule. Meshing those responsibilities with the needs of contemporary family life appears to create enormous burdens for women, as well as for those men who have substantial family obligations. It is also the case that those in power in academia are disproportionately male. Women more frequently occupy the lowest levels of the university hierarchy and carry the heaviest service loads. Finally, the denigration of women and their capabilities, especially of feminist women, is an important contribution to this "male" climate.

As a result of this study, several changes were made at this institution. A faculty women's network was developed, an ombudscommittee was formed in the school to provide complainants with assistance, and the developing of mentoring relationships was encouraged. It is unlikely, however, that changes such as these will eliminate the chilly climate quickly. We believe the climate will change only as many more women enter positions of leadership in the university.

Note

1. Grouped by academic rank, the women included 1 tenured full professor, 14 tenured associate professors, 1 untenured associate professor, 7 tenured assistant professors, 10

untenured assistant professors, and 9 untenured instructors. The men included 2 tenured full professors, 6 tenured associate professors, 10 untenured assistant professors, and 2 untenured instructors.

References

Aisenberg, N., & Harrington, M. (1988). *Women of academe: Outsiders in the sacred grove.* Amherst: University of Massachusetts Press.

Angel, M. (1988). Women in legal education: What it's like to be part of the perceptual first wave, or, the case of the disappearing woman. *Temple Law Review, 61,* 799-846.

Balogh, D. W., & Kite, M. E. (1991, May). *Evaluating the campus climate: Effects of sex and tenure status of faculty respondents.* Paper presented at the annual meeting of the Midwestern Psychological Association, Chicago.

Basow, S. A. (1995). Student evaluations of college professors. *Journal of Educational Psychology, 87,* 656-665.

Basow, S. A., & Silberg, N. T. (1987). Student evaluations of college professors: Are female and male professors rated differently? *Journal of Educational Psychology, 79,* 308-314.

Caplan, P. (1993). *Lifting a ton of feathers: A woman's guide for surviving in the academic world.* Toronto: University of Toronto Press.

Chamberlain, M. K. (Ed.). (1988). *Women in academe: Progress and prospects.* New York: Russell Sage Foundation, Task Force on Women in Higher Education.

The Chilly Collective. (1995). *Breaking anonymity: The chilly climate for women faculty.* Waterloo, ON: Wilfrid Laurier University Press.

Fandt, P. M., & Stevens, G. E. (1991). Evaluation bias in the business classroom: Evidence relating to the effects of previous experiences. *Journal of Psychology, 125,* 469-477.

Fine, M. (1992). Passions, politics, and power: Feminist research possibilities. In M. Fine (Ed.), *Disruptive voices: The possibilities of feminist research* (pp. 205-231). Ann Arbor: University of Michigan Press.

Flam, F. (1991). Still a "chilly climate" for women? *Science, 252,* 1604-1606.

Fox, M. F. (1981). Sex segregation and salary structure in academia. *Sociology of Work and Occupations, 8,* 39-60.

Fox, M. F. (1991). Gender, environmental milieu, and productivity in science. In H. Zuckerman, J. Cole, & J. Bruer (Eds.), *The outer circle: Women in the scientific community* (pp. 188-204). New York: Norton.

Kierstad, D., D'Agostino, P., & Dill, H. (1988). Sex role stereotyping of college professors: Bias in students' ratings of instructors. *Journal of Educational Psychology, 80,* 342-344.

McIntyre, S. (1995). Gender bias within the law school: "The memo" and its impact. In The Chilly Collective (Eds.), *Breaking anonymity: The chilly climate for women faculty* (pp. 211-264). Waterloo, ON: Wilfrid Laurier University Press.

McKinney, K. (1990). Sexual harassment of university faculty by colleagues and students. *Sex Roles, 23,* 421-438.

Reinharz, S. (1992). *Feminist methods in social research.* New York: Oxford University Press.

Sandler, B., Silverberg, L. A., & Hall, R. M. (1996). *The chilly climate: A guide to improve the education of women.* Washington, DC: National Association for Women in Education.

Sandler, B. R. (1991). Women faculty at work in the classroom, or, why it still hurts to be a woman in labor. *Communication Education, 40,* 6-15.

Sandler, B. R., & Hall, R. M. (1986). *The campus climate revisited: Chilly for women faculty, administrators, and graduate students.* Washington, DC: Association of American Colleges, Project on the Status and Education of Women.

Swoboda, M. J. (1990). *Retaining and promoting women and minority faculty members: Problems and possibilities.* Madison: University of Wisconsin System.

Unger, R. K. (1979). Sexism in teacher evaluation: The comparability of real life to laboratory analogs. *Academic Psychology Bulletin, 1,* 163-170.

Zuckerman, H. (1991). The careers of men and women scientists: A review of current research. In H. Zuckerman, J. Cole, & J. Bruer (Eds.), *The outer circle: Women in the scientific community* (pp. 27-56). New York: Norton.

Chapter

4

Who's Laughing? Hillary Rodham Clinton in Political Humor

Ann Marshall

Imagine hearing the following:

> Al Gore, Bill and Hillary Clinton are in a car accident. They all die and go to heaven. One by one they approach God. Al Gore goes first. God asks, "Who are you?" Gore responds, "I'm Al Gore and I'm vice president of the United States." God motions to his left and says, "Go have a seat over there." Bill Clinton approaches next. Again, God asks, "Who are you?" Clinton responds, "Well, I'm Bill Clinton and I'm president of the United States." God is impressed and tells him to have a seat in a larger chair. It's Hillary Clinton's turn and she approaches God. Again God asks, "Who are you?" Hillary responds, "I'm Hillary Clinton and what are you doing in my chair?"

Regardless of what you may think of the joke, you have just participated in a political event. We all know that politics "happens" on the Senate floor, during a presidential decree, or with a Supreme Court decision. We read *Congressional Reports* and the *New York Times,* listen to National Public Radio, watch *60 Minutes* or the evening news. But politics also happens in our everyday lives, through those acts that are not officially recorded. In fact, this domain is especially important because it is not readily seen and because the etiquette of our "casual" talk does not have to follow the rules of formal discourse. Humor in particular is a haven for those opinions that cannot be stated directly. We may dismiss such language as "only a joke," but to do so would be to miss the themes embedded in our words and to disregard humor's forceful messages.

Now that you've experienced a joke-telling event and reacted either in silence, scorn, or laughter, I want to sharpen your attention. To gain a clearer perspective on the power of political humor, we must move away from being active participants in the joke-telling event and attempt to look in from the outside. Our mission is to expose a form of narrative often free from academic scrutiny. What message does political humor bring? In particular, how do political jokes about women, in both content and context, define and redefine the limits of acceptable behavior? To what extent do political jokes reveal a subtle yet still powerful public anxiety about influential women leaders?

The Political Setting: Hillary Rodham Clinton in Perspective

To investigate such terrain, this chapter examines jokes about one highly visible female political figure: Hillary Rodham Clinton. To fully understand the political relevance of such jokes, it is necessary to consider Hillary Rodham Clinton's presence within a larger framework of electoral politics. To begin with, women remain significantly underrepresented at all levels of electoral government. The first woman was elected to Congress in 1917 and although the number of female congressional representatives has grown, progress has been slow. The number of female representatives reached 20 in 1961, then gradually increased to 33 in 1991 and 55 in 1993. Yet this most recent high adds up to just 7% of all Senate members and 11% of House members. State legislative representation is slightly higher, but far from equal at 21% (Mandel, 1995). There have been no female presidents or vice presidents. Only one female vice presidential candidate has ever been nominated by a major party.

It is important to note that the job of politician differs in crucial ways from other types of employment, however. In most occupations, an employee is chosen by either a single employer or a relatively small group of employers. But this is not the case with representative government. American democracy holds that political leaders will be "hired" by the people at large. Leaders are granted power because of the endorsement they receive from the voters.

In addition, contemporary electoral government differs from other work environments because of the involved nature of political campaigning and electoral leadership. Although candidates are at the center of their elections, they are also dependent on the financial, technical, and physical assistance of their supporters.[1] This is especially true in higher levels of government where candidates must deliver their name recognition and message to a larger number of voters. Politicians therefore work closely with their supporters to negotiate a public image in tune with their constituents (Fenno, 1978). For presidential leaders in particular, the importance of a staff and advisers, as well as political appointees, continues into the president's term in office.

In presidential politics, women have been most visible as First Ladies. As documented by Caroli (1987), the history of First Ladies is complex and these women have varied by personality and circumstance. Some early First Ladies were nearly invisible in Washington. Even in the 20th century, some presidential wives, such as Bess Truman and Mamie Eisenhower, had a strictly ceremonial presence where they had "limited contact with the public, and devoted little if any thought to communicating their ideas to the country" (Gutin, 1989, p. 2). Yet throughout history, First Ladies have also exerted significant influence in presidential politics. For example, Dolley Madison acted as a White House hostess, but did so strategically with an "uncanny ability" (Caroli, 1987) to further her husband's political advantage. Eleanor Roosevelt is well known for her public role, and Lady Bird Johnson made more than 700 appearances, gave 164 speeches during her husband's presidency, and professionalized her own staff. Betty Ford voiced opinions in opposition to her husband, and Rosalynn Carter testified on mental health care policy before a Senate committee and attended cabinet meetings (Caroli, 1987).

Regardless of how each First Lady interpreted her role, it is clear that the public has viewed presidential wives as a reflection of their husbands. The merging of a president's and his wife's identity can be seen symbolically through discussions about George Washington's permanent burial site. Congress voted to move George Washington's remains from a family grave site in Mount Vernon to a marble tomb honoring him at the Capitol. When it appeared that arrangements had not been made to move Martha Washington as well, John Quincy Adams stated that it was not Congress' intention that "one-half of General Washington's remains" be transferred to the capitol (Caroli, 1987, p. 319). In this controversy, Martha Washington had no identity separate from that of her husband.

Since Washington's time, many First Ladies have been expected to be presidential supporters instead of actors in their own right. Gillespie (1987) argues that the dutiful public wife conveys legitimacy on the male politician:

> The wife, perhaps more than any of the other satellites of a public figure, seems responsible for motivating viewers to be comfortable with the man—to reassure them that their loyalty to her husband will be a safe investment. (p. 199)

When the public wife departs from this expected role, she and her husband may face serious political repercussions. In one extreme example, Angelina Alioto, the wife of the former mayor of San Francisco, disappeared for 17 days after her husband forgot to introduce her at a political dinner. When she returned and voiced long-term frustration about her secondary status, a reporter confronted her husband by asking, "If you can't control your wife, how can you control what happens in Sacramento?" (MacPherson, 1975, p. 93).

Given the history of First Ladies, Hillary Rodham Clinton poses significant questions about the changing role of women in presidential politics. She is different from past First Ladies because of her professional career in law and politics. Because of these political credentials, many observers have raised questions about the degree to which she should be involved in her husband's political career. The complexity of this issue can be illustrated by the controversy over Hillary Rodham Clinton's name. When Hillary chose to keep her maiden name after marrying Bill Clinton in 1975, she explained to reporters that "it seemed like a sensible way of keeping my professional life separate from [Bill's] political life . . . I did not want to be perceived as a conduit to him" (Radcliffe, 1993, p. 170). However, Hillary eventually added Clinton to her name because of pressure from constituents who believed that something must be wrong with Bill Clinton's marriage if his wife kept her maiden name (Graham, 1993). Despite her caution about her role in the future president's career, many who worked with Bill Clinton welcomed Hillary's expertise. After Bill Clinton won the 1992 presidential election, campaign consultant James Carville said he hoped Hillary Rodham Clinton would be involved in the administration, and a friend commented, "[Bill Clinton] married a brain trust; it would be very wasteful not to use it" (Clift & Miller, 1992, pp. 23-24).

Although Hillary Rodham Clinton has most often appeared in the press as First Lady, she has had her own political career as well. She graduated in the top 5% of her high school class and was voted most likely to succeed by her high school classmates. She attended Wellesley College where she was the head of the local chapter of the Young Republicans before becoming involved in the Democratic party. She was the first Wellesley student ever to speak at commencement and excerpts of her remarks were printed in *Life* magazine.[2] While studying law at Yale University, she served on the editorial board of the *Yale Review of Law and Social Action* and interned at Marian Wright Edelman's Washington Research Project, which later became the Unites States' largest lobbying group for young people, the Children's Defense Fund. In 1974, she was one of three female attorneys (out of 43 total) who investigated the impeachment of Richard Nixon under special counsel John Doar. In 1974, she turned down high-paying jobs at prestigious law firms to move to Arkansas where she joined her Yale classmate and future husband, Bill Clinton, on the faculty of the Arkansas School of Law. In 1977, President Carter appointed her to the board of directors of the Legal Services Corporation, and she was later one of the first female associates hired by the prestigious Arkansas Rose Law Firm. In 1978, she campaigned for Bill Clinton in his race for governor and he later appointed her chairperson of the Rural Health Advisory Committee. In 1980, the same year that daughter Chelsea was born, Hillary was made a partner at the Rose Law Firm. Throughout Bill Clinton's 10 years as governor, she served in a variety of leadership roles and had positions on the boards of directors of several corporations. In 1988 and 1991, the *National Law Journal* named her one of the most influential lawyers in the United States (Graham, 1993).

In her book on First Ladies, Caroli (1987) is reluctant to evaluate the contributions of presidential wives, arguing that the women differed in important ways. She does state, however, that "individual First Ladies have reflected the status of American women of their time while helping shape expectations of what women might properly do" (p. xxi). Similarly, commentators have stressed Hillary Rodham Clinton's symbolic role for understanding gender dynamics in the society at large. Journalist Judith Warner (1993) wrote that "her life mirrors those women who came of age in the social upheavals of the late 1960s, married and/or built careers in the 1970s, reached professional stature in the 1980s" (p. 5). Eleanor Clift (1992) stated that "a lot of women are projecting their hopes and their fears" on the First Lady. Given Hillary's impressive résumé and the symbolic nature of the First Lady role, evaluations of Hillary Rodham Clinton offer a window into public perceptions of powerful women.[3]

Research Approach

There is an abundance of written commentary, satire, and even political cartoons about First Lady Hillary Rodham Clinton. I chose to focus on oral jokes because of the access they provide to political dialogue that takes place outside of printed or taped discourse. As Dundes (1989) explains, oral political jokes often embody public opinion that is considered too potent for newspapers, commercial radio, or television.

The jokes for my study were collected in response to a query sent to the Women's Studies List, an academic electronic listserve, in December of 1993. The list is directed to people involved in women's studies as teachers, researchers, librarians, or program administrators. I sent a message to the listserve in which I explained that I was "working on a paper concerning jokes made about women in leadership positions." I asked subscribers, "Do you know of any jokes about Hillary Clinton, Janet Reno, or other women in leadership positions?" I also asked subscribers to tell me where they had heard the joke. In addition, I collected a few jokes from informal conversations with colleagues and friends. Except for one joke on Janet Reno, all of the jokes were about Hillary Clinton.[4] The study is based on responses from approximately 20 people who sent me Hillary Clinton jokes.[5]

Discussion: The Hillary Clinton Jokes

Given the nature of women in presidential politics, Hillary Clinton jokes offer the potential to investigate a number of interesting questions. What kinds of characteristics are attributed to Hillary Clinton? How is she portrayed? What do these jokes tell us about women in influential positions? How do these jokes describe talented women who are trying to reach their career goals? In the following pages, I will analyze the Hillary Clinton jokes collected and suggest their implications.

Sexuality and Powerful Women

Several jokes focus on Hillary Clinton as a lesbian. Consider the following:

> Do you know how Bill and Hillary met? They were both dating the same girl.

> What caused the flooding in the Midwest? Hillary took the dykes to Washington.

> Why did they outlaw miniskirts on the White House lawn? So Hillary's balls wouldn't show.

The large number of lesbian jokes in this collection suggest a preoccupation with the sexuality of powerful women. Through her successful career, Hillary has become an authority in her own right. As an attorney and political advocate, she has a knowledge base and political aptitude independent of her husband's public role. Hillary's ability to act on her own and aggressively pursue political ends signals some observers that she doesn't fit the desired picture of femininity. By mocking Hillary as a lesbian, the joke teller scoffs at Hillary's influence and questions the appropriateness of all women's strength.

By demonizing lesbian relationships, these jokes distort female power. Instead of celebrating female ability, these jokes question the presence of women in Washington politics and on the White House lawn. In addition, these jokes express a fear of female solidarity. The message conveyed is that lesbian women should not be taken seriously and that bonds between women are dangerous. These jokes tell a woman that a heterosexual relationship is necessary to be normal, thereby contributing to the web of social control that Rich (1980) labels "compulsory heterosexuality." In addition, jokes about Hillary's sexuality imply that women should sacrifice their relationships with other women, their careers, and political ideals in order to appear heterosexual. Because she may jeopardize her femininity, a woman should not lead, initiate, or participate in the turmoil of a male-defined contest, that is, politics.

Such humor, therefore, ridicules both lesbians and women in powerful positions. The joke tells us to laugh at the freak, the oddity, the misfit, because "it" does not fit the "right mold." For example, consider the following:

> You know, I really feel sorry for Chelsea most of all. She must be very confused, having two parents who sleep with women they're not married to.

This joke targets not only Hillary Clinton's sexuality but also her role as mother. Because she has combined motherhood with political clout, it is assumed that Hillary Clinton's career interferes with her ability to be a good mother to Chelsea. The joke, therefore, casts doubt on any mother who cares for a child where the father is not the traditional head of household or sole breadwinner.

Certainly, these jokes have the power both to castigate and intimidate. However, the extent to which such jokes carry hostile messages depends not only on the words but on the context of the joke telling. Occasionally, my sources offered their reaction to the joke when they heard it. One woman told me emphatically how angry she was at her neighbor's rendition of a Hillary Clinton-lesbian joke. However, another woman hearing a joke with a similar theme from her brother said that she found the joke as funny as her brother did.

The different interpretations of such jokes point out how much meaning is conveyed through the dynamics of the actual joke telling. On one level, different responses to the jokes could simply reflect the listener's awareness of gender issues or the listener's attitudes about joke telling in general. This is important, but jokes and their meanings are also shaped by other specificities. To really understand a joke-telling event, we might try to capture the teller's intonation and body movements. Important, also, might be the background of the person telling the joke, the relationship of the teller to his or her listeners, and what happened directly prior to telling the joke. Given all of these factors, we can imagine any number of meanings for a particular joke. In fact, a joke seen as offensive when told by a man to a woman could potentially be empowering if told between two women.[6]

This added awareness begs the question, "In what context are these jokes being told?" Unfortunately, such detail is rarely available. However, some contacts did mention where or how they had heard the jokes. Most of my respondents were women who indicated that Hillary Clinton jokes are at least occasionally told by women to women. But often these jokes seem to come from men and originate in male-dominated structures. Some of the settings mentioned by my informants included the army reserve, an inner-city hospital in Atlanta, a relative who is a fundamentalist, the colleague of a professor, a husband who is an international target shooter, a male neighbor who sells guns and ammunition, and a husband who is an attorney.

This contextual picture is not complete without a recognition of the geographically widespread nature of these jokes. In fact, word of mouth appears to have been quite effective in transporting these jokes from one end of the country to the other. My collection came from respondents at Temple University, Florida Atlanta University, Virginia Polytechnic Institute and State University, University of Maryland, Colorado College, University of California at Berkeley, University of Miami, Cleveland State University, College of Charleston, University of Missouri in Kansas City, Emory University, and sources in Columbus, Ohio and Syracuse, New York. Hillary Clinton jokes, therefore, appear to have been a part of many people's lives, including both men and women across the country.

Hillary Clinton and Female Images

I also uncovered jokes that question Hillary Clinton's personality or intellectual capabilities. At one extreme, there are the jokes that associate Hillary with despicable female images:

> Why did Arkansas cancel Halloween and Thanksgiving? The witch left and took the turkey with her.

In this joke, Hillary Clinton is not even mentioned by name. However, the association between Arkansas and witch is enough for listeners to know that the joke is about Hillary Clinton. A similar dynamic is reflected in the following joke:

> Bill was asked to throw out the first ball at a major league game. He and Hillary were standing in their box waiting for the signal when one of the secret service agents told him it was time. Suddenly, Hillary was seen flying down the rows of seats in front of their box, and the secret service agent exclaimed, "The first *pitch,* sir!"

In this case, Hillary's name is mentioned, but the punch line relies on the listeners' quick association of Hillary not with "pitch" but "bitch" or "witch." Although these jokes are indirect, both the witch and bitch images here characterize Hillary as an evil or malicious woman.

Similarly, several jokes trivialize Hillary Clinton's professional achievements by transforming Hillary the Yale law graduate into Hillary the sex object:

> Did you hear about the Hillary Clinton special at Kentucky Fried Chicken? For $2.99 you can get two small breasts, two large thighs, and a left wing.

This joke diminishes Hillary's skills and accomplishments by emphasizing the contours of her body. Depicted with small breasts and large thighs, it is clear that Hillary Clinton's physical appearance is deemed unattractive and undesirable. In 1984, vice presidential candidate Geraldine Ferraro was, similarly, a target of political humor. Consider the sexualization of Geraldine Ferraro in the following jokes:

> Elect Mondale. Put three boobs in the White House.

> Did you hear Mondale was arrested over the weekend? He was doing 69 in his Ferraro. (Miller, 1993, p. 358)

Jokes about political women go back much further than 10 years, however. In fact, such jokes have a long tradition. Powerful women such as Queen Victoria and Catherine the Great were "drawn to look fat, unattractive or male" and other powerful women were "shown to exploit their figures rather than their brains" (Bendix & Bendix, 1992, p. 446).

Often, attacks on political women are interchanged or generalized to successful women outside the political arena. The following joke about skating champion Nancy Kerrigan parallels the Hillary Clinton joke just presented:

> What did Nancy Kerrigan order at Kentucky Fried Chicken? Two tiny breasts and a bruised thigh.

This joke shows how quickly and easily our sexual notions about one high-profile woman are transferred to another. Hillary Clinton and Nancy Kerrigan have very little in common. They are of different generations and professional backgrounds. One is an attorney and political activist and the other is an athlete. But both are accomplished women who are highly visible to the public. The jokes imply that a woman's physical features are more important than her mind or a lifetime of practice devoted to her career.

Although not as dramatic, different versions of Hillary Clinton jokes tend to stereotype the First Lady as aggressive and manipulative. Compare the following versions of the "boyfriend" joke:

> On the campaign trail, the presidential limo stops at a filling station. The man pumping the gas turns out to be an old boyfriend of Hillary's; call him Joe. They chat with Joe for a few minutes. After the motorcade drives off, Bill turns to Hillary and says, "I bet you're glad you didn't marry him instead of me." She says, "Why?" He says, "Think of how close you came to being a grease monkey's wife." She says, "No, think of how close Joe came to being president."

> Hillary and Bill are at her [Hillary's] high school reunion. She points out a guy she used to date and Bill asks Hillary what he does for a living. She replies that he's a plumber. Bill chuckles and says, "You could have married a plumber!" Hillary says, "No, Bill. He could have been president."

This particular joke, in one form or another, was sent to me by seven respondents. Each version was slightly different. In one telling, the boyfriend was named Billy Bob and in a second narration, Hillary gets "misty-eyed" when she sees her high school sweetheart. However, the core meaning behind the punch line does not change. In each version, Hillary is mocked for her (presumed) belief that she was the determining influence behind Bill Clinton's presidential success. Whether told in Pittsburgh or Florida, the First Lady's powerful persona remains at the heart of what is meant to make the story comical.

A Presidential Partnership

Several of the jokes imply that powerful women are undesirable partners in marriage. Such sentiment is clearly embedded in the lesbian jokes I discussed earlier, but it is also found in other jokes that do not specifically target Hillary Clinton's sexuality. Consider the following about an encounter between Bill Clinton and White House adviser, George Stephanopoulos:

> George Stephanopoulos comes into the Oval Office. In the office are Bill Clinton and an absolutely beautiful German shepherd. "Boss," says George, "what a gorgeous dog. Where did he come from?" "I got him for Hillary," says Clinton. "Wow," says George, "great trade!"

On a superficial level, this joke implies that a dog is a better companion than Hillary Clinton. However, the joke may be even more telling as a metaphor for what makes a good wife. It is well known that dogs are referred to as "man's best friend." In part, dogs are loved because of their loyalty and affection for their master under any circumstance. Not only does this joke assume that companionship should be based on such values, but it implies that strong women fail to live up to such expectations.

Several jokes in this collection also castigate Bill Clinton as husband to a well-educated and influential woman. Such jokes are interesting because they reveal the difficulty that many people have imagining a relationship where both partners are equally successful. One good example of this dynamic is found in the boyfriend joke discussed earlier. In the first part of the joke, Hillary's status is evaluated in terms of her husband. Bill Clinton says to Hillary, "I'll bet you're glad you didn't marry him [the gas station attendant] instead of me." In the punch line, however, Hillary challenges Bill to "think of how close Joe [Hillary's old boyfriend] came to being president." In the punch line, Hillary is the key to presidential success, but Bill is now incompetent and at the mercy of his wife. Neither of these images shows cooperation or mutual success between wife and husband.

A joke about an encounter between Hillary Clinton and a waiter mocks Bill Clinton more blatantly:

> The Clintons went out to dinner and the waiter asked for Hillary's order. Hillary responded, "I'll take a medium rare steak and a baked potato." The waiter asked, "What about the vegetable?" Hillary said, "He'll take the same."

The joke assumes that talented women like Hillary Clinton overpower their husbands. Bill Clinton is ridiculed as a man dependent on his wife for even the most minute decisions. The influential wife is the source of Bill's shame as Hillary publicly confirms her husband's incapacity. Does this joke reveal a fear that marriage to a strong woman will result in both public embarrassment and male subordination?

Women, Politics, and Joking

The jokes in this chapter are political, but not just because their subject matter is political figure Hillary Clinton. Instead, Hillary Clinton jokes are part of the substance of politics because they make claims about how women should act and what electoral politics should be about. In particular, these jokes tell women that to openly exert power in the national public arena is dangerous and that such women will be ridiculed. Although I discussed jokes about Hillary's sexuality, intellect, and marriage separately, each joke is similarly about the power of women. One final joke is particularly useful in bringing these themes together and illustrating the political relevance of Hillary Clinton jokes:

> During the campaign, Hillary was seen giving a speech to a group of Democrats. It was a routine speech and contained a number of negative comments about her husband's opponent. At a most strategic moment in the speech, Hillary suddenly stepped away from the podium and flipped up her skirt in the front, revealing that she was without undergarments and shaved clear to the waist. She then said, "Read my lips, no more Bush!"

This joke is particularly potent because it highlights an activity that is so crucial for political success. Effective speech delivery is one of the key skills needed to become elected.

In addition, this joke is disturbing because of the way Hillary delivers her political message to the audience. It is only through a strategic exposure of her body that Hillary makes her most memorable commentary about George Bush, Bill Clinton's 1992 presidential opponent. Yet the open display of her genitals in this formal setting is also a mockery of Hillary Clinton. In this joke, Hillary Clinton's private body parts are visible and Hillary Clinton is exposed as sexually disfigured, a woman without pubic hair. At the same time, the rejection of an intellectual voice in favor of a sexual voice is explicit. Using George Bush's much quoted phrase, "read my lips,"[7] Hillary speaks not by her own words but through a sex act. The implication of such a joke is clear. As an influential presenter, a woman is to be judged not by her words but by what is or is not between her legs.

This joke "works" because it conveys a juxtaposition of two or more incongruent images. It is common knowledge that the president discusses White House issues in the Oval Office and often throws the first pitch at baseball games. Similarly, Hillary Clinton is a frequent speaker at political rallies. The joke, however, is meant to entertain by mixing the real and unreal and surprising the listener with the absurd. Bergmann (1986, p. 66) writes that "an episode is funny to us if it presents us with an incongruity that we attend to in fun." The jokes in this chapter are filled with such incongruities. Bill Clinton does not throw Hillary across the field at baseball games nor is the First Lady likely to lift her skirt during the key point of her speech.

The Hillary Clinton jokes discussed here, moreover, are not based on neutral ideas about what is expected and unexpected. Instead, the jokes reinforce the belief that aggressive women are suspect, especially as leaders in presidential politics. In Bergmann's (1986) words, "shared sexist beliefs" are used by the humorist to create the incongruity revealed in the punch line. To be effective, the Hillary Clinton jokes depend on the audience's discomfort with female power. It is not necessary that the reference to female power be direct. For example, no joke simply declares that "Hillary is too much like a man," or "women shouldn't be as powerful as their husbands." Yet each problematizes Hillary Clinton's presence in a male political world by making Hillary and not the political world the butt of the joke. Because the electoral system is unquestioned, these jokes promote a complacency with the male-dominated political status quo (Mackie, 1990).

In addition, these jokes are important because they are a part of people's immediate lives and offer a comfortable forum for hostile views to be expressed and reified. Bill and Naus (1992) find that college students are more likely to see sexist incidents as acceptable if they have perceived the incident as humorous. They state that "if sexism is disguised by and delivered through humor, it is interpreted as being harmless and innocent" (p. 646). In other words, the public is less likely to question sexist hostility toward Hillary Clinton when it comes in the form of a joke. Because the effects of humor are hard to see, joking provides a subtle but effective means of exerting power. For instance, there is a growing awareness that gender-related jokes can be a form of sexual harassment when told in a work setting between an employer and employee (Hemmasi, Graf, & Russ, 1994).

The dynamics of joke telling raise questions about the consequences of Hillary Clinton jokes for women seeking political careers. Recent studies suggest that blatant sex discrimination plays a diminishing role in the election of women to office. A 1991 survey found that 86% of respondents, compared to 31% in 1937, said that they would vote for a woman president if she were qualified for the job (Darcy, Welch, & Clark, 1994).[8] In addition, Darcy and his associates report that there is no difference between male and female candidates in political fundraising, name recognition, or the ability to win votes. However, Brown, Heighberger, and Shocket (1993) suggest that women candidates have been negatively evaluated because of their gender. They find that female city council candidates are seen as more effective than men with community and social service organizations. However, male candidates are seen as better able to make decisions, work with other politicians, and provide leadership.

Given the parameters of this study, I can only speculate about the degree to which jokes about powerful women actually discourage female leadership. However, the jokes presented here do have the potential to reinforce distorted images of strong women in both the minds of potential female candidates and the voting public at large. Political women may tolerate sexist jokes, but such humor can still create extra burdens for women. Faced with an unfriendly public consciousness, women may be forced to negotiate their public image in light of jokes about Hillary Clinton or other powerful women. As women think about political campaigns, write speeches, and plan legislative initiatives, the risk of gender-based ridicule remains.

Responding to Political Jokes About Women

It is difficult to counter jokes that embody our apprehensions and are rooted in our everyday lives. In short, it is hard to argue with a joke. We might be tempted to protest that Hillary Clinton isn't a bitch and she doesn't make speeches where she lifts her skirt. But the joke teller can claim that this was not his or her intention. It was, after all, "just a joke." The listener might choose not to laugh and certainly this is an important resistance technique. However, joking is integral to everyday conversation (Norrick, 1993) and is difficult to sidestep entirely.

Many strategies exist to confront offensive jokes about women, however. For instance, electing more women to office may defuse jokes about political women. In addition, there is a renewed recognition of the importance of feminist humor.[9] Feminist humor is defined by Kaufman (1980) as humor based on the need for social change and nonacceptance of gender oppression. For example, Sheppard (1993) documents how feminist humor encouraged women's involvement in the suffrage movement and popularized the agenda of women leaders. In addition, feminist humor is sometimes subtle and may call attention to gender inequality in a subversive way. For example, Nancy Walker (1988) argues that for women to dare to be funny is in and of itself a form of resistance. She explains that "instead of passive, emotional beings, women in their humorous writings show themselves to be assertive, insightful, alert" (p. 183). In her aptly titled *They Used to Call Me Snow White . . . But I Drifted,* Barreca (1991) urges women to "come out of the humor closet" and to use humor to demonstrate self-confidence. Former stand-up comedienne Melinda Rose (1990) teaches a course called "Tongue Fu: Using Humor to Combat Stress," where students learn how to respond to a put-down with humor. She quotes Pat Schroeder as an example of the technique. When Schroeder was asked, "How do you feel about running for president as a woman?" Schroeder replied, "I didn't realize I had a choice in the matter."

Swords (1992) argues that "instead of being the obverse of male mainstream humor, with its put-downs, feminist humor is noted for its *pick-ups*" (p. 80). Swords's 1972 collection of nine cartoon drawings, titled "A woman who . . . ," traces a series of events leading up to the election of a woman to public office. One of the first pictures shows a woman next to a stack of dishes while her husband states, "But gee, hon, you're my wife. Why would you want to be county commissioner?" Another shows a man waving his arms wildly as he exclaims, "Confound it, man, women don't belong in public office! They're too emotional!" The last caption shows the newly elected woman in front of a podium surrounded by a sea of congratulators. Off to the side her husband whispers to another bystander, " . . . so I said, 'Look, you've got the qualifications, right? So, get in there and win!' " Although this form of humor is not oral, it does encourage women to use their own versions of joke telling as tools of resistance and political empowerment.

Conclusion

The exchange of humor about powerful women is itself a political act. Although joke telling can be emancipatory, it can also be destructive and disempowering. This study shows that Hillary Clinton jokes are being told between our colleagues, neighbors, and family members that demonstrate an uneasiness, at best, and hostility, at worst, toward influential women. It is important to create an awareness of the jokes that are told in our communities and to consider what messages they bring to both men and women. This study has analyzed jokes from this critical perspective. My collection of Hillary Clinton jokes reveals that exploitative images of the past are being projected on contemporary female leadership. Such jokes castigate lesbians, sexualize women in general, problematize dual-career marriages, and undermine positive images of articulate and assertive women. The joke cycle discussed here spans all corners of the country and often circulates in male-dominated settings. Hillary Clinton jokes should not be dismissed as a harmless form of entertainment. Jokes express the boundaries of public legitimacy and have the potential to threaten the political contributions of women.

Notes

1. The type of assistance I am referring to here includes such things as campaign contributions, knowledge of the district, polling, administrative support, phone bank assistance, and so on.

2. The *Life* magazine article ("The Class of '69," 1969) highlights the class of 1969 commencement speakers who spoke about political protest. In her speech, Hillary Clinton talked about the personal aspects of college and discussed protest as "an attempt to forge an identity." In addition, she harshly criticized the speaker before her, Senator Edward W. Brooke, describing his remarks as irrelevant (Graham, 1993).

3. See Sapiro (1993) for a more extensive discussion of the political significance of symbolic women.

4. In the jokes collected, the First Lady was typically referred to as "Hillary Clinton" not "Hillary Rodham Clinton." For this reason, I will use "Hillary Clinton" throughout my discussion of the jokes.

5. Other respondents described humorous bumper stickers and greeting cards about Hillary Clinton, and a few people offered a more general commentary on Hillary Clinton jokes or the nature of the project. To keep the project well defined, this study focuses strictly on jokes that appear to have been told verbally from one person to another.

6. The heaven joke at the beginning of the chapter is a case in point. The joke might be offensive if told by a male to a female colleague if the joke was seen to imply that women like Hillary Clinton are too assertive and manipulative. Yet, if told between two women, the same joke might be understood as a declaration of women's power. In this telling, the joke is on God because he was, in fact, seen as sitting in Hillary Clinton's chair.

7. "Read my lips, no new taxes" was a campaign slogan that George Bush used in his 1992 campaign for president. The joke assumes that the listener will recognize the play on both "Bush" and "lips." In the joke, "Bush" refers to the former President George Bush as well as a woman's pubic hair. "Lips" refers to the mouth as used in "read my lips," as well as a woman's vaginal lips (labia minora and labia majora).

8. Note that this question leaves the definition of *qualified* to the discretion of the respondent. Some respondents may endorse the idea of a woman president but have biased or unrealistic expectations about what makes a qualified female candidate (Brown, Heighberger, & Shocket, 1993).

9. An institutional response may be necessary to counteract some types of sexist jokes. Feminist humor should not be seen as a replacement for such efforts. Instead, I am suggesting

that feminist humor is one strategy in which women can individually and collectively respond to hostility toward women.

References

Barreca, R. (1991). *They used to call me Snow White . . . But I drifted.* New York: Viking Penguin.

Bendix, J., & Bendix, R. (1992). Politics and gender in humor and satire: The cases of Elisabeth Kopp and Geraldine Ferraro. *Schweizerische Zeitschrift für Soziologie—Revue suisse de sociologie, 18,* 441-460.

Bergmann, M. (1986). How many feminists does it take to make a joke? Sexist humor and what's wrong with it. *Hypatia, 1,* 63-82.

Bill, B., & Naus, P. (1992). The role of humor in the interpretation of sexist incidents. *Sex Roles, 27,* 645-664.

Brown, C., Heighberger, N., & Shocket, P. (1993). Gender-based differences in perceptions of male and female city council candidates. *Women and Politics, 13,* 1-17.

Caroli, B. B. (1987). *First Ladies.* New York: Oxford University Press.

The class of '69. (1969, June 20). *Life, 66,* 28-34.

Clift, E. (1992, December 28). Interview: I try to be who I am. *Newsweek, 120,* 24-25.

Clift, E., & Miller, M. (1992, December 28). Hillary: Behind the scenes. *Newsweek, 120,* 23-25.

Darcy, R., Welch, S., & Clark, J. (1994). *Women, elections, and representation* (2nd ed.). Lincoln: University of Nebraska Press.

Dundes, A. (1989). Six inches from the presidency: The Gary Hart jokes as public opinion. *Western Folklore, 48,* 43-51.

Fenno, R. (1978). *Home style: House members in their districts.* Boston: Little, Brown.

Gillespie, J. (1987). The phenomenon of the public wife: An exercise in Goffman's impression management. In M. J. Deegan & M. Hill (Eds.), *Women and symbolic interaction* (pp. 191-210). Boston: Allen and Unwin.

Graham, J. (Ed.). (1993). Clinton, Hillary Rodham. In *Current biography yearbook 1993* (pp. 116-120). New York: H. W. Wilson.

Gutin, M. (1989). *The president's partner: The First Lady in the twentieth century.* New York: Greenwood.

Hemmasi, M., Graf, L. A., & Russ, G. S. (1994). Gender-related jokes in the workplace: Sexual humor or sexual harassment? *Journal of Applied Social Psychology, 24,* 1114-1128.

Kaufman, G. (1980). Introduction. In G. Kaufman & M. K. Blakely (Eds.), *Pulling our own strings: Feminist humor and satire* (pp. 13-16). Bloomington: Indiana University Press.

MacPherson, M. (1975). *The power lovers: An intimate look at politicians and their marriages.* New York: G. P. Putnam.

Mackie, M. (1990). Who is laughing now? The role of humour in the social construction of gender. *Atlantis, 15,* 11-26.

Mandel, R. B. (1995). A generation of change for women in politics. In J. Freeman (Ed.), *Women: A feminist perspective* (5th ed., pp. 405-429). Mountain View, CA: Mayfield.

Miller, E. (1993). Politics and gender: Geraldine Ferraro in the editorial cartoons. In S. T. Hollis, L. Pershing, & M. J. Young (Eds.), *Feminist theory and the study of folklore* (pp. 358-395). Chicago: University of Illinois Press.

Norrick, N. R. (1993). *Conversational joking: Humor in everyday talk.* Bloomington: Indiana University Press.

Radcliffe, D. (1993). *Hillary Rodham Clinton: A First Lady for our time.* New York: Warner.

Rich, A. (1980). Compulsory heterosexuality and lesbian existence. *Signs, 5,* 631-660.

Rose, M. (1990). Healthy humor. *Woman of power, 17,* 40-43.

Sapiro, V. (1993). The political uses of symbolic women: An essay in honor of Murray Edelman. *Political Communication, 10,* 141-154.

Sheppard, A. (1993). *Cartooning for suffrage.* Albuquerque: University of New Mexico Press.

Swords, B. (1992). Why women cartoonists are rare, and why that's important. In R. Barreca, (Ed.), *New perspectives on women and comedy* (pp. 65-84). Philadelphia: Gordon and Breach.

Walker, N. (1988). *A very serious thing: Women's humor and American culture.* Minneapolis: University of Minnesota Press.

Warner, J. (1993). *Hillary Clinton: The inside story.* New York: Signet.

PART

II

Subtle Sexism in Organizational Settings

Most of us spend many of our waking hours in organizations. Whether the settings are formal or informal, organizations are not static clumps of hierarchical arrangements. Besides producing goods and services, organizations also produce social beliefs about racial/ethnic relationships and gender roles.

In the last section we introduced you to several types of discrimination, showed how sexism operates in interpersonal and work relationships, and how subtle sexism is embedded in much of our humor. The next four chapters focus on organizational settings with varying male/female ratios and different degrees of discriminatory motives.

How hospitable are organizations in which many members feel that they are embracing nonsexist and nonracist procedures? Is the environment more cordial and are the results more egalitarian? Not necessarily, according to Regina F. Bento's analysis of performance appraisal in Chapter 5. In "When

Good Intentions Are Not Enough: Unintentional Subtle Discrimination Against Latinas in the Workplace," Bento shows that gendered racism (or the intersection of sexism and racism) is so steeped in subtle stereotypes and cultural ethnocentrism that those who practice gendered racism are often unaware of the consequences and implications of their behaviors. Bias can slither in through perception, storage, and recall biases so that subjective evaluations are transformed into "objective facts" and *truly* objective facts may be overridden by subjective misinterpretations. For example, the cultural tradition of *respeto,* which discourages challenging authority, may be misconstrued as a lack of assertiveness on the part of Latinas. As a result, Latina employees, and especially those with high educational levels, will be evaluated as "lacking leadership potential."

The next two chapters, Lisa M. Frehill's "Subtle Sexism in Engineering" and Susan B. Murray's "It's Safer This Way: The Subtle and Not-So-Subtle Exclusion of Men in Child Care," analyze two atypical organizational settings. Does sexist behavior increase or decrease when women engineers work in a traditionally male-dominated occupation and when male child care workers labor in a traditionally female-dominated occupation?

As Frehill and Murray show, the results are mixed, but for different reasons. In the case of female engineers, whether the organizational setting is industry or academia influences whether the sexism is more likely to be blatant or subtle. If the sexism is subtle *and* unintentional *and* advocates "run interference" by pointing out the offensive behaviors to well-intentioned decision makers, an organization may be open to altering sexist settings and work relationships. The case of male child care workers seems to be even more complex. Many people view child care outside the family as not very "manly," especially when such jobs are low paying and not prestigious. When men cross the gender boundary into child care, they may encounter additional suspicions about their sexuality ("The guy must be gay") and apprehension about the children's safety ("He must be a pedophile"). In anticipation of such parental concerns, Murray shows, child care centers often establish, albeit very subtly, "protective" rules and regulations that limit the male caretaker's interaction with children.

Chapters 6 and 7 suggest that sex discrimination "makes sense" from an employer's perspective. If some categories of people, such as men, are either perceived as having (or actually have) more marketable or desirable skills, an organization will recruit them more enthusiastically and will pay them more (Becker, 1975). In other cases, such decision makers as managers may rely on "rational bias" in personnel and salary judgments because they are motivated by self-interest rather than the abilities of the subordinates. For example, if a manager *believes* that a client or customer is biased against a group of people (such as women and minorities), the manager may engage in discriminatory practices despite his or her personal preferences or membership in the disadvantaged group (Larwood, Szwajkowski, & Rose, 1988; see also Merton, 1976). Consequently, engineering environments may be less welcoming to women, and child care settings may limit men's participation because the clients are *expected* to be uncomfortable with such employees.

In Chapter 8, "Subtle Sexism in the U.S. Military: Individual Responses to Sexual Harassment," Richard J. Harris and Juanita M. Firestone document the widespread prevalence of sexual harassment in military organizations. They differentiate between *individual* (blatant) harassment, such as attempted or actual rape, sexual touching, and obscene phone calls, and *environmental* (subtle) harassment, such as suggestive looks and gestures. They note that the "distinctly masculine culture of the military," as well as a failure to implement available antiharassment policies, have discouraged people from reporting both the blatant and the subtle offenses.

The Navy, especially, according to one observer, "can't shake its reputation for misogyny" (Vistica, 1996). After the 1991 Tailhook scandal, although more than 140 Navy and Marine officers were cited for wrongdoing, none was convicted at court-martial hearings (Thompson, 1995). Since 1992, the Department of the Navy has logged more that 1,000 new harassment complaints and more than 3,500 charges of indecent assault, from groping to rape—nearly three times the national rate for the same period. The Navy acknowledges that sexual abuse is actually underreported because many women who file complaints are victims of reprisals (Vistica, 1996).

Whether the harassment is blatant or subtle, covering up the problems not only derails the victim's career plans but also wreaks enormous emotional and psychological costs. According to a faculty member at the Naval Academy, for example, when one of his students complained that her roommate was having sex with an upperclassman in their dorm room, she said she was harassed by the boyfriend and his friends for 2 years:

> When she finally sought counseling, she was sent to the psychiatric ward of the Bethesda Naval Medical Center for four days. She was classified as depressed. She became sick from medication, missed classes, received low grades and was dismissed from the academy, despite an official request that they wait until a second psychologist opinion was received. The day before

> she left, the second opinion had come back from the hospital declaring her fit for duty. With tears streaming down her face, she told me, "I just want to leave here as soon as possible and get my dignity back." (Barry, 1996, p. C4)

What is especially interesting about the response in this case is the great pains the organization apparently took to discredit the student's complaints. Wouldn't it have been more just and cost-effective, not to mention law abiding, to control the harasser's behavior rather than the target's reaction?

References

Barry, J. F. (1996, March 31). Adrift in Annapolis. *Washington Post,* pp. C1, C4.

Becker, G. S. (1975). *Human capital.* New York: Columbia University Press.

Larwood, L., Szwajkowski, E., & Rose, S. (1988). When discrimination makes "sense": The rational bias theory. In B. A. Gutek, A. H. Stromberg, & L. Larwood (Eds.), *Women and work: An annual review* (Vol. 3, pp. 265-288). Newbury Park, CA: Sage.

Merton, R. K. (1976). Discrimination and the American creed. In R. K. Merton (Ed.), *Sociological ambivalence and other essays* (pp. 189-216). New York: Free Press.

Thompson, M. (1995, October 23). An officer and a creep? *Time,* p. 42.

Vistica, G. L. (1996, February 5). Anchors aweigh. *Newsweek,* pp. 69-71.

Chapter

5

When Good Intentions Are Not Enough

Unintentional Subtle Discrimination Against Latinas in the Workplace

Regina F. Bento

The number of Hispanics is expected to grow faster than any other ethnic or racial group in the United States. By 2050, Hispanics should be the largest minority group[1] in the U.S. population and labor force (Fine, 1995). Hispanic women are also joining the labor force in ever-increasing numbers: During the 1980s, the number of employed Hispanic women grew 50%, an increase that was two and a half times greater than the growth in employment of women in general (Segura, 1992).

Despite the growing numbers, we know very little about the experiences of Latinas[2] in the workplace. Several authors have noted the remarkable lack of research on the work experiences of women of color (Bell, 1990; Cox & Nkomo, 1990; Fine, 1995). Of the existing studies, most describe the experiences of black women. Latinas, with a few notable exceptions (e.g., Amaro, Russo, & Johnson, 1987; Comas-Díaz & Greene, 1994; Rivera-Ramos, 1992; Segura, 1992), have been largely ignored in the literature.

The literature on working Latinas indicates that this research scarcity is troubling not only from a scholarly point of view but also for very practical reasons. Although affirmative action and equal employment initiatives are helping Latinas get their "foot in the door," much of the progress in the workplace is restricted by glass ceilings and "sticky floors" (Carnevale & Stone, 1995). Latinas are underpaid, underrepresented in the top layers of the organizational hierarchy, and subjected to working environments that contribute to high levels of job stress (Carnevale & Stone, 1995; Comas-Díaz & Greene, 1994; Segura, 1992). A study of highly educated, high-income Latina women in professional and managerial careers found that 82% had experienced discrimination, with negative consequences for their psychological well-being (Amaro et al., 1987). Overt racism and sexism are only partial explanations for this dismal scenario—and, to some degree, the easiest to identify, document, and address through legal remedies. Much more insidious, pervasive, and difficult to eradicate are the effects of subtle discrimination (Benokraitis & Feagin, 1995). Most times, the gendered racism encountered by Latinas is so subtle that those who practice it are even unaware of the determinants and consequences of their own behaviors. The results of subtle discrimination, however, are not at all subtle (Dovidio, Gaertner, Anastasio, & Sanitioso, 1992). Hurtful actions do hurt, even when they are not meant to.

This chapter explores performance appraisal, a critical area where unintentional discrimination can severely limit the careers of Latinas. Performance appraisal is a complex process, situated at the very center of the web of human resource decisions made in organizations. Once someone's performance is formally labeled as deficient in one or more regard, this assessment—no matter how incorrect or how subjective—becomes the unchallenged "factual" basis for a multitude of interrelated decisions about training and development, assessment of potential and career planning, compensation, promotions, and so on. Besides the significant effect of such assessment, the very nature of the performance appraisal process makes it especially vulnerable to the often unconscious workings of unintentional discrimination.

The following section examines the cognitive mechanisms behind the perception of Latinas as an "outgroup" and the stereotypes, symbolic beliefs, and forms of gendered racism directed toward that outgroup. Next, the significance and mechanisms of unintentional discrimination in the performance appraisal of Latinas are explored. The chapter concludes with a discussion of theoretical and practical changes that appraisers can pursue to move from good intentions to good results.

Perception of Latinas as an Outgroup

When forming impressions about people, we do not see all the particularities of each individual we come across. The level of detail of individual characteristics we take into account in impression formation can vary along a continuum (Fiske & Neuberg, 1990). At one end of this continuum, *individuating processes* cause our impressions of a person to be driven by his or her own personal attributes. At the other end of the continuum, *category-based processes* lead us to form impressions on the basis of attributes we associate with the category or group in which we place the person, without taking into consideration his or her individual attributes.

For example, if an American man is introduced to a Latina who speaks English with a heavy (but understandable) accent, the interaction can go in two very different directions. If he engages in an individuating process, he will perceive the Latina's accent and ethnicity as pieces of information to be added to a much more complex picture, which may emerge gradually as they get to know each other better. If, however, categorization occurs, he will automatically attribute to that specific Latina all the characteristics he associates with Latinas in general (e.g., making instant assumptions about her level of education, career potential, religious beliefs, political views, food and music preferences). Categorization will then influence how he perceives all other information they exchange, as well as how interested he will be in pursuing the interaction any further.

Category-based processes are adaptive in the sense that they are very efficient in screening and summarizing information. Not surprisingly, they are also the most commonly used in impression formation (Pryor & Ostrom, 1981). Dovidio and Gaertner (1993) point out that categorization is often automatic and spontaneous. A common form of categorization involves perceiving others as either belonging to the same group as oneself (the "ingroup") or to other groups (the "outgroups").

The literature on intergroup theory documents extensively the implications of ingroup/outgroup categorization (Alderfer, 1986; Dovidio et al., 1992). Outgroups are perceived as more homogeneous than ingroups; outgroup members are seen as more similar to each other, more interchangeable, and more different from the ingroup; members of the ingroup are perceived as similar to the self. These phenomena occur even when the categorization is arbitrary or has no social meaning (e.g., when people are randomly assigned to groups "A" and "B" in an experiment). The differences in perception of ingroup and outgroup members tend to become more pronounced when the categorization is meaningful (e.g., when it reflects commonly used categories such as race and gender).

The double minority status of Latinas means that most people in the workplace are likely to see Latinas as members of an outgroup. The combined effect of gender and ethnicity characterizes them as "different" from both white men and women as well as from other ethnic and racial minorities. Latinas are thus lumped together into an amorphous outgroup. Although people know little about them, Latinas are typically perceived to be fairly homogeneous and undifferentiated. This blurring of one's individuality can be quite uncomfortable:

> Remember the other day when that airplane crashed in Colombia? A colleague of mine, who has been working with me for years, said that she was relieved to see me at work the following morning, because she had been worried that I might have been on that plane. I felt quite funny about her concern. On the one hand, I appreciated the fact that she had worried about me. On the other hand, why on earth would she even think that I might have been on that plane? For starters, my family is not from Colombia. I guess that for my colleague people from "south of the border" are all the same. . . . Besides, I had been working side by side with her the day before the accident happened and had not mentioned any intention of traveling. Well, it all left me feeling that after all these years the fact that I'm from "down there" is still stronger in her perception of me than the fact that we are co-workers. (Luzia, an Argentinean nurse)

> Why do people think we know everyone with a Latino name? Co-workers will often ask if I know Jose Rodriguez or someone with another Latino

> name. Don't they realize that there are millions of Latinos in this city? (Blank & Slipp, 1994, p. 60)

> Not all Hispanas look alike or speak with the same accent. Not all of them are called Maria. (Nieves-Squires, 1992, p. 89)

Attitudes toward outgroups tend to be less positive than those toward the ingroup (Dovidio et al., 1992). As we will see in the next section, such unfavorable attitudes, termed *prejudice,* have significant implications for the performance appraisal of Latinas.

Attitudes have both affective and cognitive components related to specific feelings, emotions, and beliefs about the outgroup (Esses, Haddock, & Zanna, 1993). The *affective* components may include feelings and emotions such as contempt, pity, distrust, fear, dislike, and even hate. The *cognitive* components include specific stereotypes and more general perceptions about the outgroup, such as symbolic beliefs.

Stereotypes

Stereotypes refer to specific beliefs about the characteristics of members of the outgroup. The following quote exemplifies some of the stereotypes about Latinas in academia:

> 1. Thought processes of Hispanas are not as clear as those of Anglos, as betrayed by their hesitation in pursuing oral confrontations, their wide use of gesticulation, and their poor representation in refereed publications.
> 2. The Hispana's social life is entirely wound up with the Hispanic scene—thus, she would be uncomfortable if included in "mainstream" activities.
> 3. Hispana faculty come from backgrounds so totally different from Anglo faculty that it is not possible or productive to entertain their company in settings other than on campus, if at all.
> 4. All Hispanas prefer to work with their "own kind"; thus, it is impractical to place them in departments where there are no Hispanics.
> 5. Most Hispanas' names are difficult to pronounce, so it is OK to substitute more familiar ones such as "Maria." (Nieves-Squires, 1992, p. 84)

These beliefs can be widely shared in society (consensual stereotype) or held only by a particular individual (idiosyncratic stereotype). In either case, people who hold such beliefs think of them as objective "facts of life." They do not question whether there are alternative explanations for their so-called empirical evidence. For instance, *if* Latinas are reluctant to engage in oral confrontations, could there be explanations other than a faulty thought process, such as a cultural dislike for face-to-face conflict, or insecurity about their ability to use English fluently in a confrontational situation? Could gesticulation be part of the Latino culture, or even a way to further express oneself beyond the limitations of another language? Could the underrepresentation in refereed publications simply reflect styles of expression that sound "foreign" to editors or reviewers, or maybe a choice of minority-related topics that are not considered relevant by the mainstream culture? Could a Latina's apparent discomfort with her Anglo colleagues be the consequence, not the cause, of her being systematically excluded from their social interactions? These and other questions typically remain unasked and unanswered. The stereotypical beliefs are not only allowed to remain unchecked, but they often generate their own "reality" through self-fulfilling prophecies. If Latinas initially want to interact with their Anglo colleagues outside of routine work-related activities, but are never invited to do so, they may end up losing interest in associating with them. This exclusion from informal networking may have not only social but also professional consequences.

Symbolic Beliefs

In addition to specific stereotypical beliefs, the cognitive component of attitudes also includes more general symbolic beliefs about the degree to which the outgroup fits into society or contributes to it (Esses et al., 1993). For example, members of the ingroup may perceive minorities as passive people, who would rather live on welfare all their lives, if they could. When a minority family moves into a "good" neighborhood, their ingroup neighbors may take this as a signal that property values will decrease, SAT scores will drop, and all kinds of unpleasantness, maybe even criminal incidents, will start. Latinas, and especially as their numbers increase, have to contend with some strong symbolic beliefs:

> You know, I'm really tired of coming home from a hard day of work at the office and then, when I turn on the TV, what do I see? Another scary documentary about how "Hispanics" are taking over the country, how you can't find anybody in Miami who speaks English anymore, how all those pregnant women keep crossing the borders so that their kids will be Ameri-

> can, how the whole U.S. system of welfare, education and health care will soon collapse under the collective weight of the hordes of illegal immigrants. It makes me feel like Hispanics are leeches sucking out the blood of America—and in the process giving it the AIDS virus. I never hear a word about how we contribute, what value we bring to this society. (Gloria, a Latina lawyer)

Symbolic beliefs are so deeply rooted in the fundamental norms and values of the ingroup that its members may even see themselves as "enlightened" and free of any prejudice or bigotry toward racial minorities. Beneath a layer of sincere good will, however, the ingroup's perception of racial minorities may still be tainted. Having been raised in a society with a long history of oppression and discrimination, many members of the ingroup accept exclusionary practices of racial minorities as normal and acceptable.

Subtle Racism and Gendered Racism

When subtle racism is directed toward minority women—the outgroup of the outgroup—it interacts with the sexism that may also be deeply embedded in the values and beliefs of the ingroup member. The combination of racism and sexism strengthens both and results in "gendered racism" (Essed, 1991). Here, again, the ingroup member may not be aware of his—or her—sexism.

Three main forms of subtle racism have been described in the literature: symbolic, ambivalent, and aversive. They can all be applied to understanding the barriers faced by Latinas in the workplace. *Symbolic racism* is based on a combination of negative affect and abstract beliefs that racial minorities violate important ingroup values (Esses et al., 1993). If these emotions and abstract beliefs are more negative when directed toward female members of the racial minority, we may call it "symbolic gendered racism." An example of symbolic gendered racism is the perception that Latinas are lazy and lack the Protestant work ethic:

> You won't believe what happened to me today. After hours of staring into my computer monitor, I was rubbing my eyes. My boss passed by and, only half-kidding, made a comment: "What is wrong? Did you miss your *siesta*?" I'm still kicking myself because I just sat there, my jaw dropped, and I didn't know what to answer. (Denise, a Latina computer programmer)

> I was in this high-powered meeting, with other people in positions of leadership in the various campuses of my university. When it was time to put our calendars together to schedule our next meeting, several white males volunteered the information that they wouldn't be able to meet on certain dates. Everybody took their statements at face value, no questions asked. When, however, I told them the dates when I couldn't meet, one turned to me and said in a very sarcastic tone: "What is this? A vacation?" (Julia, a Latina university professor)

Racial ambivalence refers to the notion that people may experience conflicting values when dealing with racial minorities (Katz, Wackenhut, & Glass, 1986). On the one hand, they may perceive members of the racial minority as "inferior" because they presumably do nothing to improve their own lot and only complain and ask for privileges. On the other hand, they may also perceive minority members as people who have been victimized and oppressed. The first set of perceptions, by implying a violation of the Protestant work ethic, elicits rejection and hostility. The second triggers humanitarian and egalitarian values, generating sympathy and a willingness to help. If the ambivalence is even more pronounced toward the female members of a racial minority, we may call the phenomenon "ambivalent gendered racism." Exposure to such conflicting perceptions can be very disorienting for Latinas:

> My boss, Mr. Smith, sometimes reminds me of that story about Dr. Jekyll and Mr. Hyde. One moment, he is out in the community trying to recruit Latino high school girls for summer internships, giving us lectures about the importance of providing them with opportunity, and telling me that, as a Latina, I should try especially hard to help the new interns. Next thing you know, I find his secretary in tears in the ladies' room. It turns out that Mr. Smith had asked the secretary to make copies of an important document, and to deliver them immediately to top management. The secretary had passed on the task to one of the Latina interns. When Mr. Smith found out, he yelled at the secretary for being irresponsible: "I told you this was urgent! You should have done it yourself! Don't you know that these people leave everything to do *mañana*! She's probably on the phone talking to a boyfriend, and I'll be the one to pay the price." (Raquel, an advertising specialist)

Such conflicting perceptions are also present in *aversive racism* (Dovidio et al., 1992). Aversive racism reflects holding sincere egalitarian values but, at the same time, harboring unacknowledged negative feelings and beliefs about racial minorities. Aversive racism is commonly triggered by minorities who defy stereotypes by achieving high status and success. When the negative feelings and beliefs are particularly strong about the female members of a racial minority, this represents "aversive gendered racism." The following situation illustrates a Latina's encounter with aversive gendered racism:

> I was in this committee to select a new Human Resources Director. We each received copies of the candidates' resumes, and were asked to classify them into three groups: "No Way," "Maybe" and "Top Candidates." I was really excited to find this Latina with fantastic credentials, and put her right into my "top" pile. When the committee met, we were asked to list the candidates we had in the top category. Was I surprised to find out I had been the only one to place the Latina in the top list! When I asked the others, they all said that yes, she seemed to be really good, and had "almost" made it to their top group as well. But, you know, this was a really important position for the organization, and we could not take chances. It was not that they thought she was worse than the non-minority candidates; she was just not as good as the best ones. . . . It became clear to me that if she were a white man (or even, perhaps, a white woman) she would have been in most people's "top" pile. As a Latina, she would have had to outperform by far the white candidates, so that even if her achievements were underestimated, they would still be impressive enough. (Julia, a Latina university professor)

Unintentional Subtle Discrimination in Appraisals

When the sex and ethnicity of Latinas interact to firmly place them as a "particularly out" outgroup, the consequences are not limited to affective and cognitive levels. They are often translated, whether intentionally or not, into discriminatory behaviors.

The performance appraisal process is a critical example of enacting discrimination against Latinas in the workplace. Formal performance appraisals are reportedly used in over 95% of all organizations (Bernardin & Russell, 1993). The very nature of the appraisal process makes it prone to biases and subjectivity to the point that it is considered "one of the most troubling areas of human resource management" (p. 378).

Intentional discrimination can be manifested in blatant, subtle, and covert ways in the performance appraisal process (see Benokraitis & Feagin, 1995). A supervisor, for example, can express gendered racism by openly and clearly underrating the performance of a Latina employee (blatant discrimination). Or the supervisor can subtly devalue the employee's performance by carefully phrasing the appraisal in stereotypical ways. For instance, the written appraisal may refer to how "she is trying to improve her Spanish accent" or how "she is avoiding attendance problems by bringing her sick kids to work with her" (subtle discrimination). If there is a strong possibility of detecting and punishing discriminatory evaluations, the supervisor might be even more manipulative. For example, he or she might give the Latina an impossible assignment, thus setting her up for failure, and then evaluate her poor performance "objectively" (covert discrimination).

These different forms of intentional discrimination vary in the degree to which they can be identified, detected, and redressed. Their effects in performance appraisal may be reversed, at least partially, however, through internal appeals or more formal legal procedures. Intentional discrimination can also be discouraged by implementing practices that dilute the perpetrators' discriminatory motives. For example, cultural diversity programs may combat prejudice, racism, and sexism by encouraging employees from diverse racial and ethnic backgrounds to work together. Intentional discrimination can also be challenged by promoting racially neutral employment opportunities. For instance, a system of checks and balances can increase the accountability of the performance rater and the possibility of detecting bias. In addition, top management can send strong and unambiguous messages, reinforced throughout the organization, that bias will not be tolerated.

Discrimination, however, is not always intentional. As you saw earlier, even people who think themselves immune to prejudice may harbor unacknowledged beliefs and attitudes that lead to subtle forms of gendered discrimination. When they find themselves in the role of appraising a Latina, supervisors may conscientiously follow all the stated rules and procedures of performance appraisal yet still arrive at evaluations that are subtly, and unintentionally, unfair. In other words, procedural justice (observance of equitable rules) does not guarantee substantive justice (equitable results). Unintentional discrimination in performance appraisal is particularly serious because it may be subtle in its expression but devastating in its results.

Mechanisms of Unintentional Discrimination in Appraisal

The seriousness of the consequences of unintentional discrimination in appraisal makes it crucial to understand how bias may quietly creep into the appraisal process. Three types of biases will be examined here: perception, storage, and recall biases; interpretation biases; and evaluation biases.

Perception, Storage, and Recall Biases

The perceptual process is characterized by extensive filtering and summarizing of information. Research in intergroup relations has shown that the amount and type of information that is perceived, stored in memory, and later recalled by ingroup members varies depending on *who* is being observed. Some findings are particularly significant in suggesting how ingroup members perceive, store, and recall information about the performance of Latinas compared to the performance of other ingroup members: (a) More details are taken into consideration when processing information about ingroup members; (b) it is easier to recall information that confirms the perceived difference between oneself and the members of the outgroup, and these differences reinforce the perceived similarity between ingroup members; (c) the less positive the information about outgroup members, the easier it is to recall; and (d) the more salient or accessible the outgroup, the easier it is to process information about traits that reinforce stereotypes about the outgroup (Dovidio & Gaertner, 1993).

These findings suggest that appraisers (who are typically ingroup members) may perceive, store, and recall less information about the performance of Latinas than other ingroup members. In the filtering process, appraisers may be more likely to leave out information that may distinguish one specific Latina from their stereotypes about Latinas in general. When the time for performance appraisal comes around, their recollections may be more influenced by stereotypical traits attributed to the Latina outgroup than by the concrete behaviors of the particular Latina being evaluated. In this recollection, there may be an overrepresentation of negative information, because the more positive information has been forgotten or altogether filtered out of the perceptual process. All of these processes may be more pronounced in areas of the country such as Florida, New York, California, and Texas, where the Latino community is large and more visible. The effect of the stereotype may be so strong that it will override objective evidence to the contrary:

> I will never forget one time, in the beginning of the school year, when my new English teacher returned my essay ungraded. She said it was too good for me to have written it, and demanded to know where I had found it. (Ana, a Latina writer)

Another perception problem in performance appraisal is the "halo" effect. Halo errors occur when we let one characteristic of an individual influence our perception of all other characteristics of that person. In the performance appraisal of Latinas, negative halo effects—or "horn" effects—can be triggered by a variety of stimuli, such as an accent, a non-Anglo physical appearance, or stereotypes about cultural differences:

> A Puerto Rican social worker who worked in a mental health facility said, "The white doctors always seemed uncomfortable, nervous around me—as if I wouldn't know the right answers to questions. They acted as if they didn't know how to talk to me. It's funny because I grew up in an Italian and Jewish neighborhood and went to mostly white colleges. I wanted to tell the guys, 'Relax. You can talk to me like a normal colleague.' I didn't say anything because I didn't think it would work." (Blank & Slipp, 1994, p. 61)

In the appraisal of Latinas, visibility of performance can be a frequent source of unintended bias. Latino culture tends to frown on self-promotion. Latinas often feel uncomfortable calling attention to their own accomplishments or participating too visibly in meetings:

> In many American workplaces, meetings are considered an opportunity for workers to "show off," that is, to show how smart they are. Many Latinos, in contrast, have been brought up with the belief that when you play yourself up, it's at someone else's expense. (Blank & Slipp, 1994, p. 62)

> In the Hispanic value system, self-promotion is considered selfish behavior. . . . The reluctance to promote oneself may be played out in several workplace behaviors—resumes that do not adequately reflect abilities and accomplishments, the failure to negotiate a salary when first offered a position, quietness at meetings when one's past accomplishments are germane to the discussion. (Carnevale & Stone, 1995, p. 197)

Another factor that may lower performance visibility is that Latinas tend to be assigned to peripheral positions and tasks in organizations: "The assumption is made that Latinos' only competence is speaking Spanish or working with their own" (Blank & Slipp, 1994, p. 62). As commonly happens in situations of tokenism, women may be sidetracked into jobs with impressive-sounding titles, but little responsibility or opportunity for advancement (Kanter, 1977). This is also true of Latinas:

> Chicanas, like other women of color faculty, are usually "tokens" within an academic department, called on to represent two historically disenfranchised groups—women, and people of color—on committees and various forums that take time and energy away from the research and publication activities rewarded in the academy. . . . Moreover the research and community service activities women of color engage in are often devalued by academic departments. (Segura, 1992, p. 187)

Interpretation Biases

A Latina is not on safe ground even if the information about her performance makes it through the perception, storage, and recall filters of the appraiser. It is not enough for the information to be recalled correctly; it also has to be interpreted correctly.

The interpretive process is directly influenced by the cultural assumptions and norms of the appraiser. His or her own culture is the code that interprets information about others. One of the main characteristics of culture, however, is its "taken-for-granted" nature (Fine, 1995). Ingroup members are typically unaware of their own cultural characteristics and oblivious to the fact that the same behavior may carry completely different meanings in another culture.

There are several elements in the cultural background of Latinas that are particularly prone to misinterpretation by many Anglo ingroup members. For example, the cultural script of *simpatía* emphasizes friendly interpersonal relations and blurs the boundaries between personal and professional roles. This may encourage personal conversations and self-disclosure in the workplace, which may be misinterpreted as a lack of seriousness or professionalism. The cultural tradition of *respeto* fosters a reluctance to openly question authority or to disagree. Showing respect for authority may be mistranslated as a lack of assertiveness, low self-confidence, or an avoidance of leadership. The script of *aguantar*, or endurance, may be mistaken for a lack of motivation to initiate change. The deeply rooted values of loyalty to the organization may be misunderstood as a lack of career mobility and aspirations. Obligation to the family (familism) may be misconstrued as a lack of professional commitment where job and family roles conflict.

Interpretive biases may be prompted not only by not understanding Latina culture but also by perceiving Latinas as cultural outsiders. Intergroup research shows that the same behavior or outcome may be interpreted differently, depending on whether the actor is perceived as "we" or "they" (Dovidio et al., 1992). Positive behaviors and successful outcomes are more likely to be attributed to causes that are both internal and stable (e.g., personality, expertise, talent) when the actor is a member of the ingroup. If a member of an outgroup achieves similarly valued outcomes, these results are typically credited to situational factors (such as help from someone else, special favors, simplicity of the task) or to good luck. Conversely, the negative behaviors and outcomes of an outgroup member are more likely to be attributed to internal and stable causes. In short, the success of Latinas tends to be discounted and explained away by external factors (she was lucky, the task was easy, or somebody helped her). The blame for failure, however, falls squarely on Latina shoulders.

Evaluation Biases

Even if information about a Latina's performance emerges relatively unscathed from the hurdles of subjective perception, storage, recall, and interpretation, she still faces a major source of bias—evaluation. The appraiser, when forming an overall judgment of a Latina's performance, can still unintentionally engage in discrimination.

The existing research on intergroup relations suggests that being labeled as an outgroup may have several negative implications for the evaluation of Latinas (Dovidio & Gaertner, 1993). Outgroup members tend to be devalued, to receive less favorable appraisals than their ingroup counterparts, and to be associated with undesirable characteristics such as lack of professionalism and low career potential. In addition, ingroup members behave less favorably toward members of the outgroup and are more willing to help "their own kind." These findings imply that many ingroup appraisers would tend to underrate the performance of Latinas. Such underestimations may be especially likely when such valued organizational rewards as pay and promotion are scarce or highly competitive.

Symbolic, aversive, and ambivalent racism theories suggest several other factors that may increase the likelihood of underestimating Latina performance. According to the symbolic racism perspective, an appraiser's attitudes toward Latinas could be more negative when external events escalate negative symbolic beliefs about the outgroup (e.g., when there is loud public concern about immigration and the loss of jobs to "cheap labor" or outcries about reverse discrimination against white males).

According to both aversive and ambivalent racism theories, discriminatory evaluations depend on the relative cost or availability of opportunities to be either egalitarian or discriminatory toward a minority (Dovidio & Gaertner, 1993; Katz et al., 1986). In situations with clear and unambiguous norms, where rationalizing a biased decision would be both difficult and impractical, appraisers tend to be egalitarian and may be less likely to underestimate the performance. Conversely, in situations that are ambiguous or governed by weak or conflicting norms, it would be easier for appraisers to be more discriminatory.

For example, discriminatory evaluations are more likely in organizations where appraisers are not trained to do performance evaluations, particularly in regard to minority employees; where appraisers are not held accountable for the evaluations they provide; where performance is appraised in terms of subjective, poorly defined terms such as "below standard," "not up to expectations"; where there are no clearly defined mechanisms for checking the accuracy of appraisals on the basis of actual data; where there are no effective appeal procedures; and where the organizational culture condones discriminatory behaviors. To the degree that appraisers can rationalize their evaluation decisions to themselves and others, they may give Latinas an unfair evaluation without experiencing guilt or a threat to their egalitarian self-image.

Another interesting implication of the empirical findings about aversive racism is that the likelihood of underestimating the performance of a Latina may also vary with the level of performance being assessed (Dovidio et al., 1992). Ingroup appraisers may not differentiate between ingroup and outgroup members with equally low levels of performance. When, however, the comparison involves high levels of performance, ingroup appraisers tend to underestimate the performance of outgroup members. In aversive racism, appraisers do not automatically place outgroup members at the bottom of the totem pole. Neither, however, do they think that the outgroup member belongs at the top of the pole.

An example of this phenomenon is the earlier quote by Julia, a Latina university professor, about how the search committee for Human Resources Director would not place a highly qualified Latina applicant among their top candidates. The effect of level of performance on discriminatory evaluation has also been documented in numerous experiments (Dovidio et al., 1992). It can be explained from an aversive racism perspective in that most appraisers like to perceive themselves as "fair" and try to ignore the ambivalent nature of their attitudes toward minorities. Their self-image of fairness would be threatened if they gave unjustified low ratings to minorities, which explains why so many experiments have failed to find evidence of discrimination at the low end of the scale. There is no threat to self-image, however, in being "rigorous" when assessing high performance. Actually, appraisers feel virtuous when they perceive themselves as being demanding and uncompromising when placing people at the high end of the scale. This self-righteousness blinds appraisers to the possibility of bias when evaluating high performance. Appraisers do not feel that they are being hurtful toward minorities, but that they are simply abstaining from giving minorities unwarranted special breaks.

Consequences of Unintentional Discrimination in Appraisal

The results of performance appraisal—regardless of how subjective—become the "objective facts" that form the basis for significant decisions in areas such as compensation, training and employee development, promotion, transfer, discharge, and layoff (Bernardin & Russell, 1993). Once bias enters the performance appraisal process, it works like a malignant virus that, carried into the bloodstream, infects the whole body and weakens or eventually destroys other organs. Unintentional discrimination in appraisal can, in the same way, affect the professional lives of Latinas in the long run as well as in the short run.

Unfair appraisals can also have a more immediate personal and psychological effect. If a Latina perceives that her gender and ethnicity have made her an easy target for discrimination, this can have profound effects on her motivation. According to the expectancy theory of motivation (Vroom, 1964), a Latina's experience of discrimination may directly discourage future effort. If she feels that her effort and high level of performance bear little or no effect on the likelihood of obtaining valued professional rewards (such as pay and recognition), she will feel discouraged and may not work as hard in the future.

A similar response would also be predicted by the equity theory of motivation (Mowday, 1991). If a Latina perceives that the material and symbolic rewards she gets out of her job are not proportional to what she brings into it (such as her effort, expertise, experience), particularly when compared to others, she may tend to adjust this "ratio" by putting less into the job. This decreased effort, in turn, may decrease the probability of successful performance in the future, which may result in even fewer rewards. In effect, then, unfair appraisals can create a vicious cycle or even a snowball effect.

There may be different but equally significant negative psychological consequences if the Latina is not even aware that her performance appraisal is biased. When she accepts, unquestioningly, the results of a biased evaluation as fair or objective, she may experience a loss of self-esteem, self-efficacy, and self-confidence (Melville, 1980). This may, of course, affect subsequent performance and create a self-fulfilling prophecy (Cox, 1993). In addition, if she unconsciously perceives that she has been wronged, the repressed anger may be turned inward, resulting in depression or other injuries to self. It is probably no coincidence that the prevalence of depression among Latinas is higher than for Latino men or the general population (Vasquez, 1994).

Directions for Change

Unintentional discrimination against Latinas in performance appraisal hurts not only their professional and personal lives but the organization as well. Besides the ethical implications of discriminatory behavior, demographic trends make it imperative for organizations to be concerned about how they treat Latina employees. In the next few decades, as Hispanics become the largest minority in the United States, organizations may pay a heavy price if they fail to recognize, develop, nurture, and use the talent and unique contributions of Latinas.

Also, the growth of the Latino market is capturing the attention of an increasing number of organizations. Many businesses are learning, the hard way, that successfully catering to the Latino market requires much more than simply translating marketing materials into high school Spanish. For example, Latinas tend to have high brand loyalty and like to buy "top of the line" whenever possible, even when a high price does not necessarily mean high quality (Weyr, 1988). They are willing to splurge on small items (a really fancy bleach that makes the Latina mother feel she is giving her family "the best") to compensate for the large items they may not be able to afford (a fancy new car). Therefore, an ad campaign for a small item that emphasizes low price may miss its target in a Latina's household.

Another difference is that the Anglo market values product efficacy, whereas the Latino market emphasizes personal benefit. Not surprisingly, advertisements for Crest toothpaste that stressed its cavity-fighting properties did not play as well in the Latino market as the ads for Colgate, which emphasized sparkling white teeth. As a result, Colgate clobbered Crest in the Latino market (Weyr, 1988).

Moreover, the same Spanish word may have different meanings in different Latin countries. For example, an ad campaign for baby powder translated the name of the product using a word, which although perfectly acceptable in several Latin countries, was a very crude description of sexual intercourse in many parts of the Caribbe. The company discovered this error in time and was able to substitute a more widely accepted synonym. Several such million-dollar mistakes can be avoided by a more intimate knowledge of the distinct Latino subcultures and the rapidly changing preferences of the diverse Latino communities.

Demographics are not the only reason for taking Latinas seriously. Because of their cultural heritage, many Latinas possess prized organizational characteristics and skills, which include an interpersonal orientation, participative leadership, team spirit, an interest in process, a tolerance of ambiguity, adaptability to and acceptance of change, and an ability to listen and motivate. Such traits should make Latinas uniquely appealing to forward-looking organizations that are trying to become "less hierarchical, more flexible and team-oriented, faster and more fluid" (Peters, 1990).

Many major U.S. companies are already actively pursuing the "Latino advantage." They are targeting their employment recruitment efforts at Latino publications as well as colleges and high schools with significant Latino enrollments. They are also supporting Latino associations and causes, creating Latino networks inside the organization, and establishing special job-training programs (Cox, 1993; Fine, 1995; Graham, 1993; Weyr, 1988).

Some organizations are also trying to curtail intentional discrimination through various types of diversity programs as well as affirmative action and equal employment efforts. But unintentional discrimination causes just as much harm, if not more, and is harder to prevent, detect, and combat.

This chapter explored how unintentional subtle discrimination works and why it is so likely in the performance evaluation of Latinas. Given the scarcity of empirical data about Latinas in the workforce, the findings of intergroup research should signal the need for much more theory building in this area. Considerable empirical research is also needed to inform the theory-building process. A particularly promising direction for research would be to explore the individual, interpersonal, situational, and organizational factors that support or encourage appraisal bias against Latinas. Comparative studies that examine subtle unintentional discrimination toward Latinos and Latinas, as well as male and female members of other racial and ethnic minorities, are also critical.

However, well-intentioned appraisers and organizations should not wait for the full development of theoretical and empirical research to fight subtle discrimination against Latinas. Changing the status quo can include the following:

Efforts to reduce perception of Latinas as an outgroup. If appraisers can see Latinas as individuals, and not as faceless members of a homogeneous outgroup, this may prevent or moderate some of the harmful effects of categorization. Different types of situations that increase the contact of ingroup members with Latinas can help. For example, diversity workshops can bring together people from many racial and ethnic backgrounds and help them learn more about each other as individuals. Also, the inclusion of Latinas in important projects with ingroup members can move the employers' perspective from "us versus them" toward "we" (Dovidio et al., 1992).

Efforts to reframe both stereotypes and symbolic beliefs. The traditional diversity-training model focuses typically on changing stereotypical beliefs about specific characteristics attributed to minorities. This is important but not sufficient. It is also necessary to address the deep-rooted symbolic beliefs about Latinas that are at the core of symbolic, aversive, and ambivalent gendered racism.

Efforts to increase awareness and prevention of unintentional biases in the appraisal process. When discrimination in performance appraisal is unintentional, appraisers can benefit significantly from developing awareness of why, how, and when they may be biased in perception, storage, recall, interpretation, and evaluation of Latinas. Moreover, evaluation skills in preventing or detecting these biases can be improved through training. For example, appraisers can modify the quantity and quality of information that they process. They can explore alternative cultural interpretations to explain workplace behaviors and enhance their ability to perform unbiased overall evaluations.

Efforts to produce structural changes in the performance appraisal process and career management of minorities. According to aversive and ambivalence theories of racism, initiatives that decrease the ambiguity and the conflicting normative structure of the performance appraisal process should decrease the likelihood of unintentional discrimination. This can be done, for example, through carefully designing appraisal systems to improve the collection, interpretation, and evaluation of performance data that make it harder to rationalize discriminatory decisions. The use of multiple evaluators should also be helpful, particularly if they are familiar with Latino culture. Otherwise, the mere increase in the number of ingroup members in the evaluation process might even be dangerous; they might reinforce each other's biases and use consensus as proof of their impartiality.

Efforts to create a culture of inclusion. Top management should also strive, in symbolic and practical ways, to send a strong and clear message to all members of the organization that Latinas should not simply be tolerated but sincerely valued.

It is difficult but not impossible to fight unintentional discrimination against Latinas in performance appraisal. Understanding the insidious nature and mechanisms of unintentional discrimination opens a variety of avenues for improving the appraisal of Latinas and incorporating their contributions into the workplace. Knowledge and action are powerful partners in helping people and organizations move from good intentions to good results.

Notes

1. In 1990, Hispanics were already the second largest minority group in the U.S. population (9.0%) and in the U.S. labor force (7.5%), fast approaching the number of blacks (who then accounted for 11.8% of the population and 10.8% of the labor force). By 2050,

Hispanics should represent 22.5% of the population, which will make them almost as numerous as *all* the other minorities combined (Fine, 1995).

2. Policy Directive Number 15 of the Office of Management and Budget, issued in 1980, defined two ethnic groups (Hispanic, non-Hispanic) and four racial groups (white, black, American Indian/Eskimo/Aleut, and Asian/Pacific Islander). The umbrella term *Hispanic* is perceived by many to be simply a statistical label created by government bureaucrats. Many "Hispanics" would rather be described on the basis of their country of origin (Mexican American, Cuban American, etc.), or in terms that carry more political and symbolic meaning (Chicano, Chicana), or that refer to what is common in their cultural heritage (Latino, Latina).

Although some groups, such as the U.S. Bureau of the Census, use the label *Hispanic,* I prefer the terms *Latino* and *Latina* when referring to male and female U.S. citizens or residents from many different origins: Mexico, Puerto Rico, Cuba, Central and South America, and so on. These terms are more culturally acceptable, are sufficiently broad in scope, and better emphasize sex differences.

References

Alderfer, C. P. (1986). An intergroup perspective on group dynamics. In J. Lorsch (Ed.), *Handbook of organizational behavior* (pp. 190-222). Englewood Cliffs, NJ: Prentice Hall.

Amaro, H., Russo, N. F., & Johnson, J. (1987). Family and work predictors of psychological well-being among Hispanic women professionals. *Psychology of Women Quarterly, 11,* 505-522.

Bell, E. L. (1990). The bicultural life experience of career-oriented black women. *Journal of Organizational Behavior, 11,* 459-477.

Benokraitis, N. V., & Feagin, J. R. (1995). *Modern sexism: Blatant, subtle, and covert discrimination.* Englewood Cliffs, NJ: Prentice Hall.

Bernardin, H. J., & Russell, J. E. A. (1993). *Human resource management: An experiential approach.* New York: McGraw-Hill.

Blank, R., & Slipp, S. (1994). *Voices of diversity: Real people talk about problems and solutions in a workplace where everyone is not alike.* New York: AMACOM, American Management Association.

Carnevale, A. P., & Stone, S. C. (1995). *The American mosaic: An in-depth report on the advantage of diversity in the U.S. work force.* New York: McGraw-Hill.

Comas-Díaz, L., & Greene, B. (1994). Women of color with professional status. In L. Comas-Díaz & B. Greene (Eds.), *Women of color: Integrating ethnic and gender identities in psychotherapy* (pp. 347-388). New York: Guilford.

Cox, T., Jr. (1993). *Cultural diversity in organizations: Theory, research, and practice.* San Francisco: Berret-Koehler.

Cox, T., Jr., & Nkomo, S. M. (1990). Invisible men and women: A status report on race as a variable in organizational behavior research. *Journal of Organizational Behavior, 11,* 419-432.

Dovidio, J. F., & Gaertner, S. L. (1993). Stereotypes and evaluative intergroup bias. In D. M. Mackie & D. L. Hamilton (Eds.), *Affect, cognition, and stereotyping: Interactive processes in group perception* (pp. 167-193). San Diego, CA: Academic Press.

Dovidio, J. F., Gaertner, S. L., Anastasio, P. A., & Sanitioso, R. (1992). Cognitive and motivational bases of bias: Implications of aversive racism for attitudes towards Hispanics. In S. B. Knouse, P. Rosenfeld, & A. L. Culbertson (Eds.), *Hispanics in the workplace* (pp. 75-106). Newbury Park, CA: Sage.

Essed, P. (1991). *Understanding everyday racism.* Newbury Park, CA: Sage.

Esses, V. M., Haddock, G., & Zanna, M. P. (1993). Values, stereotypes, and emotions as determinants of intergroup attitudes. In D. M. Mackie & D. L. Hamilton (Eds.), *Affect, cognition, and stereotyping: Interactive processes in group perception* (pp. 137-166). San Diego, CA: Academic Press.

Fine, M. G. (1995). *Building successful multicultural organizations: Challenges and opportunities.* Westport, CT: Quorum.

Fiske, S. T., & Neuberg, S. L. (1990). A continuum of impression formation, from category-based to individuating processes: Influences of information and motivation on attention and interpretation. In M. Zanna (Ed.), *Advances in experimental social psychology* (Vol. 23, pp. 1-74). Orlando, FL: Academic Press.

Graham, L. O. (1993). *The best companies for minorities.* New York: Penguin.

Kanter, E. R. (1977). *Men and women of the corporation.* New York: Basic Books.

Katz, I., Wackenhut, J., & Glass, D. C. (1986). An ambivalence-amplification theory of behavior toward the stigmatized. In S. Worchel (Ed.), *Psychology of intergroup relations* (pp. 103-117). Chicago: Nelson-Hall.

Melville, M. B. (1980). *Twice a minority: Mexican American women.* St. Louis, MO: C. V. Mosby.

Mowday, R. T. (1991). Equity theory predictions of behavior in organizations. In R. Steers & L. W. Porter (Eds.), *Motivation and work behavior* (pp. 111-131). New York: McGraw-Hill.

Nieves-Squires, S. (1992). Hispanic women in the U.S. academic context. In L. B. Welch (Ed.), *Perspectives on minority women in higher education* (pp. 71-92). New York: Praeger.

Peters, T. (1990). The best new managers will listen, motivate, support. Isn't that just like a woman? *Working Woman, 15,* 142-217.

Pryor, J. B., & Ostrom, T. M. (1981). The cognitive organization of social information: A converging operations approach. *Journal of Personality and Social Psychology, 41,* 628-641.

Rivera-Ramos, A. N. (1992). The psychological experience of Puerto Rican women at work. In S. B. Knouse, P. Rosenfeld, & A. L. Culbertson (Eds.), *Hispanics in the workplace* (pp. 194-207). Newbury Park, CA: Sage.

Segura, D. A. (1992). Walking on eggshells: Chicanas in the labor force. In S. B. Knouse, P. Rosenfeld, & A. L. Culbertson (Eds.), *Hispanics in the workplace* (pp. 173-193). Newbury Park, CA: Sage.

Vasquez, M. J. T. (1994). Latinas. In L. Comas-Díaz & B. Greene (Eds.), *Women of color: Integrating ethnic and gender identities in psychotherapy* (pp. 114-138). New York: Guilford.

Vroom, V. H. (1964). *Work and motivation.* New York: John Wiley.

Weyr, T. (1988). *Hispanic U.S.A.: Breaking the melting pot.* New York: Harper & Row.

Chapter

6

Subtle Sexism in Engineering

Lisa M. Frehill

During the past 20 years, women have made great progress in entering professional occupations that were once largely reserved for men. However, women's inroads into the professions have been quite uneven. In the 1992-1993 academic year, for example, women accounted for 38% of all new medical doctors, 34% of new dentists, and 42% of new lawyers but only 14% of new engineers (National Center for Education Statistics, 1995). By the 1994-1995 academic year, women earned 17% of all engineering and engineering technology bachelor's degrees in the United States. Women now account for approximately 8% of the U.S. national engineering labor force (U.S. Bureau of the Census, 1995). Despite increasing global economic

AUTHOR'S NOTE: I would like to thank the interviewees, who generously gave me their time. I also acknowledge the Society of Women Engineers, especially Peggy Layne, who provided the SWE Survey data.

competition and the high salaries that even entry-level engineers command, why are there so few female engineers? Is it because many women just are not interested in engineering? Or is it because, as some observers have noted (Geppert, 1995; National Science Foundation, 1994), the United States has not developed engineering talent because of deeply entrenched gender bias in a "gendered" profession?

Women as Tokens in Gendered Professions

In contrast to several other occupations, there has been a dearth of studies of women in engineering. The available data suggest, however, that female engineers experience sexism in the classroom and the workplace because of two related characteristics. First, because there are so few women in engineering, they encounter problems associated with being a token. Second, engineering is a gendered profession. Because women were historically not permitted into the profession, and still represent only a small percentage of all engineers, engineering reflects a "masculine culture."

Rosabeth Moss Kanter (1977) conducted research in the early 1970s at "Indsco," a large industrial supply company, where women had only recently been permitted to enter managerial positions. Because there were so few women in management at Indsco, they often played the role of tokens:

> Although the token captured attention, it was often for her discrepant characteristics, for the auxiliary traits that gave her token status. The token does not have to work hard to have her presence noticed, but she does have to work hard to have her achievements noticed. (p. 216)

In this case, the "auxiliary traits" refers to gender. Although increased visibility could facilitate upward mobility at Indsco, for women this visibility due to gender rather than achievements was really a double-edged sword. Because men at Indsco had to struggle to have their accomplishments noticed, managerial men often resented the attention that women received. On the other hand, whereas men's errors could be hidden, increased visibility for women meant that even the slightest mistakes were noticed.

Because they worked in a male-dominated environment, some token women dealt with the pressure of the spotlight by overachieving. Other women tried to minimize the pressure by blending into appropriate gendered roles that their male co-workers found more comfortable. Tokenism was further exacerbated by expectations about appropriate female behavior. Kanter found, for example, that when female tokens demonstrated important managerial qualities, such as aggressiveness, they were viewed negatively rather than positively. This negative assessment was due to the token's sex (woman), which was considered to be more important than her position as a manager.

More recent studies have supported Kanter's findings that women in male-dominated workplaces often encounter sexism. Research on women who became steelworkers in the 1970s and on women in the U.S. Marine Corps in the 1980s shows that women in male-dominated occupations must "prove themselves" and minimize the differences between themselves and their male co-workers (Fonow, 1993; Williams, 1989). For example, Fonow's study of women who entered steelwork in the 1970s reported that to prove they could do the same work as their male peers, women would often overexert themselves. One worker severely injured herself when she attempted to lift a 100-pound lead box, which, she later learned, no man would have attempted without assistance. Fine's (1987) research on female cooks in restaurants concluded that women in male work settings need to become "one of the boys" to assimilate to the male work culture to both advance and to accomplish the work that must get done. Assimilation to male work culture involved being willing to engage in sexual banter common in the kitchens where Fine conducted his fieldwork.

Women Engineers in a Gendered Profession

The issues women in engineering face today are not much different from those experienced by the management women Kanter studied. In addition, women in engineering face new obstacles compared to the women who entered managerial ranks during the 1970s and 1980s. Kanter predicted that the problems women faced within the formerly "all boys network" of the corporation would disappear as more women entered managerial ranks. Although most women have not achieved parity with men at managerial levels in the United States (Jacobs, 1992), business schools graduate almost as many women as men. During the 1992-1993 academic year, women earned 47% of all bachelor's degrees and 36% of all master's degrees in business. That business schools are able to attract almost equivalent numbers of men and women suggests that ideas about the appropriateness of women pursuing business degrees have undergone some change over the past 20 years. In contrast, engineering schools continue to graduate about five men for each woman. This means that many engineering women still work in a predominantly male environment.

One important piece of research is Sally Hacker's (1981) study of the culture of engineering at a large eastern engineering college. Hacker's research discusses the linkage between gender and being "adept," an important engineering trait. Within the engineering college, jokes made by engineers most often poked fun at ineptness, with inept people, in general, as the most common target of humor. Being inept was also equated with femininity, with women being the second most popular object of humor. Engineers are expected to be knowledgeable about tools and to be able to assemble objects (e.g., put together furniture, work on cars). Just as "you throw like a girl" is an insult, the image of the "bungling female" (e.g., the "woman driver") was a model of ineptness that engineers were encouraged to avoid.

Peter Lyman (1987) has also studied jokes to examine how masculine culture emphasizes differences between men and women. He views jokes as "a theater of domination in everyday life, and the success or failure of a joke marks the boundary within which power and aggression may be used in a relationship" (p. 150). Jokes are one way of reinforcing the boundary between engineers (the adept) and nonengineers (the inept). When ineptness is equated with being a female, a boundary between engineers (men) and women is emphasized.

McIlwee and Robinson (1992) have conducted the most recent research on women's experiences in engineering. Whereas Hacker focused on the culture of engineering within academia, McIlwee and Robinson studied 406 graduates of the mechanical and electrical engineering programs from two public universities in southern California in nonacademic settings. According to McIlwee and Robinson, the culture of engineering consists of three components. First, the culture of engineering has a positive ideological focus on technology. Second, organizational power is a basis for engineering success. Finally, they found that the culture of engineering

> requires that an interest in technology and organizational power be interactionally "presented" in an appropriate form—a form closely tied to the male gender role. . . . The *style* of this interactional presentation is as important as its substance. Here gender roles are important. To be taken as an engineer is to look like an engineer, talk like an engineer, and act like an engineer. In most workplaces this means looking, talking, and acting male. (pp. 19, 21)

Although the McIlwee and Robinson study is the most comprehensive so far, the findings are limited because the research focused on the southern California area and included only mechanical and electrical engineering graduates of public universities. In addition to southern California's distinctive regional flavor, mechanical and electrical engineering account for less than half of all employed engineers, and mechanical engineering has only recently become a popular choice among women. Many women who are in chemical and industrial engineering were not included in McIlwee and Robinson's study.

The rest of this chapter will use nationwide data to examine the extent to which women in engineering experience sexism in the workplace (especially the subtle forms). The chapter will conclude with some thoughts about the future of women in engineering.

Method

I used several data collection strategies to examine the experiences of women in engineering. The primary source of quantitative data was a national survey of members of engineering societies conducted by the Society of Women Engineers (SWE) and the American Association of Engineering Societies (AAES). More than one-half million engineers belong to the 22 member societies of the AAES, roughly a third of the U.S. engineering labor force. These quantitative data were supplemented with qualitative data gathered from my experiences as an active member of the Women in Engineering Program Advocates' Network (WEPAN). My field notes reflect informal conversations with both advocates and women in engineering from conferences and training seminars, information from an organizational E-mail subscription listserve,[1] and semistructured interviews with 11 respondents (WEPAN members, academic engineers, and engineers employed by industry).

The Society of Women Engineers' Survey

The SWE Survey of the members of 22 engineering professional societies was mailed under a cover letter from the American Association of Engineering Societies (*not* SWE) in August 1992. The questionnaire asked about engineers' academic and work experiences, including ratings of work satisfaction at the respondents' current workplace. This survey is an unobtrusive way of looking at engineers' perceptions of equal treatment because the survey was conducted under the auspices of the AAES rather than SWE and included several questions about workplace equity. Respondents could also address any of the issues raised in the survey by writing additional comments to open-ended questions or to supplement answers to close-ended questions.

The survey asked several questions about equity in the workplace, two of which are most relevant to the research presented in this chapter. The first question addressed the respondents' perception of general gender inequality in their workplaces and asked: "Do you believe that female and male employees performing the same job are treated equally where you work?" The second question about equitable treatment asked: "Are you personally aware of instances where women or members of minority groups have been overlooked with regard to career opportunities?" The survey response categories allowed respondents to indicate whether their knowledge of "overlooked career opportunities" had to do with women, minorities, or both.

In addition to comparing men's and women's responses to these questions and because women's experiences of subtle sexism were expected to vary by the type of workplace, I also examined differences between engineers employed in three types of settings: academia, industry, and government. For example, although "catcalls" can still be heard on many factory floors, academic women are unlikely to get catcalls from male colleagues in academic settings. On the other hand, women in industry do not deal with the "publish or perish" pressures of academic life.

Fieldwork Observations

The results I present here are based on the field notes I maintained at the five multi-day WEPAN-sponsored programs I attended between June 1994 and November 1995. These field notes included reports from advocates at more than 40 colleges about the status of women in engineering on their campuses. I also conducted five semistructured interviews of WEPAN members whom I will refer to as "Advocates." Advocates of women in engineering are ideal key informants because they are not on the academic tenure track but still report directly to engineering college deans. In many cases, these informants are either tenured engineering faculty or employed as professional staff within the college of engineering. Faculty and students alike tend to seek Advocates' advice and guidance on a number of issues, including allegations of discriminatory behavior. Such consulting gives

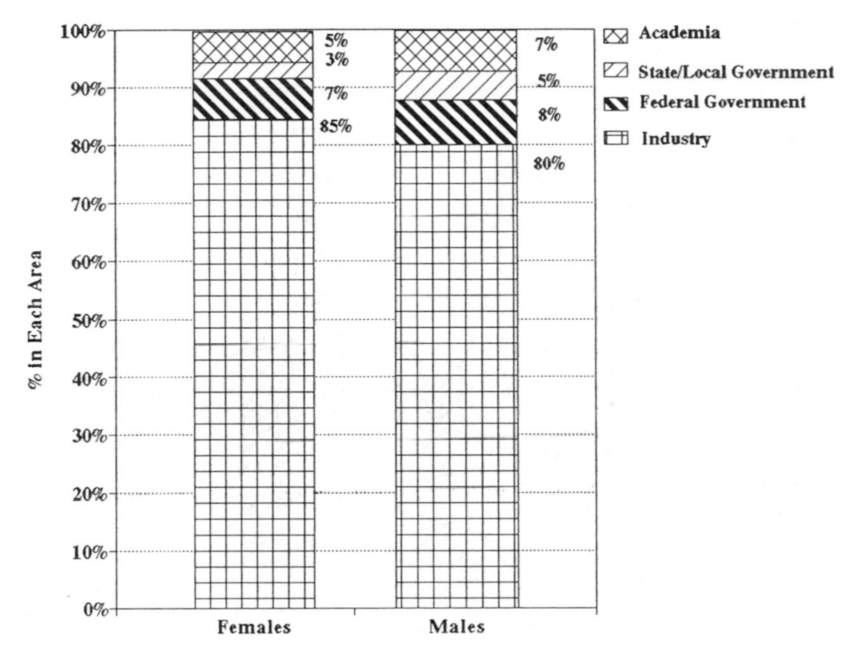

Figure 6.1. Society of Women Engineers' Survey: Respondents' Employment Area

these Advocates broad-based insight into the experiences of women in academic engineering settings. I also conducted six semistructured interviews of engineers in academia and industry who are not members of SWE or WEPAN.

Results

In this section, I'll first give an overview of engineers' attitudes about gender inequality and sex discrimination based on my analysis of the SWE Survey data. Then, I will focus on the processes of subtle sexism that were collected through my field notes and interviews.

Nationwide Attitudes About Job Gender Equity

There were no large differences between male and female engineers with respect to their area of employment (see Figure 6.1). Women are slightly

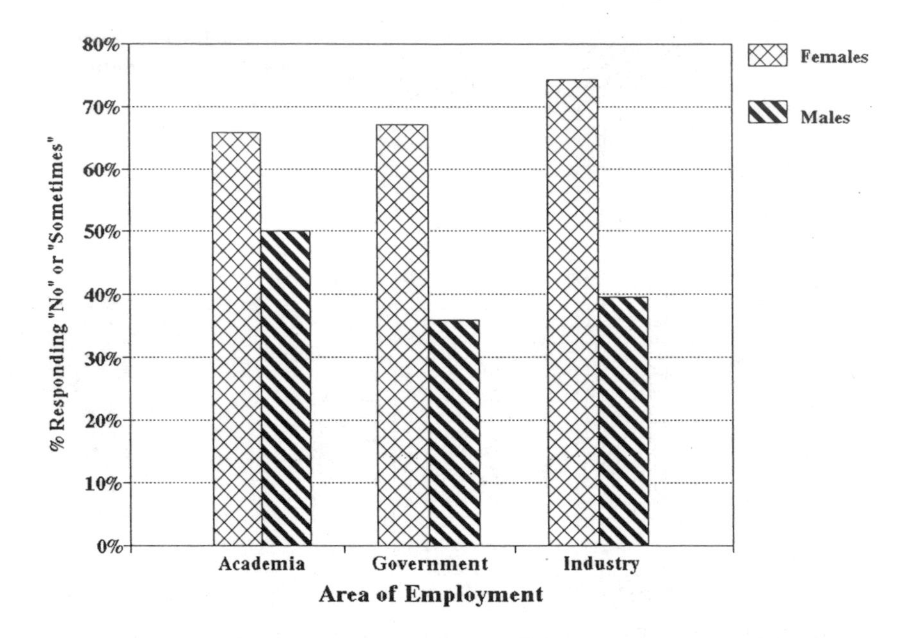

Figure 6.2. Society of Women Engineers' Survey: Respondents' Awareness of Gender Inequality

NOTE: Question: Do you believe that females and males performing the same job are treated equally where you work?

more likely to be employed in private industry than men, whereas men are slightly more likely than women to work in state or local government. This is not surprising because most engineers employed by state and local governments are civil engineers, a specialization that tends to attract proportionately fewer women than other engineering areas. Also, there was little difference in the proportion of women (5%) and men (7%) reporting they worked in academia.

Answers to the first equity question, "Do you believe that females and males performing the same job are treated equally where you work?" are shown in Figure 6.2. Within each of the three areas of employment, women were more likely than men to indicate that they felt there were either "consistent inequalities" or that "sometimes" people were treated differently due to sex. More than 60% of women in academia and government and just over 70% of those in industry felt there was gender inequality at their

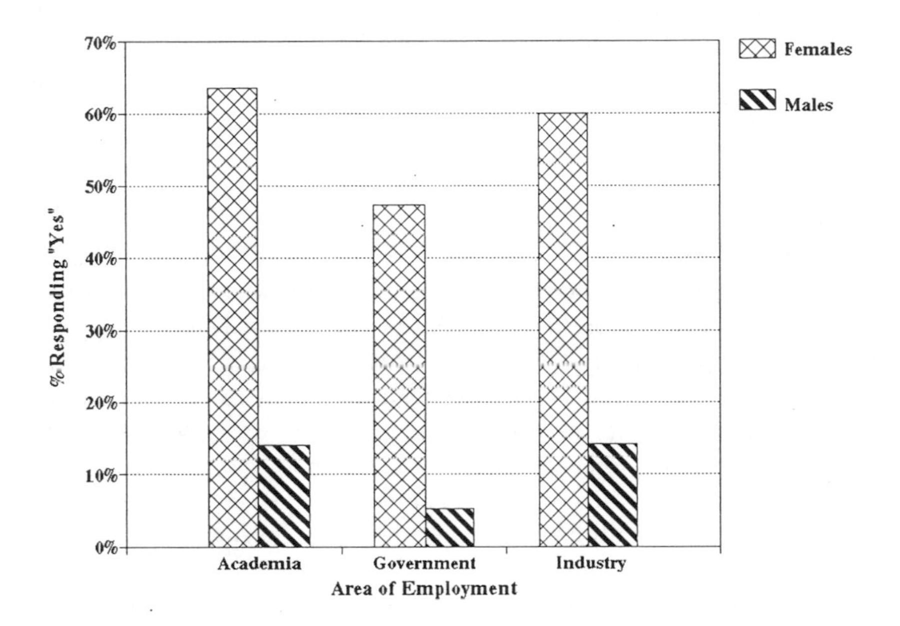

Figure 6.3. Society of Women Engineers' Survey: Respondents' Awareness of Discrimination Against Women

NOTE: Question: Are you aware of instances where women have been overlooked for opportunities?

workplaces. About 40% of the males, especially those employed in government or industry, indicated that there was gender inequality within their workplaces. Half of all academic males, however, indicated that they thought there were times when men and women were treated unequally. Thus, the sex gap is smallest among academic engineers and largest between men and women employed in industry and government.

Figure 6.3 shows the percentage of male and female respondents who reported that they were aware of instances where women had been overlooked for a career opportunity. The sex gap is striking: 59% of the women but only 13% of the men indicated an awareness of discrimination against women in career opportunities. Unfortunately, because the survey did not specify "career opportunities," we have no way of knowing if respondents were referring to promotions, advancement, or training opportunities. Women's responses varied by sector of employment. Women in government jobs were least likely to report an awareness of discrimination: 64% of those in academia and 60% of those in industry but 47% of women in government jobs reported that they were aware of some instance where a woman had been overlooked for a career opportunity.[2]

In-Depth Focus of Subtle Sex Discrimination

Subtle sexism is discriminatory behavior that is often overlooked, can be unintentional, and is built into our norms of gendered behavior. In many cases, subtle sexist behavior is consistent with our normative expectations about male-female interactions. Although subtle sexist behavior may be unintentional or "friendly," it still reinforces the boundaries between men and women (Benokraitis & Feagin, 1995). For women in the male-sex-typical field of engineering, the picture is further complicated by consciousness issues due to women's tokenism in the field. As tokens, women in engineering are under pressure to conform to both professional engineering standards, which are culturally consistent with the male gender role, and societal standards of acceptable femininity.

According to my field notes and in-depth interviews, women's experiences of subtle sex discrimination in engineering varied depending on whether they were employed in private industry or academia. Also, within academia, women's experiences as students were different than those of women who were engineering faculty members.

Women as Engineering Students

Much of the sexist behavior reported by students at engineering schools appears to be subtle. Although some of the behaviors were blatant, in many cases faculty members often did not realize that they were treating women and men differently. According to the Advocates, many female students reported that when they asked questions in class, professors' body language made them feel stupid or uncomfortable. For example, a professor might "roll his eyes" when a woman asks a question, give a curt answer, or tell her to see him after class while not responding in this way to male students' questions. As a result, women have also reported that they feel they are not "taken as seriously" as their male peers.

This is not surprising. In other studies of gender differences in education, both male and female teachers interact differently with male and female students (Sadker & Sadker, 1995; Sandler & Hall, 1986). Hence, this kind of behavior is not unique to engineering. However, because women are more likely to be few in number in any given engineering classroom, this kind of behavior is potentially more intimidating than the same behavior in a classroom where there are more women. Because the spotlight is focused on tokens, women in engineering classrooms are less likely than those in classrooms in less male-dominated areas to challenge what may be sexist behavior.

Third-party intervention can be a useful way of dealing with sexist behavior for women in engineering courses. The Advocates reported that students would often ask them about the various sexist behaviors in the classroom. In many cases, students were not sure if the behavior constituted sexism or if there was anything that could be done.

The Advocates dealt with subtle sexist behavior by discussing the matter with a professor without revealing the source of the complaint. When confronted, professors often indicated that they did not realize what they were doing and were willing to be more self-aware in the future. Indeed, an issue raised by all of the Advocates was that the vast majority of engineering faculty—mostly males—*did* want to change the "chilly" classroom environment to make it more friendly for female students. For example, Ruth, an Advocate at a large midwestern engineering college, illustrated professors' willingness to change and underscored the need to have "third parties" to advocate for women in engineering programs:

> One of our professors had a coffee mug on the bookcase behind his desk. He had received the mug as a gag gift and it had women's breasts as the handle. A student mentioned the mug to me, indicating that every time she went to see the professor in his office, the mug was just "there" and offended and distracted her. I then relayed the information about the situation to the professor's department head who then spoke with the professor. The professor had forgotten the mug was there and didn't realize it might be offensive. He promptly removed the item from his office when he heard of the problem and apologized for his thoughtlessness.

Advocates reported that engineering students indicated that in some cases faculty were actually more sensitive than fellow male students. In one climate study a respondent said: "Most of the sexist attitudes I have encountered have been from male students" (Michigan Technological University Presidential Commission for Women, 1994). That faculty were perceived as possibly more understanding than students' peers is not surprising. The data in the SWE Survey showed that among employed male engineers, academics were the most conscious of gender inequality. Male students made remarks that sexually objectified their female classmates with comments such as "Look at the tits on her!" In many engineering classes, teamwork is an important part of the learning experience. Sometimes when working on teams with men, women reported to the Advocates that they were assigned "secretarial" duties (taking notes and typing the final report) and that their ideas and suggestions were often ignored. Two comments made by students in the Michigan Technological University climate study reflect this experience:

> As far as group projects are concerned, I've been lucky enough to work with decent partners and haven't had any problems with male group members. This, however, is because I know who [*sic*] not to work with.

> The main problem I have in classes or labs is that when I do a calculation, and I say what I got as an answer, the male students in the group will ignore me and try to figure it out themselves. They question my answers.

Women as Engineering Instructors

Women in engineering face the same structural hurdles associated with the tenure track as their academic male peers. In short, academics must publish or perish. For engineering faculty, this requirement means that lab facilities, class schedules, service commitments, and access to graduate research assistants are important elements in a successful academic career.

There are a number of salient issues for women engineering faculty members that simply do not exist for their male peers. First, women tend to be tokens in their departments. Based on the information from representatives of more than 40 engineering colleges in my fieldwork, most engineering departments have only one woman on the tenure track. Although most engineering colleges employ more than one woman on the faculty, women tend to be spread out across many departments, often with little opportunity to interact with faculty outside their department. One respondent indicated that she was excited to accept a job offer from a midwestern engineering college because there already was a woman in the department: "For once, I would not have to break new ground and I would not be the only one." Academic women in engineering are often quite conscious of being the only woman in a department. In many colleges, some engineering departments do not have *any* female tenure-track (or tenured) professors. Women engineering faculty indicated to the Advocates that it was common for their colleagues to refer additional women students to them for advising, even when the student was not in their department. Besides finding herself overburdened by these advising duties, the token female professor often has additional "service" responsibilities because she is expected to represent the voice of all women on numerous committees (Meyers, 1993).

Some Advocates indicated that new faculty women in engineering felt that they had been given the least desirable lab or office space and/or the least desirable class hours. For example, Linda, an Advocate from a large eastern engineering school, said that a female faculty member felt slighted by being given the smallest lab with the oldest equipment. Also, some engineering faculty women felt that they were assigned evening courses more often than their male peers. Because research is required of all faculty, a modicum of control over one's hours of work is important in ensuring a productive research career. Furthermore, because much engineering research requires laboratory space and equipment, being given the least desirable space or equipment at the start of a tenure-track career can seem like one is being "set up" to do poorly. This kind of discrimination is especially difficult to remedy because an alternate "logical" explanation exists: that is, all new tenure-track professors get the short end of the stick. However, in the case cited above, the faculty member felt that she received the worst space and equipment because of her sex and not because of her newness; other new male professors had not received the same treatment.

How widespread are gender inequities in academics' lab and office space assignments? In my analysis of the SWE Survey data, there was no statistically significant difference in academic males' and females' reported levels of satisfaction with support facilities, job content, or support for professional/technical activities. Therefore, gender discrimination in the distribution of lab space and equipment in academic settings probably varies across institutions.

For academic women, pregnancy is often seen as more of a problem than a natural life process. The WEPAN Faculty Action Group discussed pregnancy issues as they related to tenure at conference meetings in both 1994 and 1995 (Metz, 1994, 1995). A recent survey (by another listserve member) on the WEPAN listserve asked for input about pregnancy leave policies. The inquirer indicated that she had been informed that she could not take a leave of absence for a pregnancy and stay on the tenure track at the college where she worked. Other engineering faculty have reported that they were able to hide their pregnancies, to minimize the time taken off during the pregnancy, or to plan the pregnancy so that the baby would be delivered during the summer or winter break to avoid possible confrontations with male peers and administrators, who perceived pregnancy as an indication that a woman was not "serious" about a tenured position.

Finally, in any classroom setting, instructors must establish themselves as capable and competent professionals in the subject area. In my study, women in engineering reported that students appeared to "test" them more often than their male colleagues. They felt these tests were directed toward them—often by male students—because of their sex. They recalled their own undergraduate student experiences when it was unthinkable to call a professor by his first name or not to use the titles "Professor" or "Dr." Faculty women reported that students more often called them by their first name or used titles like "Miss," "Ms.," or "Mrs." rather than "Professor" or "Dr." Women engineering professors have also reported that students more often asked about their engineering credentials or appeared more critical of in-class mistakes:

> Her audience, the students, [is] often less forgiving of her faux pas than those of [the] male professors. He can have a bad day or just get confused while working out a derivation in class; she just doesn't know the material. Similarly, this same audience will accept the standards set by male professors; he can demand high performance from students whereas she will be touted as "picky" and "unreasonable." (Meyers, 1993, p. 55)

Women in Industry

An Advocate at one college of engineering reported that students who returned from co-op positions in industrial settings were surprised that blatant and offensive displays of nude or scantily clad women were still found in engineering workplaces in the 1990s. Another respondent, an engineer who had been denied promotion in the late 1980s, was able to photograph a number of such "decorations" in her workplace as evidence of a work environment that is hostile to women. Another respondent indicated that she was "amazed" to find two young, attractive female models at a trade show booth for her company. When she asked the women if they worked for the company, they responded, giggling, "Today we do!" The engineer was offended by the company's sexist practice.

Many women in industrial settings are reluctant to complain about such practices. Because engineering women are so few in number and because women are seen as "invading" this traditionally male domain, objections to such masculine displays were often met with such retorts as: "If you can't stand the heat, get out of the kitchen!" At the 1995 National SWE Conference, one session was titled "Snappy Responses to Obnoxious Remarks." Because women in engineering are under scrutiny and are expected to adapt to male work cultures, "snappy responses" are one way of "fitting in" while also challenging sexist assumptions or behavior.

This notion of invading men's occupations was discussed by many informants, who said that males sometimes asked questions such as: "Don't you feel bad about taking a job away from a man?" The respondents indicated that such questions often placed them on the defensive. They found themselves listing their qualifications rather than confronting such insulting and offensive remarks.

Engineers tend to experience a period during which their academic credentials are not automatically accepted as proof of their engineering ability (Sobol, 1992). Especially in nonresearch settings, "book learning" is seen as less relevant to the "real world" than actual work experience. Engineering work, by definition, requires *application* of the theoretical principles of math and science. It is imperative to "prove oneself" by "doing." Women in engineering face this hurdle in qualitatively different ways than do their male peers. For example, a woman on a shop floor who cannot operate a particular machine may be teased with, "Isn't that like a woman!" As a result, her actions are stereotyped as representative of all women. A male engineer in the same situation would still be teased, but because of his general lack of experience rather than his sex.

In the United States, "tinkering" is considered a masculine characteristic, and most men are assumed to be unafraid of getting their hands dirty. Whether a male really has such interests or abilities is irrelevant, because being "mechanically inclined" is assumed to be a masculine trait. Women, on the other hand, are typically assumed to be lacking such skills and to be incapable of the physical effort required for some jobs. Therefore, women face more frequent and higher hurdles to prove themselves; they may be required to pass mechanical skills tests that are not given to men. One respondent, who had worked as an industrial engineer in an automobile assembly plant, reported that she was often asked to perform various jobs on the assembly line. She felt that although it was assumed that the male engineers could automatically perform these jobs, she, as a female engineer, was assumed to be inept:

> I used to go in on the weekends so that I could practice the most difficult jobs on the assembly line. That way, if for some reason someone would ask me to do their job, I could jump right in and do it without looking like an idiot. People were always asking me to do their jobs. In some cases, I got the sense that it was so they [the men] could just watch me. In other cases, it was clearly to see the inept woman make a fool of herself, since no woman could ever do as good a job as them. It was important that I could do the jobs *and* do them at speed in order to gain the respect of both the workers and the supervisors.

According to this informant, male engineers in the same factory were only rarely asked to demonstrate their skill in performing assembly line operations.

Conclusions and Some Thoughts About the Future

The national data analyzed here indicate that gender inequality among engineers is still pervasive. Approximately 67% of engineering women and 40% of engineering men who participated in the SWE Survey indicated that males and females were treated differently where they worked. Only 0.1% of women and fewer than 2% of the men mentioned "reverse discrimination" as a problem in their workplaces. The qualitative data collected through participant observation and interviews reveal that many women still experience gender inequality in engineering workplaces and in higher education. Whether the gender inequality is blatant or subtle, intentional or unintentional, such discrimination reinforces our cultural stereotypes about women and men in the classroom and on the job.

Many engineering women still feel that they need to fit into a male-oriented workplace culture. Advocates and other respondents reported that women in engineering often view sexist behavior simply as "obnoxious" rather than as a form of discrimination. Whereas men often contend that women are too quick to "jump" to conclusions of discrimination, many women in engineering feel that sex discrimination is de-emphasized or ignored. For example, one academic engineer observed that

> at regular [engineering professional society] conferences you don't hear too much talk about sexism at the sessions or during the socialization and networking periods between sessions. You *do* hear a lot of talk about sexism and discrimination in the ladies' room, though.

The prognosis for the future is mixed. On the one hand, some engineering faculty appear to be genuinely interested in creating a "warmer" climate for women students. Organizations such as WEPAN and SWE have also turned their attention to making systemic changes in educational institutions to warm the climate for female students. Rather than "fitting women into engineering," the Advocates I interviewed said that it was increasingly important for the engineering profession to reflect the "diversity of the world." This is an important shift in the guiding philosophy of WEPAN Advocates. Prior to focusing on systemic change, Advocates tended to counsel individual women on how to fit in and "not make waves." Now, however, Advocates are more willing to intervene with engineering faculty and administrative personnel on behalf of women engineering students and faculty members. The Advocate's role is vital because the token status of women in college engineering programs makes self-advocacy quite difficult.

On the other hand, engineering women in industry settings are likely to continue to face the pressures associated with token status, especially because women continue to represent less than 20% of all engineering college graduates. Unlike engineering women in some academic settings, moreover, their female counterparts in industry do not have third-party advocates. In many cases, the pressures of working in the spotlight as a token in a male-dominated culture discourages identifying and rectifying both overt and subtle sexist practices.

The persistence of women as tokens in engineering and the perceived penalties of confronting sexism imply that the masculine culture of engineering is likely to change slowly. According to Kanter's (1977) theory of relative numbers, as women come to represent a larger portion of a group, the pressure of the spotlight and of token status should diminish. This means that, eventually, as women become more common in formerly male-dominated occupations, the gendered meanings of the professions should change. There is little evidence for such optimism, however. Although business schools graduate almost as many men as women, sex discrimination in the business sector is still widespread (Blum & Smith, 1988; Chaffins, Forbes, Fuqua, & Cangemi, 1995; Jacobs, 1992; Tucker, 1985; Wright, Baxter, & Birkelund-Gunn, 1995). In male-dominated occupations, a lack of advocacy *combined* with women's status as tokens suggests that sexism—and especially subtle sexism—may persist for many years.

Notes

1. The Internet has become an important source of communication, especially among academics and technical professionals. People subscribe to listserves, on which messages are posted and sent to subscribers around the world. Organizations such as WEPAN have established listserves to encourage dialogue and to disseminate news ranging from statistical information to queries about maternal leave policies to job notices.

2. I also compared the responses to the equity questions of women who were members of SWE to women who were not members of SWE. The SWE membership list was a convenient way to locate enough women so that comparisons of male and female engineers would be possible. However, this oversampling technique could have resulted in bias. For example, the SWE women who responded might be more sensitive to equity issues than engineering women in general. By comparing the responses of SWE and non-SWE women, then, I was able to check for this possible bias. I found that there was no statistically significant difference between the SWE and non-SWE engineering women's perceptions of equity.

References

Benokraitis, N. V., & Feagin, J. R. (1995). *Modern sexism: Blatant, subtle, and covert discrimination.* Englewood Cliffs, NJ: Prentice Hall.

Blum, L., & Smith, V. (1988). Women's mobility in the corporation: A critique of the politics of optimism. *Signs: Journal of Women in Culture and Society, 13,* 528-545.

Chaffins, S., Forbes, M., Fuqua, H. E., Jr., & Cangemi, J. P. (1995). The glass ceiling: Are women where they should be? *Education, 115,* 380-386.

Fine, G. A. (1987). One of the boys: Women in male-dominated settings. In M. S. Kimmel (Ed.), *Changing men: New directions in research on men and masculinity* (pp. 131-147). Newbury Park, CA: Sage.

Fonow, M. M. (1993). Occupation/steelworker: Sex/female. In L. Richardson & V. Taylor (Eds.), *Feminist frontiers III: Rethinking sex, gender, and society* (pp. 209-215). New York: McGraw-Hill.

Geppert, L. (1995, May). The uphill struggle: No rose garden for women in engineering. *IEEE Spectrum,* pp. 40-50.

Hacker, S. (1981). The culture of engineering: Woman, workplace, and machine. *Women's Studies Quarterly 4,* 341-353.

Jacobs, J. A. (1992). Women's entry into management: Trends in earnings, authority, and values among salaried managers. *Administrative Science Quarterly, 37,* 282-301.

Kanter, R. M. (1977). *Men and women of the corporation.* New York: Basic Books.

Lyman, P. (1987). The fraternal bond as a joking relationship: A case study of the role of sexist jokes in male group bonding. In M. S. Kimmel (Ed.), *Changing men: New directions in research on men and masculinity* (pp. 148-163). Newbury Park, CA: Sage.

McIlwee, J. S., & Robinson, J. G. (1992). *Women in engineering: Gender, power, and workplace culture.* Albany: State University of New York Press.

Metz, S. S. (Ed.). (1994). *Proceedings: Women in engineering conference.* West Lafayette, IN: WEPAN Member Services.

Metz, S. S. (Ed.). (1995). *Proceedings: Women in engineering conference.* West Lafayette, IN: WEPAN Member Services.

Meyers, C. W. (1993). The role of faculty in women's engineering programs. In S. S. Metz (Ed.), *Proceedings: Women in engineering conference* (pp. 55-60). West Lafayette, IN: WEPAN Member Services.

Michigan Technological University Presidential Commission for Women. (1994). *A study of the climate for women at Michigan Technological University, Volume I.* Houghton: Michigan Technological University.

National Center for Education Statistics. (1995). *Digest of education statistics.* Washington, DC: Government Printing Office.

National Science Foundation. (1994). *Women, minorities, and persons with disabilities in science and engineering, 1994* (NSF No. 94-333). Arlington, VA: Author.

Sadker, M., & Sadker, D. (1995). *Failing at fairness: How our schools cheat girls.* New York: Touchstone.

Sandler, B. R., & Hall, R. M. (1986). *The campus climate revisited: Chilly for women faculty, administrators, and graduate students.* Washington, DC: Association of American Colleges, Project on the Status and Education of Women.

Sobol, S. (1992, October). Excuse me, what are your credentials? *Graduating Engineer* [Special issue: Minorities], pp. 74-80.

Tucker, S. (1985). Careers of men and women MBAs: 1950-1980. *Work and Occupations, 12,* 166-185.

U.S. Bureau of the Census. (1995). *The statistical abstract of the United States.* Washington, DC: Government Printing Office.

Williams, C. (1989). *Gender differences at work: Women and men in nontraditional occupations.* Berkeley: University of California Press.

Wright, E. O., Baxter, J., & Birkelund-Gunn, E. (1995). The gender gap in workplace authority: A cross-national study. *American Sociological Review, 60,* 407-435.

Chapter

7

It's Safer This Way

The Subtle and Not-So-Subtle Exclusion of Men in Child Care

Susan B. Murray

Child care is "women's work." Men workers make up only 3% to 6% of all child care workers in the United States. This scarcity of men probably reflects the dearth of available literature on men in child care occupations (e.g., Clarke-Stewart, 1993; Hartmann & Pearce, 1989). As a feminist scholar, my commitment has always been to put women at the center of my research. In my decision to focus my research on women by studying child care workers, I inadvertently bought into the notion that women are, in fact, the expected workers in this occupation. My subsequent research has shown me, however, that the experience of these workers as women workers is

AUTHOR'S NOTE: An earlier version of this chapter, "We All Love Charles: Child Care and the Social Construction of Gender," was published in *Gender & Society,* Vol. 10, No. 4, 1996.

made most visible by contrasting their experiences with the experiences of men workers. In other words, to see the differential treatment of women, it is sometimes necessary to focus on the differential treatment of men:

> Feminist scholars must avoid analyzing men as one-dimensional, omnipotent oppressors. Male behavior and consciousness emerge from a complex interaction with women as they at times initiate and control, while at other times, cooperate or resist the action of women. Clearly, researchers need to examine men in the context of gender relations more precisely and extensively than they have at the present time. (Gerson & Peiss, 1985, p. 327)

This chapter is about the experiences of men who do child care work. It is about the seemingly innocuous, yet "subtlety sexist,"[1] everyday encounters that men workers face in the child care setting. These messages, concerning the inappropriateness of men doing child care work, form the normative backdrop for all the workers in this setting. In this way, then, the organization of child care and its gendered status[2] as women's work systematically pushes men away from nurturing responsibilities and attaches them to women workers.

Method

My approach to this research was inductive. That is, I began with my position as a feminist sociologist wanting to conduct research on an issue that was central to women's lives. I had recently completed 2 years of research on battered women's shelters (Murray, 1988). I decided to shift my research focus from a description of inequality toward a solution to inequality.[3]

As more and more families use center-based child care, child care workers play an increasingly significant role in the lives of young children. Child care workers fulfill the caregiving obligations for young children when parents are unavailable to parent. So I began my research by asking who these workers are, and how their working conditions shape the care they give to young children. I found that 95% of all child care workers nationwide are women, and that these workers often experience very poor working conditions (Murray, 1995). My next step was to ask why these workers are mostly women, and how child care's positioning as women's work shapes the experiences of both women and men workers. To really see the effect of the gendering of child care on its workers (and subsequently on the children in their care), I turned my attention to men workers.

Data for this chapter were collected as part of my larger dissertation project on child care workers (Murray, 1995). In my research, conducted primarily in northern California between June 1988 and June 1992, I used a combination of participant-observation field methods, focused interviews, and survey methods. The data collected were analyzed using a combination of principles derived from Becker's (1970) discussion of "quasi-statistics," Glaser and Strauss's (1967) formulation of "grounded theory," and Katz's (1983) description of "analytic inductive" methods.

My primary field sites included two child care centers, a group of child care union organizers, and an informal group of gay and lesbian child care workers. Using a "snowball" sampling technique,[4] I conducted 18 focused interviews with child care workers between June 1990 and September 1994; 12 of these interviews were with women, and 6 were with men.[5] I also distributed 50 mail-back surveys to gay and lesbian child care workers at the Gay and Lesbian Caucus of the National Association for the Education of Young Children meetings in Washington, D.C., in November 1990. These surveys contained 16 open-ended questions about child care work and a number of demographic items. I received 35 usable questionnaires from respondents in 16 states and Canada: 63% of the respondents were women, 37% were men.

Results

When men enter child care settings, their participation is often "marked" as men's experiences. To be marked by gender means that you are viewed as a man or woman first before any other status you may occupy. The marking of men workers in nontraditional occupations is often accomplished through the practice of "subtle sexism." Subtle sexism, according to Benokraitis and Feagin (1995), has the following characteristics:

> (1) It can be intentional or unintentional; (2) it is visible but often goes unnoticed because it has been built into norms, values, and ideologies; (3) it is communicated both verbally and behaviorally; (4) it is usually informal rather than formal; and (5) it is most visible on the individual rather than the organizational level. (p. 4)

In the case of child care, the presence of men workers violates normative (generally accepted and acceptable) conceptions about who should be doing this work. These violations are routinely marked by co-workers and parents (and sometimes by the men workers themselves) through interactional practices that reflect subtle and pervasive sexism.[6] As the rest of this chapter shows, men in child care are marked in three primary ways. First, the occupation of child care reveals a gendered division in wages, in the positions held by men and women, and a token status where men workers in this setting are inordinately praised for simply being present. Second, the roles that men are expected to fill in this setting are often restricted in their emotional caregiving contributions. Finally, the act of "crossing over" to do women's work puts most men in a suspect category regarding the children they care for and severely limits men's physical access to children.

The Child Caring Context: "They Like Having a Man Around"

In child care occupations, wages differ by sex. Women child care workers earn wages that average 69% of those earned by men, with full-time women workers earning even less (Hartmann & Pearce, 1989, p. 26). These differences in wages "could reflect differences in experience and education, more likely [they reflect] differences in the types of jobs held, with men able to secure the better positions within child care" (Hartmann & Pearce, 1989, p. 27).

Although the child care occupation is dominated by women numerically, one of the reasons why men have higher wages and salaries is that the men who work in child care are often found in director and administrative positions and have risen to those positions more rapidly than their women counterparts. They encounter what Williams (1992) characterizes as the "glass escalator"—which moves them quickly up the occupational hierarchy. Each of the men I interviewed (except for the substitute teacher) talked about their rapid movement into teaching positions, and many—quite consciously—attributed their rapid rise in position to their sex. As Calvin, a head teacher at a college-based preschool, recounted:

> I was able to jump right into a head teaching job and I didn't quite follow all the steps . . . they were looking for a man.[7] If there were a man and a woman equally qualified for a [child care] position, I would probably get the job.

In my observations of child care workers and parents, this type of gender bias was most visible during hiring decisions. In both informal conversations and in formal discussions of potential job candidates, it was quite common to hear staff and parents openly discuss giving men preferential treatment in hiring.

Other researchers (e.g., Acker, 1990; Coltrane, 1989) have found similar cases of the positive valuation of men who enter woman-dominated workplaces. In my research, I found that this "positive valuation" of men workers permeated the daily child care working environment. As Tom, a white man and a substitute caregiver at an infant toddler center, notes:

> I get all these strokes for just showing up at my job every day. They are built in. And it has nothing to do with me. It's just because I'm a man showing up in this realm where basically there aren't any. I know they call me [to sub] 'cause they like having a man around.

In the child care setting, men receive an inordinate amount of positive feedback in comparison to women workers. Women's presence in this woman-dominated setting is taken for granted (i.e., "only natural"), but men's presence is highly valued. There are many examples in my field notes where, in the course of casual conversation, men were singled out and stroked for simply being present in child care (cf. Coltrane, 1989). The following excerpt from my field notes on Beach Side Preschool illustrates such a moment:

> Lunch is ending, Robin and Jane (the two morning teachers), are discussing who will clear the lunch dishes from the table, and who will start napping kids. Some of the children are on the deck, and some have gone down into the yard. As Robin grabs the milk pitcher off the table, she takes Gina's hand and they start walking inside. Mandy and Charles (the afternoon teachers) arrive together at the side gate. As Charles enters the gate, Gina lets go of Robin's hand and runs to Charles, as do two other kids on the deck. Jane comments, "Boy are we glad to see you." Robin follows with, "We are always glad to see Charles." And Mandy pipes in, "Yeah, we all love Charles."

These comments, though made casually, are significant to the extent that they form the context in which Charles works. These comments and others like them form a supportive and collegial net for this worker.[8] This was not an isolated incident. Similar interactions happened time and time again in the classroom when one man and two or more women workers were present.

This is not to say that women workers receive no positive or encouraging feedback from co-workers. However, in my observations at different centers, it appeared that men received such comments much more frequently than women workers. In fact, on any given day in a classroom where I observed for more than 2 hours, and if there was a man worker present, he enjoyed at least one supportive or appreciative remark by his female counterparts. It was almost as if the women workers perceived men as needing additional inducement to stay in this setting.

If such positive reinforcement is indeed typical of men's experiences in child care, then it suggests that the working environment for men workers has the potential of being quite different from that of women workers. Moreover, this type of subtle yet consistent support for men's presence in the child care setting sends a clear message to workers of both genders as to the positive valuation of one gender over the other.

Men's Caregiving Contributions: "Someone to Do Truck-Play With the Boys"

Even though men have some advantages in the child care occupation, they also face a number of obstacles. In this woman-dominated field, gender becomes a "master status" for men workers (Hughes, 1945). A master status is one that cuts across the other statuses a person may hold. In the college classroom, for example, a person's status as a student may take precedence over his or her status as daughter, friend, lab assistant, sorority sister, and so on. In child care, men workers are men first and foremost. Men are limited in what they are allowed to bring to the children emotionally in this setting. Perceptions about men's roles are limited to those available to fathers. "Father" appears to be the only appropriate role context within which men are allowed to love and care for children. The men workers I studied likened their relationships with the children under their care to fathers' relationships with children. Mark, a head teacher at a preschool, commented that "some of the kids really take to me. It's like they don't get enough male attention at home." Frank, a teacher at a college-based preschool, characterized his relationships with the children at the center in a similar way:

> I think some of the kids here just look at me and see daddy. The boys especially seem to really thrive on my attention. I think about all the kids that don't have fathers, and I wish there were more men doing this work.

Frank sees himself as cast in the role of father by the children in his center. It is not, however, only the men who hold themselves accountable to normative conceptions of "essential" manly natures in the child care environment. It was not uncommon to hear women workers attributing the benefits of having male co-workers to the masculine roles they play within the family.[9] As noted earlier, and as illustrated by my field notes, both workers and parents openly discussed men's gender as a deciding factor in hiring decisions:

> Beach Side Preschool needed a new afternoon head teacher to replace Charles, who was leaving. We interviewed three teachers for this position, two women and one man. The following excerpt is taken from the conversation that took place between the two board members, two teachers and myself (all women) following our interview with Bill.
>
> **Katherine [Board member/parent]:** I liked him. I mean I like Sandra [one of the other candidates] better, but I think we need to keep a balance around here.
>
> **Sarah [Board member/parent]:** I think it is good for kids to be around male energy, to have male models for kids to look up to.
>
> **Robin [Head teacher]:** I know. Some of the kids are really drawn to Charles.
>
> **Mandy [Assistant teacher]:** I know. I watch him with the kids and I think about what I missed not having a father around.

Although in this particular instance Bill was not offered a position at Beach Side Preschool (the two other candidates had more experience), all other things being equal, Bill would have been offered the job. In the child care environment, men are often sought as workers because of the perceived need to have "male role models" for children. As illustrated by a comment a co-worker made to Jeff on his first day of work at a new job: "Oh good, now we'll have someone to do truck-play with the boys." To the extent that "manly" qualities are sought in the woman-dominated environment of child care, men, by virtue of their sex category, will be given opportunities over and above those given women.

Perceiving men in this setting as simply "fathers," or as role models for childhood socialization, however, obscures what else might be going on in this setting. Although men see themselves as being called on to "do" masculinity in the child care setting, they view their contributions to child care differently. When they talked about what they see themselves as bringing to child care (outside of the perceptions of others), all of the men interviewed framed their contributions as intellectual and academic in nature. For example, although Frank sees the children putting him in a "daddy" role, he views his role differently:

> [My role is] to set up an environment where children can discover the physical world and the social world. . . . We also set up a classic nursery school environment; we do the corny stuff with turkeys and Halloween. But really my role is to set up an environment and social climate so they can learn to manage their own world.

Similarly, when asked about his favorite moments in the classroom, Mark responded:

> [My favorite moments] probably would be in the yard and not in the classroom. In the last 2 years I have been especially interested in large motor development because it is something that is measurable, and we can see sequence happen. I started videotaping children over and over doing something and moving with it. It is a visual look at development: swinging on the bar and falling, swinging on the bar and falling, swinging on the bar and finally getting his knee up. Charting that development over several months on a video camera, it's just so thrilling to watch.

Although one might argue that even these conceptions are very gendered in that they emphasize intellectual (masculinized) contributions over emotional (feminized) ones, the men did not perceive them that way. Developmental analyses are not seen as something that men, in particular, bring to child care. Being marked by their sex category in the child care setting masks other contributions that men might make. In our culture, normative conceptions of appropriate manly behaviors in interaction with young children are very restricted. In child care work, these restrictions constrain men and narrow the possible contributions men can make to children's lives.

Working in a Climate of Suspicion: "Why Are *You in This Field?"*

> I think that being a man there is more curiosity, like, why are you in this field? And it generally comes from the point of view of what's wrong with you? Because basically you're not in it to make big bucks, and there is very little status, and virtually no power. What I do know about the child care profession in general is that men generally end up in positions of authority. I mean that's how the hierarchy works. If you are a man and you are in child care, well, you at least better be the director.

When men cross the gender boundary into child care, they challenge assumptions about heterosexual masculinity. In addition to the positive strokes men receive for their child care work, there are also penalties. The occupational and personal sanctions placed on them for choosing child care work reveal much about the ways in which sexist and heterosexist behaviors get obscured by seemingly "helpful" and "protective" policies.

There are few socially acceptable reasons for men choosing to involve themselves in lower-status women's work. The choice to do child care means an almost certain movement down the ladder of power and prestige (or, for those men who have not yet achieved high status, a reduced potential for establishing it). Moreover,

> the man who crosses over into a female-dominated occupation upsets the gender assumptions embedded in the work. Almost immediately, he is suspected of not being a "real man": There must be something wrong with him ("Is he gay? Effeminate? Lazy?") for him to be interested in this work. (Williams, 1993, p. 3)

When men chose child care, their motives for making such a choice are questioned. In child care settings, this questioning manifests on those occasions where men get judged negatively for engaging in the same behaviors as their women counterparts. Men are often suspect just for doing their jobs.

In my study, many workers, both men and women, talked about how the men are subject to different unwritten rules regarding their physical access to children. Specifically, in many centers men are more restricted in their freedom to touch, cuddle, nap, and change diapers for children. As one worker stated, "I have worked in centers that employ male caregivers. Parents have on occasion been hesitant to accept them. One parent explicitly asked that a male caregiver not rub her daughter's back at nap time." In my observations of workers, I paid careful attention to those interactions focusing specifically on men's caregiving. What I noticed was a tendency in some centers toward a division of labor among teachers, which resulted in men having less access to certain moments in a child's day. Ostensibly, such divisions were designed to protect men from potential accusations of child abuse. In their effect, however, they upheld the sexist assumptions they purported to be working against. For example, at a Head Start program (where I observed several times over a period of 3 months) I noted the following patterns:

> Arrived at 12:30 and began observing while the children were still eating their lunches. Three people were working: Michelle (head teacher), Michael (teacher), and Juanita (assistant teacher). As the children began finishing their lunches, Michael got up from the table and directed them outside. He followed them outside and, standing to one side of the yard, he watched them. Michelle and Juanita remained inside helping the remaining children finish their lunches. When all the children had finished eating (about half were outside playing and half remained in the classroom), Michelle and Juanita each took a group of four kids and began getting them ready for their naps. They sent the others outside. Michael continued to watch the kids outside. As Michelle and Juanita got the children in their groups to lay on their mats quietly, they went outside and got another group of kids to nap. As the last group of children (there were 18 present) went inside with Juanita, Michael followed them and began wiping the tables from lunch and moving the chairs back to the side of the room.
>
> Though the teachers at this Head Start program often rotated other duties (like greeting parents, doing circle time, directing art projects), this napping routine did not vary—each time I observed at this center Michael never napped the kids. I asked Michelle about this one evening as she was closing the center. She replied: "It's safer this way. You just never know what the parents might think, what kids might say. We really like Michael, and we've just always done it this way."

The established routine at this center, although not written into center policy, was to exclude men providers from an activity that might lead to parental accusations even though there were no grounds for such accusations. As was true for all the centers I observed, the napping routine is often a very physically interactive process for teachers and children. Napping the children can involve changing their clothes (removing pants, shoes, socks, jackets), changing diapers, assisting them in going to the toilet (helping to pull on and off underwear or wiping them), laying down next to them, rubbing their backs, holding them, rocking them, or any other techniques that might help them to relax and fall asleep. It can be a very intimate routine, and a rewarding one for teachers. It can provide an opportunity for teachers to connect with otherwise difficult and disruptive children.[10] In the illustration above, the head teacher was not questioning Michael's competence to nap kids. Nor was she concerned that kids might not be safe with him. Her concern was with "what parents might think" and "what kids might say." Michelle's concern was to protect Michael from potential accusations of child sexual abuse. Excluding him from the napping procedure decreased the opportunities for his behavior to be suspect. This form of subtle discrimination though "friendly" on the surface follows the oxymoronic pattern suggested by Benokraitis and Feagin (1995, p. 83): Michael's exclusion from the napping procedure appears to be a case of helpful, yet condemning, protective indictment.

Child care centers also have very explicit policies about what men can and cannot do in caregiving activities. Surveys of lesbian and gay child care workers suggest that restrictions on men caregivers are quite blatant in some cases. One worker wrote, "I was teaching in a center when all of a sudden my taking a little girl to the bathroom became an issue. I think it was because an administrator at the center thought I was gay. My head teacher defended me, but after that none of the male workers were allowed to help kids in the bathroom." Still another wrote: "When I first came to work at my center the head teacher told me I shouldn't lay down next to the kids while napping them. She said I needed to sit up while napping kids. This didn't apply to the women." Other respondents similarly mentioned restrictions about napping routines, diapering, and "unnecessary" or "excessive" touching of children.

Inasmuch as centers develop unwritten policies to "protect" men workers from potential accusations by parents, there were also occasions on which men excluded themselves from their routine duties to avoid interactions with parents. Such was the case with Tom, who intentionally dodged the "morning greeting" with one of his parents to avoid a potentially uncomfortable interaction:

> I have been filling in for someone for almost a month. Robbie is one of my kids. He's really grown fond of me, and I really grew fond of him. His mother

> is the one that I have met a number of times. She was a little edgy at first but has since gotten friendlier. But when the father dropped him off, he was just like "Who are you?" and he was checking me out, I mean on so many levels. It was really uncomfortable. He was holding his son in his arms and saying "What do you think of this guy?" and Robbie can barely talk. You know he [the father] was putting Robbie in a really uncomfortable situation because Robbie loves his father and he's barely awake—it takes Robbie a while to be awake anyway—so he's kind of looking at me and you know being weird and stuff. And he finally hands Robbie over to me, but Robbie is one of those kids who usually runs up to me in the morning. So it was weird. So the next time he dropped Robbie off, normally I do the greetings in the morning, I asked the head teacher to greet him because he was obviously so uncomfortable with having to hand his kid over to another man.

In sidestepping this caregiving routine, Tom has, in a sense, compromised his ability to deliver quality care to this child because "greeting" parents is an important component of quality. It is in the morning greeting that the parents let the caregiver know what is happening with their child. Parents report on whether the child slept well, ate breakfast, fell down, had a tantrum, or whatever else might have occurred since they were last at the center. Such information is important in maintaining caregiver/parent rapport. Unfamiliar caregivers may miss important cues from the parent. Although the head teacher can report the greeting with Robbie's dad to Tom, she has not been privy to Robbie's history in the same way that Tom has. Therefore, she may overlook information that she did not perceive as relevant. Fortunately, not all centers give in to pressures from parents and others to shape the caregiving rules concerning men caregivers. For instance, the director of the Tiny Tot Toddler Center told me about several situations involving David, a long-term caregiver. Some parents had asked that their child be given a different caregiver because they were not comfortable with the idea of a man caring for their children. She said she refused all such requests from parents involving regular staff. As a result of these incidents, the Board of Directors at the Tiny Tot Toddler Center implemented a nondiscrimination policy for caregivers.

Responses to men caregivers can be organized along a continuum of access to children. Subtle and blatant sexism and heterosexism form the core of this continuum composed of no access at one pole, partial access in the middle, and open access at the other pole. Regarding the no-access pole, my data showed numerous cases where parents clearly did not want their child taken care of by a man at all. Sometimes parents requested another caregiver for their child. Other times, parents refused to enroll their child, or withdrew him or her once they discovered a man was working at the center. The following excerpt from my interview with Jeff, the afternoon head teacher at a preschool, illustrates the no-access pole:

> There have already been a couple of incidents here. As soon as parents find out a man is working here, they decide not to enroll their child. The last one was really weird. This parent spent 2 hours with the director, she had gone through the whole admissions procedures and was signing her child up. She had come in the morning to visit the center, but it was an all-day child, a little girl. Finally, the director had the parent come in around noon to meet me. She introduced me saying, "This is Jeff. He is the afternoon head teacher. He works with the younger children, and your child will be with him in the afternoon." I knew right away just from looking at her face, and when she shook my hand, that something was wrong. When the woman left and the director came back in the center she said, "You won't believe this but she decided against our center because she does not want to leave her child with a man."

Although it is impossible to say for certain why this woman did not want to leave her child with a man, the outcome of her decision is the same regardless of her reasons. For Jeff and for his director, the line has been drawn around his maleness as an undesirable quality of a caregiver. For other parents, a phone call to the center was enough for them to decide not to enroll their child in a center employing men caregivers. It is my contention that such blatant discrimination—usually found in cases of no access—make cases of subtle sexism more difficult to discern. Clearly, there is evidence to suggest that men caregivers might need protection from false accusations. But the form and content of that "protection" needs to be carefully scrutinized because it may harbor sexist assumptions.

Situations involving partial but limited access of men caregivers to children abound in the child care setting. Any occasions where men are asked to modify their caregiving routines, where established routines have a gendered division of labor, or where men are "warned" against behaving in a certain way around children constitute cases of subtle and not-so-subtle sexism. Typical of such cases was the situation Tom encountered during a substitute job where the head teacher explained to him that men caregivers were not allowed to let the children sit on their laps or to nap them.

At the other end of the continuum are cases of open access. Here men have the same responsibilities, rights, and caregiving routines as women caregivers. In the case of the Tiny Tot Toddler Center, where the director upheld David's right to care for children despite the pressure from parents, men caregivers' open access to children was written into center policy by the Board of Directors. Open access, in other words, had to be legislated by the center.

When normative expectations of appropriate attitudes and activities for a particular sex category are breached, as is the case of men doing child care, the expectations, usually tacit, become explicit. The restrictions placed on the men who work in child care regarding physical contact with the children they care for shows that their presence in this setting violates normative expectations. Doing child care is still women's work. That the men in this occupation are subject to a different set of rules than women provides further evidence of its gendered structure and the subtly sexist practices that uphold that structure.

Conclusion

It is my contention that heterosexism lies at the core of the idea that white men who do child care are "suspect."[11] Men, both gay and straight, who work in child care challenge our culture's dichotomous normative conceptions associated with "essential manly and womanly natures" (West & Zimmerman, 1987). The claim that child care is women's work may appear an oversimplification of reality. When that boundary is crossed, however, there are consequences. When gender boundaries are penetrated, interactions may take on a subtly sexist tone.

When gender is tied to sexuality, actions take on a heterosexist flavor as well as a sexist one. In the case of men in child care, just the act of their caring for children may raise questions about their sexual orientation. Their interest in child care may make them vulnerable to homophobic reactions from others in that situation. In a hetero-dominant culture like ours, accusations of "homosexuality" can have far-reaching and negative consequences for people.

Men's actions become suspect because they are choosing to do something that women do, and even worse, because child care is undervalued employment in our society. Gay is a sexualized identity. When a man admits to being, is discovered to be, or is suspected of being gay, his gay identity may define everything else. The so-labeled individual is seen as someone who is guided by sexual practices, thoughts, and feelings in all undertakings. Within the child care setting, anything having to do with adult sexuality is strictly off-limits. Thus, when a person's identity as a gay person is discovered or even suspected (as may be the case with straight men doing women's work), his competence as a teacher/caregiver is called into question. To the extent that being gay is viewed as a perversion, it is linked with other perversions, such as child sexual abuse.

The survey data I collected from members of the National Association for the Education of Young Children's Gay and Lesbian Caucus affirmed that the equating of "gay" and "child molester" is not uncommon. In response to the question, "Have you ever seen or experienced instances of homophobia at your center?" several people who answered yes described instances where people in child care settings equated being gay with being a child molester. One woman responded that "I have often heard remarks about all 'homos' being interested in molesting children." Another gay man who was "out" at his center stated that "a couple of times I have worked in places where staff or parents were blatantly anti-gay, refusing to leave a child alone with me." In several cases, survey respondents noted that such accusations were ludicrous, and especially where gay men were charged with molesting young girls. The facts are irrelevant in countering homophobic myths.

The final repercussion is the effect that "being suspect" has on individual men who do child care. Working in a climate of suspicion causes men to question themselves, their motives, and their behaviors. As Frank noted:

> One particular time, there was an allegation about a fellow in the community. Men came together; there were 9 or 10 of us and we had a meeting. And a lot of us began thinking, the witchhunt is on, and we should start looking at ourselves. So I started looking at how physically close I was to children. I started thinking, well, "Why is she on my lap?" "Why did I bring her on to my lap?" "Do I feel something down there, or whatever?" "Do I get any kick out of this?" I had to go through that soul searching. I didn't come up with anything, but you know, you really start questioning yourself.

Subtle heterosexism—the cultural push for people to adhere to heterosexual norms—is one of the more effective tools in maintaining gender inequality. Pressuring people to adhere to normative conceptions of "essential manly and womanly natures" (West & Zimmerman, 1987) relegates them to permanently unequal statuses. What is true for men who cross gendered boundaries is also true for women who cross into men's territories. Whereas men suffer accusations of "faggot" and get pushed out of a caring role in the lives of children, they do not seem to suffer economically from the act of crossing over.[12] Women, however, who cross into men's territories encounter a "glass ceiling," preventing them from advancing through male-dominated workplaces. Thus, some of the same subtly sexist and heterosexist practices that keep men in their place also ensure that some occupations will remain female dominated.

Notes

1. For a more extensive discussion of the concept of "subtle sexism," see Benokraitis and Feagin (1995).

2. See Acker (1990) for a discussion of gendered organizations.

3. Drawing from the work of Thorne (1994), I surmised that the lessons of gender inequality—inequality that I contend often results in violence against women—are often learned very early in life. Child care centers seemed to be the earliest public sites for "recruitment to gender identities" (Cahill, 1982). In my research on battered women's shelters, I had concluded that shelters are a response to the problem of violence against women, not a solution (Murray, 1988).

4. It was my initial intention to interview workers who had some longevity in the field, and who were involved in the child care community. My first interviews were conducted with workers in the centers where I was doing fieldwork. I selected these workers because they fit my criteria of longevity in the field and involvement in the community. During their interviews I asked if they knew of other child care workers who had been in the field a long time who might be interested in being interviewed. Each interviewee gave me a few names of people to contact. I asked this same question of each subsequent interviewee, and thus my sample began to "snowball" as each of my interviewees suggested others.

5. All the names appearing here (of both individuals and child care centers) have been changed to preserve the confidentiality of those involved.

6. Later in this analysis, I extend the concept of subtle sexism to include "subtle heterosexism." I conceptualize subtle heterosexism as the cultural push for people to adhere to dichotomous normative conceptions associated with "essential manly and womanly natures" (West & Zimmerman 1987), and for transgressions from such dichotomies to be negatively sanctioned by linking transgressors to a gay identity, as if such an identity were synonymous with perversion.

7. The first step for most workers is to enter the occupation of child care as aides or assistant teachers. They become teachers, and only after spending time on the floor are they promoted to the position of head teacher. Head teachers still work on the floor with children, but they have the added responsibility of supervising the assistant teachers and teachers on their shift.

8. The supportive comments made about Charles are indicative of the fact that in child care men workers are more valued than women workers. In society, in general, white men have more status than either white women or women of color, and this status differential is carried over into the child care setting.

9. Men also reported that their women co-workers frequently assumed that men workers would be responsible for manly chores around the center like taking out the trash, lifting heavy boxes, and moving furniture. In one case I observed an afternoon head teacher toss her car keys at the morning head teacher (a man) and say, "There's some cement bags in the trunk of my car I need you to bring in."

10. As a head teacher at Neighborhood School, Robin was given responsibility to nap three of the most difficult children at the center. I often observed these children in the yard and in the classroom, fighting with other kids, hitting them, screaming at teachers, yelling obscenities, and having tantrums. Observing these same children in their nap room with Robin I would often find the four of them lying on the floor (on mats), side by side, with Robin in the middle rubbing two backs at once and telling a story.

11. In my research, white men were the only men I found doing child care in the child care setting. Hence, I can only draw conclusions from the cases I studied.

12. Men who do child care do not seem to suffer economically relative to women who do child care. However, men in child care, relative to other men not in child care, put themselves in a position of inferior status by entering a woman-dominated occupation.

References

Acker, J. (1990). Hierarchies, jobs, bodies: A theory of gendered organizations. *Gender & Society, 4,* 139-158.

Becker, H. S. (1970). *Sociological work: Method and substance.* Chicago: Aldine.

Benokraitis, N. V., & Feagin, J. R. (1995). *Modern sexism: Blatant, subtle, and covert discrimination.* Englewood Cliffs, NJ: Prentice Hall.

Cahill, S. (1982). *Becoming boys and girls.* Unpublished doctoral dissertation, University of California, Santa Barbara.

Clarke-Stewart, A. (1993). *Daycare.* Cambridge, MA: Harvard University Press.

Coltrane, S. (1989). Household labor and the routine production of gender. *Social Problems, 36,* 473-490.

Glaser, B. G., & Strauss, A. L. (1967). *The discovery of grounded theory: Strategies for qualitative research.* Chicago: Aldine.

Gerson, J., & Peiss, K. (1985). Boundaries, negotiation, consciousness: Reconceptualizing gender relations. *Social Problems, 32,* 317-331.

Hartmann, H. I., & Pearce, D. M. (1989). *High skill and low pay: The economics of child care work.* Washington, DC: Institute for Women's Policy Research.

Hughes, E. C. (1945, March). Dilemmas and contradictions of status. *American Journal of Sociology,* pp. 353-359.

Katz, J. (1983). A theory of qualitative methodology: The social system of analytic fieldwork. In R. M. Emerson (Ed.), *Contemporary field research: A collection of readings* (pp. 127-148). Boston: Little, Brown.

Murray, S. B. (1988). The unhappy marriage of theory and practice: An analysis of a battered women's shelter. *NWSA Journal, 1,* 75-92.

Murray, S. B. (1995). *Child care work: The lived experience.* Unpublished doctoral dissertation, University of California, Santa Cruz.

Thorne, B. (1994). *Gender play: Girls and boys in school.* New Brunswick, NJ: Rutgers University Press.

West, C., & Zimmerman, D. H. (1987). Doing gender. *Gender & Society, 1,* 125-151.

Williams, C. L. (1992). The glass escalator: Hidden advantages for men in the "female" professions. *Social Problems, 39,* 253-267.

Williams, C. L. (1993). Introduction. In C. L. Williams (Ed.), *Doing "women's work": Men in non-traditional occupations* (pp. 1-9). Newbury Park, CA: Sage.

Chapter

8

Subtle Sexism in the U.S. Military

Individual Responses to Sexual Harassment

Richard J. Harris
Juanita M. Firestone

Sexual harassment was first defined as a concept in the late 1970s (Farley, 1978; MacKinnon, 1979). Several court cases during that period led to the use of Title VII of the Civil Rights Act of 1964 as a basis for prohibiting such behavior. In 1989, the Equal Employment Opportunity Commission (EEOC) issued guidelines that define sexual harassment:

> Unwelcome sexual advances, requests for sexual favors, and other verbal or physical conduct of a sexual nature constitute sexual harassment when

> submission to such conduct is made either explicitly or implicitly a term or condition of an individual's employment, submission to or rejection of such conduct by an individual is used as the basis for employment decisions affecting such individual, or such conduct has the purpose or effect of unreasonably interfering with an individual's work performance or creating an intimidating hostile, or offensive working environment. (EEOC, 1989)

This definition recognizes two types of sexual harassment: "quid pro quo," where someone predicates employment opportunities on a sexual relationship with the employee or applicant, and "hostile environment," where unwelcome sexual conduct or comments have either the purpose or effect of interfering with an employee's effort by creating an intimidating, abusive, or insulting working environment. In 1986, the Supreme Court, in *Meritor Savings Bank, FSB v. Vinson,* ruled that both forms of sexual harassment violated federal laws against discrimination.

In spite of antidiscrimination laws, sexual harassment in the workplace is still a serious problem (Paetzold & O'Leary-Kelly, 1996). The Clarence Thomas hearings and the Navy's Tailhook scandal provide public examples of harassing behaviors.

Social science research also establishes the pervasiveness of the problem. Most surveys suggest that 50% of women say they are currently being harassed at work; between 80% and 90% say they have been harassed at some point in their careers (Martin, 1989). Donald and Merker (1993) surveyed nurses certified by the Kentucky Board of Nursing and found that 35% described being harassed in their workplaces. Using data collected in 1989 at the university where she worked, Grauerholz (1996) found that 25% of female college professors reported being harassed by superiors, peers, and students. Results from a 1988 Department of Defense (DoD) survey found that over 70% of the women in the U.S. military, across all service branches and ranks, had experienced some form of sexual harassment during the 12 months just prior to the survey (Firestone & Harris, 1994). Sexual harassment is widespread in Canada and Europe as well (Cockburn, 1991; Gruber, Smith, & Kauppinen-Toropainen, 1996). It seems evident that, legal barriers notwithstanding, harassment continues to negatively affect women in a variety of countries, organizational settings, and hierarchical positions in organizations.

There are a number of myths about sexual harassment that make it difficult for women to report the problem. These myths reflect a tendency to blame the victim. For example, one myth implies that sexual harassment is not very common. As documented earlier, this is obviously not true. Another myth is that victims "ask for it" by their behavior and/or dress. Sexual harassment is not experienced only by young, attractive women. Studies show that sexual harassment threatens all women, and some men, regardless of age, race, marital status, or appearance (Caruthers & Crull, 1984; Grauerholz, 1996; Siegal, 1991). Another myth is that women often make false claims of sexual harassment, especially if they are angry with a man for personal reasons.

Sexual harassment has nothing to do with mutual desire, love, attraction, or affection between women and men. It is, instead, a matter of power and reflects domination and humiliation (Colatosti & Karg, 1991; DiTomaso, 1989; Paetzold & O'Leary-Kelly, 1996).

The prevalence of such myths suggests that implementing policies to provide a nonthreatening procedure for making complaints may be particularly important. According to MacKinnon (1987), legal and policy initiatives can also make a difference in how victims respond to sexual harassment, but they have to reflect "women's real experience of violation." To be effective, policies must be designed and implemented in such a way as to ensure that those experiencing harassment do not believe they are being held responsible for their own victimization.

Unfortunately, implementation in the past has often reinforced rather than challenged myths that blame the victim. For example, the individual who complained of harassment was frequently fired, demoted, or transferred, whereas the harasser typically remained at the same job during what can be a lengthy investigation. Furthermore, people who file harassment complaints are often labeled "troublemakers." Such labels can follow them to new jobs or different work settings. Thus, fear of being blamed (either for the harassment or for filing charges against the perpetrator) may prevent many women from labeling a behavior as harassment, which, in turn, may discourage using official channels to report incidents. Thus, often only those who label experiences as sexual harassment will report them (Malovich & Stake, 1990; Stockdale & Vaux, 1993).

There are a variety of responses to sexual harassment, which range from ignoring the situation to directly confronting the harasser to filing formal complaints. Previous research suggests that personal rather than formal responses to harassment are the norm, regardless of work climate, or even the nature of the harassment (Bingham & Scherer, 1993; Grauerholz, 1989; Livingston, 1982; Terpstra, 1986; see also McAllister, 1996). The type of harassment experienced, individualized (blatant) or environmental (subtle), may also affect the response.

In addition to work climate, the type of harassment people experience could affect their responses. Baker, Terpstra, and Larntz (1990) found that sexually coercive experiences (like demanding sexual favors or dates, or touching) were more likely to be reported than more general harassment (like sexual teasing, jokes, and whistles). In contrast, Bingham and Scherer (1993) reported that type of harassment had no significant effect on responses. Both of the above studies confirm that clearly defining the situation as harassment, with no uncertainty possible, is important in predicting type of response. That is, people may take stronger actions when they are certain that the situation will be perceived as sexual harassment by others (Bingham, 1991). Fitzgerald, Swan, and Fischer (1995) argue that a victim's response depends on whether she or he desires to change the situation or to reduce personal stress. If changing the situation is the preferred result, then individuals are more likely to report the problem through official channels, whereas ignoring the harassment or joking about it are supposed to reduce the victim's stress level.

This chapter compares the frequency of and responses to blatant and subtle forms of sexual harassment in the U.S. military. We are interested in determining (a) if the type of harassment affected whether an incident was reported through official channels, (b) if the type of harassment affected how the victim reacted, and (c) if policies against sexual harassment affected victims' responses. The behavioral responses provide a context for evaluating the effect on both victims and perpetrators as well as the policies and regulations in place at the time of the survey. Our analysis is important because it provides empirical rather than anecdotal evidence for beliefs about harassment that are prevalent in both academic and other work settings.

Data and Method

The 1988 DoD Survey of Sex Roles in the Active-Duty Military, conducted for the Office of the Secretary of Defense by the Defense Manpower Data Center, provides the database for this analysis. This was a "worldwide scientific survey of how men and women work together in the four DoD Active-Duty Military Services" (Martindale, 1990, Appendix A). The purpose of the survey was to ask about "observations, opinions and experiences with *all kinds* of sexual talk and behavior that can occur at work." The instrument emphasized the importance of responses both from those who have not been sexually harassed as well as those who have been harassed. Responses were voluntary, but the questionnaire noted that "maximum participation is encouraged so that data will be complete and representative" and that the "information will assist in the formulation of policies which may be needed to improve the working environment."

A stratified random sample of 20,249 respondents was drawn for the survey, representing male and female enlisted personnel and officers in the Army, Navy, Marines, Air Force, and Coast Guard. The original sample included 10,752 males and 9,497 females, illustrating the oversampling of women.[1] Marines and Coast Guard members were also oversampled. To compensate for the oversampling, we used a weighting scheme developed by the original survey team at the Defense Manpower Data Center tied to branch of service, rank, sex, and race.[2]

Defining Sexual Harassment

The survey provided respondents with a detailed framework to evaluate conditions in the work site. Before beginning, respondents were asked to read a one-page statement:

> This survey deals with sexual talk and behavior which can range from apparently casual remarks (like "Mary (or Joe) looks sexy today") to the serious crimes of sexual assault and rape.
>
> Sometimes this sexual talk and behavior is considered sexual harassment and sometimes it is not.
>
> Certain kinds of *uninvited* and *unwanted* sexual talk and behavior occurring at work can be considered sexual harassment. Examples are:
>
> *Actual* or *attempted rape* or sexual assault.
>
> *Unwanted, uninvited* pressure for sexual favors (Example: Someone tried to talk you into performing a certain sexual act with them or for them, maybe promising a reward).
>
> *Unwanted, uninvited* touching, leaning over, cornering, pinching or brushing against of a deliberately sexual nature.
>
> *Unwanted, uninvited* sexually suggestive looks, gestures or body language (Example: Someone at work kept staring at your sexual body parts).

Unwanted, uninvited letters, telephone calls, or materials of a sexual nature (Examples: Someone at work called you and said foul things; someone at work brought nude pictures for you to look at; someone sent you letters suggesting that you and the person have sex).

Unwanted, uninvited pressure for dates (Example: A superior kept pressuring you to go out).

Unwanted, uninvited sexual teasing, jokes, remarks or questions (Examples: Someone told you that you have a nice body; someone asked you how your sex life is; someone told crude jokes to embarrass you; someone jokingly made some comment about how you might perform in bed).

Unwanted, uninvited whistles, calls, hoots or yells of a sexual nature (Example: One or more persons whistled at you or yelled some sexual things at you from a window or from a car driving past you).

Unwanted, uninvited attempts to get your participation in any other kinds of sexually oriented activities (Examples: Someone tried to get you involved in group sex, or to pose for nude films, or to seduce someone for fun).

Both men and women can be victims of sexual harassment; both women and men can be sexual harassers; people can sexually harass persons of their own sex.

Types of Sexual Harassment

As these items show, respondents were provided with a framework that would allow them to make meaningful and reasonably comprehensive judgments about workplace conditions. With these definitions in mind, it is also possible to identify individualistic forms of sexual harassment that are frequently physical in nature and leave little room for misinterpretation by either the victim or the perpetrator. This form can be differentiated from the broader category of environmental harassment. Firestone and Harris (1994) classified the harassment experienced in the military into two major types: environmental (sexual teasing, jokes; suggestive looks, gestures; sexual whistles, calls, hoots) and individual (actual or attempted rape; pressure for favors, dates; sexual touching, cornering; phone calls, letters). The empirical evidence that linked those classifications together reinforces the fact that two types of harassment exist in the workplace.

In general, the individual forms of harassment are more blatant and more likely to be perceived as wrong. The environmental forms are more subtle and may be defined as ambiguous or as typical gender role behaviors, and as a result environmental forms are more likely to be considered acceptable behaviors (Benokraitis & Feagin, 1995). Although both are key to understanding harassment in the military (and other organizational settings) and developing effective policies for prevention, we focus on environmental forms to illustrate the process of subtle sexism. We describe the experiences reported by the respondents overall and then explore the patterns that had the greatest effect on the respondents. Almost all results comparing differences between men and women are statistically significant due to the large sample size; therefore, a comparison of the magnitude of differences in results is the key to interpreting our data.

Findings

The results of this investigation are presented in two parts. First, the prevalence of sexual harassment is documented, and then various responses to the harassment are discussed.

Prevalence of Sexual Harassment

The following evidence shows that sexual harassment is widespread in the military. In general, women were much more likely than men to indicate that they experienced both subtle and blatant harassment, although men also encountered both forms. For all respondents the most likely response to being harassed was ignoring the behavior, with making a joke of the incident a close second. Respondents were far more likely to ignore or joke about subtle forms of harassment than the more blatant forms.

One of the questions asked whether the respondent had received uninvited and unwanted sexual attention from someone at the work site during the past 12 months. As Figures 8.1 and 8.2 show, women were much more likely than men to report experiencing both subtle and blatant harassment. The environmental forms of harassment were most prevalent, and females were more likely to report experiences of sexual harassment in all categories of behavior, although some males reported problems in each area.

Figure 8.1 shows the proportion of men and women experiencing various types of subtle harassment. The sexual teasing and jokes category was the most prevalent for both males (13%) and females (58%). Suggestive looks and gestures was the next most frequently reported category, but much

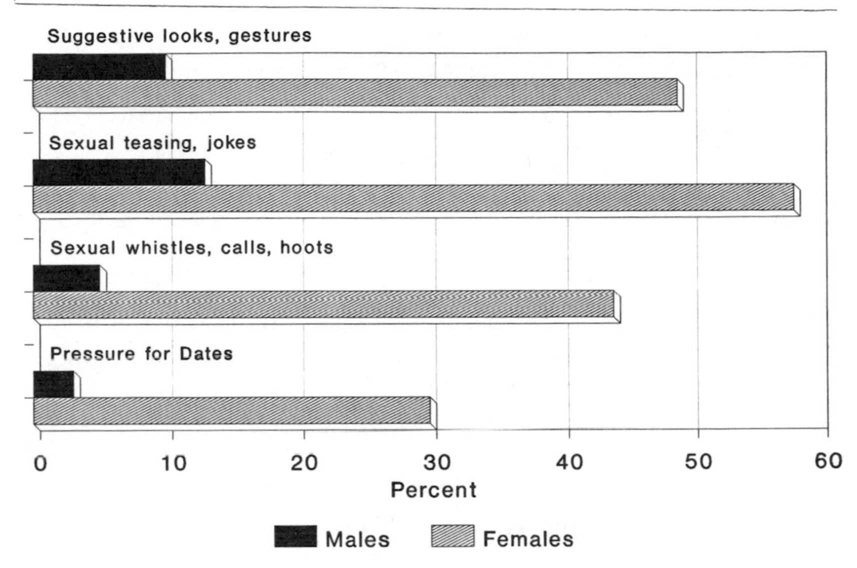

Figure 8.1. Males and Females Experiencing Subtle Harassment in the U.S. Military
SOURCE: Data from 1988 DoD Survey.

higher for women (49%) than for men (10%). Sexual whistles, calls, and hoots were mentioned by over 40% of the women. This was also the third most frequently mentioned area for the men, with 5% reporting sexual whistles, calls, and hoots. Pressure for dates was the fifth most frequently mentioned harassment behavior for the women (30%), although this was much less likely to be mentioned by the men (3%).

Figure 8.2 focuses on more blatant forms of harassment, providing a basis for comparison with the more subtle forms in Figure 8.1. Although overall the blatant forms are less prevalent, receiving sexual letters and phone calls and experiencing sexual touching and cornering were experienced by over 40% of the women.

Sexual touching and cornering, at 9%, was the most frequent blatant form experienced by the men. Pressure for sexual favors or being asked to have group sex, pose nude in films, or seduce another person affected over one in six of the women, but only about 3% of the men.

In their book *Sound Off! American Military Women Speak Out,* Dorothy Schneider and Carl Schneider (1988) report that the women they interviewed said that "men also harass women by name-calling, heavy duty teasing, and 'joking' . . . [men use] a lot of foul language, dirty jokes, sexual innuendos"

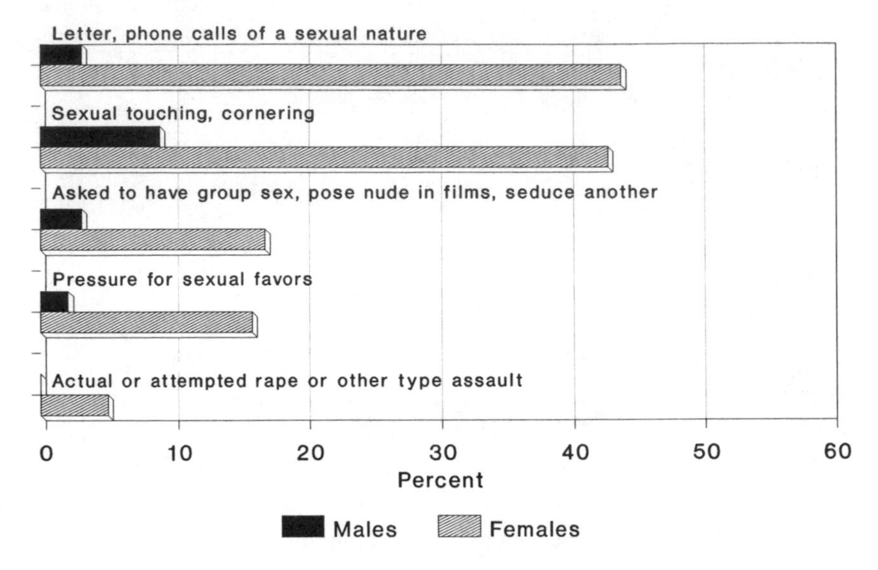

Figure 8.2. Males and Females Experiencing Blatant Harassment in the U.S. Military
SOURCE: Data from 1988 DoD Survey.

(p. 44). Such behaviors are often used to belittle women's accomplishments by implying they used sexual favors to move up the ranks, or to make it clear that women do not belong in a man's world:

> A lot of old crusty sergeants just have this straight, narrow thinking, and it's really funny. They always say, "In my Army, I wouldn't have any women." I tell 'em, "Well, it's not your Army." (Schneider & Schneider, 1988, p. 40)

In the minds of such men, it is clear that woman do not fit the role of soldier. This perception can then become a justification for such subtle forms of harassment as ignoring women, assigning them meaningless tasks, and refusing to teach them necessary skills for their assignments, all of which can have serious negative consequences for a woman's career.

Responses to Sexual Harassment

The military organization is unique in several important ways that may exacerbate the problems of responding to sexual harassment. First, the military is governed by the U.S. Code of Military Justice rather than by the national and state laws that regulate other organizations. Although sexual harassment is illegal in the military as well as in civilian organizations, the differences in the justice systems, coupled with the "military culture," may produce different perceptions of and responses to the problem.

Second, organizational cohesion is very highly valued within the military. Therefore, divulging negative information about another soldier is considered taboo.[3] Finally, harassment in general is part of the culture of the military. Thus sexual harassment is sometimes a subset of general harassment (see, e.g., Patrow & Patrow, 1986; Rogan, 1981; Schneider & Schneider, 1988; Steihm, 1989; Zimmerman, 1995). All of these factors may combine to create an organizational climate that is neither open to informal complaints nor a safe place for lodging formal charges.

Strikingly, 73% of the women and 18% of the men reported some form of sexual harassment in the past 12 months. What were the reactions to these incidents? Respondents were asked about "the one experience that had the greatest effect on you." Possible responses ranged from doing nothing at all to pursuing formal charges against the alleged perpetrator. It is possible, of course, to have reacted in several different ways to the same incident. For many people a sequence of responses might be expected, beginning with individualistic reactions and progressing to formal, institutional charges.

Starting with a base of 100% for those indicating any type of sexual harassment in the previous 12 months, the vast majority of men (89%) and women (67%) report no formal or official response to the incidents. Formal responses were rare: Only 33% of the women and 11% of the men who were harassed reported the incident to an official. Only 11% of the women and only 5% of the men filed formal charges against the perpetrators.

Figures 8.3 and 8.4 illustrate four types of responses separately for males and females by type of incident—ignoring the behavior or doing nothing, joking about it, reporting the behavior to an official, and finally, filing formal charges against the harasser(s). Over 60% initially did nothing about the sexual harassment, regardless of type. The men were more likely to ignore sexual assault and the women were more likely to ignore pressures for sexual favors. Overall, however, both men and women were very likely, at least at first, to do nothing about the sexually harassing experience. In fact, 64% of the women and 80% of the men initially ignored even actual or attempted rape.

At the next and more public level, large percentages of respondents attempted to make a joke of the incident. Nearly 38% of those reporting actual or attempted rape reacted to the episodes by making jokes of them.

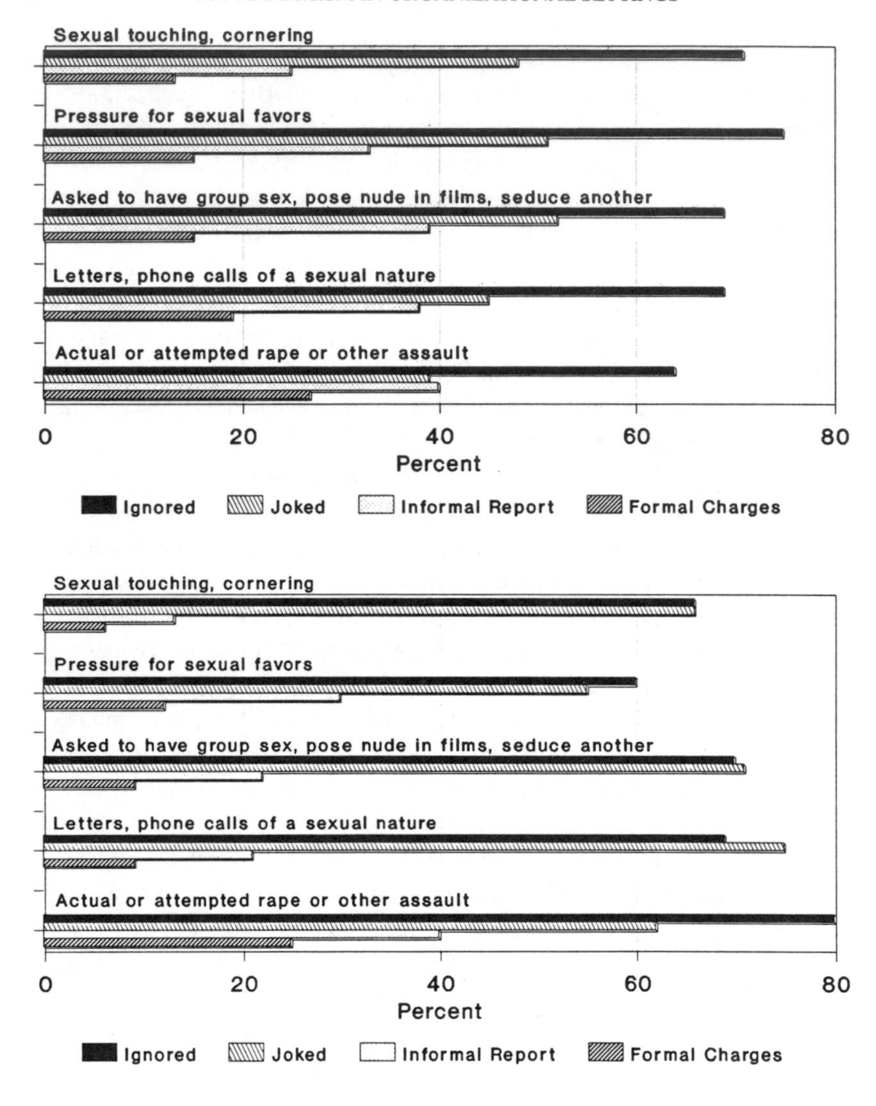

Figure 8.3. Responses to Blatant Harassment in the U.S. Military (female: top panel; male: bottom panel)
SOURCE: Data from 1988 DoD Survey.

For most of the other types of subtle and blatant incidents, about half of the women responded to the incident by joking about it. The likelihood of dismissing sexual harassment is substantially higher for men in all sexual

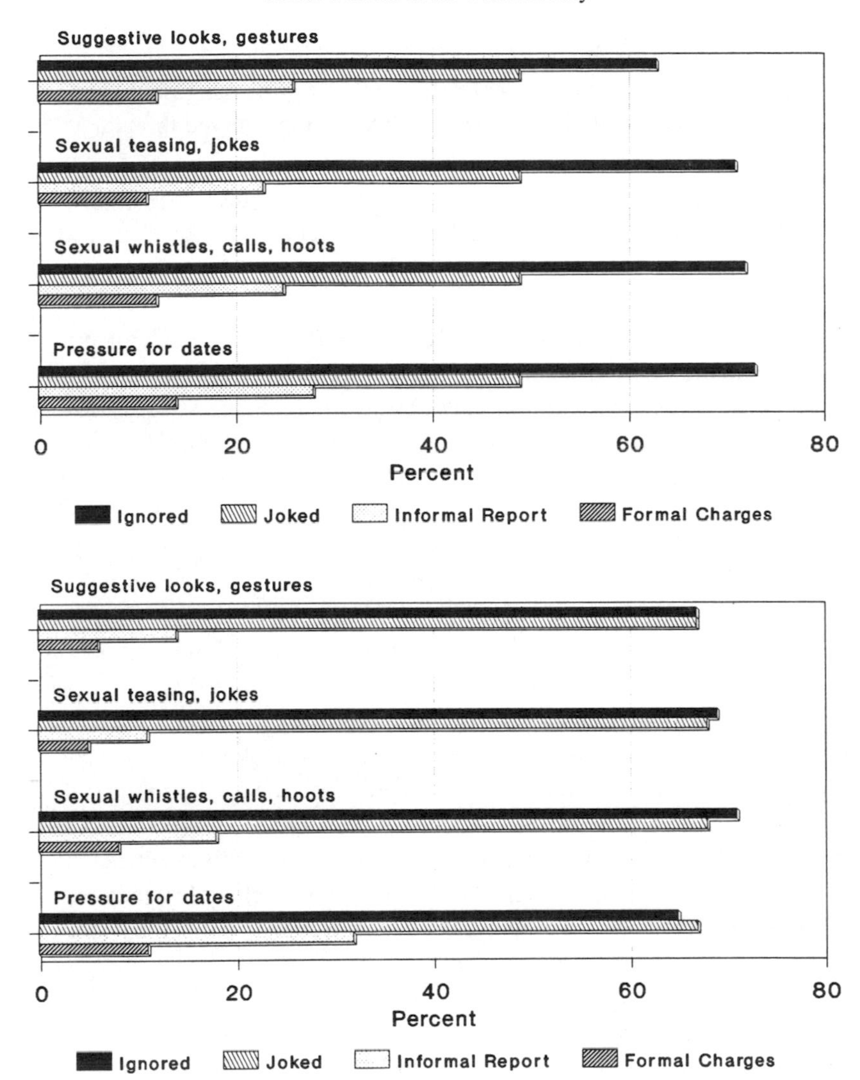

Figure 8.4. Responses to Subtle Harassment in the U.S. Military (female: top panel; male: bottom panel)
SOURCE: Data from 1988 DoD Survey.

harassment categories. Men may use joking as a means of redefining the situation and thus alleviating personal stress. A study of U.S. Navy personnel found that generally men considered harassment incidents as less serious than did women (Thomas, 1995). Perhaps joking seems an appropriate response to men when they do not define a situation as dangerous. Women, on the other hand, might use joking to reduce any perceived threat:

> A Marine captain talked about how she treats "a senior officer that constantly makes kind of suggestive remarks. My initial reaction is to play along with it and tease." (Schneider & Schneider, 1988, p. 60)

The danger here is that the perpetrators fail to take such responses seriously or understand the problem in their behavior. As the woman above noted, if the dialogue continues to the point where he may be "getting the wrong idea," she finally resorts to saying, "Sir, I really just don't appreciate these types of comments" (p. 60). That is the end of the incident until the next time.

Figure 8.4 shows the responses of men and women to subtle forms of harassment. Filing a formal action or reporting the incident to an official was very rare for subtle forms of harassment. For example, only 11% of men and 23% of women reported sexual teasing or jokes to an official, and only 5% of men and 11% of the women filed formal actions against such behavior. Notice the dramatic decrease in the proportion of respondents who take public versus individual action. Although the subtle forms of harassment are the most prevalent, they are the forms least likely to be filed through official channels. There may be several explanations for this finding. First, victims may be ambivalent about interpreting the action as harassment. As mentioned earlier, victims are less likely to report harassment unless they clearly define the incident as such in their own minds. Second, victims may believe that by ignoring the situation or joking about it they may reduce the amount of stress they could experience (Fitzgerald et al., 1995). This is especially true in environments where victims fear retaliation or where harassing behaviors seem more accepted (Hulin, Fitzgerald, & Drasgow, 1996).

The data we analyzed did not have information about whether the person who was harassed made some initial attempts to get someone in the organization to listen but found that their complaints were ignored. However, this is exactly what happened when Paula Coughlin tried to make someone in Washington listen to her account of the Tailhook incident. It took her over 5 weeks to break through the system and get Admiral Dunleavy to listen to her complaint. This was in spite of repeated attempts to tell superiors and co-workers alike how disgusted and miserable she was over what happened.

She described the men who participated in attacking her in this way: "Those jet pilots are a bunch of animals." Yet her superior officer continued to blame her for the incident: "That's what you get when you go to a hotel party with a bunch of drunk aviators" (Zimmerman, 1995, p. 40).

Reporting the behavior to the unit commander or another official is a move away from individualistic and toward institutional responses. The percentages pursuing this pattern of response were much lower for both males and females. With only a few exceptions, however, females were more likely than men to report the incidents to officials, but only in the case of actual or attempted assault did the proportion reach as high as 40% (see Figure 8.3). Sexual harassment is classified as a form of sexual assault (Gutek, 1985).[4] The pattern of responses by victims in our analysis is very similar to the responses to sexual assault reported for the civilian population (Basow, 1992; Cleveland & McNamara, 1996).

Why are victims generally unlikely to report harassing behavior? Reporting the incident can create a threatening backlash from those in charge, as Paula Coughlin described after disclosing the Tailhook scandal:

> "This was a learning experience," the admiral told her at one point. "Now you know the hatred and chauvinism that exists in the TACAIR[5] community." He voiced his concern—a warning which somehow came across as a threat—that Coughlin might be blackballed by her fellow aviators if word got out that she had raised the issue of culpability. (Zimmerman, 1995, p. 41)

Strikingly, only about one fourth of both males and females who experienced actual or attempted rape filed formal charges. This pattern of not filing formal charges is also evident for each other type of harassing incident. Whereas women were somewhat more likely than men to file charges, the basic finding is that few of those harassed ever pursued formal actions.

Conclusion

Because sexual harassment is embedded in the gender-power dynamics of male-dominated cultures, our findings, although consistent with earlier case studies, are striking in that they provide large-scale generalizable evidence of the extraordinary prevalence of sexual harassment, at least in the U.S. military. Many women may define sexually harassing behaviors as "normal," typical of their expectations of male-female relations, and therefore "to be expected" and not worth reporting. Women are often blamed for the sexual harassment they receive. That is, women who claim harassment are asked what they themselves did to bring on the harassing behavior. This response is even more prevalent for subtle forms of harassment because the focus on the individual makes it easier to "blame the victim" (Benokraitis & Feagin, 1995). Ignoring the behavior is also typical of people who hold very traditional gender stereotypes (Malovich & Stake, 1990). Fear of being blamed may prevent women from labeling a behavior as harassment. Yet labeling is important because only those who label experiences as sexual harassment will report them (Bingham & Scherer, 1993; Malovich & Stake, 1990; Stockdale & Vaux, 1993; Terpstra & Baker, 1987).

The distinctly masculine culture of the military may mitigate against people who report sexual harassment in general and the more subtle forms in particular.[6] Furthermore, the more overt the harassment, the more likely that the offense will be reported (Terpstra & Baker, 1987). Thus, blatant sexually coercive experiences, such as touching, cornering, and pressure for sexual favors, are more likely to be reported than the more subtle forms of environmental harassment, like sexual teasing, jokes, and whistles (Baker et al., 1990; Fitzgerald et al., 1995; Stockdale & Vaux, 1993). Firestone and Harris (1994) demonstrate that such subtle, environmental harassment is strongly predictive of personal, even physical, sexual harassment. In other words, the blatant, individually coercive forms of sexual harassment almost never occur unless environmental harassment is also present.

Additionally, these results support the necessity for viewing subtle and blatant types of sexual harassment as two sides of the same coin. These findings are consistent with previous research and provide strong empirical evidence for the contention that subtle sexual harassment should be treated equally as importantly as other more blatant forms such as sexual assault. Policies designed to remedy the negative consequences of sexual harassment must confront both the more subtle environmental and the blatant individualistic experiences to be effective.

The data presented here strongly suggest a failure of U.S. military policies that were in place in 1988 and/or the implementation of those policies. Individuals were unwilling to operate through institutional channels to deal with the pervasive sexual harassment experienced in the military. We have no data to suggest that the situation has improved since that time.[7]

Notes

1. It is important to oversample women (and Marines) because they are such a small proportion of the total armed forces. Simple random sampling techniques could produce biased results for underrepresented groups because of the small numbers that would be included.

2. The full weights provide estimated numbers of respondents that approximate the total active force at the time of the survey. For the analyses that follow, the full weight was divided by the mean weight, retaining estimates of the approximate total number of cases in the original survey (see Firestone & Harris, 1994, for more detail).

3. Although cohesion is highly valued in the military, it has been used to exclude rather than include women into the organization. Thus, women are accused of intruding on the male bonding that creates strong cohesion among members.

4. Sexual harassment, as with all forms of sexual assault, is an abuse of power where sex becomes the instrument through which power is realized.

5. This acronym refers to Tactical Air Command units.

6. Hulin et al. (1996) state that organizational cultures that are more tolerant of harassing behaviors are settings where more frequent harassment occurs, and where fewer incidents are reported through formal channels.

7. In a 1993 report, researchers for the U.S. Navy found that even though overall harassment was lower than in previous years, it was still prevalent. Compared to previous years, the rate of rape and sexual assault had not changed, women officers reported being harassed by civilian contractors/employees, and stalking or invasion of residence were now reported (Thomas, Newell, & Eliassen, 1995).

References

Baker, D. D., Terpstra, D. E., & Larntz, J. (1990). The influence of individual characteristics and severity of harassing behavior on reactions to sexual harassment. *Sex Roles, 22,* 305-325.

Basow, S. A. (1992). *Gender stereotypes and roles* (3rd ed.). Pacific Grove, CA: Brooks/Cole.

Benokraitis, N. V., & Feagin, J. R. (1995). *Modern sexism: Blatant, subtle, and covert discrimination.* Englewood Cliffs, NJ: Prentice Hall.

Bingham, S. G. (1991). Communication strategies for managing sexual harassment in organizations: Understanding message options and their effects. *Journal of Applied Communication Research, 19,* 88-115.

Bingham, S. G., & Scherer. L. L. (1993). Factors associated with responses to sexual harassment and satisfaction with outcome. *Sex Roles, 29,* 239-269.

Caruthers, S. C., & Crull, P. (1984). Contrasting sexual harassment in female and male-dominated occupations. In J. Sacks & S. Remy (Eds.), *My troubles are going to have trouble with me* (pp. 209-228). New Brunswick, NJ: Rutgers University Press.

Cleveland, J., & McNamara, K. (1996). Understanding sexual harassment: Contributions from research on domestic violence and organizational change. In M. S. Stockdale (Ed.), *Sexual harassment in the workplace: Perspectives, frontiers, and response strategies* (pp. 217-240). Thousand Oaks, CA: Sage.

Cockburn, C. (1991). *In the way of women: Men's resistance to sex equality in organizations.* Ithaca, NY: ILR Press.

Colatosti, C., & Karg, E. (1991). *Stopping sexual harassment: A handbook for union and workplace activists.* Detroit, MI: Labor Education and Research Project.

DiTomaso, N. (1989). Sexuality in the workplace: Discrimination and harassment. In J. Hearn, D. L. Sheppard, P. Tancred-Sheriff, & G. Burrell (Eds.), *The sexuality of organization* (pp. 71-90). Newbury Park, CA: Sage.

Donald, C. G., & Merker, S. (1993). Medical alert: Sexual harassment in the health care industry. *International Journal of Public Administration, 16,* 1483-1499.

Equal Employment Opportunity Commission. (1989). *EEOC guidelines,* 29 C.F.R. Section 1604, 193-203.

Farley, L. (1978). *Sexual shakedown.* New York: McGraw-Hill.

Firestone, J. M., & Harris, R. J. (1994). Sexual harassment in the U.S. military: Environmental and individual contexts. *Armed Forces and Society, 21,* 25-43.

Fitzgerald, L., Swan, S., & Fischer, K. (1995). Why didn't she just report him? The psychological and legal implications of women's responses to sexual harassment. *Journal of Social Issues, 51,* 117-138.

Grauerholz, E. (1989). Sexual harassment of women professors by students: Exploring the dynamics of power, authority, and gender in a university setting. *Sex Roles, 21,* 789-801.

Grauerholz, E. (1996). Sexual harassment in the academy: The case of women professors. In M. S. Stockdale (Ed.), *Sexual harassment in the workplace: Perspectives, frontiers, and response strategies* (pp. 29-50). Thousand Oaks, CA: Sage.

Gruber, J. E., Smith, M., & Kauppinen-Toropainen, K. (1996). Sexual harassment types and severity: Linking research and policy. In M. S. Stockdale (Ed.), *Sexual harassment in the workplace: Perspectives, frontiers, and response strategies* (pp. 151-173). Thousand Oaks, CA: Sage.

Gutek, B. A. (1985). *Sex and the workplace: The impact of sexual behavior and harassment on men, women, and organizations.* San Francisco: Jossey-Bass.

Hulin, C. L., Fitzgerald, L. F., & Drasgow, F. (1996). Organizational influences on sexual harassment. In M. S. Stockdale (Ed.), *Sexual harassment in the workplace: Perspectives, frontiers, and response strategies* (pp. 127-150). Thousand Oaks, CA: Sage.

Livingston, J. A. (1982). Responses to sexual harassment on the job: Legal, organizational, and individual actions. *Journal of Social Issues, 38,* 5-22.

MacKinnon, C. A. (1979). *Sexual harassment of working women.* New Haven, CT: Yale University Press.

MacKinnon, C. A. (1987). *Feminism unmodified: Discourses on life and law.* Cambridge, MA: Harvard University Press.

Malovich, N. J., & Stake, J. E. (1990). Sexual harassment on campus: Individual differences in attitudes and beliefs. *Psychology of Women Quarterly, 14,* 63-81.

Martin, S. E. (1989). Sexual harassment: The link joining gender stratification, sexuality, and women's economic status. In J. Freedman (Ed.), *Women: A feminist perspective* (3rd ed., pp. 54-69). Palo Alto, CA: Mayfield.

Martindale, M. (1990). *Sexual harassment in the military: 1988.* Arlington, VA: Defense Manpower Data Center.

McAllister, B. (1996, March 13). Harassment case took 5 years to resolve. *Washington Post,* p. A19.

Meritor Savings Bank, FSB v. Vinson, 06 S. Ct. 2399 (1986).

Paetzold, R. L., & O'Leary-Kelly, A. M. (1996). The implications of U.S. Supreme Court and circuit court decisions for hostile environment sexual harassment cases. In M. S. Stockdale (Ed.), *Sexual harassment in the workplace: Perspectives, frontiers, and response strategies* (pp. 85-104). Thousand Oaks, CA: Sage.

Patrow, J. L., & Patrow, R. (1986). The leathernecks: A few good men . . . and women. In D. R. Segal & H. W. Sinaiko (Eds.), *Life in the rank and file: Enlisted men and women in the armed forces of the United States, Australia, Canada, and the United Kingdom* (pp. 153-183). Washington, DC: Pergamon-Brassey's.

Rogan, H. (1981). *Mixed company; Women in the modern army.* Boston: Beacon.

Schneider, D., & Schneider, C. J. (1988). *Sound off! American military women speak out.* New York: E. P. Dutton.

Siegal, D. (1991). *Sexual harassment: Research and resources.* New York: National Council for Research on Women.

Steihm, J. (1989). *Arms and the enlisted woman.* Philadelphia: Temple University Press.

Stockdale, M. S., & Vaux, A. (1993). What sexual harassment experiences lead respondents to acknowledge being sexually harassed? A secondary analysis of a university study. *Journal of Vocational Behavior, 43,* 221-234.

Terpstra, D. E. (1986). A framework for the study of sexual harassment. *Basic and Applied Social Psychology, 7,* 17-34.

Terpstra, D. E., & Baker, D. D. (1987). A hierarchy of sexual harassment. *Journal of Applied Psychology, 121,* 599-605.

Thomas, M. D. (1995). *Gender differences in conceptualizing sexual harassment.* San Diego, CA: Navy Personnel Research and Development Center.

Thomas, P. J., Newell, C. E., & Eliassen, D. M. (1995). *Sexual harassment of Navy personnel: Results of a 1993 survey.* San Diego, CA: Navy Personnel Research and Development Center.

Zimmerman, J. (1995). *Tail spin: Women at war in the wake of Tailhook.* New York: Doubleday.

PART III

Subtle Sexism as Social Control

As you saw in previous chapters, sex discrimination serves a number of related functions. It relegates many women to low-paying jobs, which ensures that much of our society's necessary "dirty work" gets done (Chapter 1). It enhances many men's productivity because women perform unrewarded and time-consuming tasks (Chapter 3). Sex discrimination also assures many men (and some women) that competition for the high-paying positions will be limited despite women's entry into male-dominated political and economic arenas (Chapters 4 and 6). Sex discrimination also allows gatekeepers to contain women, and especially racial/ethnic women, to lower-level jobs by not recognizing or rewarding their accomplishments (Chapter 5).

Thus, an overarching function of sex discrimination is social control. In employment, sex discrimination can restrict entry into jobs, discourage job mobility, and secure incumbents in upper-level ranks. Many women's *job entry* is often restricted because many occupations are still sex segregated. For example, 98% of all secretaries, stenographers, and typists are women; 93% of all nurses are women; and 86% of all elementary school teachers are women (U.S. Department of Labor, 1994). Some might argue that women choose to work in such "women's jobs" as nursing and teaching because the jobs have more flexible work hours and workers can slip in and out of the workforce between childbirth and raising children. Why is it, however, that men's jobs do not have such "options"?

The employment situation is not much better for women in other "progressive" countries. In Japan, for example, and despite a severe labor shortage, men are almost twice as likely as women to get job offers after graduating from college. Women are not hired (or hired only in temporary and part-time positions and fired because of economic downturns, whereas men are perceived as "lifetime employees") because they are expected to quit their jobs within 10 years of graduating from college to get married and raise children. Thus, "a male applicant will always be chosen over a female applicant, even if she scores high on the company entrance examination and his score is barely average" (Findlay-Kaneko, 1995, p. A43).

Sweden is often touted as the most enlightened country in the world in terms of women's equality. The enlightenment is not all-encompassing, however. Although 84% of all Swedish women work outside the home, for example, only 48% have full-time jobs because part-time work is far more plentiful, women who do work full time earn 80% of what men earn, and only 7% of university professors are women. Many women are reluctant to take full advantage of maternity leaves because they fear being passed over for a promotion or missing vital training that their employers refuse to make available later on their return (Sloane, 1995).

Sex discrimination also discourages many women's *job mobility.* For example, a 1995 survey done for the Council for Advancement and Support for Education (see Mercer, 1996) found that—and controlling for years of experience—although women hold 55% of the jobs in college advancement positions (such as fundraising and public relations and alumni relations) at all levels of education, men earned almost $13,000 a year more than their female counterparts ($60,169 for men compared to $47,198 for women). One of the major reasons for the salary difference is that most women in college advancement positions are given such dead-end jobs as orchestrating minor public relations work. The higher-status and better-paying jobs, such as fundraising, usually go to men.

Finally, sex discrimination can solidify *seniority and job security* for men in positions that have traditionally excluded women. Because many of the most recent job entrants are women, they are among the first to be laid off during "downsizing." In higher education, for example, because women outnumber men at only the lecturer rank and are the first to be fired because of budget cuts, most of the senior-level and tenured faculty members remain overwhelmingly male (U.S. Department of Education, 1996). As a result, there are few women who might challenge established hiring and promotion practices. As colleges and universities lose resources, moreover, politicians and other groups have more power in limiting the types of faculty who get tenure:

> To control how [the] changing faculty distributes itself . . . private institutions are being targeted for financial pressure through narrowly tailored contributions for professorships, endowed chairs and academic program supports. Public institutions are experiencing some of the same pressures, but are also being subjected to severe budget cuts, at both state and federal levels, with conservative legislators pushing them to restrict or abandon tenure as one way to stay solvent. The net effect of these tactics, hopes the Right, will be the containment of the nation's changing demographics, at least on campus. (Kolodny, 1996, p. 23)

Although social control is common in employment, the chapters in this section show that women are often controlled in other settings as well. In Chapter 9, "Racial Masques: Black Women and Subtle Gendered Racism," for example, Yanick St. Jean and Joe R. Feagin describe how many black women are plagued by gendered racism in higher education, intermarriages, and social situations. St. Jean and Feagin maintain that many of us partake in "racial masquerades" that reinforce subtle gendered racism. For example, a young black female at a high school may be discouraged from doing well in biochemistry because "she is going to get married." Chapter 9 also demonstrates that much of the subtle gendered racism comes from white women. Wilson and Russell (1996) echo this sentiment:

> The issues are real and are not subject to quick fixes. Spouting platitudes such as "sisterhood is global" and issuing desperate pleas to "just get along" do little to change Black and White women's realities. Real work must be done if progress is to be made in cross-race relations. (p. 272)

There are no precise figures, but it has been estimated that 40% of U.S. households seek counseling at one time or another ("What's Happening to American Families?" 1988). Because many counselors (both female and male) have internalized cultural stereotypes about gender roles, they may not be effective in diagnosing and treating gender-related problems. In Chapter 10, "Feminist Family Therapy: The Battle Against Subtle Sexism," Carolyn I. Wright and Linda Stone Fish show that some family therapists control women by "medicalizing" their emotional problems (if you feel depressed after childbirth, take an antidepressant or get counseling). Others ignore the balance of power in marriages and families that often make a woman feel inadequate and unimportant in family life. Even worse, many family therapists fan the "It must be my fault" feelings on the woman's part by reinforcing gender stereotypes.

A very interesting form of social control is simply ignoring women as a credible source of information. In Chapter 11, "Credibility in the Courts: Why Is There a Gender Gap?" Lynn Hecht Schafran maintains that many women's complaints are dismissed by both attorneys and judges because of the "Three Cs of Credibility": collective credibility, contextual credibility, and consequential credibility. Using experiential and anecdotal data, Schafran shows that courts often control women by ignoring their complaints: Women are often not taken seriously, many judges and attorneys may not understand what women are talking about because they do not know about women's life experiences, and the crimes against women are often trivialized and devalued.

In the final chapter of this section, "Some Unanticipated Consequences of Women Guarding Men in Prisons," Richard C. Monk shows how female prison guards are often controlled and manipulated within correctional institutions. Although the numbers of female guards in male prisons have increased substantially during the past few decades, women still represent a small proportion of guards. Because prisons are closed systems, most of us know little about what goes on behind prison walls. In their review of the literature on women and corrections, Martin and Jurik (1996) note that "as old forms of gender subordination have eroded, new and sometimes invidious forms have emerged" (p. 157). In this revealing research, Monk identifies some of the invidious ways in which prison administrators, inmates, and guards try to diminish the formal authority that women guards have over male prisoners. Typically, for example, male inmates and male guards try to control female guards through jokes, excluding women from information, and sexual rumor mongering.

References

Findlay-Kaneko, B. (1995, September 15). Corporate recruiters in Japan shun female graduates. *Chronicle of Higher Education,* p. A43.

Kolodny, A. (1996). Why feminists need tenure. *Women's Review of Books, 13,* 22-24.

Martin, S. E., & Jurik, N. C. (1996). *Doing justice, doing gender: Women in law and criminal justice occupations.* Thousand Oaks, CA: Sage.

Mercer, J. (1996, February 9). Philanthropy notes. *Chronicle of Higher Education,* p. A32.

Sloane, W. (1995, November 1). Sweden's liberation goes only so far. *Christian Science Monitor,* pp. 12-13.

U.S. Department of Education. National Center for Education Statistics. (1996). *1993 national study of postsecondary faculty.* Statistics provided in boxed materials in *Chronicle of Higher Education,* February 2, 1996, p. A17.

U.S. Department of Labor. (1994). *Employment and earnings.* Bureau of Labor Statistics. Washington, DC: Government Printing Office.

What's happening to American families? Report from the editors. (1988). *Better Homes and Gardens.*

Wilson, M., & Russell, K. (1996). *Divided sisters: Bridging the gap between black women and white women.* New York: Anchor.

Chapter

9

Racial Masques

Black Women and Subtle Gendered Racism

Yanick St. Jean
Joe R. Feagin

In *Modern Sexism,* Benokraitis and Feagin (1995) describe subtle sex discrimination as

> the unequal and harmful treatment of women that is typically less visible and obvious than blatant sex discrimination. It is often not noticed because most people have internalized subtle sexist behavior as "normal," "natural" or customary." However liberated we might like to be, many of us—men and women alike—often feel deep down that women are *really* not as good, capable, competent, and intelligent as men. (p. 41)

The sexist attitudes and actions black women in the United States face are in a number of ways similar to those that confront many white women.

However, the hybrid identities of black women expose them to a complex of "inferiorizations," difficult and often disguised in the dress of honesty, like characters in a masquerade. These dressed-up inferiorizations can be intricate and subdued, and often barely visible. Beneath the disguise, as a rule, there is an old, historically dominant, persistent racist practice that has learned to hide in a subtle presentation and that often remains silent about its motivations.

So common is disguise in racial masquerades that it may not be noticed. Or, if noticed, the disguise may not be questioned or seen as deceitful in daily life. That people mimic a false character and hide genuine identities are conditions of participation. In the everyday interracial context, discriminatory behaviors are often disguised and thus appear normal and customary. Like characters in a masquerade, the costumed, subtle forms of discrimination targeting black women can be overlooked, especially by outside observers. Low visibility is one notable feature of subtle discrimination (Benokraitis & Feagin, 1995). Subtle racism is sometimes defined by its rejection of racial groups for ostensibly *nonracial* reasons (Pettigrew & Meertens, 1993; Wieviorka, 1991). In many such cases, whites, and especially white men, provide reasons for their discriminatory actions that ignore race or gender. The explanations are so embedded in the racialized and gendered context that most people in the dominant groups have internalized these behaviors as normal and natural. Subtly biased behaviors facing black women usually are unquestioned by those in dominant groups, or they are explained by reasons other than race and gender. In the racial masquerade, *gendered racism*—the intersection of sexism and racism (Essed, 1990, 1991)—is camouflaged under intricate and deceptive costumes.

We use the term *subtle gendered racism* for certain types of subtle discrimination that target black women. One of our respondents, a black counselor at a university, noted how racism in this society is often gendered:

> But this society shows its racism in a sexist way. Black women may be tolerated, so that then they may be more likely to be let in the door and hired. But *then* they're devalued, because we still devalue women in general . . . women, then, are perceived as less of a threat to male-dominated systems.

Devaluation is at the heart of the negative treatment of black women by whites. This respondent further noted that black men can face a type of gendered racism because (in contrast to black women usually regarded as manageable) they are seen by many white men as competition or as intimidating: "They invoke lots of fear and threats from white men" (see

Dollard, 1957; Roberts, 1994). There is *subtle masculinized racism* as well—the sex-typed practices that harm black men. A discussion of this latter type will not be possible in this chapter because of space limitations, but it is important to keep in mind that both black men and black women encounter gendered racism (see Reid, 1988).

We now turn to black women and listen to their views on subtle racism and subtle gendered racism.

Research Procedures

We draw here primarily on interviews with 101 of the women from a national data set of 209 interviews with middle-class African Americans. This group of women has a median age of just under 40 years, and a median income of $47,000. About 90% have a college degree, a graduate degree, or have attended a graduate school. We also draw on comments by one black male in this national sample and on comments by a white male and two black female participants in focus group interviews with racially intermarried couples in Nevada. The focus group participants had at least a year of college work and a median family income of $50,000. Our respondents are middle-class black Americans.

For this chapter we searched interviews for the use of the term *subtle* in connection with discrimination and for incidents where racial and gender meanings were blurred or less obvious. Out of a large pool of incidents, we use statements from 17 respondents whose demographic characteristics match those of the broader sample. Some statements are about the general nature of discriminatory practices, whereas others recount specific instances of discrimination. Although there are occasional reports of sexual harassment, the women's primary concern is not with particular expressions of gendered racism but racism in general that originates from whites, including some white women. For that reason, we often refer to white society, or to whites, instead of a white male society. This is part of our attempt to see as black women see, and to speak as they do.

Black Women's Experiences With Subtle Racism

We first turn to the racialized discrimination that black women face every day. These accounts contextualize the discussion of gendered racism that follows. Significantly, the most blatant door-slamming and exclusionary forms of racial discrimination have all but disappeared from U.S. society. However, many forms of overt and covert discrimination have persisted, and subtle and sophisticated forms have developed, as this female respondent noted:

> I think discrimination still exists, I just think it's a different way that it's shown. It's more subtle, I guess. I always see myself, though, always having to be a little bit better than my counterparts. So, it's still there, but it's better, it's better.

Our respondents periodically underscored the point, made by Pettigrew and Meertens (1993), that contemporary racism no longer uses explicit Jim Crow symbols but often promotes exclusion for allegedly nonracial reasons. One black woman put it this way:

> Well, you don't see signs, we don't see signs anymore that say "For Whites Only" or "Blacks are not allowed." But I see things like, I don't know, I guess people find ways in which they can discriminate against you. They find other things in order to keep you out, or "We're looking for a man for this job" or "Do you have these qualifications?" or whatever. And sometimes those qualifications may or may not be necessary. It's just a way of screening. . . . I think it's like that everywhere. People find ways to screen out what they don't want.

This modern type of exclusion accents the gender of the applicant rather than her race or uses the screen of (often arbitrary) credentials. In such cases, the outsider racial group is seen as violating established white traditions. Subtly racist behaviors are customary responses that are rooted in old racist traditions.

Contemporary racist practice is so rooted in U.S. history and culture that even whites who genuinely believe in equal rights can be perpetrators, without necessarily being aware of their role in transmitting subtle racial messages. Laughing a bit, one respondent noted:

> Subtle racism is what I notice among all kinds of [whites], whether it's professional, peers, whatever. Just racial attitudes and assumptions that

> people make, and usually they aren't even aware that they're revealing this to you, obviously.

Although the subtle assumptions behind differential treatment are often perceived by black women to be racial, at times these motivations may be so obfuscated and entangled in multiple meanings that they pose a dilemma even for veterans of racism, as in this case:

> You have to be on the lookout and cannot be a fool. You know, you have to be aware of what's going on, the dynamic. And the thing about [it] is that the dynamics are so damn subtle, and so damn invisible, and you've really got to keep your eyes open.

Maintaining a defensive shield is commonplace for black Americans. In a conversation that one of the authors had with a retired music teacher, one older black woman noted that like most white women she dresses and puts on her cosmetics before leaving home. However, unlike white women, she said that she puts on her "shield" before she leaves home (see Feagin & Sikes, 1994). When quizzed about this, she noted that she has to be prepared psychologically for white discrimination and hostility, a point underscored by another respondent:

> I feel as though most of the time I find myself being in a guarded position or somewhat on the defense. I somewhat stay prepared to be discriminated against because I never know when it's going to happen to me. So I sort of keep myself on the defense in preparation for discrimination because I think it exists. I think it exists all the time—it's just that the middle-class [white] people are educated about [doing] it—I just think that it happens in a subtle way, and I think you still have to be on the defense.

Proposed here seems to be a connection between middle-class status and subtly racist behavior. Some previous research has suggested that educated whites in middle-class settings may be more inclined to engage in less obvious discrimination than their less-educated counterparts (Wieviorka, 1991). The experience of our respondents with mostly middle-class discriminators raises serious questions about the general perception that education reduces racial intolerance.

Although there seems a conviction among most women in our sample that racism is rampant, they sometimes question their assessments, wanting to know if they see things clearly or construct a racist reality that does not exist. For example, commenting on the workload at her place of employment, one woman said: "I don't know if that's my paranoia or if, in fact, the work is not distributed equally." Black Americans often ponder and take second or third looks at their everyday experiences with white Americans. The issue of "paranoia" raised here is important because it attests to the sophisticated and confounding nature of much modern racism. Like the white perpetrators, this woman seems to have so internalized assumptions about blacks' suspicious personalities that even when confronted with evidence of racism, she expresses doubt and is ready to define herself, as whites might, on the basis of customary assumptions of black paranoia.

Self-doubt means that black women frequently question their abilities and accomplishments, a point underscored in the following comment:

> It's like, god, is that person better than me? What do they have that I don't have, in terms of, say, their performance, or the attention that they received? Or if I did a project, and they did a project, and mine, "Oh, Carol that was OK," and theirs, "Oh, that was super, that was fantastic," you know. And it's just kind of some of that subtle stuff. And it may be even direct, but it happens so much after a period of time that you subconsciously begin to doubt yourself. And I've had subconscious doubts and I've had . . . just really questioned myself, "Carol, are you *really* with the program? Should you *really* be here? Do you deserve to be doing what you're doing, and living where you're living?"

One of the serious costs of modern racism is the huge psychological and energy loss. Such internal questioning is painful and comes on top of life's ordinary struggles. Racism is not just about discriminatory actions but also about the long-lasting effect and costs for those who are daily victimized by those actions. The effect is cumulative as well, for one who questions herself may not be able to perform as well as white peers not faced with racial oppression.

Harboring and nurturing old historical characterizations of black Americans in a subtle or even polite way, modern racial practices not only target these black women in ways similar to those faced by their ancestors but also reproduce the old arrangements and arguments, albeit often in new dress. Subtle racist practices are confronted by these women like disguised characters at a masquerade ball—like questions of "Guess who I am?"—but they remain at base only variants of the old blatant racism.

Experiences With Subtle Gendered Racism

In the case of black women today, the discriminatory actions of whites frequently entail gendered aspects, although these are not always apparent. Gendered racist behavior comes in many masks and some surprising costumes.

Backstage With Gendered Racism

One white husband we interviewed, whose wife is black, spoke passionately of how influential whites covertly hold black women in contempt: "I am dead serious. Because I've sat with some very predominant leaders of that church. And them not knowing that my wife is black, and I know how they think here." Not only is this man pointing to dangerously false notions about black women that are held by some influential whites in this western city but, also, on the basis of these notions, inferring what the attitudes of these whites might be toward marriages uniting a black woman and a white man. Whites have access to white constructions of black women, which are often unknown to the latter (Feagin & Feagin, 1996). Here white testimony supports the conviction among black women that gendered racism is alive in even the most unexpected of places. In religious settings, the crude type of racism might be frowned on, yet such institutions foster conformity and thereby protect negative subtle white constructions of black women. In this way they are fertile grounds for the rapid spreading of gendered racism.

Interracial Dating and Marriage

The masquerade of gendered racism is perhaps most clear in cases of interracial dating, sex, and marriage. The following comment from a black wife with a white husband illustrates this:

> We would be in a car—and like you said, people make remarks. I'll never forget we were driving in the car, and you know, people are looking and looking . . . this old couple, and I know they were talking [about us] because Mitch and I were—and we were just talking and I was kissing him a little on the cheek. And this lady, and they were just talking, so I went like, I was looking like this, and I went like this, I went, "Bang." [She indicates by pointing her finger like a gun and laughs.] Of course, you don't do that now.

> I think the lady must have had a heart attack. She grabbed herself. And Mitch was laughing so hard he couldn't drive the car. Or one time [at a governmental function] . . . and I knew they were talking about us across the room and [behind] Mitch's back and went—and they were embarrassed because they probably didn't think I was aware they were looking. But you are. You become attuned to the room.

Both incidents are likely rooted in the culturally devalued femininity of this black woman, whose presence in an interracial relationship violates customary white expectations. For most whites, intimate racially mixed associations are inappropriate or outrageous. To see and understand these white reactions, one must be attuned to the historical and cultural contexts of U.S. racism.

One black female student's description of a relationship with a white student illustrates how old stereotypes of black women flow into contemporary situations:

> First of all, he only saw me as what I call the jungle bunny syndrome. He only saw me as his black female sexual object, something to try, something new or different, you know. And I realized that too late. And I really, really felt bad. I mean, I felt horrible.

Sexual Harassment

As in the case of this student, many white men seem to view black women as exotic or accessible sex objects, as was the case for this black female entrepreneur:

> They think they get so familiar with you that they can say certain things, or do certain things. It's just like my husband worked with this guy, Anglo guy. And he called [on us] one night, and he was drunk, and my husband was not at home. And I told him that my husband wasn't at home, and I said, you really need to go home, because you seem like you need to get off the streets. You know, he made a pass at me. Hey, don't put your hands on me, I don't want your white hands on me. Don't touch me, no!

She then added a comment about another white man:

> I'll never forget a state representative, a white state rep. He didn't mean anything, we were just standing up talking at the Capitol. And he walked up and placed his hands on my shoulders. Hey, that was an insult to me. Hey, don't put your hands on me, OK. It was like, "don't become familiar with me." Even though he might have meant nothing about it, it's just that psychology of the thing. It would just be all the hurt and the pain. It would just be very hard for me to develop that kind of relationship. . . . So, I just have real problems with [white people]. And they always want to get off into the most intimate things about your life. They're always searching, because they don't really know the essence of black people.

She is uncertain as to the second white man's motivation but her prior experience makes her suspicious. In both cases the problem from the black point of view was not really subtle, but bristled with danger and potential pain. The subtlety of racism varies with the perspective of the interpreter. What is "common" or "normal" from the white point of view often will not be taken that way by the black victim. Note, too, that in the last two cases a black woman's experience makes it difficult for her to have even casual relationships with white men. The past creates or contaminates the future.

Subtle gendered racism takes on greater meaning because it is part of a larger context in which the female ancestors of black women were routinely subjected to slaveholders' blatant sexual improprieties (Fox-Genovese, 1988). Subtle gendered racism is also part of a context in which black women continue to face very blatant harassment, as in this account provided by a black teacher:

> I had a problem at school. Harassment. I had a white assistant principal. He was really making me feel miserable. Sexually harassed, you know. Chasing me around the room. . . . It started off as, "I want you to know that I really like you, and I mean in more than a professional way." . . . I was in the workroom, and . . . he grabbed me. . . . My sister told me, she said, "This man is dangerous. If you don't go and tell somebody, you're gonna end up raped."

Then the teacher explained the ramifications of her experience: "I was really trying to deal with *that* and come home and not tell my husband." She was concerned that her husband might go after the harassing white man, perhaps endangering himself.

Significantly, black men can also contribute to the devaluation of black women, as one respondent noted:

> Maybe I'm just very naive about this, but I didn't know that there were pornographic magazines that were for black men, that had all black females. I didn't know this. I saw one the other day, and I asked the person who had it, and he said, "Yeah, this has been out a long, long time." And I was sick. Because it's like, OK, black people want to strive, they want to excel, and to a certain extent they admire white people, but they take the worst things about white people to emulate, exploiting their women! I don't get it. I just don't get it. Obviously, there is some hatred going on there, big time.

The lives of black women are shaped not only by the direct gendered-racist actions of white men but also by the actions of black men who mimic negative aspects of white male culture.

Problems in the Workplace

Despite their long-standing presence in the workforce (Malson, 1983), black women still encounter many subtle devaluations by whites. These devaluations occur during and after hiring, or even when self-employed (Essed, 1990; Feagin & Sikes, 1994).

Job Hunting

Gendered racism can hit its targets in most of life's situations and settings. In this example, a black woman was looking for work. Although she was dressed more professionally than white applicants, she still encountered subtle rejection highlighting her race and gender:

> When we first moved here [a western city] about 3 and a half years ago, I thought I was going to semi-retire, you know? But I went out looking for a job. And so I would go in and I'm sitting in the entryway, and I still have a suit on. . . . And I'm sitting there, and I'm looking at all these people, half-naked—that's to just [go] to a job interview. And we're all going for the same job. They call out my name and I get up, and they're shocked because they think Suzie Jones sitting next to me, who's half-naked, is the person that they want to interview. So then they're stumbling over them-

> selves. So the point that I am making is they don't know what they're getting until I get to the door, and when I open the door they're shocked.

The untrained eye may not see this experience as a subtle form of inferiorization. The cues seem to have been nonverbal—a facial or other bodily message obvious only to attentive, culturally trained observers. It is likely that only the respondent, looking directly at the white interviewer, could see, feel, and relive that message on the basis of *prior experience.* Even if this incident were captured on camera, the untrained eye might suggest other possible interpretations. Situational ambiguity (multiple or fuzzy meanings) is a recurring characteristic of subtle feminized racism in many contemporary social settings.

There seem to be both racial and gender aspects to this job incident. Traditional white values were violated by a black woman who stepped "out of her place." Because Suzie Jones is presumably a white woman, this out-of-place-ness is linked to a complex of factors (primarily the interaction of race and gender) and not just the black woman's gender. The white interviewer's reaction likely derives from notions of blacks and/or black women. Even though we cannot *know* for sure what the interviewer was thinking, the reaction reflects active participation in a racial-gender masquerade.

At Work

Once hired, black women typically encounter many subtle devaluations. There are many types of racial barriers in the workplace. White "exceptionalism" is a common aspect of the contemporary workplace, as one respondent made quite clear:

> It ranges across all kinds of things . . . of saying, intimating that "Oh, you must be very different from the rest of them." That sort of thing. Or the kinds of statements that [white] people make about affirmative action, and the fact that "blacks can get all kinds of things, but they [whites] can't."

The common white image targets the "rest of them" as incompetent and demanding and only a few black women are allowed to transcend these stereotypes. One common image, which may be implied in many statements by whites, is that of the "black welfare queen." Even very distinguished black women have had to face such stereotypes, often at great personal and professional cost. For example, just after he came to office President Bill Clinton nominated Lani Guinier, a successful law professor and scholar, for the post of assistant attorney general. Labeled a "Quota Queen" by a *Wall Street Journal* headline writer, Guinier became the victim of the thinly disguised reference to the "welfare queen." Subliminal association with "welfare queen" gives the label Quota Queen a pejorative meaning. Nationally, white politicians and journalists picked up this epithet, which suggested that Guinier was really like the "rest of them." Although no questions were raised explicitly about her ability to do the job, she did not get the position in part because of the image of an incompetent black woman (Garrow, 1993). Assumptions about black women are so webbed into the social fabric that these images effectively pervade workplaces and many other spaces in U.S. society (Collins, 1991; Morton, 1991).

In some cases it is unclear whether the negative white reactions come primarily from gender or racial stereotypes. A black teacher at a predominantly white school commented on the prejudice she faces this way:

> Sometimes when I'm at the school, and I'm talking to a white male, I don't know whether I'm being put in certain positions because I'm a female or because I'm black. It's very confusing.

Another black teacher with a dream of having her own business in construction first noted the same point and then underscored another problem for black women:

> In terms of the thing about becoming a general contractor, I think that I get subtle [discrimination] when I talk to people. I think many times it's hard for me to tell if it's because of my race, of my being black, and second, because I'm a woman. I'm faced with that a lot. Not only being black, but being a woman, too. So it's like, sometimes you don't know if the discrimination is because you're a woman or because you're black, or a combination of both. Probably a combination of both. A lot of times people just don't think you know what it is that you're talking about. I'm faced with that a lot, trying to convince people that I'm *real* sure of what it is that I'm talking about.

She noted that this constant scrutiny of the presentation of self to doubting whites has heavy energy costs.

> I find myself almost exerting myself to the point of stress, you know, to make sure that all my bases are covered. Because as a black person, whatever it is that you're trying to accomplish, if there are any mistakes along the way, you won't be viewed as "Well, you didn't cover all your bases." You'll be viewed as "Well, you know, it was a black person doing it, so that's why it happened." So I think when you're trying to accomplish something as a black person, you deal with even more stress, because you cannot afford to make any mistakes.

Everyday practices frequently reflect gendered racism. As a corporate manager stated about differentially heavy workloads: "I think as I look back on what I've been asked to do and what others, some of my [black] peers, have been asked to do, seems to be a disproportionate share of the workload." But even as she recognizes the work imbalance, she hesitates to conclude that it is calculated:

> And I don't know, I can't say that I believe that that's deliberate. It just seems that if you look at what blacks are asked to do in the organization, it always seems to be a very troubled area, or one that has a lot of work or one that has some people that aren't as effective as they ought to be, etc. And so I don't know if that's a vote of confidence or discrimination. [She laughs.] [Interviewer: Well, do you think that kind of gets at the old adage that, you know, if you're black you've got to be nine times better?] Yeah, and I realize you're talking to me about my situation, but I also know that that's happened to some friends of mine, too, that have very responsible jobs. And they would comment sometimes that it seems that we're expected to do more, and I'm not sure whether that's self-imposed or if that's coming from within or without. . . . I just really have not decided, but I will tell you that, as I look back on it, it does seem to be out of balance.

Such ambivalent reactions attest to the difficulties often involved in recognizing the subtleties of everyday gendered racism.

From the standpoint of white notions about black women, the assignment of a heavy workload makes sense. Heavy workloads force conformity to traditional work values that white stereotypes assert black women lack. Demanding higher workloads become a means of purifying black women so they can be worthy in the eyes of white society. Black women, especially, may be given more difficult job assignments:

> When I used to work for another company, prior to coming here, in sales, then I was the only black there . . . and in my training class. . . . And of course they gave me the worst territory, and I had to work a little bit harder. And I had to fight for what I wanted, although I didn't get it. And it's always been there, and it's really sad to see that, but it really exists. I think a lot of blacks don't know that because they might not be at certain levels where they can really see it, and see how whites manipulate the system, and manipulate us, and we fall into those little holes there. So, it's been real difficult, to some degree.

As at a masquerade ball, such experiences are shaped, largely, by racial-gender views. Supervisors or outside observers might offer nonracial, gender-blind explanations—for instance, that this territory was the only one available. Men who see themselves as liberal might even suggest that assigning a black woman to the "worst territory" is a vote of confidence in her ability to take on a tough assignment. As we see it, such an explanation still reflects racial-gender thinking because if black women can expect the poor assignments by virtue of their racial-gender characteristics, the thinking is disingenuous, deceitful, and a ruse.

One's racial designation is commonly highlighted at work by white men and white women. One respondent noted this about her white female supervisor:

> I had some real good incidents when I had a female boss who did not like black people. I shouldn't say that. When I went to work for her, and we sat down to talk to each other, and she said, "I think we're going to get along well together, even if you are black." And I said, "What difference does that make with us working well together?" And she said, "Oh, well, you know what I meant." I said, "No, I don't know what you meant."

Previously held images of black women influence white women's interactions with black women at work and elsewhere (Essed, 1991). Although the importance of race is obvious here, there are confounding factors. From the comment "I think we're going to get along well together, even if you are black," it is not possible to say if this white woman is expressing racial or racial-gender thinking. Her discourse is linked to a common white symbolic code that is customary. It is reflective of that code.

Invisibility is another negative condition that many black employees experience. It may be worse in the corporate workplace because of black women's recent and token entrance:

> I don't think it makes it any easier that I'm female, because until recently, there were no women in the board room, and definitely no people of color in the board room. And I have been in meetings where it's almost like I was invisible.

Black women often struggle just to be seen and heard in the monocultural corporate workplace.

Moreover, the notion that black women will sooner or later fail is a common assumption in many corporate settings and other workplaces. This may be one reason why many black women are ignored or subtly deterred by "supportive discouragement" (Benokraitis & Feagin, 1995). Such actions conceal the disingenuous intentions of many white employers. Consider, for example, one black professional woman's exchange with her white supervisor:

> "I hope *you* make it." Emphasis on *you*. And I told my new supervisor right then and there. I stopped her right in her tracks and I said, "What do you mean? I detect some sort of implication here regarding the pronoun *you*. I don't feel that you're addressing it singularly, but plural. And there's nobody here but me and you."

In reply the supervisor said that "we never had a black person make it." This respondent then noted that such experiences made her feel bad, "like you've got this black cloud coming over your head through the probation period. They don't think I'm going to make it anyway." The comment "I hope *you* make it" might at first seem to be positive. Yet this appears to be another disguise for gendered racism:

> I just felt like if I did make a mistake, it was like, "See, we expected that anyway. No black has ever made it anyhow." Instead of looking at it as a learning experience, or, I don't know, maybe they did feel that way. All I'm saying is this: This is the fact, that's what was told to me, and why would anyone feel—how would you feel if you were working for a corporation that you noticed was predominantly black, and someone told you, "I hope *you* make it," and you . . . ask them to elaborate. What did they mean by that?

> And they say, "Well, no white has ever made it." Wouldn't you feel uncomfortable if they single out something about you, the person? No redhead has made it, no female has made it. Now if she had said, "It's a hard position. Not many people have what it takes." If she had said something objective, I wouldn't have felt anything. But to single something [out] about me, you know, that confused me, and I didn't know if I'd make it or not.

A skeptical white observer might ask, "Since there is ambiguity, why does the black woman feel that a dark cloud is hanging over her head? Why isn't she more positive about the comment?" For this black woman the "black cloud" symbolizes the widespread racial mistreatment of blacks by many whites. Black women are familiar with white culture and its symbolic codes and often have little difficulty in attaching meaning to white actions. The black cloud alludes to white prejudice and discrimination that many black Americans recognize despite the masks.

Cultural characterizations of whites usually command that they, as the reference points for this society, can be expected to adhere to the work ethic and to succeed. A white employer who sees himself (or occasionally herself) in terms of such a positive work ethic portrayal will likely view, at least initially, a white employee in terms of these positive traits. In contrast, a black woman is preceded in traditionally white workplaces by negative stereotypes that suggest she will perform poorly. Because these prejudices shape her treatment, opportunities are typically limited, as one respondent described:

> In another position which I had, I think that my boss may have been a little bit threatened by me in my own particular style. And so, from time to time different opportunities that I wanted to take advantage of, you know, I was told, "No, you can't do this or you can't do that." But not necessarily overt discrimination. I worked for an insurance company for many years, saw a lot of things happen, did a lot of training of people who became my supervisors, that kind of thing. Got transferred from certain things. There was always something that you could figure out. It was subtle; it would be there, but it wouldn't have a name. Those kinds of things: To get missed for promotions. You know, just little things that probably you could say are not really very much, but after you've been sitting there for a while, or you have somebody that comes in and you've been with the company for, say, 8 or 10 years, and been in various departments, and then here comes somebody in off the street, and they sit over here with you for a couple of weeks and you've got to train them, and you do this, this, and this, and then the next

> thing you know, they get to be the supervisor. And it makes you [think], "Well, I wonder why."

This "I wonder why" may include an element of self-doubt, as was evident when a previous respondent asked herself: "Should you really be here?" This doubt seems to be associated with lack of access to employment opportunities. The slower the access, the more intense the victim-blaming-victim thinking on the part of these black women.

Self-doubt is strengthened by other work-related matters. One example is the phenomenon of rules changing rapidly and unexpectedly:

> And sometimes they wouldn't tell me, and I would do things thinking I was going under a set of rules, and the rules had been changed. And they would say things like, "Oh, didn't you know that? Oh, you screwed up!" And she [the supervisor] would walk out of her room and stand at her door and say, "Get it right!" You know, things like that.

Rule changes alone do not constitute subtle discrimination. The changes become suspect when, despite their significance for performance and promotion, they are withheld only from black female employees. Here, too, unprejudiced reasons could be suggested by outside observers, such as forgetfulness on the part of an incompetent supervisor or complacency on the part of black women who do not take steps to stay current. As we have noted previously, there is often no way to resolve this ambiguity completely. But the prior experiences of black female employees and their families with whites constitute the relevant collective memory, the reservoir they draw on to assess racial-gender discrimination.

Self-Employment

Given the many problems black women experience in interactions with whites in the workplace, one might surmise that self-employment would be a good alternative to economic success. Self-employment would afford these women greater control over their work and would remove them from predominantly white settings where decisions are often based on arbitrary cultural characterizations. However, even self-employed black women encounter subtle gendered racism. Subtle gendered racism may partially explain the consistently low rates of self-employed black women when compared to rates for white women. Of all self-employed women, 3.8% were black in 1975 and 3.9% in 1990 compared to 94.2% and 91.7% (respectively) for white women (Devine, 1994).

A single face-to-face encounter with a white client may sometimes neutralize any number of previously successful contacts:

> I do a lot of work over the phone and I make appointments. So when I have to go out and meet a client, I make the appointment. And then when I go, they [clients] are completely shocked when—first of all, my name—I say my name and they're expecting me. And then I'll say, "I'm here to see Mr. Such-and-Such, and I'm such-and-such" and they look, and then they stop and then they [say], "Oh yes, by all means, but . . ."

Because of the prior phone contact, gender is not the only factor triggering shock; racial factors interacting with gender are likely at work. In these incidents whites are conforming, if unthinkingly, to the dictates of their society about what is "normal." This account reinforces our interpretation of an earlier incident where a job interviewer did not expect a black woman and expressed surprise on seeing her. In both situations the women are subtly reminded of their inferior societal placement by whites with power.

Gendered Racism Outside the Workplace

Subtle offensive behavior persists outside the workplace, including at work-related functions, where some whites are not receptive to black women. Here is an account of a black female professor:

> There are certain colleagues that I have hardly any relationship with because they teach in a different sector [discipline] or whatever. And it's very obvious that some of those people haven't gone out of their way to . . . they haven't been unfriendly, but they certainly haven't taken it upon themselves to welcome me or something else. I'd be waiting around a long time. [Laughs.] So it's not a big, overt sort of thing. . . . And some, a couple of those certain people, like if there's a social event at the beginning of spring and these are males, white male professors, and their wives are there it's just a whole subtlety of never bothering to introduce their wives to you. But there are subtle things like that you would pick up on, but it's been the minority, certainly, but you find that sort of thing in any group, I think, with white people.

Here again, nonracial reasons could be offered for what happened. Who has time these days? People may seem unfriendly because they are busy. The behavior was a faux pas. But this veteran at predominantly white universities observes it to be subtle gendered racism. That this behavior is not an isolated instance of discourtesy or just an oversight is clear from the fact that it recurs in many white settings. We define this problem as white because black women see it as such.

By no means is subtle gendered racism limited to work associates or the workplace itself. It also exists in housing, education, and elsewhere. Consider this mother's description of her daughter's experience in an elementary school classroom:

> Sometimes I'm not sure whether there's more sex discrimination, or whether there's more racial discrimination. I had a teacher of my daughter just tell me that girls didn't do well in calculus. And my daughter was perfectly competent. And I was concerned with the methods of teaching that were going on in that classroom. And she was not the only one having difficulty. There were lots of blacks and lots of whites in the class. And he just said, "Girls have problems." And that was certainly not the case, and that concerns me greatly. Or, I had another teacher tell me, "Don't worry how she's doing in biochemistry, because she is going to get married." And I said, "Well, so what, I'm married, but I work too!" And that annoyed me greatly.

At first reading, the subtle inferiorization here seems to be based on gender. However, the comment "Girls have problems" may have implied in that particular context that "black girls *could* have even more problems." And the comment "Don't worry how she's doing in biochemistry" suggests there are alternatives to getting an education for black girls. "Girls have problems" may also be a veiled reference to assumptions about black intelligence. In any event, the white commentator revealed ignorance of the fact that the large majority of black women have always had to work and have not had the opportunity to "just get married and stay at home."

Black female students face many problems in historically white colleges and universities (D'Augelli & Hershberger, 1993; Essed, 1990; Feagin & Sikes, 1994). The following account by a black student at a major white university illustrates how subtle racism and sexism can overlap. The student wrote a column in the student paper explaining how white Americans grow up with racist ideas that are so accepted that whites do not know they are being ignorant when they express such attitudes. Some of the racist reactions to her column were very blatant:

> I had people calling me up and hanging up. I had a couple of heavy breathers, and some guy called me "black bitch" a lot, you know, and hung up the phone. White people were very hostile to me. . . . Honors program people. Well, white people in general, but specifically honors program people because those were the white people that I saw most of the time.

Then she described more subtle discriminatory reactions of fellow students:

> But, they were very cold. They didn't know what to say to me. It was like "Oh my god, who is this black female, how dare she say this!? She's black and she's female; she has no right to come out and question me." You know, so I got that kind of attitude.

She continued with a discussion of the odd and disconcerting ways that even white liberal students treated her after she wrote the column. This student's experience with gendered racism is not unusual. Recent research has found that white students are frequently a serious source of racial barriers at white universities (Feagin & Sikes, 1994; Feagin, Vera, & Imani, 1996).

Black women also face problems in the area of housing (Essed, 1990; Leigh, 1989), where they encounter rejections disguised in various costumes:

> I guess one funny thing happened when I took an apartment in [a major city], and I did the application for the apartment over the telephone. When I went in to sign the lease, the owner, in fact, emphasized the fact that I did the application over the telephone. I distinctly felt as though they didn't know I was black. Then when I showed up and I was black, he just came right out and said, "Oh, you did the interview over the phone." I think he said it without really thinking about what he was implying when he said it.

Again, one can see how its deceptive character makes this racial-gender discrimination fluid and hard to prove. It was not her woman-ness alone that got her into trouble, but her black woman-ness. By emphasizing that this renter did the application over the phone, the white landlord implied (or stereotyped) deception on her part. She seems to be reproached for having stepped out of her place and having violated traditional white customs—for not having let the owner know somehow that she was black. The likely cues indicating subtle discriminatory treatment included his tone of voice, his facial expression, and his negative reaction to her application.

Conclusions

Our analysis of black women reveals that subtle gendered racism:

1. Takes many forms, including heavy workloads, difficult assignments, workplace invisibility, positive discouragements, and various interpersonal slights.
2. Is wily and often difficult to separate from racism in general.
3. Sometimes confuses its victims. Although it is clear, at times, that the rejections are not entirely anchored in gender, gender is so interwoven with race that it is often impossible to determine whether or when gender is more significant than race in the white discriminator's thought or actions.
4. Often receives less attention from black women, who tend to emphasize racism when describing racial-gender interactions with white men.
5. May shape negative conceptions of black women among some black men.
6. Is a "normal" and "customary" mechanism for protecting historical racial arrangements and reproducing the old symbolic codes of white Americans.

Social masquerades do end. Eventually, people go home. Costumes come off. Genuine identities surface. Yet the U.S. racial masquerade persists, with daily rehearsals that produce and reproduce a protean, though ancient, racial reality. In the everyday racial-gender routines, the masks and costumes are often deceptive and subtle. The white characters are sometimes difficult to recognize as racist. Yet the old persistent and blatant habits hide beneath the masks and costumes as they fuel and cheer on new forms of gendered racism.

References

Benokraitis, N. V., & Feagin, J. R. (1995). *Modern sexism: Blatant, subtle, and covert discrimination.* Englewood Cliffs, NJ: Prentice Hall.

Collins, P. H. (1991). *Black feminist thought: Knowledge, consciousness, and the politics of empowerment.* New York: Routledge.

D'Augelli, A. R., & Hershberger, S. L. (1993). African American undergraduates on a predominantly white campus: Academic factors, social networks, and campus climate. *Journal of Negro Education, 62,* 67-81.

Devine, T. J. (1994). Characteristics of self-employed women in the United States. *Monthly Labor Review, 4,* 23-24.

Dollard, J. (1957). *Caste and class in a southern town.* Garden City, NY: Anchor.

Essed, P. (1990). *Everyday racism: Reports from women of two cultures.* Claremont, CA: Hunter House.

Essed, P. (1991). *Understanding everyday racism: An interdisciplinary theory.* Newbury Park, CA: Sage.

Feagin, J. R., & Feagin, C. B. (1996). *Racial and ethnic relations.* Upper Saddle River, NJ: Prentice Hall.

Feagin, J. R., & Sikes, M. P. (1994). *Living with racism: The black middle class experience.* Boston: Beacon.

Feagin, J. R., Vera, H., & Imani, N. (1996). *The agony of education: Black students at white colleges and universities.* New York: Routledge.

Fox-Genovese, E. (1988). *Within the plantation household.* Chapel Hill: University of North Carolina Press.

Garrow, D. (1993). Lani Guinier. *The Progressive, 9,* 28.

Leigh, W. A. (1989). Barriers to fair housing for black women. *Sex Roles, 21,* 69-84.

Malson, M. R. (1983). Black women's sex roles: The social context of a new ideology. *Journal of Social Issues, 39,* 101-113.

Morton, P. (1991). *Disfigured images: The historical assault on Afro-American women.* New York: Praeger.

Pettigrew, T., & Meertens, R. W. (1993). Le racisme voilé: dimensions et mesures [Masked racism: Dimensions and measurement]. In M. Wieviorka (Ed.), *Racisme et modernité* (pp. 109-126). Paris: Éditions de la découverte.

Reid, P. T. (1988). Racism and sexism: Comparisons and conflicts. In P. A. Katz & D. A. Taylor (Eds.), *Eliminating racism* (pp. 203-219). New York: Plenum.

Roberts, S. (1994, October 31). Black women graduates outpace male counterparts. *New York Times,* p. A12.

Wieviorka, M. (1991). *L'Espace du racisme* [The arena of racism]. Paris: Editions du seuil.

Chapter

10

Feminist Family Therapy

The Battle Against Subtle Sexism

Carolyn I. Wright
Linda Stone Fish

The field of mental health is based in the scientific paradigm that organizes medicine. This "disease model" attempts to understand individuals by studying that which is failing. "Medicalization," then, permeates the mental health field as it continues to be grounded in this disease model. The medicalizing of women occurs when the normal things that distinguish a female as female, either biologically or culturally, are regarded as diseases or are seen as abnormal and are open for medical intervention. "Female normality may be stolen and replaced by medical needs and dependency, perhaps even a debt of gratitude toward the medical experts" (Malterud, 1993, p. 368). When medical experts work with women and face a perplexing diagnosis, they may inadvertently "pathologize" the patient and infer a psychological problem. Such is the case for Mary, whose "feeling tired" reflects the normal developmental stage for most high school seniors:

> Mary was a 17-year-old high school senior. Along with being a cheerleading captain, she was taking a full load of honors courses, including physics, psychology, and computer science. She worked weekends for a national fast food restaurant. Her goals seemed to center on a role in medicine. Mary also had many friends, an active social life, and was close to her family. Recently she had experienced some difficulties in her relationship with her boyfriend and she had expressed some grief about moving on from high school, which she loved, to college. During the middle of basketball season, Mary noticed she was very tired. She wondered if she was ill. Mary's mother made an appointment for her at the local HMO with Mary's usual health care provider. Blood work was done and a routine exam. No physical problems were noted. The physician suggested Mary might be depressed and offered her a prescription for an antidepressant. When Mary refused, the physician gave her the prescription and suggested she think about it further. (Authors' files)

The physician did not recognize the biological and cultural pressures on Mary's life. Rapid hormonal changes were occurring at the time. Mary was also responding to a cultural demand for teenagers to increase their achievement and activity. Add to that the cultural demand for young women to maintain and increase their social connections at this stage of adolescent development. Instead of addressing any or all of these intense pressures, drugs were offered as a panacea.

The process of medicalizing complaints also occurred for Anna, whose stressful transition to parenthood is defined as her problem of depression:

> Anna delivered a healthy baby boy and was now feeling depressed and inadequate as a parent. She made an appointment with her general practitioner and described feeling tired, negative toward her son, and generally in need of time away from parenting. The physician placed her on an antidepressant and encouraged her to seek counseling with a psychiatrist he recommended. (Authors' files)

The above examples show bias in the medical and mental health care arena in two ways. In each case, either subtly or not so subtly, the bias was shown through the medicalization or the ignoring of the women's symptoms.

Mary's response to cultural mandates to be social, fully engaged, and competent was pathologized. She was tired and feeling under pressure. It is unlikely that a man in similar circumstances would have been prescribed antidepressants. Instead, he probably would have been told either that he needed more medical tests or more rest. The physician assumed depression, which subtly suggests that Mary is psychologically deficient.

Anna's physician both pathologized her feelings and ignored her social context. Women experience more change during the transition to parenting than men. Mothers generally feel more responsible about the happiness of their children and receive more blame when things go wrong for their children than do their husbands. Mothers' stress typically increases when their spouses are not supportive (McBride, 1990). Empirical research that supports these findings is ignored by Anna's health care provider. Anna's negative feelings about herself and parenting were exacerbated by her critical husband and her history of abuse. In other words, her feelings made sense in the context in which she lived. Instead, the social context was ignored and she was put on medication. Some authors (Bernardez, 1984; Brown, 1994) suggest that there are members of the medical profession who drug women (pharmacological therapy) to reduce the perception of stress and to increase the women's passivity to their socially induced condition.

Subtle sexism occurs, then, when we pathologize women for attempting to live within the cultural mandate of womanhood and when we ignore the social context. Subtle sexism also occurs when we have "insufficient medical knowledge" about female health problems (Malterud, 1993, p. 368):

> Jane's father had died when she was 16. When she was 19 her uncle, a man whom she saw as a father replacement, also died. Now at 28 she was the mother of two boys and pregnant with her third child. Jane was a low-income patient receiving care at an outpatient family practice clinic. During her second pregnancy she had been cared for by a family practice resident who considered her his "special patient." She felt very connected to him and was looking forward to his delivering what would be her third and last child. In her last trimester she developed high blood pressure and was transferred to an obstetrical group of five physicians all of whom would need to see her on a rotating basis. This was hospital protocol for high-risk pregnancies but Jane was feeling abandoned by another significant man in her life. This manifested itself in her sudden fear of dying in childbirth and in her noncompliance with treatment. (Authors' files)

Jane's emotional needs were not understood. There was insufficient medical knowledge about the need for consistent care during her high-risk pregnancy. When medical providers ignore the concerns of women, the message reinforces what women have already come to "know": that they should hide their feelings, thoughts, and concerns and that they should be silent. This silence could result in cutting off painful feelings. "The feelings may be transformed to illness, especially if the woman has to hide her feelings out of concern for herself or others" (Malterud, 1993, p. 370).

Many of the psychotherapy referrals come from health care professionals. Psychotherapists can anticipate that many women will be referred to and enter into therapy with feelings of being blamed and disapproved of, invalidated, and ill (Walters, 1988). It will be up to the therapist, then, to highlight a woman's deficits or construct a context that repairs the "social messages and life experiences" that destroyed her self-esteem (Walters, 1988, p. 309). Unfortunately, many psychotherapists are not immune to their own subtle sexist practices.

Sex Differences in Defining Mental Health

Since the inception of the concept of mental health, there has been a double standard of what is seen as healthy for men and what is seen as healthy for women. Mental health research has found evidence for sex differences in the incidence, diagnosis, research, practice, treatment, and outcome of psychiatric disorders, which may directly and negatively affect the health of women individually and as a group (Bayes, 1981; Caplan, 1987; Mark, 1981; Nadelson, 1993; Pugliesi, 1992; Robbins, 1983; Smyth & McFarlane, 1985; Tavris, 1992; Ussher, 1991; Walker, 1989; Webster, 1990). Western male characteristics of mental health—including independence, competition, objectivity, and hierarchy—that have been presented as synonymous with those of the mentally healthy adult are discriminatory against women (Bograd, 1986; Broverman, Broverman, Clarkson, Rosenkrantz, & Vogel, 1970; Caplan, 1992; Chesler, 1972; Robbins, 1983; Voss & Gannon, 1978). Women are caught in a double bind: They are seen as significantly less healthy if they take on male characteristics of agency (the ability to actively make decisions in one's own best interest), self-focus, and independence, and less healthy if they show such socially female proscribed characteristics as interdependency, nurturance, and connection (Tannen, 1990). Women's culturally acquired attributes of empathy, nurturance, facilitation (as opposed to order-giving), and networking are not generally recognized as attributes to which healthy adults should aspire.

Feminist criticism of the Western male model of health as it is applied to women has led to new theories of female development (Miller, 1976). These theories "describe the structuring of women's sense of self [which is] organized around being able to make and then to maintain affiliations and relationships" (Holmes & Anderson, 1994, p. 42). Such theories build a more pluralistic model of mental health that limits neither men nor women. Developmental feminists cherish interdependence and independence. They understand that there are negative and positive consequences for women who emphasize connection. This relational model of mental health suggests that both women and men can be rational, emotional, interdependent, nurturing, assertive, sexual, independent, and instrumental. The movement is toward an integration of roles and needs as well as flexibility and balance in lifestyles and behaviors. It is a theory of health that respects men's and women's interactional gifts as it challenges to incorporate both instrumentation and expressiveness as well as autonomy and intimacy (Holmes & Anderson, 1994).

Generally, feminists have concluded that the lens through which we view women and men and their social contexts has been and will continue to be colored with the biases of unequal gender expectations. The field of mental health, similarly, is not immune to such biases. Practitioners and consumers of mental health services have become increasingly aware of biases in male-oriented traditional models of developmental and psychological theory and increasingly cognizant of academic training and professional organizations that transmit sexism both through the content itself and the way the content is presented (Bayes, 1981). But sex biases among clinicians, supervisors, and trainers, even when exposed, are still deeply entrenched in the mental health field (Ault-Riche, 1987; Caplan, 1992). Feminist theorists and clinicians, although varying in their theoretical approaches, recognize both the unique contextual experiences of women as well as the gender stereotypes labeling them. Their work has challenged the field of mental health.

Family Therapy as a Mental Health Institution

Family therapy was created in the 1950s as a response to traditional therapy practices that emphasized individuals but excluded a relationship perspective. Family therapists view the world through relationship dynamics. They are committed to a systemic perspective, which means that everyone involved in the family system is a part of the dynamics in which interactions are embedded. The family is seen, then, as the main focus for treatment. If the family dynamics change, individuals in the family are expected to change in response.

Family therapy is a flourishing institution. As it rose in stature, more women were drawn to the field. Whereas most women felt disenfranchised from traditional psychotherapy practices, they saw in family therapy a way to challenge the status quo. As they became more involved in the family therapy field, however, women, and especially feminist women (as well as some feminist men), began to recognize the ways in which family therapy was quickly becoming another sexist institution. They saw that family therapists were engaged in practices that further invalidated women's experiences and women's ways of being. For example, mothers were scapegoated or blamed for not protecting daughters (Bograd, 1990; Walters, 1988). Social factors were ignored in explaining women's health status (Pugliesi, 1992). Violent acts of men were being blamed on the interactional functioning of the couple without regard to the social messages about the value and entitlements of women compared to those of men. That is, when men are socialized to believe that they have the right to control women, they may act on that belief even through the use of violence. Women, as a consequence, may feel less valuable and simultaneously less empowered to change their conditions or keep themselves safe (Walker, 1989).

Subtle Sexism in Family Therapy

Family therapists have engaged in subtle sexism in two major ways. They have defined women solely in terms of the couple or family and have thus measured women's growth, health, and emotional functioning from that vantage point. In addition, they have been so focused on the family as an institution that they have ignored not only the individual needs of family members but also the imbalance of power between those individuals.

Clinicians working with couples often support the existing imbalance of gender power within the couple or the family. Their own socialized beliefs that women are responsible for the family's emotional health lead them to (a) make the woman responsible for bringing the family into therapy, (b) define couple therapy as effective only when the husband is present, (c) undervalue what the woman does in session and overvalue what the man does, and (d) define masculinity as agency and expect that men are less capable of empathy than women.

When the family does not attend therapy, the woman is seen as having failed. If the husband refuses to attend marital therapy, the woman is seen as not powerful enough to have an impact on the system by herself. Clinicians, failing to envision women as being able to create actively the kind of relationships they want, support the message that the man has the power. Men who *do* enter therapy are seen as extraordinary. Their contributions are punctuated as important and the issue of male privilege is ignored. Men are typically praised for their courage to show up, to show affect, or to help out the relationship. In contrast, women's contributions are often negated or overlooked because women are expected to be active therapy participants.

Once couples are in therapy and are committed to change, therapists may continue to use subtle sexist interventions:

> Sally and Tom went to couple therapy for 3 months. Sally complained that Tom was not doing his share of the housework or child care. Tom defended himself by stating that even though they both worked full time, he made more money and had a more demanding job than Sally so should not be responsible for half of the housework and child care. Sally agreed, and the therapist helped the couple define what both felt would be equal. They listed all the tasks that had to be done and then negotiated around which ones both were willing to accomplish. By the end of treatment, Tom was doing more work around the house while Sally was still dissatisfied with the relationship, tired, and withdrawn. The couple decided to terminate therapy because they had accomplished their goals. (Authors' files)

Clinicians who use a model of *quid pro quo* (an eye for an eye) negotiation or contracting interventions with couples typically assume that both partners are equally committed to the relationship and have equal power within the relationship. However, power use and abuse rears its ugly head in domestic violence and financial areas as well as presumably less volatile issues of parenting and household tasks. Clinicians, assuming that a couple can equally negotiate and contract on household tasks and child care, fail to recognize that couples often do not enter the arena on an equal playing field. Sally, for example, was afraid to be too demanding lest she push Tom into a divorce. A divorce would hurt both her and the children emotionally and financially. She was even afraid to broach the unequal power differential during sessions for fear of Tom's disapproval. Clinicians also must be aware, when contracting on household tasks, that not all chores have equal weight and that some tasks are more "political" than others. That is, some jobs take more time, thought, or energy than other jobs; some chores have more negative consequences for the responsible party; some jobs are seen as important, whereas others are undervalued; some chores may be perceived as more appropriate for women to do than for men to do. Cleaning the toilet may not be equal to cleaning the sink. Rocking the baby to sleep may not be equal to changing her diapers. Doing the grocery shopping for a family of four every week may not be equal to waxing the car twice a year.

Another example of subtle sexism is the way that some couple therapists treat sexual problems:

> Brenda and John went to couple therapy for over a year because Brenda had inhibited sexual desire (ISD). She never desired sex with John, never initiated sexual relationships, and was cut off entirely from all sexual thoughts and feelings. John, on the other hand, thought about and wanted sex daily. He compromised with Brenda to have sex every other day but was still dissatisfied with the amount of sex and with Brenda's inability to enjoy sex. The couple therapist worked on sensate focus exercises with Brenda and encouraged her to be more comfortable with her own sexuality. She also worked on couple dynamics and was able to equalize some of the power imbalances that were exacerbating Brenda's ISD. At the end of treatment, Brenda was enjoying sex more often with John and he was more satisfied with their sexual relationship. (Authors' files)

ISD is one of the leading sexual complaints in couple therapy. Unfortunately, the label itself is a form of subtle sexism. By implying that one person has a problem because she or he is dissatisfied with the sexual relationship does not focus on the reasons behind the dissatisfaction with the entire sexualized relationship. The therapist treating ISD often fails to honor individual differences or to recognize that both partners have bought into a male-dominated view of sexuality. One partner, usually the male, may claim to have a "normal sexual desire." The other, usually the female, may be labeled as "cold" or "frigid." Whereas one partner may want sex on a routine, on-demand basis, the other may need to *feel* loved to "make love." Each individual in the couple must respect each other's needs to create a relationship where sexual desire is no longer inhibited. The male may need to learn new ways to please his partner in bed. Or he may have to increase his share of household and child care responsibilities so that his partner is not only less tired but feels cared for on a regular basis. She may be defining sexuality as feeling appreciated, attractive, cherished, and valued rather than being treated as a sexual object. Together, the couple may need to change their narrow definition of sexuality, which also includes, but is not limited to, equating sex with having intercourse and orgasm.

The Feminist Challenge to Marriage and Family Therapy

With the advent of family therapy's rise in the mental health field, feminists have had ample opportunity to observe overt and subtle sexism. Those viewing the field of family therapy are concerned with sex-role stereotypes as they affect the perception, diagnosis, and treatment of both sexes (Caplan, 1985; Fausto-Sterling, 1985; Franks, 1986; Hafner, 1986; Smyth & McFarlane, 1985; Tavris, 1988). Other concerns include the following:

1. Failure to see gender as a primary variable in therapy (Goldner, 1988);
2. Viewing the family as separate from its "historical, social, economic, and political contexts" (Avis, 1987);
3. Mother-blaming as a common perspective (Lerner, 1988);
4. Reinforcement of stereotyped, gender issues in training (Walker, 1989);
5. The "no fault" view of family problems that dismisses the unequal gender power imbalance within the family structure and behaviors (Goldner, 1988; Pittman, 1985);
6. The political dimensions of therapy and clinicians themselves that can sustain the traditional patriarchal family structure and behaviors (Avis, 1987; Bograd, 1986); and
7. Lack of feminist research on families to challenge the androcentric biases that measure females against male behavior as the norm and ignore the experiences of women (Avis, 1987).

Some writers have questioned whether feminism can be integrated into a family therapy systems perspective (Braverman, 1987; Pilalis & Anderton, 1986; Walrond-Skinner, 1987; Wheeler, 1985). Some feminists feel that couple and family therapy are forums that support sexism. They are wary of any integrative efforts because they maintain that most family therapists view the family unit as always more important than the individuals in the family. As a result, many feminists argue, family therapists rarely teach women how to have a voice to transform their uncertainty and silence or give women the tools to expand their verbal space. Instead, women's voices are often muted, ignored, or pathologized.

Although there are reservations about the integration of feminist thought and family therapy, feminists have nevertheless had a great effect on the field. There is a subgroup of family therapists who consider themselves feminist or feminist informed. This subgroup encourages family therapists to challenge women to expand their expressive and relational gifts outside the family circle and to develop new or expanded instrumental skills. They validate men's need for affiliation and their instrumental skills while supporting the development of their expressive and relational skills. Feminist family therapists do not assume that the family is always supportive. They do not always assume that women are better off married; instead they value negotiations and alternatives in relationships. Feminist family therapists negotiate the equal distribution of household and child care tasks in relationships and hold both genders equally responsible for change. Whereas feminist family therapists affirm family life, they also move to transform its oppression (Mirkin, 1990).

Feminist family therapists have also encouraged the family therapy field to expand the walls of the therapy office. They have promoted the recognition of gender as a primary variable in relationships. They have also encouraged therapists to intervene in challenging the power differential between men and women as well as between classes and between cultures. Feminist family therapists examine the gender power imbalance in economics, law, divorce, employment, relational responsibilities, child care, household responsibilities, and violence. In essence, feminists demand family therapists to construct worlds that do not exclude men or women but empower all people. Feminism does not promote "the needs and experiences of women as normative or universal but [makes] visible the varying experiences and perspectives that masculinist thought denies" (Kaschak, 1992, p. 11).

Feminist-informed family therapy encourages the field to view couples and families from a socially constructed, context orientation. Feminist family therapy calls for taking responsibility, even in systems models, for such violent acts as battering, rape, and intimidation; the sexual abuse of children; as well as for drug and alcohol abuse. Therapists overtly acknowledge that women are individuals within a family and that a family can often be oppressive, and they help the family ask itself what it does for and to women (Bridenthal, 1982). They boldly state that the individual will not be sacrificed for the family unit *and* that a healthy family unit can be beneficial to all individuals in it.

Eliminating Subtle Sexism in Treatment

Feminists have had a great effect on the family therapy field. They have identified such forms of subtle sexism as defining women solely in terms of their relationships with family members and not recognizing the effects of gender, power, and culture. Individual idiosyncratic issues in couple and family work can be remedied with a feminist-informed lens. Once therapists recognize that most clients begin therapy after referral from sexist institutions and often in sexist ways, therapists can begin addressing and changing the subtle forms of sexism reproduced in the therapy office.

Subtle sexism permeates how family therapists negotiate change in relationships. Returning to the earlier example of the couple negotiating household tasks, a therapist attempting to eliminate subtle sexism would recognize the unequal distributions of power that permeated the couple relationship. Assuming that couples come to therapy as equal partners in the relationship is often a faulty assumption. Feminist family therapists combat subtle sexism by making the covert overt. For example, the commitment in a relationship may be unbalanced because of the financial stability that one of the partners, usually the male, provides. A woman may be more likely to invest heavily in a relationship because she is aware that if the relationship were to end, her financial status would decrease rapidly. Asking questions about commitment is also critical. It is important to discuss the fact that if the relationship were to end, each person might be affected differently. Bringing such issues to the table is also essential to the power dynamics inherent in the couple's negotiation process.

Couple therapists also need to remember that conflict may not always be safe. The threat of or actual violence in couple and family relationships needs to be addressed so that therapists are not escalating conflict with the potential of doing more harm. Feminist family therapists, then, may be more likely to meet with individual members of the couple alone to determine the risk of violence in the relationship before escalating conflict in couple sessions. It is often unsafe to admit violence in front of the partner. Most women, even when the partner is not present, find it difficult to admit to violence in the relationship. Therefore therapists must ask for information about safety in a patient and respectful way.

A therapist could also eliminate subtle sexism in the ISD case described earlier. For instance, the therapist could address the issue as a couple dynamic. Although ISD is often seen as one partner's problem, a feminist family therapy could directly confront this subtle sexism. Feminist family therapists could ask specific questions that enlarge the boundaries of the problem and the dynamics between the individuals. Why is it that sex is only defined as an act that leads to intercourse and orgasm? Why is sex not examined in its context of a sexualized relationship? Why is it that she is undersexed and he is not labeled as oversexed? How does the culture inform the way we think and act sexually? How does the fact that women's bodies are used to sell products influence this couple's sexual relationship? Is he substituting sex for something else? Does he "need" sex or want intimacy? What parts of her and his bodies are part of the relationship?

Feminist family therapists also help challenge subtle sexism in family therapy with children. Subtle sexist practices include holding mothers responsible for everything that occurs in the family. Often children, who have internalized patriarchal beliefs, tend to do the same. Rather than "blaming mom" for all that goes wrong, feminist family therapists challenge all family members to take responsibility for their own behavior and the consequences of that behavior. Feminists are also apt to talk about how the family is embedded in the larger sociocultural context. They may question families about their values and beliefs and ask them to think about the ways that these attitudes have been shaped and reinforced by the larger culture. Then, they encourage the family members to decide if they want to maintain these values or change them.

Family therapists can also help to eliminate subtle sexism by encouraging each member of the family to be actively involved in relationship maintenance, rather than expecting mothers to do it all. Although it is known that women take more responsibility for much of what occurs in the family after the children are born, subtle sexism occurs when family therapists expect and encourage such expectations to continue. Women cannot be expected to have fulfilling lives unless everyone in the family is contributing to the well-being of the family unit. Feminist family therapists confront sexism when they challenge men who see family work as women's work. Feminist family therapists also challenge sexism when they encourage everyone in the family to reexamine the ways in which rigid gender roles limit each family member's contribution to family life.

Conclusion

The feminist critique of mental health has been at least partially successful. For the first time, women's varying experiences and perspectives have been included in many psychological theories and practices about "how women perceive themselves or others, about who women are and especially about who and what women can be" (Kaschak, 1992, p. 10). Part of this change is the result of the women's movement and women's struggle to inform and have an effect on the world and part comes from the fact that women's numbers as students and therapists in mental health areas have increased.

Feminists first had to expose patriarchal biases, and they then had to challenge them. This challenge continues. As Caplan (1992) states: "I am told that women need therapy as a safe place to practice speaking their minds before they try it in the 'real world.' Shouldn't we wonder if it's time to make the real world safe for women who speak their minds?" (p. 14).

References

Ault-Riche, M. (1987). Teaching an integrated model of family therapy: Women as students, women as supervisors. *Journal of Psychotherapy and the Family, 3,* 175-192.

Avis, J. M. (1987). Deepening awareness: A private study guide to feminism and family therapy. *Journal of Psychiatry and the Family, 3,* 15-16.

Bayes, M. (1981). The prevalence of gender-role bias in mental health services. In E. Howell & M. Bayes (Eds.), *Women and mental health* (pp. 83-85). New York: Basic Books.

Bernardez, T. (1984). Prevalent disorders of women: Attempts toward a different understanding and treatment. *Women and Therapy, 3,* 7-28.

Bograd, M. (1986). A feminist examination of family therapy: What is women's place? *Women and Therapy, 5,* 95-106.

Bograd, M. (1990). Scapegoating mothers: Conceptual errors in systems formulations. In M. Mirkin (Ed.), *The social and political contexts of family therapy* (pp. 69-88). Boston: Allyn & Bacon.

Braverman, L. (1987). Feminism and family therapy: Friends or foes. *Journal of Psychotherapy and the Family, 3,* 5-14.

Bridenthal, R. (1982). The family: The view from a room of her own. In B. Thorne & M. Yalom (Eds.), *Rethinking the family: Some feminist questions* (pp. 225-239). New York: Longman.

Broverman, I., Broverman, D., Clarkson, F., Rosenkrantz, P., & Vogel, S. (1970). Sex role stereotypes and clinical judgments of mental health. *Journal of Consulting and Clinical Psychology, 34,* 1-7.

Brown, L. (1994). *Subversive dialogues.* New York: Basic Books.

Caplan, P. (1985). Sex-based manipulation in the clinical psychologist's workplace. *International Journal of Women's Studies, 8,* 175-182.

Caplan, P. (1987). The psychiatric association's failure to meet its own standards: The dangers of self-defeating personality disorder as a category. *Journal of Personality Disorder, 1,* 178-182.

Caplan, P. (1992). Driving us crazy: How oppression damages women's mental health and what we can do about it. *Women and Therapy, 12,* 5-28.

Chesler, P. (1972). *Women and madness.* New York: Avon.

Fausto-Sterling, A. (1985). *Myths of gender.* New York: Basic Books.

Franks, V. (1986). Sex stereotyping and diagnosis of psychopathology. *Women and Therapy, 5,* 219-232.

Goldner, V. (1988). Generation and gender: Normative and covert hierarchies. *Family Process, 27,* 17-31.

Hafner, R. J. (1986). *Marriage and mental illness: A sex role perspective.* New York: Guilford.

Holmes, S., & Anderson, S. (1994). Gender differences in the relationship between differentiation experienced in one's family of origin and adult adjustment. *Journal of Feminist Family Therapy, 6,* 27-48.

Kaschak, E. (1992). *Engendered lives.* New York: Basic Books.

Lerner, H. G. (1988).*Women in therapy.* New York: Harper and Row.

Mark, E. (1981). The ubiquitous male standard. *Professional Psychology, 12,* 667-668.

Malterud, K. (1993). Strategies for empowering women's voices in the medical culture. *Health Care for Women International, 14,* 365-373.

McBride, A. (1990). Mental health effects of women's emotional roles. *American Psychologist, 45,* 381-384.

Miller, J. B. (1976). *Toward a new psychology of women.* Boston: Beacon.

Mirkin, M. (Ed.). (1990). *The social and political contexts of family therapy.* Boston: Allyn & Bacon.

Nadelson, C. (1993). Ethics, empathy, and gender in health care. *American Journal of Psychiatry, 150,* 1309-1313.

Pilalis, J., & Anderton, J. (1986). Feminism and family therapy: A possible meeting point. *Journal of Family Therapy, 8,* 99-114.

Pittman, F. (1985, November/December). Gender myths: When does gender become pathology? *Family Therapy Networker,* pp. 25-33.

Pugliesi, K. (1992). Women and mental health: Two traditions of feminist research. *Women and Health, 19,* 43-68.

Robbins, J. H. (1983). Complex triangles: Uncovering sexist bias in relationship counseling. *Women and Therapy, 2,* 159-169.

Smyth, M., & McFarlane, G. (1985). Sex-role stereotypes by psychologists and psychiatrists: A further analysis. *International Journal of Women's Studies, 8,* 131-139.

Tannen, D. (1990). *You just don't understand: Women and men in conversation.* New York: Ballantine.

Tavris, C. (1992). *The mismeasure of women.* New York: Simon & Schuster.

Tavris, C. B. (1988). *Women and health psychology: Mental health issues.* Hillsdale, NJ: Lawrence Erlbaum.

Ussher, J. (1991). *Women's madness: Misogyny or mental illness?* Amherst: University of Massachusetts Press.

Voss, J., & Gannon, L. (1978). Sexism in the theory and practice of clinical psychology. *Professional Psychology, 9,* 623-632.

Walker, L. (1989). Psychology and violence against women. *American Psychologist, 44,* 695-702.

Walrond-Skinner, S. (1987). Feminist therapy and family therapy: The limits to the association. In S. Walrond-Skinner & D. Watson (Eds.), *Ethical issues in family therapy* (pp. 71-86). London: Routledge & Kegan Paul.

Walters, M. (1988). Single-parent, female-headed households. In M. Walters, B. Carter, P. Papp, & O. Silverstein (Eds.), *The invisible web: Gender patterns in family relationships* (pp. 289-332). New York: Guilford.

Webster, D. (1990). Women and depression (alias codependency). *Family and Community Health, 3,* 58-66.

Wheeler, D. (1985, November/December). The fear of feminism in family therapy: The risks of making waves. *Family Therapy Networker,* pp. 55-57.

Chapter

11

Credibility in the Courts

Why Is There a Gender Gap?

Lynn Hecht Schafran

This chapter is about the credibility of women in the justice system. To begin, I would like each reader to make a decision in a case that came to my attention from Wisconsin. This case may not seem to you to be about credibility, but by the end of this chapter, I hope you will see that it is. Please jot down your decision.

Imagine that you are an employer. There has been an incident of sexual harassment at your court or law firm, and now you must decide what, if any, disciplinary measures should be taken against the harasser.

The incident was this. A male employee with an unblemished work record was talking on the telephone. He put the receiver down, walked up behind a female co-worker standing nearby, grabbed and squeezed her breasts, returned to the telephone and said, "Yup, they're real." What, if any, sanction should be imposed on this employee? Should the incident be ignored? Will you or someone else in the chain of command talk to him about his behavior? Will you put a letter of reprimand in his personnel file? Will you dock his pay? Suspend him? Fire him?

Take a moment to jot down whatever your response as the employer would be.

I am going to talk about credibility by focusing on three aspects of this issue, which I call the Three Cs of Credibility: collective credibility, contextual credibility, and consequential credibility.

Before I explain these three categories, let me define *credible*. It is a word that encompasses many meanings: truthful, believable, trustworthy, intelligent, convincing, reasonable, competent, capable, someone to be taken seriously, someone who matters in the world. *Credible* is the crucial attribute for a lawyer, litigant, complainant, defendant, or witness. Yet for women, achieving credibility in and out of the courtroom is no easy task.

Collective Credibility

This brings me to my first category, collective credibility, by which I mean belonging to a group that has credibility. Simply put, women, as a group, do not.

Custom and law have taught that women are not to be taken seriously and not to be believed. For most of this country's history, the law classed women with children and the mentally impaired and forbade us to own property, enter into contracts, or vote. The rape laws were a codified expression of mistrust. Although the laws have changed, social science and legal research reveal that women are still perceived as less credible than men.

In an often replicated experiment, two groups of matched participants evaluate an identical set of essays, one group believing the essays to have been written by a man, the other group believing them to have been written by a woman. Those essays believed to have been written by a man are consistently evaluated as better written and more persuasive.

Student evaluations of college and graduate professors reveal that although both male and female students often rank their women teachers as superior in the sense of being better prepared, having mastery of the material, and being more responsive to students, students give significantly more weight to the views of their male professors, evaluating them as more credible, authoritative, and persuasive than those of their female professors. Moreover, male students are much more dramatically prejudiced in favor of their male professors than are female students.

Even youngsters are acutely conscious that women and girls are not as credible as men and boys. In 1982, two thousand Colorado schoolchildren in Grades 3 through 12 were asked, "If you woke up tomorrow and discovered that you were the opposite sex from what you are now, how would your life be different?"

Both boys and girls exhibited a fundamental contempt for being female and women's traditional role in society. The boys perceived being a girl as a disaster because they would be valued for their appearance and would have to give up all but the most stereotypically feminine activities. The girls saw being a boy as vastly liberating. Their comments included, "I would get paid more," and "My dad would respect me more."

Where this perception of men as the more credible sex takes us is brilliantly revealed in a Canadian hit film called *Wisecracks.* The film is about female comedians and combines clips of their performances with interviews in which they discuss how hard it is to be taken seriously as funny women. One of the comedians observes that when a male comic takes the stage, the audience assumes he will make them laugh. But when a female comic takes the stage, the audience's attitude is "show me."

This perception of men as competent to do the job and women as not is not confined to comedy clubs. A few years ago I presented a program for the Missouri judiciary at which a male appellate judge said to his colleagues: "Gentlemen, let's tell the truth. When a male attorney we do not know appears before us, we assume that he can do the job. But when a female attorney we don't know appears, our attitude is 'show me.' "

The American Bar Association (ABA) Commission on women in the Profession has written:

> Women report that they are often treated with a presumption of incompetence, to be overcome only by flawless performance, whereas they see men attorneys treated with a presumption of competence overcome only after numerous significant mistakes. Minority women testified that adverse presumptions are even more likely to be made about their competence.[1]

The legal system's dichotomous view of women's and men's credibility and competence affects not only assessments of women lawyers but of women litigants and parties as well. The most striking example I can give you is a study of right-to-die cases.

Dr. Steven Miles, a Minnesota physician specializing in gerontology, identified 22 appellate court decisions from 14 states in the years 1979-1989 in which courts were asked to construct the wishes of individuals who were legally incompetent because of an accident or terminal illness and who had not left living wills.[2] These individuals had all said essentially the same thing to family and friends in discussions about illness, accidents, and others' right-to-die cases: If I am ever reduced to a vegetative state, don't let them keep mc on life support.

Eight of these decisions dealt with men, 14 with women. Dr. Miles found a sharp difference in the way courts viewed incompetent women and incompetent men. Women were referred to by their first names and constructed as emotional, immature, and unreflective. Men were referred to by their surnames and constructed as rational, mature, and decisive.

In the large majority of cases involving a man, the courts constructed the patient's wishes based on his previous oral statements to family and friends and allowed withdrawal of life support. But in the large majority of cases involving a woman, the courts directed that the decision be made by a male parent or guardian, the treating physician, or a government agency.

In describing the language used in these 22 opinions, Dr. Miles wrote, "A jargon of childlikeness is used to discount the maturity of persons when a preference is not constructed. Only women are described as being in *fetal* positions or in an *infantile* state. . . . The legal familial relationship of *'parens patriae'* is only asserted in relation to women." In other words, men's moral agency must be respected even when they are legally incompetent, but women are still only children.

Contextual Credibility

The second aspect of credibility is contextual credibility, by which I mean credibility that depends on understanding the context of the claim. How can you assess someone's credibility if you literally do not know what she is talking about, which is often the case when the matter is about women's life experiences? Our justice system, like our entire society, is unused to hearing women talk about their lives. An individual has a hard time being perceived as credible when she is talking about an area about which people—both men and women—have few facts and many mistaken opinions.

In October 1991, we were riveted to our television sets watching the Senate Judiciary Committee hearings into Professor Anita Hill's allegations of sexual harassment against then-judge, now U.S. Supreme Court Associate Justice Clarence Thomas. Public opinion polls showed that respondents believed him over her by a two-to-one margin.

In October 1992, I sat at the National Association of Women Judge's luncheon honoring Professor Hill and thought about the sea change in public opinion about her credibility that occurred over that year. Current polls show that the public now perceives *her* as the credible witness.

How do we account for this massive shift? I believe it is because of national teach-ins about sexual harassment. Before the hearings my colleagues at the NOW Legal Defense and Education Fund urged the Senate Judiciary Committee to begin the hearings with an expert witness to explain what sexual harassment is, how it affects its victims, how victims respond, and that sexual harassers come from all walks of life, including the judiciary. The committee ignored our advice, and Anita Hill testified in a vacuum. The result was that she faced the same kind of incomprehension as do victims of child sexual abuse and rape when they seek justice.

She was vilified, for example, for her failure to file a sexual harassment complaint. Yet those who report sexual harassment, child sexual abuse, and sexual assault are the extreme rather than the norm. Data from numerous highly reputable studies indicate that only about 5% of those who identify themselves as victims of sexual harassment[3] and 10% to 15% of rape victims ever file complaints.[4]

The traditional insistence on a "prompt report" in sex crimes cases has always been the bane of rape victims, who find themselves confronted with police, prosecutors, judges, and juries for whom waiting equals fabricating. There is a wholesale failure to understand that victims of any kind of sexual abuse feel so deeply and personally violated and so fearful of retaliation that they resist disclosure, fearing that they will not be believed and that their humiliation will be compounded. Many never tell anyone. Others will wait days, weeks, months, and even years before telling a friend or seeking help from a rape crisis center, much less going to the police.

The judicial system is beginning to recognize that the so-called common sense about women's issues such as how a battered woman will behave is so contrary to reality that expert witness testimony is needed to educate the judge and jury. Canada's Supreme Court decision in *Regina v. Lavallee*[5] illustrates this point.

A woman shoots her husband in the back of the head. She insists this was not the cold-blooded murder it appears to be but rather an act of self-defense. Can we credit that this is the act of a reasonable woman? Her defense is *in*credible until an expert witness explains the battered woman syndrome.

It is only by viewing the situation through the woman's eyes that we can understand her response and that she becomes a credible witness. The movement toward assessing women's responses from women's points of view is one of the most significant advances in the effort to achieve gender equity in the courts.

A recent United States case involved a female Internal Revenue Service (IRS) employee who was receiving obsessive letters from a male co-worker, which, although not overtly sexual in content, frightened her. Then he showed up at an off-site training program that only her husband and supervisor were supposed to know she was attending. When the IRS took what she considered inadequate action to protect her, she filed a sexual harassment suit. The trial court dismissed, but the Ninth Circuit Court of Appeals reversed, stating:

> Because women are disproportionately victims of rape and sexual assault, women have a stronger incentive to be concerned with sexual behavior. Women who are victims of mild forms of sexual harassment may understandably worry whether a harasser's conduct is merely a prelude to violent sexual assault. Men, who are rarely victims of sexual assault, may view sexual conduct in a vacuum without a full appreciation of the social setting or the underlying threat of violence that a woman may perceive.[6]

In a similar vein, Canada's Court of Appeal recognized in *Regina v. McCraw*[7] that a letter sent to three cheerleaders threatening to rape them was not, as the trial judge found, "an adoring fantasy," but rather a terrifying threat to cause bodily harm.

The dissenting appellate opinion states that the "outcome depends upon the reaction of the reader to the letters which constitute the criminal acts alleged. To me, they are simply obscene: to my brother Brooke, they are a threat to rape." I was struck by the dissenting judge's description of these letters as if they were some kind of literature published for all to read and interpret individually. In fact, these letters were directed to three specific women, with a fourth letter to one of them demanding that she meet the writer at a specific place or he would hunt her down at her home. The only interpretation of these letters that is material is that of the women to whom they were sent.

Because I have developed a model judicial education curriculum about rape and have done extensive research in this area for many months, I feel compelled to drop a footnote to my remarks on the *McCraw* case. The notion on the part of the trial judge and the appellate dissenter that the defendant's letters are "more of an adoring fantasy than a threat to cause serious bodily harm" not only ignores the letters' effect on the victims, it ignores the fact that such "fantasies" should not be taken lightly. The research on sex offenders demonstrates that rapists spend a great deal of time fantasizing about the acts they will commit. It is estimated that 25% of rapists are literally "acting out a fantasy in which they force a woman to have sex, and then she falls in love with them."[8]

The disparate views of the majority and minority in *McCraw* reminded me of a story told at a program on gender equity presented by the Supreme Court of British Columbia at which I was a speaker in 1991. During a discussion of how women's behavior is circumscribed by fear of rape, a male judge explained how he came to understand the difference in women's and men's perceptions of the world.

This judge had always left his doors and windows open. Then he got married. Each night as he was about to go to bed, his wife asked if he were sure the doors and windows were locked, and each night he said to her, "I don't know what you are worried about. We don't have anything worth stealing." This went on for a while until it dawned on him that although his wife was too shy to say it, she was not worrying about a thief stealing their material possessions. She was worried about being raped.

Consequential Credibility

The third aspect of credibility I call consequential credibility. *Consequential* is the opposite of *inconsequential.* Part of having credibility is being seen as someone of consequence, someone who matters, someone to be taken seriously. Part of being taken seriously is having your harms and injuries taken seriously—not devalued and trivialized.

Recently, a Wyoming judge told me of a case in which she asked a man accused of assaulting a woman whether he wished to say anything in his defense. The defendant rose and said, "I don't see what all the fuss is about. It was only a woman."

This man's attitude is no aberration. Every study of the justice system's response to domestic violence has found myriad cases in which wife batterers who inflict serious injuries receive no meaningful punishment. This widespread trivializing of injuries to women is a stark expression of women's lack of consequence in the world.

Minimization of harms to women is also a factor in rape sentencing, especially cases involving nonstrangers. Eighty percent of rapes are committed by someone known to the victim[9] and often these rapists have no other criminal record, even though there is a high likelihood they are recidivists.[10] There is a supremely mistaken assumption that for a woman to be raped by someone she knows is nothing more than "bad sex," nothing worth sending a nice guy to jail for. But research shows that victims of nonstranger rape usually suffer even more severe and long-lasting psychological trauma than victims of stranger rape. They experience greater societal and self-blame for not avoiding the rape, and their ability to trust other people in any context is destroyed.[11]

I began this chapter by asking you to decide what disciplinary measures, if any, should be taken against a male employee who sexually harassed a female co-worker by grabbing her breasts and then making a comment about her breasts to a crony on the telephone. This is the type of situation that might come to your attention in a sexual harassment case, or in an administrative proceeding involving judicial or nonjudicial court personnel who are sexual harassers.

I asked you to make a decision about this case as a prelude to telling you about a case in which the Chrysler Corporation fired a harasser for precisely this behavior, but was overruled by an arbitrator. The arbitrator stated that the punishment was too severe for a first offense because this was not the equivalent of "extremely serious offenses, such as stealing money or striking a foreman."[12] Sexual harassment, even when it is strictly verbal, causes significant harm to the victim. This case of sexual harassment was legally a sexual assault. Yet to this arbitrator it was less serious than taking money or committing a nonsexual assault against a man in a position of authority.

This perception that sexual assault is less serious than theft is appalling, and it is not unique to this case. Under sentencing guidelines for the U.S. federal courts, rape is punished less severely than robbery.[13] Many of the state supreme court task forces on gender bias in the courts have urged that the state sentencing guidelines for rape be increased to take account of the profound psychological trauma of sexual assault.

How we sentence tells us who we value. What could be a clearer expression of women's lack of consequence in the world than *de minimis* sentences for the archetypal crime against women, rape.

Conclusion

Women lack collective credibility, contextual credibility, and consequential credibility. As a group we are perceived as less competent than men; the context of the harms for which we seek redress in the courts is often completely foreign to the trier of the fact; and even when the harm is acknowledged, it is often minimized by a *de minimis* punishment for those who injure us.

Changing this requires an intensely conscious effort. Some steps that other judges have taken include monitoring their response to the lawyers who appear before them to see whether they are surprised when a woman is able and a man is not, and mentally switching the sex of the individual they are evaluating to ask themselves whether they would respond the same way if this woman were a man and vice versa.

But I believe the most important thing you can do is to educate yourselves and permit expert witnesses to educate your juries, so that you, and they, can see women's cases through women's eyes and in light of the voluminous research that now exists about matters such as wife beating, sexual harassment, rape, and the myriad other criminal, civil, and family law issues that I have not had room to address.

No one, and I include women, is born with this knowledge. Often, the reality is counterintuitive. But we now have information to enable the justice system to correct the credibility imbalance that has hampered women's access to justice for so long.

One chapter is only the beginning of a complete exploration of gender issues and the courts. In 1990, I published a book called *Promoting Gender Fairness Through Judicial Education: A Guide to the Issues and Resources,* which covers 60 substantive and procedural areas ranging from law and psychiatry to judicial writing in which gender bias may be a factor. Only by incorporating this material throughout judicial education will it be possible to address all the issues that need to be studied, and to make clear that gender equity issues are not a discrete subject for a single training program but an integral part of the mainstream, daily concerns of the courts.

Notes

1. ABA Commission on Women in the Profession, *Report to the House of Delegates,* 1988, at 12.

2. Steven H. Miles and Allison August, *Courts, Gender and the "Right to Die,"* 18 Law, Medicine and Health Care 85 (1990).

3. E.g., U.S. Merit Systems Protection Board, *Sexual Harassment of Federal Workers: Is It a Problem?* Government Printing Office (1981); *Sexual Harassment of Federal Workers: An Update* (1987).

4. E.g., Crime Victims Research and Treatment Center, *Rape in America: A Report to the Nation* 7 (1992) [hereinafter *Rape in America*]; Majority Staff of the Senate Committee on the Judiciary, 102d Cong. 1st Sen., *Violence Against Women: The Increase of Rape in America* 7 (Comm. Print 1991).

5. 1990 S.C.R. 852

6. *Ellison v. Brady,* 924 F.2d 872, 879 (9th Cir. 1991).

7. 51 C.C.C. (3d) 239 (Ont. C.).

8. Daniel Goleman, New Studies Map the Mind of a Rapist, *New York Times,* December 10, 1991, at C1.

The judicial education curriculum, *Understanding Sexual Violence: The Judicial Response to Stranger and Nonstranger Rape and Sexual Assault,* is available from the National Judicial Education Program, 99 Hudson Street, 12th Floor, New York, New York 10013; (212) 925-6635. The cost is $60, which includes domestic postage.

9. *Rape in America, supra* note 4, at 5.

10. Gene R. Abel, et al., *Self-Reported Sex Crimes of Nonincarcerated Paraphilliacs,* 2 J. Interpersonal Violence 3 (1987). The 126 rapists in this study averaged seven victims each.

11. Sally I. Bowie et al., *Blitz Rape and Confidence Rape: Implications for Clinical Intervention,* 44 Am. J. of Psychotherapy 180 (1990).

12. *In the Matter of the Arbitration Proceedings Between Chrysler Motors Corp. and Local 793, Allied Industrial Workers of America, AFL-CIO,* involving the Discharge of Ronald Gallenbeck (July 24, 1989), at 9.

13. U.S. Senate Committee on the Judiciary, Majority Report, Analysis of Federal Rape Sentences 1, 3 (1992).

Chapter

12

Some Unanticipated Consequences of Women Guarding Men in Prisons

Richard C. Monk

A paradox of the 1990s is that on the one hand significant gains in civil rights are being achieved by racial, gender, ethnic, and religious minorities. Political and legal protections are in place so that, in theory, abuses of the past—especially in the workplace—no longer have to be "put up with." On the other hand, in spite of a plethora of publicized outrages against women by naval officials, Supreme Court nominees, and U.S. senators, patent sex discrimination persists. Although it is perhaps becoming more subtle, it has hardly even gone underground let alone disappeared (Benokraitis & Feagin, 1995). Another paradox is that in spite of solid criminological research showing that prisons do not necessarily reduce the crime rate, the number of prison inmates in the United States has more than doubled since the 1980s.

Since 1990, state prison populations have increased 9.1% per year. Currently, there are over 1 million inmates in state prisons compared to 501,886 in 1980 (Marvell, 1996). The percentage of inmates who are black has increased significantly and the length of sentences are greater than in the past (Silverman & Vega, 1996). Yet serious crimes, including violence by and against the young, continue to escalate. Prisons are increasingly seen (falsely) as a "solution."

Not only is the number of inmates growing, but paralleling increases in civil and economic rights, the number of female correctional officers within male prisons is increasing as well. Specifically, among both blacks and whites since the 1970s, the number and institutional distribution of female guards in all-male prisons have increased. Beginning with Title VII of the Civil Rights Act of 1964 and followed by several amendments prohibiting hiring discrimination on the basis of "race, color, religion, sex, age, national origin, or disability," women have a legal basis for exercising their right to be hired as prison guards including at male institutions (Belknap, 1996a; Rubin, 1995a, 1995b). Historically, women's role in corrections was limited either to female institutions, to juvenile facilities, or as clerical staff within male prisons (Morton, 1992, 1995). Not only was such sex segregation insulting and demeaning, but practically, it prevented women access to most jobs within corrections. For instance, 94% of all prisons in the United States house male offenders. Of the 460,000 inmates in jail in 1994, 90% were males. At the beginning of 1994, there were 859,227 males compared to only 50,853 females in state prisons. Of the projected 114,579 inmates housed by the Federal Bureau of Prisons by the end of 1996, about 106,000 will be males (U.S. Department of Justice, 1995).

In terms of the analytical categories of sex discrimination developed by Benokraitis and Feagin (1995), *overt* discrimination in the hiring of females as guards within male institutions has been greatly reduced. In the 1960s, there were few or no females guarding males in most prisons. At the end of the fiscal year for 1994, out of a total of 205,453 correctional officers in adult facilities, approximately 36,000 were females and about 1,100 of the 10,248 federal guards were women. Black females number 13,812 compared to 19,864 white females in state institutions and 438 blacks compared to 581 white females in federal prisons. Hispanic female correctional officers numbered 1,982 in state and 104 in the federal systems (U.S. Department of Justice, 1995). All states now have female officers guarding males, and several states, as well as the Federal Bureau of Prisons, have females supervising male prisons (Feinman, 1994; Martin & Jurik, 1996).

Yet compared with the other two major components of the criminal justice system, the courts and the police, corrections remains by far the most sex-segregated workplace (Feinman, 1994). In addition, almost all previous studies of women guarding men have indicated at least some elements of continuing sex discrimination within custodial settings. These ranged from *quid pro quo* harassment (supervisors or others with power demanding sexual favors for promotions, hiring, desirable assignments, or even providing basic support) to hostile work environments. The latter is creating and/or allowing verbal and/or physical abuse that creates "an intimidating, hostile, or offensive work environment" (Rubin, 1995a, 1995b). Hostile work environment harassment, which can consist of overt, covert, or subtle sex discrimination, is in the 1990s far more common within correctional institutions than quid pro quo harassment (Feinman, 1994; Martin & Jurik, 1996; Pollock, 1995).

A widely publicized recent case of hostile work environment is the District of Columbia (D.C.) Correctional Treatment Facility that houses both men and women and has male and female guards. Recent allegations were made by female inmates of sexual assault by a supervisor who was linked with past harassment of female officers (Locy, 1995). In early 1995, a jury awarded six guards $1.4 million on the basis that male guards and supervisors had "groped them, pressured them for sex or retaliated against them when they complained" (Locy, 1995, p. B1).

As indicated above, the number of white female officers in state prisons is 19,864 compared to 13,812 black female officers. Combined, women constitute approximately 17% of the guard force. However, relative to the total number of black females in the general population, there is a far greater proportion of black females than white females who are guarding males. Also, in many urban prison settings, especially on the East Coast, black female officers greatly outnumber white female officers (American Correctional Association, 1994). An extreme example of this is the D.C. Department of Corrections, which has 726 black female officers compared to 13 white female officers (U.S. Department of Justice, 1995). As a point of interest, that system also has a high rate of female officers to males (approximately 30%), yet it, too, is obviously plagued by severe sex discrimination. As important as these studies are otherwise, it is ironic that within the slowly emerging literature on females working within male correctional institutions very little is said about black female correctional officers.

Some studies touch on aspects of race and sex among prison guards (see Feinman, 1994; Martin & Jurik, 1996; Owen, 1985; Van Voorhis, Cullen,

Link, & Wolfe, 1991). Maghan and McLeish-Blackwell's (1991) chapter is relatively unique because it provides an overview of black females in corrections. Yet, as indicated earlier, most studies of correctional officers, including females, say little about black female officers. This is especially striking because there is a disproportionately high number of such officers. In many prisons, the majority of inmates are black males. Yet, it appears, the consequences of being in the prison setting for either black female officers or black inmates are rarely directly examined. The negative unanticipated consequences of women guarding men have yet to be considered systematically.

It is also ironic that other than providing labels for different types of female guards (e.g., "iron maidens," "innovators"), few researchers have used existing analytical categories to clarify and explain the emergence, maintenance, and modification of sex discrimination against female officers guarding males. These categories might include subtle as well as covert and overt strategies by males to maintain their hegemony within a formerly male preserve. Benokraitis and Feagin (1995), for instance, have delineated such a helpful typology. Their work has been largely ignored by criminologists and criminal justice scholars, however. An exception is Hale and Menniti's (1993) discussion of women in policing.

This chapter will examine, then, subtle and other variants of sex discrimination against women guarding men. The primary focus will be on sex discrimination against black female officers. Part of the analysis will include strategies used by male guards in the workplace to discriminate against female officers through "dividing and conquering female officers and inmates" by playing them off against each other.

Research Design and Data Collection

The data reported here are part of a larger, ongoing study of correctional institutions. The findings are based on interviews conducted with 20 inmates, 16 female correctional officers, 6 male officers, and 4 administrators. Several of the interviews were recorded. The sample came from three maximum-security institutions, one medium- and one minimum-security prison, and two detention centers. Six of the institutions are in an East Coast state and the seventh is in a deep south state. The majority of the officers are black.

Two thirds of the East Coast participants were interviewed in the late 1980s. The remainder were interviewed in late 1995 and early 1996. Interviews in the deep south prison were conducted in the early 1990s. The interviews were open ended, in-depth, consisted of 32 questions, and used frequent probes.

Although this is a "work in progress" report, there are sufficient data to generate a rudimentary typology for an analysis and explanation of a *divisa et imperia* (divide and conquer) strategy used by many male guards against female officers and male inmates. The typology will serve to clarify subtle, overt, and covert gender discrimination in a unique occupational setting.

Findings

There are roughly four clusters of findings that emerge from this study: (a) verbal and sexual abuses that are primarily overt; (b) subtle, overt, and covert jokes and sexist humor by male guards to undermine female guards' work; (c) subtle, overt, and covert attempts to segregate female officers from needed institutional information and general access to basic operations; and (d) sexual rumor mongering by male officers that sabotaged the reputations of female officers.

Analytically, these behaviors are readily distinguishable. Empirically, though, there is frequent overlap. Verbal abuse, as will be shown, frequently consists of direct, overt name-calling but it can be subtle as well as shade into overt or covert sexist humor.

There are some differences in harassment based on the security levels of the facilities. At times, for instance, the higher the security level, the less subtle and more hostile (both overt and covert) the sex discrimination. As one female guard put it:

> At the prerelease facility they both [inmates and guards] are kind of nice and easygoing . . . they get along with the female officers. . . . At a maximum-security facility they are kind of hostile because they really do not want to see a female.

The data seem to indicate that sex discrimination resulting in a hostile work environment is pervasive enough, however, to warrant collapsing the findings from all six institutions.

There were also some minor differences between the two time frames (approximately 7 years) during which the data were gathered. These differences appear marginal and will be considered in the final section, which addresses some policy implications of the findings. It should be noted that staff at most prisons refer to themselves as correctional officers. Zimmer (1986), however, insists that prison guards do not correct anyone; thus, she uses the term *guard.* Belknap (1996a) follows this pattern. In this research, somewhat similar to Johnson (1996), we use the terms interchangeably.

Verbal Abuse as a Hostile Work Environment

The most common form of male guard harassment is blatant verbal abuse. In spite of the possibility of formal complaints and/or lawsuits by female officers, offensive comments were frequent. The open attack of female guards was almost taken for granted by a minority of the male guards and the majority of the females. The latter more or less simply "got used" to it:

> None of us like it but we know it's a fact of life . . . part of the job. Some of them [male guards], no matter what you do or say, are going to come down on you whenever they feel like it. They are going to say nasty, mean things.
>
> [Such as?]
>
> They're going to call you a bitch. They are going to ridicule your work, your being there. They even will say things about how defenseless and stupid you are in front of the residents [inmates]. They just don't care. Even when they are not calling you names or saying bad things, then they are laughing either to your face or to other guards [males] so you can't help overhear it.
>
> [Do they call you "bitch" right in front of the residents?]
>
> No, not that way. They'll just say to each other, "What do we have to have that bitch working here for? They trying to get us killed?" Or they'll say after another guard or resident reports on something we did like a check on a cell block or transporting an inmate to the infirmary, "That dumb bitch," meaning that we didn't do it right because we are females.

These are obvious examples of overt sex discrimination that at times may contain elements of covert actions. The latter would be abusive verbalizations deliberately uttered even if the speaker (male guard) did not believe them. These comments become weapons to undermine another officer who is female. Her credibility to inmates is weakened.

Examples of subtle verbal sex discrimination in this setting include comments that on the surface appear to be benign. These would be matter-of-fact observations that female officers might have a place in the facility but that they should not be expected to do many of the more important things as well as male guards. For instance, several participants complained about male guards and supervisors who routinely suggested that male officers were more effective than females. One female guard indicated how she confronted such subtle abuse:

> I questioned one particular officer. I asked him what he means by "effective." I told him, I said I can go up on the tier, lock it down, count it, and be back in 5 minutes without incident. You can go up on the tier, strong arm them, threaten, be threatened, come down with five infractions that you had to write somebody up, and you consider yourself more effective?

A considerably more complex example of subtle verbal abuse in the workplace is the attribution of female superiority in certain contexts. Whereas empirically such "superior effectiveness" may be problematic, the connotation is invariably linked to a gender-based stereotype. In police work, both practitioners and many scholars maintain that female police officers are more able to defuse potentially violent situations, especially those related to domestic disputes (e.g., Belknap, 1996b; Pollock, 1995). In correctional settings, both male staff and often female guards claim that females function as a "calming effect" to defuse potentially violent situations (Martin & Jurik, 1996; Owen, 1985). This attribution of "positive femininity" (mothering, comforting) may have initially been stressed to counteract charges that females in male prisons would be extremely upsetting.

Regardless of the reasons why it emerged or its empirical accuracy, this perception is now often verbalized by criminologists and practitioners. One widely respected male warden explained:

> When I first started, male institutions had no female officers . . . in some respects that is one of the reasons they had so many riots because there is a challenge that a male poses to another male that a female does not. . . . You either rise to the challenge or you are a punk. . . . Female officers see things a little differently. They deflect problems, they do not go for challenges . . . their approach is a lot different than a male.

At the very least, it would seem, this widely circulated assertion may reinforce beliefs that female correctional officers are "different" and hence should be treated differently. Feinman (1994) is one of the few to challenge this perception directly suggesting that it may be a form of subtle discrimination. She insists that the empirical evidence to support this claim is weak at best, and at worst it may be supporting gender stereotypes.

There are multiple organizational or structural features of the prison work environment that are directly and indirectly conducive for open verbal harassment. First, the cast of players in this setting, both inmates and guards, are in a tension-ridden, conflict-prone environment. Among males, and regardless of socioeconomic background, it is normative to express sentiments through emotional, violently charged expletives. Verbal anger laced with name-calling and obscenities is often part of work environments that are traditionally male dominated. The prison is no exception. Thus, regardless of the fairness or legality, openly complaining about others, including female officers, in front of other guards as well as inmates remains a frequent practice for some male guards. In extreme cases, male guards will openly ridicule female guards in the presence of inmates as well as other guards. This, too, divides females from inmates and co-workers.

Hostile Humor and Jokes

In organizational settings that are prone to uncertainty with the possibility of mistakes or simply unpredictable actions having disastrous consequences, the role of humor takes on great importance. It can have multiple functions that range from the simple safety valve mechanism of tension release to sharpening mental intensity and alertness among guards. For instance, among minority groups the ability to joke and to engage in witty responses often functions not only to make intolerable situations tolerable but to provide survival mechanisms such as rapid verbal responses to hostile power holders.

Humor, jokes, and repartee in prisons can also informally rank guards' popularity among each other and the inmate world. This results from their displaying their abilities to make others laugh, to make adversaries the butt of jokes, to put others down by a quick comeback, and to diffuse a difficult situation through humor. Although there is a thin line between those who are quick-witted and "cool" and those who are simply "smart asses" and nasty, both guards and inmates appear to place a premium on jokes and humor.

Unfortunately, male guards' jokes and laughter against female correctional officers become a convenient and constant source of verbal abuse. The introduction of female guards presented male guards with a novel and difficult situation. However, the males' ridicule of and laughter about female officers, both in their presence and otherwise, went considerably beyond releasing tensions and structuring and controlling a new, ambiguous situation.

One female officer pointed out:

> When I heard one of them [male guards] talking about me behind my back as a "dumb bitch," or even coming close to saying it to my face, it hurt. . . . But when they laugh at me, especially when I don't know what the joke is and they [the inmates] join in, it is worse. If they are just mean to me I always know some of the residents are going to take up for me, even if it is just being a little nicer to me and signaling to me that they don't like what they are hearing, either. When the other guards laugh at me or girls in general, it is much worse. We don't get pity from anyone then. It really comes down to men against women.

Within traditional male preserves the telling of "dirty jokes" has been one of many informal mechanisms to encourage male bonding. Using humor and jokes against female guards often represented a combination of overt and covert sex discrimination, sometimes obvious, intentional, and blatant (speaking in loud tones so that others would be sure to hear insulting comments). At other times the use of humor directed toward females in the prison setting was more subtle. For instance, one officer commented that both the inmates and male officers were always "playing with her." At times this included "good-natured kidding." It also was a form of reality testing: attempting to see how far they could push the officer until she became angry.

Joke telling that was intentionally harmful, as indicated above, could be most effective in dividing female officers from male inmates (as well as potentially helpful male guards). At other times, though, reflecting behavior that would probably never be directed against male officers, it could be more "playful." An example of this was given by an officer who had other officers, including males, attend a party over a weekend at her home:

> The next shift I was on some of the inmates told me exactly who was at my party, what we did, what was served . . . everything.

She was bothered that the male officers shared this with inmates but decided not to let it "get to me": "I just looked the inmate in the eye and said, 'Funny, I don't remember seeing you there. Where did you sit?' "

Excluding Females From Information and Resources

Other sexist tactics that contributed to an offensive or hostile work environment included various expressions of the "silent treatment," such as ignoring female officers and refusing to answer all but the most basic inquiries. This problem is often reported in the literature (Feinman, 1994; Zimmer, 1986). In this study, it seemed to be a greater concern in the late 1980s than in the follow-up research. Other tactics of exclusions entailed not inviting female officers to guards' activities and meetings, placing them in situations in which they have little or no interactions with other guards, or not including them in social functions both on and off the grounds. However, it is interesting to note that several female respondents indicated they do get invitations to social events but follow a strict policy of not attending such social activities:

> I do not really interact that much . . . when I leave . . . I try not to intermingle work with my personal life.

More strategies making the work environment hostile include giving female guards wrong information, complaining to supervisors about trivial infractions that male guards engaged in and were not reported, and failing to caution female officers or to provide them with vital information. Examples of the latter include recent disturbances (such as immediately prior to a female officer's shift), threats made by inmates, and a shortage of guards on a particular shift. These forms of male guard sabotage were far more likely than the silent treatment reported in other studies. Hostile males typically spoke all too much to female officers.

A common concern that a majority of the female officer participants voiced was the objections of male guards and supervisors about females "talking too much" with inmates. Sometimes the complaints would be made in a written report. Many females argued that they saw such interactions with the inmates as part of their role as officers. They pointed out, in addition, that such concerns were not made about male officers interacting with inmates:

> Things . . . will be more acceptable for men . . . but if a female is doing the same thing, then it is perceived as getting too close. . . . You are expected to perform the same job although no one may verbalize it to you . . . you know how they feel. This all brings that sense of females being kind of inferior.

Sexual Rumor Mongering

> They make it rough . . . some of them are not much older than my teenage son. Their [the male guards] calling me "baby" and that shit is not so bad. But when they insinuate right in front of the others that they slept with you the night before . . . it gets to you.
>
> [They say that in front of other guards or inmates?]
>
> Both. It doesn't matter to them.

Rumor mongering can be roughly divided into alleged activities of female correctional officers outside the correctional setting and those within the prison. The East Coast state prison system in our study appears to have had by far the higher rates of sexual harassment. These facilities were located close to or in a large urban area. Many of the guards and inmates were from the same parts of the city. Most had at least some knowledge of the general communities and neighborhoods where many black female guards grew up or were currently living while working at the correctional facility.

The first form of rumor mongering was based on the alleged home or community relations and experiences of female correctional officers. These rumors included charges of extensive use of drugs, drug dealings, or having unsavory boyfriends. Parenthetically, in the southern state prison, several male guards alleged that a dynamic white female counselor "either lived with a black man or was married to one, no one knows for sure which it is." These same guards, however, unlike those in the East Coast system, would rarely, if ever, verbally attack any female staff members. Their explanation for this "chivalry" was that "you just don't talk that way to a woman around here." Inmates concurred with this informal rule. Why this difference exists is unclear. On the one hand, it may simply reflect regional cultural differences. However, the deep south prison was only 2 years old when this research was conducted. It was unique compared to most of the prisons studied, which were several years old, one over a century. This variation is simply noted here to indicate that additional research and analysis are needed.

In the East Coast state prisons, especially the maximum-security prisons, the most common rumor mongering was the creation of the label "street prostitute." Male guards, inmates, and female guards all acknowledged this charge. It was generally manufactured about black female guards. In many ways, it reflected the structural conditions of high crime, high drug sales and use, and high rates of prostitution that characterize the neighborhood from which many inmates and guards came from or lived in.

It is difficult to respond to such charges. Technically, they would fall under slander. Legally, they would be the basis for a civil service or civil rights complaint. The charges would be transmitted in a variety of forms including direct telling to other male guards or inmates, bantering about the female officer so that others could overhear, and more rarely, making such statements directly to the victimized officer.

According to the female guards we interviewed, such rumor mongering had several common characteristics and responses. At times only subtle hints were made, but more typically sexual rumor mongering was overt. There was general agreement that these charges were frequent. Sometimes they were made by male guards directly to females. At other times they were made behind the female's back. It was also generally agreed that they were among the most painful and humiliating slurs possible. Yet the victims rarely responded formally to these charges. On a few occasions, anger was expressed through verbal confrontations. These might include bitter name-calling and threats if the male guard did not "watch your month."

Inmates sometimes spread the rumor of female officers being "known" on the street as current or former prostitutes and encouraged guards to make such allegations. They rarely repeated these charges either in the presence of the female or called her a "whore" to her face. However, even when angry, male guards themselves were much more likely to refer to disliked females as a "bitch" instead of a "whore." This probably reflects a ranking of the negativeness between the two words. It may also indicate, in part, the tenuous lower-middle-class in contrast to lower-class status earned with great difficulty by both male and female guards. Hence, any threat to such middle-class respectability such as directly calling a female officer a whore was seen as too risky; it called into question the newly acquired working-class status of male guards themselves who were often from the same communities.

Sexual rumor mongering based on acts allegedly originating within the prison itself were more common. Male guards would brag that they had seduced or even paid a female officer for sex. Other rumors depicted females as having sex with inmates. In addition, rumors were spread that female officers were lesbians or "dykes." Such rumors are widely reported in the literature (Martin & Jurik, 1996; Zimmer, 1986). However, previous research does not identify the bearing that neighborhoods of guards may have on their interactions within prisons. This was found to be an important source at times for ridiculing female officers through sexual and other rumor mongering. It appears that the only previous study that considers specifically incidents of neighborhood or community of origin influences on black female officers' interactions with either inmates or other guards deals only with the fact that some officers have friends or relatives who are incarcerated (Maghan & McLeish-Blackwell, 1991; Martin & Jurik, 1996). Although this can be a source of pain and difficulty for some correctional officers, there clearly are additional important neighborhood factors that influence prison workplace interactions, including sex discrimination.

The remainder of this chapter will briefly discuss policy implications of these findings.

Policy Implications

In the 20 years that females in large numbers fought to become correctional officers in all-male institutions, vast changes have occurred. Virtually all significant legal impediments have been overcome, females guard males in every state, and many prisons, including federal ones, have female wardens as well as correctional officers. In the several years between our study of prisons in an East Coast state and a follow-up study, there have been positive changes. More females are hired, most though not all have access to posts that male guards work, and there are more females in supervisory roles. These changes somewhat parallel those reflected in later editions of similar studies or readers dealing with women in corrections (e.g., Feinman's second edition in 1986 compared with her third edition, 1994; Price & Sokoloff's first edition compared with their second in 1995).

In spite of positive changes showing that the consequences of women guarding men are greater opportunities, destruction of former myths about the capabilities of women in tough "masculine" jobs, and probably in at least some cases a new and badly needed alternative perspective to prison work, problems persist for women. Many studies, including this one, concur with Zimmer's (1986) findings that virtually all female officers are at least occasionally victims of sexual harassment. In varying situations, these include subtle, overt, and covert. The argument could be made that in terms of the extreme expression of harassment in a formerly all-male preserve, what would be viewed as overt and even blatant harassment in other occupations is now in prisons relatively "mild" or subtle. However, to many including the staff and administrators of the two sampled prison systems, no sex discrimination is acceptable. What can be done, at least in the East Coast state facilities, to bring the ideal in line with the realities that has not been tried so far?

It would appear that a helpful policy change, though subtle, would be to build more explicitly and deliberately on what is already being done in the way of monitoring and sensitivity training. Unlike during the first interviews, almost all female guards in 1995 and 1996 mentioned the importance of "how you carry yourself." This manufacturing of body language implies that to obtain respect from both inmates and male guards the female officer must show a physical and mental confidence. Although teaching and encouraging females to achieve this appearance, which implies *more* than the self-confidence necessary for effective male officers, is subtle sex discrimination, it seems effective. Female officers were proud that they had achieved the ability to "carry myself." Many attributed their success largely to this ability. Hence, it clearly gives sensitive administrators something on which to build. For females, it is an operational goal that "makes sense" and can be achieved (though for outsiders, like so many aspects of prison work, it may appear elusive if not mystical). It is also recognized and acknowledged by both inmates and male guards.

Our proposal is that the rudimentary construct of "carry yourself" be expanded in training, in everyday monitoring of guards, both males and females, and as a source of discussion in routine gender sensitivity training sessions. What does it mean to carry oneself? How do males carry themselves that is positive? negative? (The latter was widely understood by female officers who pointed out that males, as did the warden cited earlier, often gave off hostile body language in interactions with inmates.) Discussions, then, would assist both males and females in identifying their respective strengths and weaknesses as individual officers. The construct provides an easily understandable nexus for comparisons that do not have to have an invidious connotation (what females do is "weak" or "wrong," what males do is "correct" or "better").

There are obviously many other policy recommendations possible (see Henderson & Monk, in press). However, this basic one is presented here as it is one that logically grows out of both this study and many others cited. It is implementable and seems to constitute a positive addition to the existing efforts to reduce sex discrimination in male prisons.

References

American Correctional Association. (1994). *Vital statistics in corrections.* Laurel, MD: Author.

Belknap, J. (1996a). *Invisible woman: Gender, crime, and justice.* Belmont, CA: Wadsworth.

Belknap, J. (1996b). Policewomen, policemen, or both? Issues of recruitment and training for responses to woman battering. *Journal of Contemporary Criminal Justice, 12,* 215-234.

Benokraitis, N. V., & Feagin, J. R. (1995). *Modern sexism: Blatant, subtle, and covert discrimination.* Englewood Cliffs, NJ: Prentice Hall.

Feinman, C. (1994). *Women in the criminal justice system* (3rd ed.). Westport, CT: Praeger.

Hale, D. C., & Menniti, D. J. (1993). Discrimination and harassment: Litigation by women in policing. In R. Muraskin & T. Alleman (Eds.), *It's a crime: Women and justice* (pp. 177-189). Englewood Cliffs, NJ: Regents/Prentice Hall.

Henderson, J., & Monk, R. C. (in press). *Criminological and criminal justice theories and policies.* Englewood Cliffs, NJ: Prentice Hall.

Johnson, R. (1996). *Hard time: Understanding and reforming prison* (2nd ed.). Belmont, CA: Wadsworth.

Locy, T. (1995, November 21). Inmate accuses D.C. correction official of sexual assault. *Washington Post,* pp. B1, B3.

Maghan, J., & McLeish-Blackwell, L. (1991). Black women in correctional employment. In J. B. Morton (Ed.), *Change, challenge, and choices: Women's role in modern corrections* (pp. 82-99). Waldorf, MD: St. Mary's.

Martin, S. E., & Jurik, N. C. (1996). *Doing justice, doing gender: Women in law and criminal justice occupations.* Thousand Oaks, CA: Sage.

Marvel, T. B. (1996). Is further prison expansion worth the cost? *Corrections Compendium, 21,* 1-4.

Morton, J. B. (1992, August). Women in corrections: Looking back on 200 years of valuable contributions. *Corrections Today,* pp. 76-142.

Morton, J. B. (1995, August). The agency of women—Women and the American Correctional Association. *Corrections Today,* pp. 77-84.

Owen, B. A. (1985). Race and gender relations among prison workers. *Crime & Delinquency, 31,* 147-159.

Price, B. R., & Sokoloff, N. J. (Eds.). (1995). *Criminal justice system and women* (2nd ed.). New York: McGraw-Hill.

Pollock, J. M. (1995). Women in corrections: Custody and the caring ethic. In A. V. Merlo & J. M. Pollock (Eds.), *Women, law, and social control* (pp. 97-116). Boston: Allyn and Bacon.

Rubin, P. N. (1995a, June). *Civil rights and criminal justice: Employment discrimination overview.* Washington, DC: National Institute of Justice.

Rubin, P. N. (1995b, October). *Civil rights and criminal justice: Primer on sexual harassment.* Washington, DC: National Institute of Justice.

Silverman, I. J., & Vega, M. (1996). *Corrections: A comprehensive view.* St. Paul, MN: West.

U.S. Department of Justice. (1995). *Sourcebook of criminal justice statistics.* Bureau of Justice Statistics. Washington, DC: Government Printing Office.

Van Voorhis, P., & Cullen, F. T., Link, B. G., & Wolfe, N. T. (1991). The impact of race and gender on correctional officers' orientation to the integrated environment. *Journal of Research in Crime and Delinquency 28,* 472-500.

Zimmer, L. E. (1986). *Women guarding men.* Chicago: Chicago University Press.

PART IV

How to Change Subtle Sexism Practices

So far, you've probably found this book pretty depressing. Sex discrimination is not inherited genetically, however. Because sexism is constructed socially, it can also be deconstructed socially. The next four chapters show how subtle sexism, specifically, can be eliminated (or at least decreased) through individual, institutional, community, and national efforts.

In the first chapter in this section, "Transforming the Classroom: Teaching Subtle Sexism Through Experiential Role-Playing," Melissa Kesler Gilbert shows how involving students actively in the classroom can transform "the landscape of the traditional classroom, making it a space where all of us can begin the process of exposing the subtle sexisms of our everyday lives" (p. 245). This transformation includes role-playing, sharing the responsibility of learning (instead of relying, exclusively, on the instructor as the authority), and encouraging students to work together in "coming to grips" with such issues as subtle sexism.

Some of us feel more comfortable than others with classroom role-playing techniques. Gilbert does not use the suggested teaching strategies spontaneously or in a vacuum, however. Instead, and after considerable reading and group preparation, the classroom exercises illustrate theoretical concepts, apply traditional research techniques, and interpret empirically based studies. The point here is that students and faculty can use the classroom in innovative ways to transform "book reading" into memorable class presentations that explore students' personal experiences with sex discrimination.

In fact, college may be one of the few (and safe) opportunities to enact and discuss such problems as subtle sex discrimination without being labeled a "wimp," "nerd," "lesbie," or "libber." In a national, longitudinal study of women and men students attending 4-year institutions, for example, Morrison and Wolf (1994) found both predictable and surprising changes between the first year of college and 4 years later. Not surprisingly, for example, men were more likely to start out higher in self-ratings and finish higher than the women on such variables as academic ability, intellectual self-confidence, leadership ability, social self-confidence, mathematical ability, and a drive to achieve. Female students were more likely than their male counterparts to be more socially conscious and more concerned about relationship issues. Over the 4-year period, however, both the women and the men became less status and success oriented and moved "in the direction of greater commitment to social concerns." Although, according to Morrison and Wolf, the college experience is still a gendered one, college is also "a time when an impact can be made and when institutional values can make a difference" (p. 723). Thus, both classroom experiences and campus activities can change sexist perspectives and practices.

Moving from the individual to the organizational level, Mary E. Kite and Deborah Ware Balogh show that sexist institutional practices can be ameliorated despite numerous obstacles. They cochaired a task force on the status of women in the College of Sciences and Humanities at Ball State University "to find out what, if any, institutional barriers existed that interfered with the career advancement of women" (p. 267). The task force experienced both support and resistance. Despite a number of impediments (e.g., suspicion, defensiveness, turf battles, committee disagreements, and hostility), Kite and Balogh were successful in challenging both subtle and blatant discriminatory practices. This chapter shows that the inequitable campus practices described in Chapter 3 *can* be decreased. Objecting to existing sexist behavior is not an easy task. But, as Kite and Balogh show, the barriers are not insurmountable.

In Chapter 15, "The Cultural Politics of Abuse in Lesbian Relationships: Challenges for Community Action," Janice L. Ristock shows that community action can be effective in diminishing some of the subtle and blatant discrimination that many lesbians encounter. Ristock begins the chapter with a discussion of how the film media reinforce heterosexism (an ideological system that denigrates and stigmatizes any nonheterosexual form of behavior, identity, or relationships) and misogyny (a hatred of or contempt for women). Using popular films as a backdrop, Ristock reviews the research on violence in lesbian relationships and then describes how the Coalition of Lesbians on Support and Education worked to overcome the community's subtle stereotypes about abusive partners. Ristock shows that community organizing is an effective tool for fighting sexist and heterosexist attitudes and actions.

In the final chapter, "Comparable Worth: When Do Two Jobs Deserve the Same Pay?" Carolyn J. Aman and Paula England contend that not paying women and men comparable salaries for comparable work is one of the most pernicious types of subtle and legal discrimination on the national level. According to Aman and England, the idea behind comparable worth is simple: "The pay level of a job should not be affected by the sex of those doing the work, but it may be affected by the demands of the job" (p. 301). Sounds fair and straightforward, doesn't it? Why, then, don't people earn the same salaries in similar jobs regardless of whether they have a vulva or a penis?

According to Aman and England, a major reason for salary differences is the "similarity principle." Given extensive sex segregation in the labor force, "women in predominantly female jobs will usually compare their pay to others in the same or a similar job that is also filled by women" (p. 302) instead of comparing their jobs to those of men in "male" jobs. For example, a secretary might compare her salary to another secretary's salary rather than the groundskeeper who is earning much more despite the fact that the groundskeeper's job does not require literacy, computer skills, or enduring a stressful work environment. Aman and England note that in virtually every state where comparable worth studies have been done, the studies have revealed systematic and systemic underpayment of female jobs. In effect, then, this form of subtle wage discrimination contributes to the sex gap in pay: It affects millions of women and a smaller number of men in predominantly female jobs (see Chapter 7). Despite this inequity, the United States has no comprehensive legislation prohibiting this form of discrimination.

Can you do anything? Of course! As the chapters in this section show, you can take action on the individual, organizational, community, and national levels. Among other things, you can speak out against subtle sexism, encourage other women and men to join you, support groups that are trying to change discriminatory behavior, investigate the possibility of launching a class-action lawsuit, and connect with groups that are trying to change legislation (for a broader discussion of these issues, see Benokraitis & Feagin, 1995). Remember that some of the most effective efforts to transform behavior—including drunken driving and victims' rights—started with *one* person who was determined to change the status quo.

References

Benokraitis, N. V., & Feagin, J. R. (1995). *Modern sexism: Blatant, subtle, and covert discrimination.* Englewood Cliffs, NJ: Prentice Hall.

Morrison, D. E., & Wolf, L. E. (1994). College as a gendered experience: An empirical analysis using multiple lenses. *Journal of Higher Education, 65,* 696-725.

Chapter

13

Transforming the Classroom

Teaching Subtle Sexism Through Experiential Role-Playing

Melissa Kesler Gilbert

When I walked into my classroom last Spring, a group of five women in their pajamas was sitting on the floor in a circle listening to an Indigo Girls song while eating popcorn, red licorice ropes, and pretzels. One of my students handed me a soft drink and a flyer printed in big, bold print: "You are invited to a slumber party." This was a scene from a student group presentation in my gender roles course where the traditional classroom was transformed into a woman's dorm room for the purpose of teaching about the subtle forms of sexism that limit women's educational aspirations.

Teaching about sexism has always been the work of the feminist teacher. Since the early 1970s, we have been using feminist pedagogy in our courses to educate our students about the subordination of women by creating student-centered, nonhierarchical, and cooperative classroom communities (Shackelford, 1992). But unmasking even the blatant forms of sexism in our classrooms has been a difficult challenge given that many of our students are convinced that "sex discrimination is no longer a problem" (Benokraitis & Feagin, 1995, p. 3). To teach about the more subtle types of sexism that are less visible and more informal, we need new and innovative teaching strategies that demystify sexist practices and heighten our students' awareness of both the roles they and others play in creating, maintaining, and reproducing sexism.

In my courses, students were responsible for teaching others about sexism by forming small collaborative learning groups and organizing their own student presentations. Through experiential role-playing, they came to know themselves as objects of sexism and began to understand how others experience sexism in myriad ways. The three following examples of student presentations from both a gender roles course and a women and work course illustrate how my students and I have transformed the landscape of the traditional classroom, making it a space where all of us can begin the process of exposing the subtle sexisms of our everyday lives. From a Supermom Contest, a Slumber Party, and Kitchen Talk, we see how students examined the self through role-playing and began to understand the diversity of women's everyday experiences with sexism. Throughout this chapter, I have incorporated the voices of students who have stepped out of their roles to write reflections on their teaching experiences.[1]

Sharing the Responsibility of Learning

During the second week of my courses, students read three articles that address the issue of student responsibility in the learning process: Adrienne Rich's (1977/1995, 1985) "Claiming an Education" and "Taking Women Seriously" and Jane Kenway and Helen Modra's (1992) "Feminist Pedagogy and Emancipatory Possibilities." Together we discussed the importance of negotiating authority in the classroom and sharing the responsibility for learning.

At first, students were usually apprehensive about their own abilities to teach the material. They resisted, arguing that they barely had a grasp on the scholarship to begin with and needed me to guide and interpret it for them. When Rich (1977/1995) suggested that "responsibility to yourself means refusing to let others do your thinking, talking, and naming for you" (p. 17), the students responded that they thought that learning from "experts" was what going to college was all about.

The first step in giving away some of our power and authority as teachers (Shackelford, 1992; Thorne, 1989) includes emphasizing that students can learn from one another, rather than just passively receiving "teacher-imparted truths," and allowing students to shape the "rules of talk" in the classroom. Early in the semester, encouraging dialogue between students about their personal experiences was an important way to convince students that they are capable of teaching one another. Engaging students in dynamic interactive dialogue about their personal campus experiences of sexism (e.g., tokenism in science classes, the silencing of women in political debates, the double standards of dating rituals, and advising students to downscale their academic choices) helped them to recognize that they are "both (and often simultaneously) subject and object of knowledge generated and transmitted" (Klein, 1995, p. 38). Students began to recognize the inequities of their own experiences within the educational system, compared them to each other's experiences, and came to see the centrality of their collective insights in relation to the scholarship (Brunner, 1992; Kenway & Modra, 1992; Rutenberg, 1983/1995). When students are encouraged to grasp their autonomy and independence in the learning process and to see both the teacher and the other students as actors who are negotiating the process of decoding sexisms, the classroom becomes a space where most participants feel present, respected, and ready to speak (Hesse-Biber & Gilbert, 1994; Thorne, 1989).

Collaborative Learning: The Group Process

"The peer interaction was very positive. We became friends. We cried together."

Once students felt comfortable with one another and began to respect each other's knowledge and positions, they began working on their group presentations. I encouraged students to start where they were in their own lives and to choose a topic from the syllabus that they felt personally interested in and wanted to explore. Based on their interests, students formed collaborative learning groups. Each group was assigned an ethnography that they worked with as the basis of their presentation. They met their group for the first time in class early in the semester to exchange phone numbers and decide on meeting times outside of class.

Because students had already come to recognize the importance of learning from one another, they often began the group work by "getting to know each other": "Our first meeting was marked by a lot of social interaction outside of the project. We learned each other's names, where we were from, and some other personal aspects of each other." Students often went on their own field trips. For example, a group of students studying sex work met on a Friday night and visited a strip club. Another group working on discrimination in women's sports went to several women's basketball games, took a tour of the locker rooms, and talked to the women athletes. These experiences gave the students the opportunity to socialize with one another outside of the classroom and to "work and become more intimate with people in the course."

Part of the assignment for the group presentation was to decide how they wanted the other members of the class to participate. Although I provided a bibliography for the group, it was up to them to choose readings for the class that directly pertained to their presentations. They could also select outside readings that they felt were important (e.g., reviews of the books, related research, and studies that contradict the findings of the author). The groups prepared discussion questions in advance and assigned homework for their classmates. Often, part of the homework was to write a personal reflection on an experience that related to a concept from the text or to discuss an issue from the readings with a friend or a partner at home. The students usually demanded a great deal from their classmates; they often started their presentations with such hopeful remarks as, "We assume you have done the readings and have thought about the questions for discussion."

Students were also asked to address the biases of the research. This process often led the group to try to broaden the scope of the study they were presenting. For example, some students interviewed women of color who were ignored by the author's original sample. Others interviewed students on their own campus to provide a sample of experiences for their age group. One student described how much she learned from doing additional research with her roommates on the effects of media stereotyping in television programs from the late 1970s: "We sat around discussing programs we watched as children and the group benefited from the input of my roommates and my friends. Their experiences gave us more current data to discuss with the class." In other instances, students' own interactions with their group provided concrete examples of the topic they were teaching. In this example, one student reflected on her group's communication prior to teaching Deborah Tannen's (1990) *You Just Don't Understand*:

> There was an equal number of each sex in the group. . . . Our topic dealt with the inability of men and women to communicate with each other clearly. . . . At times I found myself thinking whether or not I was communicating my point clearly to Bill and Rob and wondering whether Jill and I tended to agree on many things. . . . I believe that all of us have a better understanding of why people miscommunicate and how each sex can communicate better with each other because we have read the book and we also experienced it.

On the day of their group projects, students presented their own findings along with those of the author. They brought in videotaped interviews and charts summarizing the responses from student surveys.

Providing collaborative experiences for students in our courses helps to eliminate more competitive notions of learning. It also provides a sense of community characterized by mutual respect, collective inquiry, trust, and caring (Ayers-Nachamkin, 1992; Billson, 1986; Fisher, 1987; Rosser, 1989; Schniedewind, 1983; Thompson & Disch, 1992). Collaborative learning creates a comfortable classroom that enhances the personal relationships between students (Ruth, 1995). As one student noted, "This was an excellent way to not only engage in the material, but to engage with the class as a whole. I was much more comfortable with the class after the first presentation."

The Supermom Contest: Transforming the Classroom Landscape

Scene One

On the doors to the room there are bright yellow signs that announce a Supermom Contest. A woman in a dark navy suit, her hair tied up in a bun, is waving a microphone and hands out ballots to each person as they enter. In the center of the room are three stations: (1) a laundry station covered with towels, laundry baskets, and jugs of laundry detergent; (2) a window washing station with paper towels and window cleaners; and (3) a nursery station with teddy bears, children's books, and diapers (see Figure 13.1). Around the periphery of the room, chairs are arranged like a television audience where students are encouraged to take a seat and review their ballots. After an introduction by the contest hostess, the contestants enter and are introduced one by one. First, we meet Nancy Holt, a small woman dressed in slacks and a blazer, a social worker and mother. We are told that she has an egalitarian gender ideology and that her life with her husband, Evan, is unusually happy except for her son Joey's "problem." Next we are introduced to Nina Tanagawa, who came directly to the contest from her position in a personnel office. She is dressed in a white skirt and a jacket and we are told that both she and her husband are "transitionals." The final contestant is Carmen Delacorte, a spirited woman who walks into the room pregnant and full of sarcasm. She tells us she wanted to be a "milk and cookies mom," but had to take up some day care work, leaving her grateful for whatever her husband Frank does around the house. As the contest unfolds, the women engage in short humorous competitions, racing to fold clothes, to wash windows, and to read to their children. In between each contest they are interviewed by the show's hostess and the audience members about gender ideologies, family myths, their personal second shift, and their relationships with their husbands. The audience takes breaks to watch prerecorded commercials about the joys of housework on a monitor in front of the room. As the contest comes to a close, the audience is asked to rank each woman on her ability to be a supermom. The audience comes to the consensus that there is no winner.

The student presentation above was based on Arlie Hochschild's (1989) *The Second Shift,* an ethnography grounded in interviews with families and observations of mothers, husbands, and children interacting with one another. In these families, women performed a second shift of housework and child care in addition to the work they did outside of the home. The students chose to transform the class into a contest to address the supermom strategies that Hochschild argues lead working mothers to do all the work at home. Hochschild suggests that the supermom image appealed to many women because it offered a "cultural cover-up" to accompany the family myths that couples construct to cope with family conflict. The supermom image is a form of "liberated sexism," a type of subtle sexism where society "appears to be treating women and men equally but that, in practice, increases men's freedom while placing greater burdens on women" (Benokraitis & Feagin, 1995, p. 103).

Turning the classroom into a television contest worked in a number of important ways to teach about liberated sexism. The contest format transformed the physical space of the classroom by placing the lives of the women

Figure 13.1. The Second Shift

from the book at center stage and the teacher and the other students at the periphery. Gray (1989) suggests that we should take down the lecterns in the front of the classroom and regroup the isolated desks. Such changes dispel the notions that the teacher is the dispenser of knowledge and that education is a solitary, isolated experience. In our newly designed gender roles classroom, the central location of women's work and family lives drew attention to the legitimacy and importance of women's everyday problems and the knowledge women gain from personal experience.

The students also moved the action around the room, making each work station into a space where women competed with one another. The competitive, isolated nature of the women struggling to win mirrored the individual approaches the women in Hochschild's study used to cover-up or resolve family issues. For example, as Carmen was folding her towels in the contest she acted like she became ill, dragging an unsuspecting male from the class up to center stage to play her husband Frank. The student created this scene to illustrate that many women use illness to get help around the house while maintaining the myth of traditional separate spheres for husband and wife. The student playing Nancy provided another explanation for the division of household labor in her home. After she finished cleaning the classroom windows, the contest hostess asked her if her husband ever did chores like window-cleaning around the house. Nancy responded, "Sure he does, but only if you mean the windows in the basement or the car windows. You see,

I do the upstairs, Evan does the downstairs, the garage, the car, and the dog." This student's scene illustrated how the Holts created a family myth that appeared to divide the chores equally between them, whereas in reality they left Nancy with the majority of work. By struggling alone in front of the class to outdo one another and by pretending that things are equitable at home, the students effectively acted out the tensions women face every day to be supermoms who can handle it all.

Regrouping the other students into a studio audience created a collective space where students were expected not only to listen to the experiences of the women but to rank them on their ability to live up to the cultural expectations of being a supermom. Students were asked to judge a woman on her individual ability to fulfill both her traditional role as mother and her modern role as careerwoman. For example, could she balance her work and family responsibilities effectively? Did she keep her boss, her husband, and her children happy?

Scene Two

> When none of the women are chosen as the contest winner, the presenters turn to the audience and ask them what societal institutions can do to support the new roles women are taking on. A discussion of day care initiatives, family leave policies, job sharing, and gender role socialization follows. Students describe growing up with parents who struggled with the same issues. A presenter steps out of her role and discusses how it felt to "play" a traditional pregnant woman with career and family aspirations very different from her own.

In the Superwoman Contest example, the physical boundaries of the classroom became fluid and dynamic. Once the classroom space was disrupted, students felt free to continue to jump in and out of the spaces they occupied. Students who described their experiences at home moved from the periphery of the room to the center of the discussion. Presenters shed their roles and took seats in the audience. They commented on the life of the character they played and critiqued the lack of societal solutions to the second shift.

Transforming the classroom into an alternative space that reflects a landscape where sexism is lived and reproduced served other important purposes as well. It provided students with the opportunity to leave college behind by stepping out of their everyday lives and moving through other institutional settings that they may or may not have experienced before. One student wrote: "While participating . . . I almost forgot that I was in a classroom, watching people role-playing. It was realistic and it really touched me. It was just like being there. It brought the material to life, into my life." Changing the classroom setting also shifted the role of the instructor. I have shown up in class not only to find myself casting a ballot for the best supermom but also to be asked to play a jury member in a courtroom, a customer in a diner, a potential employee at a stewardess training workshop, a working-class cannery operative at a union meeting, and a victim of date rape at a support group counseling session.

The Slumber Party: Renegotiating the Self

Scene One

Students dressed in pajamas, sweats, and bunny slippers are sitting on the classroom floor in a circle. They are listening to music, snacking on pretzels and soda, and talking endlessly (see Figure 13.2). Around them is another circle of students listening intently to the discussion among the five women. Those of us in the outer circle are reading the Slumber Party flyer we were handed as we walked in the door: "Five middle class junior and senior females get together for an overnight of food and fun. While this gives them a chance to get away from the guys, they'll learn more about one another and what each is up to at S.U." We listen as Andie, an accounting major, tells her roommates that she has had to do "everything possible" to get good internships. This includes sleeping with guys on campus to learn about internship opportunities. Jessica, an Art History major, hugs Andie and says she knows how she feels. Jessica reveals that she does everything to please her football player boyfriend because "her status at school depends on him." She does his laundry, types his papers, and goes to all his home games. Christy jumps up out of the circle and says that she just can't keep her secret any longer! She shows everybody the diamond ring on her finger. When Andie asks her if she is still going to graduate, Christy explains that she and her boyfriend decided it would be best if she did, but she changed her major from English to education to accommodate the "big family plans" that she and Ron have made. Kathy mutters that she "doesn't want to hear any more of this garbage." Andie glares at her and says, "Well, you dated the Big Man

Figure 13.2. Educated in Romance

on Campus. Whatever happened to the two of you, anyway?" Kathy reveals to the group that she fell in love with a woman on campus. Since then, her new lesbian lifestyle has forced her to be much quieter and reserved. But, she remarks, "The two of us are much more serious about school—I'm back in the pre-med program again." Melinda gives Kathy a hug and says how proud she is of Kathy. Melinda isn't looking for a serious relationship on campus. She doesn't have time for romance. She tells everyone she has a boyfriend at another school. It helps her concentrate on her biology degree without having to constantly answer to the "culture of romance."

The five students in this inner circle were playing out dialogue from Holland and Eisenhart's (1990) *Educated in Romance.* These group members chose to blend their own college experiences with those of the women from the ethnography. Their objective was to teach the class about the culture of romance that exists at the university level. This culture, according to Holland and Eisenhart (1990), reproduces "traditional gender roles and a system of male privilege" (p. 5).

The women in Holland and Eisenhart's study downscaled their academic aspirations because of multiple forms of subtle sexism: a peer-imposed system of gender relations where sexual attractiveness mattered most, a sexual auction block on campus that ranked women's status by their attractiveness (symbolic capital), and peer-enforced ranking that reflected the degree of physical intimacy between dating partners. This culture of romance represents a dangerous form of subtle sexism that Benokraitis and Feagin (1995) describe as "supportive discouragement" where "women receive mixed messages about their abilities, intelligence, or accomplishments" (p. 86).

The students chose to replicate an intimate setting where they could openly discuss these mixed messages. According to Benokraitis and Feagin, many women are often discouraged from pursuing their academic objectives because they are believed to be less serious about their education than men ("She's only in college to a find husband"). As a result, advisers, mentors, and peers often accept and even encourage women who lower their academic ambitions. The students in this group were able to illustrate effectively the contradictory messages that both the women in the ethnography and they themselves were receiving about their schooling. During the presentation, each of the presenters and many others in the classroom reevaluated each woman's personal position about her educational goals. Many of the students also reexamined their own academic aspirations and began a process of renegotiating the self.

Gerda Lerner (1995) suggests that we all live on a stage where we act out our assigned roles. Feminists, she argues, are now consciously pointing to that stage, its sets, its props, its director, and its scriptwriter. Lerner challenges all of us to tear down the stage and reconstruct the roles we play. By role-playing in the classroom, students did just that, and they began to see their own parts in the play more clearly. As one student noted:

> It was very easy to role-play because it was my life. We are in the midst of being educated in romance, but it was difficult emotionally to see your life fit so easily into a role—so clearly to be a product of constraints based on gender.

Role-playing was a form of self-examination where students were raising their own level of consciousness and heightening their awareness of "the feelings, behaviors, and experiences surrounding sex roles" (Ruth, 1995, p. 14).

By integrating the self into the roles they played, the students perceived how their personal experiences fit within an academic framework. The students went through an identification process where they recognized their own feelings of oppression and learned to trust the knowledge that emerged from personal experience (Rutenberg, 1983/1995). Students described the role-playing as helping them voice their own feelings about their everyday experiences:

> The experience was amazing. I feel as if it had a lot of therapeutic value for me. The presentation helped me to vocalize a lot of my feelings by role-playing. I made Elaine's feelings my own and found out that it was all right to have a spectrum of emotions about my life.

> My character reflected my views to some extent, mainly that she was doing the same things I am—getting married and majoring in education. We are both going through the same stuff. I spoke for both of us.

And it helped students to see that they were not alone in their experience of being the object of sexism:

> I felt comfortable with the character I role-played because she was not that far from who I am. . . . I grew up watching sexist television shows and listening to sexism in music all my life. The reality is that I had no idea how stereotypical and oppressive the media is toward women, toward me.

By making the consequences of sexism explicit in the classroom, students also began to internalize the importance of change. They inevitably began to tear down the stage: "All of us learned how close to the characters we were and the consequences of our decisions." They started the process of change by first finding support for their views in their groups and in the class as a whole. One student noted, "I absolutely loved interacting with the members of my group as characters. I feel we all supported each other." Out of a new comfort with each other came an ability to name the dimensions of sexism that they can change:

> The group dynamic worked so well for several reasons. One, we are so different. Two, we chose to play roles similar to our own experiences. Three, we were all comfortable with each other. This comfort allowed some real emotions to surface about what some of our real regrets are and our

justifications about our decisions for our own lives. We helped each other think of new directions for our lives. The class did that, too. We are going to demand more from life now, I think.

Scene Two

After the women discuss their own college experiences through the lives of their characters, they take a break to dance the twist (a slumber party favorite) with their classmates. Then they take a seat on the floor in the wider circle, step out of character, and ask their peers to talk about their own experiences on campus. After numerous women share their stories about friends bugging them to go out instead of studying, doing their boyfriend's laundry, and skipping classes to go shop for clothes, the discussion turns to ways to counteract the culture of romance on their own campus.

Rich (1977/1995) reminds students that the "contract on the student's part involves that you demand to be taken seriously so that you can go on taking yourself seriously" (p. 17). When the students in this class decided that they had to demand an education and refuse to take their position on the sexual auction block on campus, they rejected the attitudes Rich names as "take it easy," "why be so serious," and "why-worry-you'll-probably-get-married-anyway." Through self-examination the students renegotiated a self that was going to "get the education I came to college to get."

Kitchen Talk:
Renegotiating Differences Among Women

Scene One

We find ourselves in the kitchen of an upper-middle-class white woman who is giving her black domestic worker a paper bag full of used clothing and a pair of worn-out shoes. The maid graciously takes the hand-me-downs from her mistress, looks down to the floor with deference and says quietly, "Thank you Ma'am." The domestic is dressed in an old brown skirt, a sweatshirt, an apron, and a kerchief tied around her hair. As she polishes an old pair of shoes she found in the bag, she turns to all of us in the classroom and says, in an aside, "My mother always said that no matter what they give you, you take it because one day they're going to give you something worth having.

Usually, I just thank her like I just did, then I walk out of here, go around the corner and the first trash can I get to, I throw it in there. You have to take it. It's part of the job, makes them feel like they're being so kind to you. You have to appear grateful. That makes them feel good, too." A voice from an offstage observer describes the scene we have just witnessed. The observer is a student playing Judith Rollins, the sociologist who wrote the book from which this dialogue comes. The character Judith tells the audience that the domestic is putting up with the maternalism of her mistress, even though she recognizes that the one-way gift exchange reinforces the inequality of the relationship. In scene after scene, we witness interactions between the domestic and the mistress. We also continue to hear from Judith, who provides the sociological explanations for the experiences of both the white mistress and the black domestic.

In *Between Women: Domestics and Their Employers,* Judith Rollins (1985) examines the dehumanization of black women within the domestic-mistress relationship. The students in this presentation vividly depicted the subtle, negative, and controlling images of black women that reinforce their subordinate role in our society. Patricia Collins (1990) argues that these "controlling images are designed to make racism, sexism, and poverty appear to be natural, normal, and an inevitable part of everyday life" (p. 68). As a form of subtle sexism and racism, this "subjective objectification" of black women includes being categorized as nonpersons, classified by their ascribed characteristics, "devalued as an individual, seen as decoration, or depersonalized as a sexual acquisition" (Benokraitis & Feagin, 1995, p. 99). In this presentation, by enacting their character's standpoint, students challenged their own understanding of other women's situations.

Barrie Thorne (1989) suggests providing learning experiences for students so they can "discover that one's own experience is not the measure of all things . . . come to see white, middle-class, male, and heterosexual assumptions as limited and not the universal, and . . . explore the experience of other groups" (p. 316). One part of this learning process is the initial discovery by students that they are experiencing their education through the lenses of their race, class, or gender (Annas & Maher, 1992). One student noted the importance of switching our positions in the classroom: "Role-playing forced all of us to look at our topic through the eyes of other people."

Students came to realize that the generic woman actually "obscures the heterogeneity of women" (Ruth, 1995, p. 3). They had to figure out not only where they fit in this heterogeneous category of woman, but they also went a step further by trying to understand the situations of women who fit in differently than they do: "I felt this role-playing experience was a positive one. In playing a transitional woman, I felt that I could thoroughly understand her position, once I actually had to be her. OK, well, almost." Whereas role-playing did heighten an awareness of the self, it also seemed to raise student consciousness about the roles others play on a daily basis. Students used their imaginations: "I put myself in other people's situations. I tried to imagine myself being in the shoes of these women. Sometimes I liked my situation. Other times I hated it." Another student wrote: "Playing the role of a pregnant woman was interesting. It felt strange, too, because I can't imagine being (a) pregnant or (b) a woman who wants to stay home. At least I didn't think I could imagine it until I actually tried to."

To make sense of the realities of other women and to see the effect of the controlling stereotypes that function in many women's lives, students had to become engaged in discussions of difference. Sometimes these discussions were very painful. Students felt guilty for participating in a system that oppresses others. Other times they discovered that their own privileged position has protected them from sexism that others have encountered:

> Role-playing allowed us to truly evaluate and understand the profound pain that victims of racism go through. It was a very painful experience trying to be someone else, especially because I felt at times somewhat guilty because I couldn't possibly completely understand the experience.

> Getting into her role was quite emotional for me. It was one thing for me to just read about what she went through, but after practicing and practicing her role, I was physically drained because it was so traumatic just thinking about all she went through and surviving. . . . We all realized how lucky we were that it was *just a role* for us.

We need to work closely with students during this process to help them understand their feelings about difference. We can do this by helping them create a comfortable classroom where everyone's voice is valid and legitimate. Most of the time my students tried to create safe spaces for emotional talk themselves, but sometimes there were risks involved in taking center stage in the classroom.

Student-Identified Risks in Role-Playing

"This kind of presentation is not for everyone."

For some students, speaking in front of a classroom was a challenging assignment. One student wrote, "I have a difficult time speaking in front of people so I found the experience unnerving, but fun." Although students are often asked to present material in their courses, the presentations are often factual, such as a review of the literature or a summary of readings. My students indicated that having to put themselves "out there" in front of others in the context of emotional, painful, and controversial ideas was sometimes very risky.

Thorne (1989) suggests that students may fear the judgments of others and use their own silence as a way to avoid taking risks in the classroom. My students were no exception. They were apprehensive about playing parts similar to themselves because they thought their own voices would be recognized. A group of women athletes who played the roles of college athletes from Bissinger's (1990) *Friday Night Lights* noted, "It was risky because everyone knew we weren't just playing parts. . . . It was exactly how we felt and maybe they disagreed with us."

Other students who played a role entirely different from their own were afraid of losing their own identity: "I did feel some discomfort in my role. Not that I was uncomfortable with the thought of playing a lesbian, but I felt labeled. I tried to imagine myself as a lesbian and how people would treat and react to me. What I imagined—it scared me." Another student was very upset with a classroom debate about child custody by lesbian couples that followed her presentation. She felt that even though she played the attorney for the lesbian parents, her real voice, a more conservative position, was lost in the debate: "I felt uncomfortable being in front of the class getting yelled at. . . . People didn't seem to realize that we were just role-playing and attacked us. Now I think before I speak." Other students not only hesitated before saying anything to the class but were silent: "I felt that I might offend someone. I was intimidated and felt it was difficult to share my opinion for fear of offending."

Coming to Grips With Subtle Sexism

Ellsworth (1992) argues that we "need to come to grips with issues of trust, risk, and the operations of fear and desire around issues of identity and politics in the classroom" (p. 105). Bringing our students together in small collaborative groups where they are able to create more comfortable relationships with their classmates is an important first step in this process of coming to grips with controversial issues. Teaching our students that they can be the teachers of their own personal knowledge and the scholarship of others is another important characteristic of the learning process. By changing the classroom landscape and providing spaces for open and reflective dialogue, we can begin to explore our students' understanding of the subtleties of sexism that exist in our society. My students recognized the value of bringing their knowledge to their peers:

> We were worried that when we gave the presentation we wouldn't be able to go through with it, but we managed because we knew how important it was to get this information out to our fellow students who would greatly benefit from it.

Although the fear, guilt, and discomfort that accompanies role-playing in the classroom can be a negative experience for some students, it can also enhance the process of knowing ourselves better and understanding others' positions in society. Activist and scholar Robin Morgan suggests that any kind of change that involves bringing together people with different experiences and positions "involves respect, courtesy, risk, curiosity, and patience. It means doing one's homework in advance, being willing to be vulnerable, and attentively listening to one another" (cited in Ruth, 1995, p. 4). Students need more of this kind of homework in our classrooms to unmask sexist myths and uncover new strategies for change.

Note

1. Students' contributions were taken from 82 reflection papers written in both my gender roles and my women and work courses between 1994 and 1995.

References

Annas, P., & Maher, F. (1992). Introduction. *Radical Teacher, 41,* 2-3.

Ayers-Nachamkin, B. (1992). A feminist approach to the introductory statistics course. *Women's Studies Quarterly, 20,* 86-93.

Benokraitis, N. V., & Feagin, J. R. (1995). *Modern sexism: Blatant, subtle, and covert discrimination.* Englewood Cliffs, NJ: Prentice Hall.

Billson, J. M. (1986). The college classroom as a small group: Some implications for teaching and learning. *Teaching Sociology, 14,* 143-151.

Bissinger, H. G. (1990). *Friday night lights: A town, a team and a dream.* New York: Addison-Wesley.

Brunner, D. (1992). Dislocating boundaries in our classrooms. *Feminist Teacher, 6,* 18-24.

Collins, P. H. (1990). *Black feminist thought: Knowledge, consciousness, and the politics of empowerment.* New York: Routledge.

Ellsworth, E. (1992). Why doesn't this feel empowering? Working through the repressive myths of critical pedagogy. In C. Luke & J. Gore (Eds.), *Feminisms and critical pedagogy* (pp. 90-119). New York: Routledge.

Fisher, B. (1987). The heart has its reasons: Feeling, thinking, and community-building in feminist education. *Women's Studies Quarterly, 15,* 47-58.

Gray, E. D. (1989). The culture of separated desks. In C. Pearson, D. Shavlick, & J. Touchton (Eds.), *Educating the majority: Women challenge tradition in higher education* (pp. 335-345). New York: Macmillan.

Hesse-Biber, S., & Gilbert, M. K. (1994). Closing the technological gender gap: Feminist pedagogy in the computer-assisted classroom. *Teaching Sociology, 22,* 19-31.

Hochschild, A. (1989). *The second shift: Working parents and the revolution at home.* New York: Viking.

Holland, D., & Eisenhart, M. (1990). *Educated in romance: Women, achievement, and college culture.* Chicago: University of Chicago Press.

Kenway, J., & Modra, H. (1992). Feminist pedagogy and emancipatory possibilities. In C. Luke & J. Gore (Eds.), *Feminisms and critical pedagogy* (pp. 138-166). New York: Routledge.

Klein, R. (1995). Passion and politics in women's studies in the nineties. In S. Ruth (Ed.), *Issues in feminism* (pp. 37-46). Mountain View, CA: Mayfield.

Lerner, G. (1995). A new angle of vision. In S. Ruth (Ed.), *Issues in feminism* (pp. 20-21). Mountain View, CA: Mayfield.

Rich, A. (1985). Taking women seriously. In M. Culley & C. Portuges (Eds.), *Gendered subjects: The dynamics of feminist teaching* (pp. 21-28). Boston: Routledge & Kegan Paul.

Rich, A. (1995). Claiming an education. In A. Kesselman, L. McNair, & N. Schniedewind (Eds.), *Women images and realities: A multicultural anthology* (pp. 16-18). Mountain View, CA: Mayfield. (Original work published 1977)

Rollins, J. (1985). *Between women: Domestics and their employers.* Philadelphia: Temple University Press.

Rosser, S. V. (1989). Teaching techniques to attract women to science: Applications of feminist theories and methodologies. *Women's Studies International Forum, 12,* 363-377.

Rutenberg, T. (1995). Learning women's studies. In A. Kesselman, L. McNair, & N. Schniedewind (Eds.), *Women images and realities: A multicultural anthology* (pp. 18-20). Mountain View, CA: Mayfield. (Original work published 1983)

Ruth, S. (1995). *Issues in feminism.* Mountain View, CA: Mayfield.

Schniedewind, N. (1983). Feminist values: Guidelines for a teaching methodology in women's studies. In C. Bunch & S. Pollack (Eds.), *Learning our way: Essays in feminist education* (pp. 261-271). Trumansburg, NY: Crossing.

Shackelford, J. (1992). Feminist pedagogy: A means for bringing critical thinking and creativity to the economics classroom. *Alternative Pedagogies and Economic Education, 82,* 570-576.

Tannen, D. (1990). *You just don't understand: Women and men in conversation.* New York: Ballantine.

Thompson, B., & Disch, E. (1992). Feminist, anti-racist, anti-oppression teaching: Two white women's experiences. *Radical Teacher, 41,* 4-9.

Thorne, B. (1989). Rethinking the ways we teach. In C. Pearson, D. Shavlick, & J. Touchton (Eds.), *Educating the majority: Women challenge tradition in higher education* (pp. 311-325). New York: Macmillan.

Chapter

14

Warming Trends

Improving the Chilly Campus Climate

Mary E. Kite
Deborah Ware Balogh

As the data from women's career studies and anecdotes from personal experiences of women professionals begin to accrue, one of the questions that arises is not "Why are there so few successful professional women?" but rather, "How have so many been able to survive the vicissitudes on each rung of the career ladder?"

Dorothy Zinberg (1973, p. 129)

AUTHORS' NOTE: The order of authorship for this chapter is arbitrary; we contributed equally to the preparation of the work presented here. We wish to thank Associate Dean Donald Van Meter and Dean Ronald Johnstone for their many forms of support of the College of Sciences and Humanities Task Force on the Status of Women, and, especially, former Dean Marjorie Smelstor, now at the University of Wisconsin–Eau Claire, whose vision and leadership made the concerns of women in our college a priority. We also wish to acknowledge the contributions of many supportive colleagues, both members and nonmembers of the task force, who have diligently worked to maintain our college's focus on the institutional climate for women.

Despite steady increases in the number of women obtaining academic positions, women continue to face obstacles that limit their potential for success in the academy (Bentley & Blackburn, 1992; Gallant & Cross, 1993; Ottinger & Sikula, 1993). Even though the number of women in the professoriate has risen to 32% of full-time faculty positions, women still comprise only 15% of full professors and women are less likely to hold tenure than men (Ottinger & Sikula, 1993). Hence, women are gaining admission to the academy but are not advancing at the same rate as their male counterparts. Moreover, a gender-based salary differential favoring men continues to exist at all academic ranks, with the greatest discrepancy occurring at the full-professor rank where, on average, women earn 88.5% of what men earn (Ottinger & Sikula, 1993).

Impediments to academic advancement have traditionally been defined in terms of salary, rate of promotion and tenure, and representation of women in upper administrative positions. Sandler and Hall (1986) used the term "chilly climate" to describe interpersonal and institutional barriers facing women faculty. Within their chilly climate conceptualization, they refer to Rowe's (1977, cited in Sandler & Hall, 1986) assertion that various "micro-inequities" affect the career advancement of women. Micro-inequities consist of day-to-day behaviors reflecting gender, age, and ethnic stereotypes that, in subtle ways isolate, discount, and ignore members of underrepresented groups. The cumulative effect of these behaviors results in an unsupportive work climate that interferes with occupational achievement. If women must continuously direct their attention toward coping with professional isolation and an unsupportive occupational environment, for example, they may have little time for activities that are rewarded by tenure and promotion (Yoder, 1985). This problem may be compounded if men in their departments experience a comparatively hospitable environment; their productivity is thus not compromised by the effects of a chilly campus climate.

Sandler and Hall (1986) examined the effect of the chilly campus climate on faculty women in their summary of various campus commission findings, anecdotal reports from women, and studies of discrimination

---

AUTHORS' NOTE (*continued*): During the preparation of this chapter, we learned of the death of our friend and colleague Bernadette Perham, who served as Chair of the task force for a number of years. Bernadette was a strong advocate for the group and a successful leader. She was also a frequent source of personal support for both of us. We dedicate this chapter to her memory. Correspondence concerning this work may be addressed to either author at the Department of Psychological Science, Ball State University, Muncie, IN 47306.

available in the literature. They presented evidence that women's professional competence is often devalued, that women are denied access to the academic and political networks of their institutions, and that women are often pigeonholed in stereotypic roles. These findings, based largely on the perceptions and observations of women in academic settings, may help to explain how the underrepresentation of women in higher academic ranks can occur.

Several studies confirm Sandler and Hall's (1986) report that women's competence and their contributions in academia are devalued (Clark & Corcoran, 1986; Kahn & Robbins, 1985; Kierstead, D'Agostino, & Dill, 1988; Lott, 1985; Paludi & Strayer, 1985), and there is little evidence that these patterns have changed significantly over time (Caplan, 1994; Gallant & Cross, 1993; Sandler, 1991). Moreover, a complex interaction of factors appears to be associated with differential performance appraisals of women and men. For example, when performance evaluations are conducted in personnel decisions, male raters view male instructors as significantly more effective than female instructors, even though their actual performance is very similar (Dobbins, Cardy, & Truxillo, 1986). This process led Dobbins et al. (1986) to conclude that in the context of personnel decisions, males evaluated by other males may enjoy an unfair advantage and that "such prejudicial evaluation policy could be partially responsible for the 'wage gap' between the salaries of men and women . . . and may result in organizations promoting undeserving men and ignoring competent women" (pp. 236-237). Because males comprise a majority at most academic institutions and are also often the majority in groups making personnel decisions, these findings suggest that many women encounter more formidable obstacles than their male counterparts in pursuing careers.

Repeated findings in various occupational settings, including academic institutions, have shown that women can experience a chilly climate characterized by less support for their scholarship, devaluation of their scholarly contributions, less favorable teaching evaluations, less access to the social and political networks within their academic units, and generally condescending, demoralizing, and harassing interactions with colleagues (see Benokraitis & Feagin, 1995, for a description of some of these studies). These findings prompted us to approach the dean of our college to consider how the college might address such inequities. This discussion led to the formation of a Task Force on the Status of Women to examine these issues at Ball State University. The remainder of this chapter documents the history and evolution of the task force and its mission, our strategies for evaluating and improving the climate for women in the College of Sciences and Humanities, and our successes and failures. This case history provides both anecdotal and objective evidence that should be useful to the many colleges universities that are planning to develop similar groups.

History and Development of the Task Force on the Status on Women

Although to a large extent chilly climate issues are similar across colleges and universities, the mission and structure of individual institutions may vary considerably. We provide some contextual information so readers can judge which of the strategies we used might be adapted to their setting. Ball State University is a comprehensive, state-supported institution of higher education. Academic programs are offered through one of six colleges. Our task force represented the College of Sciences and Humanities, which, with 27 departments, is the largest academic unit on campus. All Ball State students complete a general studies sequence, and most of that sequence is taught by faculty within our college. Thus, regardless of major, students have considerable contact with faculty in our college.

The Task Force on the Status of Women in the College of Sciences and Humanities was convened after the authors approached then Dean Marjorie Smelstor about campus climate issues. The goal of the task force was to find out what, if any, institutional barriers existed that interfered with the career advancement of women within our college. Our task force did not directly address racial/ethnic issues because a separate group was to be convened for that purpose. We believe, however, that the issues we raised apply to other underrepresented groups on campus.

Six women and three men met during the Spring of 1989 to begin addressing the climate for women in our college. The authors served as co-chairs of the original group. Since then, the membership and the tasks and goals of the group have changed. Neither of us is currently a member of the task force for reasons we discuss later. The task force continues to be active, but we summarize here only our experiences as members and leaders of that group.

At its inception, the task force was met with both support and resistance by individuals and administrative units across the campus. We were often applauded for our initiative during informal interactions, but some of our colleagues were unwilling to join the task force. Some faculty simply did not believe that a chilly climate existed at Ball State. Some junior faculty felt they were vulnerable as untenured assistant professors, and therefore could not be associated with a group addressing such a highly politicized agenda. Several senior faculty members, although sensitive to chilly climate issues, already felt overburdened by their many committee responsibilities. Despite these concerns, we were able to convene a group of junior and senior men and women who were committed to addressing the campus climate in our college.

One of our first goals, to collect demographic data regarding salary, rank, and gender, was often viewed suspiciously, and the information was provided only reluctantly. Also, a variety of "turf" issues arose early on. Comments like "The university has already looked at this stuff before," "This is what our Affirmative Action officer does," and "Shouldn't the Women and Gender Studies Program be in charge?" suggested that our goals overlapped those of other campus groups. We responded to this criticism by inviting the campus Affirmative Action Officer and a representative from the Women and Gender Studies Program to join the group. We found it helpful to restate our purpose regularly, to comment on the complementary nature of our college-based mission relative to that of other campuswide groups, and to emphasize the differences between the college task force and those of other campuswide groups. For example, it was useful to portray our mission as exploratory rather than as policy making, to reiterate that we could not speak to the concerns of women in other colleges, and to point out that we were concerned with the work environment for women, not curricular issues. This strategy kept our group focused on its primary goals and helped to prevent our concerns from becoming diluted.

Activities and Findings of the Task Force

Our group's first task was to determine whether women's experiences at Ball State were different from those of men, and whether women perceived less support than did men. We took several approaches to this issue. First, we gathered data from existing sources on salaries, distribution of travel funds, merit-based raises, and distribution of other resources. Second, we developed an 80-item Likert-type scale (called the Quality of Life Survey)

TABLE 14.1 Sample Items From the Quality of Life Survey

I have an opportunity to teach courses in my specialty area.
I have received praise from students for my teaching ability.
Students in my class expect me to lower my performance standards for them.
Students in my class do not call me by the name I use to introduce myself.
I have adequate resources to conduct my scholarly work.
Compared to my colleagues, I have received less than my share of departmental resources for scholarly productivity.
I have been elected to critical (i.e., powerful) departmental committees.
My contribution in committee meetings is not acknowledged.
I am outside the departmental information network.*
My colleagues make seemingly helpful comments to me that imply that I am incompetent.*
My colleagues interrupt me when I am speaking in a meeting.*
The atmosphere in my department is demoralizing.*
My colleagues doubt my professional commitment.*
My colleagues attribute my success to factors other than my ability.*
My colleagues do not speak to me in a condescending manner.*
My salary reflects my ability relative to that of my colleagues at the same rank at Ball State University.

*Items from the Interactions With Colleagues subscale.

to assess faculty views of teaching, service, research activities, the availability of resources, salaries, and interactions with students and colleagues. Table 14.1 presents sample items from this survey.

We pretested the scale with faculty outside our college and then administered the survey to all 298 tenured or tenure-track faculty (242 men and 56 women) within the college during the Fall of 1989. Sixty-two percent of tenured or tenure-line males (n = 151) and 84% of tenured or tenure-line females (n = 45) provided usable data. All responses were anonymous. The data collection and analysis were conducted by an independent survey research center on campus.

University records showed no evidence of gender-based discrimination in the distribution of such resources as salaries, travel funds, and merit increases. We did find, however, that women were underrepresented in most academic departments and that women were overrepresented in contract/

part-time positions. For example, women comprised 43% of full-time contract faculty, yet comprised only 27% of tenured or tenure-track faculty at our university the year the survey was conducted. We also found little evidence that resources, salaries, teaching loads, or contributions to service were *perceived* as inequitable between women and men. Analysis of the 30-item Interactions With Colleagues subscale told a different story, however. This subscale was largely composed of statements that reflected Sandler and Hall's (1986) findings about the chilly campus climate. They also reflected our own experiences and those reported to us by our colleagues. Sample items are noted with an asterisk in Table 14.1.

We analyzed the responses to this subscale in two ways.[1] First, we examined responses collectively to determine if sex of respondent, tenure status, or the interaction of these two variables resulted in differences in the overall pattern of responding. Second, when an overall effect was statistically significant, we examined the data on an item-by-item basis. The presence of a statistically significant effect for sex of respondent indicated less satisfaction among women as compared to men when items were considered collectively. Subsequent analysis yielded significant effects for 23 of the 30 items; women reported more negative interactions with their colleagues than did men on all of these items.

A significant interaction between sex and tenure status also emerged for the items when they were treated collectively. Although women were more likely to report negative experiences than men, untenured women expressed the greatest dissatisfaction. In fact, untenured men expressed the same degree of satisfaction as their tenured male colleagues. We also obtained evidence that sex of respondent and tenure status had a significant, combined effect on responses to 10 of the 30 items. Our findings were remarkably consistent across the items on the Interactions With Colleagues subscale (summarized as subscale total means in Figure 14.1).

Why do female faculty, compared with their male counterparts, report significantly more negative experiences? Although women and men at Ball State enjoyed equitable access to resources after being hired, such parity seems to disappear quickly. From our perspective, this occurs when subtle forms of discrimination, such as a chilly professional climate, result in a devaluation of women's competence that prevents them from sustaining the same level of satisfaction with their work environment as men.

Why do tenured women report more satisfaction with the job climate than untenured women? There are several possible explanations for this finding. One is that now-tenured women may have perceived a chilly climate when

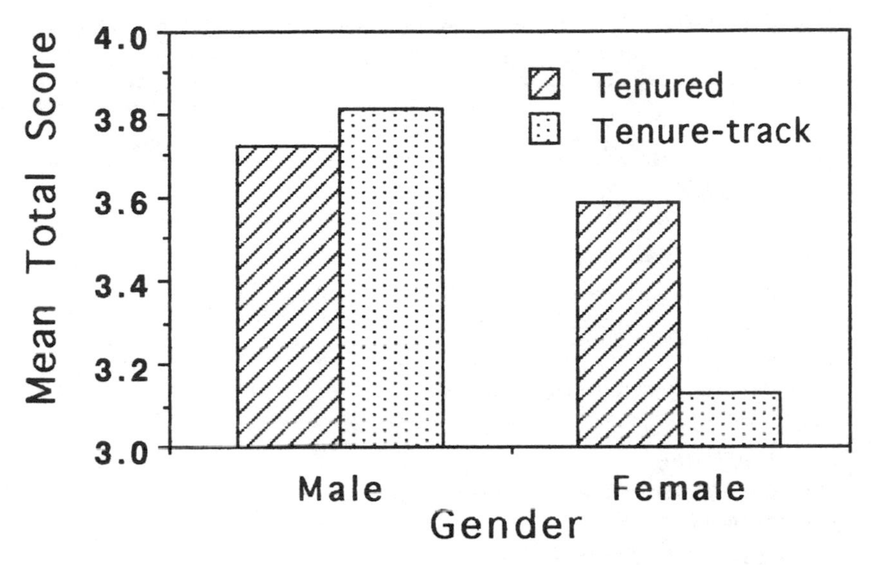

Figure 14.1. Responses of Tenured and Untenured Men and Women to Questions on the 30-Item Interactions With Colleagues Subscale Expressed as Mean Total Scores

first hired, but subsequently adapted and no longer perceive it to be unsatisfying. Another possibility is that the most dissatisfied women have left and those remaining perceive the environment to be more supportive. Finally, it may be that tenured women have been fairly isolated within their departments and simply assume that their career experiences and those of men do not differ. Of course, all three explanations might be operating. Whatever the explanation, tenured women still report more negative experiences than tenured men in this sample, suggesting that surviving a chilly climate does not eliminate it.

A third strategy that we used to evaluate the chilly campus climate involved a survey of the office staff in our college; all office staff who responded were women. We found that in a few departments, women reported a great deal of dissatisfaction related to chilly climate issues. Representative questionnaire items from this survey are presented in Table 14.2.

These results raised a conflict for us, particularly because some office staff had reported serious problems. We had promised these staff members confidentiality and were well aware that any breach of confidentiality could, in fact, make their situation even worse. Having collected the data at all affected some lives; we know, for example, that one chair demanded that his secretary tell him how she had responded. Our goal was to improve any problems, but

TABLE 14.2 Items From the Survey of Office Staff That Indicated Problem Areas for Secretaries

	Percentage Who	
Item	*Agreed*	*Disagreed*
People take unfair advantage of my willingness to do extra work.	40	43
People respect my desk/office space.	57	36
People ask me to do tasks outside my job description.	57	31
People expect me to work overtime and give up breaks.	46	46
People expect me to cover for their mistakes.	67	26
I have been treated very rudely by people in my department.	21	62
People in my department have made sexually suggestive comments to me.	12	86
University procedures protect me from being treated unfairly by my supervisor.	42	35

NOTE: *N* = 44, representing 89% of full-time office staff in the college. Percentages do not add to 100% because neutral responses were excluded.

presenting data that directly spoke to those issues could easily create more problems than it solved. Our group discussed at length how to handle this dilemma and agreed that we could not risk violating confidentiality.

Representatives of the task force presented the data in summary form to the chairs. That meeting was unpleasant for all involved because it raised what one colleague labeled the three reactions to chilly climate data: bafflement, denial, and defensiveness. People, understandably, also wanted to know whether their department was the problem. We also presented the more egregious data to the dean of our college and feel confident that he addressed the problems without compromising individual staff members. Even so, the issues raised are troubling: How does one improve the status of women without at the same time jeopardizing individual women?

Experiencing the Chilly Climate Firsthand

With the data concerning perceptions of a chilly climate for women faculty in hand, we presented our findings to various campus groups, including department chairs within our college, higher-level administrators, and a general campus audience. Response to our results was mixed. Some people readily accepted the data, others were completely silent, and a minority were hostile. In preparing this chapter, we looked at the minutes summarizing one presentation and were surprised to discover that our remarks took up 2 1/2 single-spaced pages of those minutes. Yet reaction to the material was nearly complete silence. Comments in presentations ranged from demands to see our data so the analyses could be checked, to the charge that our survey was "concocted" and the results "home cooked."

Another common criticism was that we did not study departments that had primarily women faculty to examine the effect that the chilly climate had on men. We also received a letter that stated that "I feel discrimination is a fact of life and that the best we can do is prevent those actions which are illegal and unethical." The author of this letter argued that factors other than gender account for our results, stating that our findings might be an artifact of variables such as differences in numbers of doctorates across research areas. Additionally, at least one colleague reacted with an "is-that-all-there-is?" comment, suggesting that it was good to learn that we had found no evidence of legally defined discrimination. The biggest criticism levied against our survey, however, was that we measured perceptions, not behaviors. We think it is fair to say that whenever we presented our data at Ball State, at least one audience member made comments that demonstrated the reality of the chilly climate. A particularly memorable comment was that perceptions of a chilly climate perhaps stemmed from "cat fighting" among women.

We often left such presentations feeling demoralized. Not only were the comments difficult to hear, but they often came from high-level university officials. Our perception that our remarks were discounted was echoed in letters from two administrators, both of whom apologized for their colleagues' behavior and the "chilly climate you encountered." In contrast, when we shared our experiences with the task force, their support renewed our spirits. We concluded that the results of our survey would need to be conveyed in numerous ways by numerous people before we would see any changes. We found it helpful to set realistic expectations about negative reactions as a way of maintaining morale. We compared our small successes to tossing pennies on a pile that would slowly, but steadily, accumulate.

To that end, we and others met with chairs, presenting the findings in different ways. For example, far and away the most successful meeting occurred when we invited students to talk to the chairs about *their* chilly climate experiences. These students, male and female, were members of the College Student Advisory Council and had been selected by the chairs themselves to represent the students in their major. The stories that students reported concerning the chilly climate for women in their classes were heard and taken quite seriously by the chairs. For example, female students reported being told by their professors that papers concerning "feminist issues" would not be acceptable in completing course requirements. The students also described situations in which nontraditional women were questioned about why they were in school rather than at home raising their children. A male student recalled his physics class where men were referred to as "Mr." but women were called by their first names.

Even when such blatant examples were reported by students, some chairs still expressed disbelief that such experiences happened in the 1980s and few recognized the similarities between student and faculty perceptions. Thus, we were successful to the extent that people were discussing the issues. Whether we successfully changed behavior or led chairs to consider the possibility that chilly climate issues affected their own departments, we cannot know. It is important to note, however, that a small group of these chairs, a few years later, proposed that physical contact between faculty and student participants during the graduation ceremony should not be allowed. This proposal, which was accepted by the college, arose in reaction to the practice of some male faculty embracing female degree recipients when they came on stage to receive their diplomas. Also, word of our efforts traveled across campus, and this year faculty members in another college at our institution are planning to evaluate the climate for women in their unit. Finally, we have received numerous requests for information from those at other colleges and universities who are addressing chilly climate issues.[2]

One clearly successful endeavor was bringing Dr. Susan Basow, a psychologist who studies gender bias in teaching evaluations, to our campus. She spoke to academic deans, department chairs, members of college- and department-level promotion and tenure committees, and a general audience. Because good teaching evaluations are imperative at Ball State, her talk was well received. We also believe that our colleagues were more receptive to the chilly climate message underlying Basow's presentation because the messenger was someone external to the university.

Some Political Considerations

University committees rarely operate in a vacuum. For example, they may be charged with responding to legislative questions about faculty workloads, developing curricular offerings that reflect "high tech" innovations in our society, or planning retrenchment strategies because of shrinking budgets. Task forces such as ours are also affected by both budgets and external political climates. In our case, an important issue was the structure of the committee and how it affected our group's work.

One structural issue was that our task force existed at the discretion of the dean of our college. There are both costs and benefits from this arrangement. One major benefit was the financial support we received. This support allowed us to conduct surveys of the faculty and students and to bring in many excellent speakers. As mentioned previously, the advantage of outside speakers is that they can be more frank about controversial issues, but they are typically not perceived as having an ax to grind. Another benefit was having the stated support of the administration of our college. During our tenure, we worked with three deans who were supportive of our efforts both personally and financially. Even so, the task force's objectives were circumscribed when our university, for the first time in recent memory, faced serious budget cuts. Understandably, this limited our dean's ability to support our group financially. He also vetoed other plans to continue our work. We understood our dean's reasons for these decisions. Nonetheless, we were discouraged, and for several months our group's progress effectively stalled because budget issues necessarily took priority.

Our direct link to the Dean's Office also made it difficult, if not impossible, for us to get involved in promotion and tenure appeals that affected individual women at Ball State. As a result, we were criticized in some arenas for "not practicing what we preached." By virtue of our membership on the task force, we were associated with advocating practices and policies that minimize the chilly climate and were therefore expected to have the power to affect negative promotion and tenure decisions involving women across campus. The expectation that we had the power to resolve such disputes was clearly unrealistic, yet it existed and was a significant challenge to our credibility. Despite this dynamic, overall, being connected to the administration had more benefits than liabilities.

We raise these political issues for readers considering a similar group on their campus. A group that is external to the administration may better serve your goals. Some of the turf issues that we raised earlier will also vary depending on the structure of the committee and the scope of its mission. Committees that are university sponsored, whose charge is broadly stated, and whose authority is greater may be more likely to avoid turf battles than our college-based task force, whose mission was relatively narrow and whose authority was limited to our academic unit. Anticipating these issues avoids many problems later.

Another structural issue is that unlike many faculty campus committees, we were appointed rather than elected. We believed that electing members would dilute the effectiveness of the group because at least some of the participants would not be committed to the issues. One down side, however, is that some people across the campus do not take an appointed group seriously, assuming that such a group reflects a view that is not widely relevant on campus. A related issue is that once selected by the dean, a member might continue with the task force yet contribute very little, thereby limiting the task force's effectiveness. Finally, although an appointed committee is beneficial because it permits committed people to remain with the group, such a committee has no mechanism for healthy turnover among members. Thus, there is little opportunity for fresh perspectives and alternative strategies to surface, unless current members elect to be replaced.

A third structural issue concerns the group's leadership. As we mentioned earlier, the chapter authors served first as co-chairs of the task force. We strongly believe in the practice of having co-chairs and in the practice of rotating chairs. This belief was quickly reinforced by our discovery that when we presented the task force's findings to various groups, the issues we raised were often attributed to us personally. In fact, we achieved "lightening rod" status rather quickly. Yet because the messengers varied over time, it became more difficult for others to minimize the task force's message or to attribute it to one or two individuals. Also, on a personal level, it was emotionally draining to be repeatedly on the defensive, as we often found ourselves. Sharing the responsibility for communicating the goals and concerns of the task force by selecting new chairs annually helped to maintain the vitality of the task force.

For reasons linked to these structural issues, we both decided, individually and at different times, to resign from the task force. We did so because we believed the nature of the group's work can easily lead to burnout and that new people bring new ideas and perspectives to any committee. In our particular case, we hoped that new leadership would provide directions for the group that we had not considered but that would be beneficial to the task force. We admit that it was difficult to let go. We worried that the group would not continue without us. We are pleased that the task force is still active and that its membership is at its largest ever.

Conclusion

To conclude, we quote a letter from an academic dean, written in response to one of our presentations:

> The information you brought us was irritating, uncomfortable, and forces us to confront a problem. But the information you brought us was true, and according to the Pearl Theory, we can plan for something beautiful and valuable to grow once the oyster is irritated, uncomfortable, and shaken.

Our task force, and other committees like ours, continues to raise issues that some of our colleagues may not want to hear. At the same time, we provide a voice for women on campus. It is difficult to evaluate our progress from within, but in writing this chapter, we had an opportunity to review our work and see that we had made progress. Our accomplishments included validating women's concerns that a chilly climate existed in our college; provoking discussion among administrators who have the authority to initiate policy changes; and promoting the idea that chilly climate issues are widespread, similarly affecting women in faculty, staff, and student roles. The problems we encountered were similar to those faced by other groups who challenge existing practices that negatively affect underrepresented groups. We close by saying that groups such as ours need support, encouragement, and constructive feedback about their work. As we have noted, the voices of dissent are clearly heard and it is difficult, at times, to hear the voices of consent. We hope you will support others who are taking on these issues and that those of you addressing these questions on your campus are getting the support you need.

Notes

1. A complete summary of the analyses is available on request from the authors. Readers may also request a copy of the Quality of Life Survey.

2. We welcome such requests. Also, two additional documents, which were prepared and distributed by the task force, are available from the authors: "Recommendations for Improving the Quality of Life for Faculty, Staff, and Students" and "A Field Guide for New Faculty."

References

Benokraitis, N. V., & Feagin, J. R. (1995). *Modern sexism: Blatant, subtle, and covert discrimination.* Englewood Cliffs, NJ: Prentice Hall.

Bentley, R., & Blackburn, R. T. (1992). Two decades of gains for female faculty? *Teachers College Record, 93,* 697-709.

Caplan, P. J. (1994). *Lifting a ton of feathers: A woman's guide to surviving the academic world.* Toronto, Canada: University of Toronto Press.

Clark, S. M., & Corcoran, M. (1986). Perspectives on the professional socialization of women faculty: A case of cumulative disadvantage? *Journal of Higher Education, 57,* 20-43.

Dobbins, G. H., Cardy, R. L., & Truxillo, D. M. (1986). Effect of ratee sex and purpose of appraisal on the accuracy of performance evaluations. *Basic and Applied Social Psychology, 7,* 225-241.

Gallant, M. J., & Cross, J. E. (1993). Wayward puritans in the ivory tower: Collective aspects of gender discrimination in academia. *Sociological Quarterly, 34,* 237-256.

Kahn, E. D., & Robbins, L. (Eds.). (1985). Sex discrimination in academe [Special issue]. *Journal of Social Issues, 41*(4).

Kierstead, D., D'Agostino, P., & Dill, H. (1988). Sex role stereotyping of college professors: Bias in students' rating of instructors. *Journal of Educational Psychology, 80,* 342-344.

Lott, B. (1985). The devaluation of women's competence. *Journal of Social Issues, 41*(4), 43-60.

Ottinger, C., & Sikula, R. (1993). Women in higher education: Where do we stand? *ACE Research Briefs, 4,* 1-11.

Paludi, M. A., & Strayer, L. A. (1985). "What's in an author's name?" Differential evaluations of performance as a function of author's name. *Sex Roles, 12,* 353-361.

Sandler, B. R. (1991). Women faculty at work in the classroom, or why it still hurts to be a woman in labor. *Communication Education, 40,* 6-15.

Sandler, B. R., & Hall, R. M. (1986). *The campus climate revisited: Chilly for women faculty, administrators, and graduate students.* Washington, DC: Association of American Colleges, Project on the Status and Education of Women.

Yoder, J. D. (1985). An academic woman as a token: A case study. *Journal of Social Issues, 41*(4), 61-72.

Zinberg, D. (1973). College: When the future becomes the present. In R. B. Kundsin (Ed.), *Women and success: The anatomy of achievement* (pp. 129-137). New York: William Morrow.

Chapter

15

The Cultural Politics of Abuse in Lesbian Relationships

Challenges for Community Action

Janice L. Ristock

> The pain and humiliation of living with violence went deeper than any other hurts that I have experienced. The violation of being abused by a woman I loved has shaken the very roots of my lesbian being. I know that I will never again have the same understanding or faith in womyn or sisterhood or lesbian utopia. I know in my heart today that we are all children of this violent patriarchy, and that our healing of ourselves, one another, and this planet is far more complicated than I ever imagined.
>
> *Istar (1986, p. 163)*

Discourse about the nature of women's sexuality as passive, submissive, and frequently masochistic abounds in popular culture and society at large, maintaining, as feminists argue, misogynist misrepresentations about women (see, e.g., MacKinnon, 1992; Segal, 1992; Vance, 1992). Predictably, then, in this sexist environment, most representations of lesbian sexuality in North American popular culture reinforce negative notions of lesbianism. Our knowledge is fraught with demeaning stereotypes of (so-called) "mannish" women who hate men and who are more than likely "radical feminists." Until recently, North American constructions of lesbians have been blatantly and uniformly homophobic. These representations have not just been found in popular culture but in formal institutions: Religious groups have presented lesbians as sinful; the psychology professions, as sick; and some U.S. states outlaw sex between women and withhold basic human rights entitlement (such as freedom from discrimination in employment and housing). It is no wonder, then, that very few lesbians have been inclined to acknowledge publicly their sexual identities, let alone disclose their experiences of abuse in intimate relationships.

Lesbians in Popular Culture

Despite widespread current homophobic attacks by the Religious Right, homophobia is less straightforwardly the rule than before. We point to many fronts where progress has been made, both in how lesbians have been represented and in the achievement of more rights (e.g., as I write this, Canada's parliament has at last written sexual orientation into the country's Human Rights Code, a code comparable to the U.S. Bill of Rights). Popular culture, too, seems less rigidly heterosexist in its scripts for women's lives. One example is showing lesbian possibilities in "female buddy films" during the 1990s. As epitomized by box office successes such as *Boys on the Side, Thelma & Louise, Fried Green Tomatoes,* and *Leaving Normal,* these films portray women as (asexually?) bonding with one another and rallying against male violence.

Less welcome is the reemergence of the powerful but murderous femme fatale of films such as *Fatal Attraction, The Hand That Rocks the Cradle,* and *Basic Instinct.* The twist in *Basic Instinct* is that the blonde bombshell is a lesbian. I will focus in some detail on these films to sketch in one representative piece of the social backdrop against which lesbian lives are lived. The popular view of lesbians as sick, unhappy, or homicidal shows how homophobia continues to make it difficult for lesbians in abusive relationships to ask for help or to get the help they deserve.

The "psycho-femmes" in these recent films elicit a different response from the male characters who usually dominate sexy, blonde females. Men in psycho-femme films are intrigued, often frightened, and always controlled by these dangerously powerful women. Despite their provision of truly leading roles for female actors—a clear step forward—these films still point to the continued homophobia and misogyny (not to mention racism as evident in the predominance of white characters) operating in mainstream Hollywood. No new messages about women's sexualities are being developed in this narrative discourse.

Reactions to these 1990s Hollywood films are varied and complex. Some women and some gays and lesbians like the characters in these films. They see the female buddies, and even the psycho-femmes, as a positive development, showing women as sexually aggressive, independent, strong, and capable—forces to be reckoned with. In addition, many see the mere inclusion of gay and lesbian characters in mainstream films as a step forward. Others view these films as more of the same old song—misogyny and heterosexism—but with a subtler beat.

Female Buddy Films

Three recent female buddy films—*Leaving Normal, Fried Green Tomatoes,* and *Thelma & Louise*—have a common plot in which women bond in response to male violence. In *Leaving Normal,* we meet Marianne, a 27-year-old, hysterical woman who has been married twice and is being brutalized by her current husband. She hits the road, meeting Darly, a tough, world-weary waitress, and they head off for Alaska. Similarly, *Fried Green Tomatoes* is a story set in the 1930s about two women, Idgie and Ruth, who open the Whistle Stop Cafe in Alabama. Life-long friends, they first bonded when Idgie—described as a daredevilish tomboy—rescues Ruth from an abusive, physically violent marriage. Finally, *Thelma & Louise,* the most popular film of the three, is a story of two women on the run for murder. Louise, discovering Thelma being raped in a parking lot, shoots the attacker. Together the two women travel across the southern states, their friendship intensifying while they elude the police.

The messages from this new genre of female buddy films seem to be contradictory. On the one hand, each film shows women responding to male violence, taking control of their lives, and benefiting from the friendship of other women. *Thelma & Louise* has apparently had a far-reaching effect on many women's lives. It has been called a feminist film; there have been presentations about the characters at women's studies conferences. A presentation at the 1992 National Women's Studies Association conference in Austin, Texas, was titled "*Thelma & Louise:* Feminist Education Shifts Hollywood's Portrayal of Women." The characters became role models of sorts for their response to male violence. T-shirts were sold that proudly proclaim "Graduate of the Thelma and Louise finishing school," a blunt warning to any man who has seen or heard about the film.

The film has also been accused of promoting man-hating. Some observers argue that such changes demonstrates male fear of losing control over women's sexuality when women bond; two women together is seen not as an affirmation of same-sex love but as a rejection of heterosexuality. Living independently from men is linked to man-hating. Man-hating in turn is equated with lesbianism. These films, then, are evidence of Lindsay Van Gelder's (1992) suggestion that lesbians in our society receive all of its generalized fears of what it would be like if women cut off their focus on men. The homophobia may be less blatant than before, but the message prevails.

Thelma and Louise must die at the end if they are autonomous and resist male control. A further interpretation of this ending is that they commit suicide because women loving women is itself, ultimately, unviable and self-destructive. Idgie and Ruth, and Darly and Marianne can be happy in their relationships—but they cannot be sexual. The invisibility—or impossibility—of lesbian sexuality in these films may in part be a way to temper male anxieties about not having control over women's sexualities. Although it is difficult to prove that fictional buddies are lesbian lovers who are desexualized for some audience-appeasing box-office motive, we should note that in the novel *Fried Green Tomatoes at the Whistle Stop Cafe* by Fannie Flagg (1987), it is clear that Idgie and Ruth have a sexual relationship. Furthermore, the film *Leaving Normal* had the potential to show Marianne and Darly as lovers, but instead falls short with a contrived ending disclaiming any lesbian content to their ardent embraces and passionate devotion.

Thus, the heterosexist and misogynist messages conveyed by these films, and ironically by the portrayal of female friendship, is that lesbians do not (cannot) exist; when women love women they are asexual. In those rare occasions when lesbians are depicted, their characters are warped, even malevolent. According to Van Gelder (1992), "In the thirty years that the motion picture code has allowed depictions of lesbians at all, most images have involved either homicidal women or their flip side, suicides" (p. 82). A recent example of this continued trend can be seen in the psycho-femme film *Basic Instinct.*

Psycho-Femme Films

Basic Instinct has been described as a 1990s film that deals with women's changing sexuality by showing sexually aggressive women and by explicitly addressing lesbianism. The three central characters are Nick, a San Francisco cop investigating a murder; Catherine, the bisexual woman whom Nick becomes involved with; and Catherine's girlfriend Roxy, the "true" lesbian in the film. Although both women are attractive, intelligent, successful, and sexually "exotic," they are also ice-pick-wielding "killer dykes." Needless to say, there has been a great deal of debate about this film and its depiction of women's sexualities.

Once again, the messages are contradictory. On the one hand, some women like the in-control, sexually assertive characters and see them as a satisfying flip of the old porn cliché of male voyeurism about lesbian sex: In this film the lesbian watches, not the man. On the other hand, gay and lesbian activists have boycotted this film for what they see as its blatant homophobia. Richard Goldstein (1992) in an article for *The Village Voice,* "Base Instinct," discusses Hollywood as a contradictory liberal institution. Many actors, directors, and producers are gay and lesbian, and Hollywood sports red ribbons in support of AIDS, yet at the same time it produces a film with "man-haters with ice-pick dicks . . . [who] may actually quiet the anxieties of heterosexuals" (p. 37). That is, as in the female buddy pictures, *Basic Instinct* reasserts the rightful dominance of men/heterosexuality by showing sexually assertive women/lesbians as homicidal (i.e., "abnormal").

The ignorance and denial of gay and lesbian experience is common. Research on gay bashing (Comstock, 1991; Herek & Berrill, 1992) indicates that gays and lesbians, like other minorities, are often presented as preying on society or trying to recruit new members. This in turn is seen as a justification for violence against them (Van Gelder, 1992). Furthermore, lesbians have long been typecast as "mannish murderers or dragon ladies" (Faderman, 1988). For example, a great deal of media attention has been given to the trial of Aileen (Lee) Wuornos, a Florida prostitute accused of murdering five johns, sensationalizing her as a lesbian serial killer. My own local newspaper in Winnipeg had this to say about Wuornos: "Detectives found that Aileen had a long criminal record, which included disorderly conduct, armed robbery and prostitution. She was the constant companion of Tyria, whom she referred to as her wife. Authorities soon found out that the pair were lesbian lovers, who hung around rough tough bars in the

Daytona area" (Haines, 1992, p. 24). Rather than being interested in why and how a woman who suffered a great deal of abuse throughout her life took on a more typically male predatory pattern, the media has focused on her sexuality as an "explanation" of her actions.

Van Gelder's (1992) analysis of the media's view suggests that "lesbians are [presented as] male-violence wanabees who can only pathetically aspire to the real thing—what might be called the Dildo Theory of Serial Murder" (p. 80). Thus, the recent focus on women's sexualities in films and the responses in the media and popular culture reflect what Durbin and others have come to see as a heterosexual crisis: "This is a crisis provoked by feminism and augmented by gay liberation, a crisis of power and legitimacy. Who has the power now that it's not all on one side? And what is legitimate now that our notions of bad women and good, normal and deviant, of male and female are crumbling?" (Durbin, 1992, p. 48). The many contradictory messages within the films and the public's reaction can be understood as symptoms of a crisis in heterosexuality. This means that even though depictions of lesbians and woman may be similar to those seen in more solidly heterosexual moments in history (Faderman, 1988; Van Gelder, 1992), the social context affecting audience reception is shifting.

Abuse in Lesbian Relationships

I have presented a sketch of some recent films and commented on two predominant themes—the denial of lesbianism, on the one hand, and the view of lesbians as pathological, on the other—to help bring the social backdrop of lesbian lives into focus. Any lesbian who comes out has to negotiate her social status in this context of a popular culture that represents and misrepresents lesbians. But the effect of this social backdrop is perhaps most felt by lesbians who have been abused in relationships. The issue of violence in a lesbian relationship plays resoundingly into dominant discourses in popular culture that represent lesbians as masochistic, really like men (as is the reaction to the lesbian serial killer), or sick.

Although violence in lesbian relationships has been discussed openly within feminist and lesbian circles since the early 1980s, intense debate about the dangers of acknowledging this issue continues within lesbian communities. Breaking the silence about this form of abuse remains very difficult for individuals living with it and for researchers. Very few empirical studies have examined the extent and nature of violence in lesbian relationships. Those that do exist recognize that it is a problem that deserves further attention and reveal that all forms of abuse (e.g., physical, sexual, emotional, and economic) can occur in abusive lesbian relationships (Lie & Gentlewarrier, 1991; Renzetti, 1992; Ristock, 1991).

Although recent research suggests that abuse may more often take a nonphysical rather than a physical form, battered lesbians who have experienced both report that the emotional abuse and diminished self-esteem are often more difficult to endure than painful physical injuries (Hammond, 1989; Hart 1986; Lockhart, White, Causby, & Isaac, 1994). The need for more work in this area is evident. Yet researchers face a serious problem: We cannot simply build on previous literature and deal with a particular issue in abusive lesbian relationships (as is the case in research on abuse in heterosexual intimate relationships) without having our work misread.

Such misrepresentations do not arise only from our dominant culture's patriarchal heterosexism; feminist discourses contribute their own misrecognition and misrepresentation. That being said, my own understanding of abuse in lesbian relationships is congruent with a feminist analysis of violence. The same abuses of power, ownership, and control can exist in lesbian relationships as in heterosexual relationships because of the systemic and institutionalized forms of dominance in our society.

A feminist analysis of violence against women in intimate relationships often assumes a male perpetrator and sees the roots of violence in misogyny and patriarchy (Kelly, 1988; Koss et al., 1994). Male gender and its relation to violence is often the focus rather than power and its relation to gender (Holloway, 1996). The analysis creates a situation where lesbian abuse is either seen as impossible or the lesbian perpetrator comes to be seen as male-like for the analysis to fit. Similarly, there is often a reverse discourse within feminism that valorizes lesbians and lesbian relationships as untouched by patriarchal forces (Ristock, 1991). Despite some gains in our understanding (many new texts on violence against women include a chapter addressing abuse in lesbian relationships), abused lesbians continue to fear that no one will believe them, particularly because lesbian relationships have been presented as utopian by some strains of feminism (Hart, 1986; Lockhart et al., 1994). As a result, many abused lesbians tend not to report their abuse to other lesbians, let alone police, shelter workers, or counselors.

Despite much trepidation about speaking out on the issue, lesbian groups in various communities are trying to dispel some of the common misconceptions about lesbians and abusive relationships. For example, blatant heterosexist misconceptions include seeing lesbian relationships as mimicking heterosexual relationships and assuming that abuse only occurs in "butch/femme" relationships where the butch is the batterer and the femme is the victim. More subtle misconceptions (that are just as harmful) may see violence as occurring only in nonfeminist lesbian relationships (Chesley, MacAulay, & Ristock, 1992; Elliot, 1990) or see all lesbians as feminists.

Many other writings about lesbians' experiences in abusive relationships highlight the silence and the shame that victims feel and the impact of a heterosexist social context that discourages them from talking freely about their lives (e.g., Chrystos,1991; Lobel, 1986). In my own survey research, testimonies from responses to open-ended questions clearly show how homophobia and heterosexism are part of lesbians' experiences of abuse:

> Her shame in being lesbian was strong and I was sexually, physically and emotionally abused on numerous occasions for being a "proud lesbian" . . . the wounds from this relationship went very deep for they were inflicted on my identity, as well as on my sexuality. I'm too embarrassed to relate the impacts of abuse on my sex life, but I can say that I went back to the closet for 2 years. Although I'm now working my way to being a "proud lesbian," I honestly don't know if I'll ever be able to completely reclaim such a label. (And this is almost 8 years after the fact.) I guess I'm saying that the homophobia that one is left having to deal with is one of the most painful and persistent things that I've ever encountered.

Sexuality, then, is often central to the experience of abuse, which means we cannot simply see lesbian abuse as the same as heterosexual abuse. Lesbians will only be able to reveal the pain (never mind the joy) in our lives when constraining heterosexist discourses, both mainstream and feminist, are unsettled.

Acknowledging and understanding the existence of abuse in lesbian relationships and raising consciousness about lesbian sexuality require a paradigm shift, dislodging the dominant heterosexist, racist, and misogynist world order. But they also require that we resist seeing heterosexual battering as the framework for explaining all abusive intimate relationships (Ristock, 1994). We know comparatively little about the dynamics of abusive lesbian relationships or about the role of women as perpetrators of violence in intimate relationships with partners, children, and elderly relatives (Carlson, 1992). For example, some abused lesbians have felt constrained by the dominant feminist analysis of gender inequities and power and control as the key components of violent relationships. One woman, from my interview research project, wrote to me about her different interpretation of control:

> People say abuse is a matter of control, and that's true. But it isn't control in the sense of her saying "do this" and then I do it. It's much more complicated than that. It's to do with both of you being controlled by her emotional agenda—her lack of control. So always she feels like a victim of her pain and anger. If she isn't in control of herself, then, she thinks, who is? Who else but her lover? So she has to fight to wrest this control away from you. But you don't have it, so it doesn't work. She feels more and more powerless, less and less in control. At the same time there is, at least, the emotional catharsis of being able to let out the anger and pain. Even if it's toward the wrong object, this release, I think, becomes addictive to her. Both of you are trapped by this in the end.

Seen through the lenses of a heteronormative analysis of abuse (one that keeps heterosexual experiences as the norm), this description might conjure up an abusive male role and a manipulated female role as the actors that form this couple. These gendered assumptions might apply in no way to how these two women live their lives or imagine their relationships, however. If we leave gender differences aside, we see a richly evoked scene not at all central to gendered analyses of abuse but perhaps pivotal to lesbian experience. Learning to expect differences, then, between heterosexual and same-sex dynamics, is an important step in dislodging misrepresentations of lesbians and, in this case, of learning more about lesbian abuse and asymmetries of power in lesbian relationships. For example, Sandra Butler, a lesbian, feminist therapist writes:

> If a heterosexual woman walked in and said she was in a battering relationship, I'd assume I knew what she meant, and 98% of the time I'd be right. If a lesbian said the same thing, I'd have to ask a bunch of questions before I knew what she was talking about. (as reported by Kaye/Kantrowitz, 1992, p. 34)

Butler's comments point to the difficulties we have had in responding to, naming, defining, talking about, and giving meaning to lesbian abuse. Often, we are fearful that we will add to the negative stereotypes about lesbians or that we will disrupt feminist theorizing that we have developed about male violence against women. Many tensions have erupted over how we understand the etiology of this form of violence. Shelters that have been leaders in the battered women's movement have often been reluctant to respond to abuse in lesbian relationships. Often, they are worried about the homophobic responses of other residents in the shelter, and they struggle with not always knowing who should be able to use the shelter—should the perpetrator as well as the victim be allowed? Because it is not readily apparent who the perpetrator is, issues of safety also arise (Eaton, 1994; Irvine, 1990). We seem to get stuck, then, in our theorizing and action because of the limited discourses that are available to us to talk about and understand this type of violence.

Paying attention to the discursive conditions (including how the language practices of dominant culture benefit some people and marginalize others) that affect our organizing efforts is one way that might help us "unfreeze" the political chill that often blocks work in this area. This is part of a strategy we used in our local organizing efforts to address abuse in lesbian relationships.

Using Discourse Analysis to See Subtle Sexism

My research and community organizing experiences suggest that we cannot understand abuse in lesbian relationships using current theories of violence that are based exclusively on heterosexual relationships and male perpetrators (Ristock, 1994; Ristock & Pennell, 1996). Some of the women whom I have interviewed in my research have described being abused in one relationship and being abusive in another; others have reported that their relationship is mutually abusive.[1] Many feminists have interpreted these claims as examples of false consciousness in the sense that many women are often initially unable to consciously acknowledge the abuse that they are experiencing. In my mind, however, self-reports raise serious questions about the limitations of our constructions of abuse. For example, how do our assumptions about the causes and effects of violence, about the perpetrators and victims of it, shape our research and analysis?

In asking this question, I am turning to analytical practices such as *deconstruction* (taking apart social categories as a way of seeing how one's world is constructed) and *discourse analysis* (examining language and ideologies as a way of understanding how meanings are produced) and their implications for theorizing violence. Often, the theories that we have developed to explain violence prevent us from thinking creatively about this issue. Discourse analysis, in contrast, allows us to look at how language operates to sustain oppressive practices.

For example, "battering" is a thoroughly constructed notion that excludes lesbian abuse from its dominant definitions (Ristock, 1991, 1994; Ristock & Pennell, 1996). Seeing how the concept of battering is constructed does not in any way lessen the effect of being battered. At the same time, deconstructing the category "battering" can move us past existing definitions and their dangerous social consequences. For example, most lesbians do not seek help in abusive relationships because our current constructions of battering include only heterosexuals (Ristock, 1994). Focusing on how categories and social relations are constructed by language offers greater insight in understanding and changing behavior. Discourse analysis, then, can be an effective tool that allows us to see other routes for social action. I think it is particularly useful for seeing the ways that subtle oppressive relations work. The effect of these kinds of analyses became very clear through work I was engaged in with a committee in Winnipeg called CLOSE (Coalition of Lesbians on Support and Education).

The Politics of Responding to Abuse: The CLOSE Project

A group of lesbian service providers (CLOSE) formed in Winnipeg, Manitoba (a prairie city of about 650,000 in central Canada) to discuss a range of issues having to do with lesbian abuse and the relatively subtle forms of homophobia and heterosexism found in social services. We applied for and received federal funding from Health Canada for a 1-year project called Training and Education: Responding to Abuse in Lesbian Relationships. The project involved conducting a needs assessment of lesbians and shelter workers (including those working in second-stage houses where battered women can stay for a longer period of time after leaving the shelter) in Manitoba around the issues of homophobia and heterosexism and, more specifically, abuse in lesbian relationships. Based on the outcome of the needs assessment, we designed and implemented a 3-day training program for shelter/second-stage housing workers. We designed a project that in our view was consistent with feminist participatory research (see also Renzetti, 1995) and that had an empowerment philosophy. By that we meant that we were committed to a project that would raise consciousness, develop solidarity, and promote action (Ristock & Pennell, 1996). We designed our project so that it would attend to lesbians' experiences of abuse and the difficulties they faced in accessing services. At the same time we wanted to understand the realities of shelter workers and their working conditions in a range of geographic locations (rural, northern, urban).

We designed our documentation of current conditions to feed into an action component: a training session for shelter workers that would be designed based on the information that we gained from the needs assessment with both lesbians and shelter worker communities. Our research was to be a pedagogical project where we would try to represent lesbians in ways different from the demeaning or limiting characterizations in popular culture.

We used a combination of a public forum, focus groups with established lesbian groups, and surveys in lesbian communities throughout Manitoba as a way to try and reach as many lesbians as possible. We reached 53 lesbians in our short time frame. This number was certainly far lower than we had hoped but perhaps is indicative of the difficulties that still exist in coming forward to speak about these issues. We worked with the Manitoba Association of Women's Shelters (MAWS) and were able to interview two staff members (one front-line worker and one director) from 11 shelters in Manitoba as well as distribute surveys for any other staff member who wanted to respond. We heard from a total of 36 shelter workers.

In developing our training intervention, it became clear that we needed to pay attention to discursive as well as material conditions if our education on lesbian abuse, homophobia, and heterosexism was to have a significant effect on a shelter's service delivery. Many of the barriers mentioned by lesbians were in fact subtle: Typically, the services assumed heterosexuality rather than blatant antilesbian treatment:[2]

> It's like you don't exist.

> We get the feeling that our needs aren't being met as lesbians; there isn't an acknowledgment of our existence.

> We are not seen as part of the public, we're just on talk shows.

The invisibility here parallels the theme of invisibility/impossibility in recent Hollywood films. However benign or pointed the motive for omitting lesbians, invisibility is a frustrating and painful experience:

> Ignorance is brutal. It's irritating to explain to someone your sexual orientation and what it means.

> We're tired of educating service providers; they don't know what it means to be lesbian. And then service providers can't refer you because they don't know the issues or the resources.

> It's hard to talk about lesbian abuse when they [service providers] haven't dealt with lesbianism.

Yet in contrast, most respondents to our shelter survey suggested that lesbians were welcome to use the services of shelters and residential second-stage housing programs, because their mandate is to provide services to all abused women. This mandate is firmly rooted in an ideologically liberal and supposedly nondiscriminatory view. None of the services, however, specifically named lesbians as being welcome in their brochures, nor were they included as part of their public education or outreach work. For that matter, there were no "out" lesbians (lesbians who were open about their sexual orientation) on staff at any of the Manitoba shelters. The following comments from the needs assessment of our final report (Balan, Chorney, & Ristock, 1995) reflect the view of many shelters that their use of language was adequate and inclusive. Therefore, their approach to addressing violence was not viewed as heterosexist or racist. Yet their comments also show their awareness of how homophobia in the larger community had an effect on them:

> It [our service mandate and brochure] doesn't specifically ever say that we welcome lesbians, which I think is a product of where we are and general feelings and homophobia that runs in our communities surrounding us.

> If they came in they would be treated the same as everyone else. I have to admit that if we did make it explicit that lesbians are welcome in our area we would probably not be around very long.

> In our brochures and forms it's inclusive language in the sense that we don't refer to the abuser as male. But I think that the language we use as staff when talking to women, I think we often make a real assumption that the abuser is male.

Heterosexism is fairly subtle in shelters; these are not likely locations for blatant antilesbian feeling or talk. Yet these comments reflect the way that discourses within shelters (and other services) based on male violence against women make lesbian experiences or identities hard to hear while not blatantly repressing or forbidding their articulation (Alcoff & Gray, 1993). More important, the comments show that the needs assessment was a consciousness-raising tool in itself: Shelter workers were beginning to see how their language choices, though meant to be nondiscriminatory, were in fact influenced by the surrounding homophobic communities in which they worked. We sustained our attention to discourses within shelters in the training component of our work with them. Our approach to training incorporated lesbians' experiences, and their multiple voices. Some of the comments indicate that we perhaps created an opening in their thinking:

> I know that for other parts of our service, until staff had training . . . or developed their own comfort level with different parts of our services that are offered . . . it's almost like once we have that in place, then the women will approach us. We are the ones that need to have training. We need to develop an awareness here as staff in order for it to be a safe place for lesbians to come.

> While I feel I have a fairly good understanding of the above issues, I believe that this will be an ongoing learning process which will help me in the work I do, but also ensure that I and my staff receive ongoing training in abuse in lesbian relationships and how our services can be made accessible.

These examples show that we needed to reveal to participants the subtle workings of homophobia and heterosexism. Shelters do their work with good intentions and feel that they are actively responding to male violence against women. Our project was able to show that despite their good intentions they were not doing enough to address lesbian abuse or to ensure that lesbians would feel welcome in their services. They could not stop at simply seeing lesbians as being "the same" as heterosexual women. Our intervention helped to alter their services and practices. At the same time, I became aware of how constructing the category of lesbian abuse within shelters, running a special training workshop, and developing specialized brochures could contribute to the false compartmentalizing of experiences of abuse: lesbian abuse/heterosexual abuse/women of color abuse/women with disabilities abuse. In other words, a subtle effect of naming lesbian abuse is that it can mean we see issues facing lesbians and those issues facing women of color as separate, special cases, while keeping heterosexual and white women's issues as the norm and at the forefront. This leaves the status quo solidly in place, instantly ready to subsume issues of homophobia, heterosexism, and racism into a framework that sees all women as the same:

> The issue would be that there's violence and safety. It wouldn't matter whether she was lesbian or Native [Aboriginal], so it really hasn't been an issue here. If a woman came who was lesbian, we would deal with her the same as we would deal with any other female.

Differences are ignored and subtle forms of discrimination are perpetuated. But in educating about differences, the challenge is to have shelters not only respond to lesbian abuse but to see how the intersection of oppressions operates and affects their service delivery (Crenshaw, 1992).

We know how important language has been to the feminist, antiviolence movement; how important it has been to name experiences like sexual harassment accurately; to move beyond euphemisms like spousal violence to woman abuse. At the same time we have to see the area of lesbian abuse as an opportunity to disrupt and transform our thinking about violence even further. We have to be willing to ask new questions: What is the connection between this form of violence and other forms of violence against women; other forms of violence where women are perpetrators? What is the connection between abuse in lesbian relationships and abuse in gay male relationships? Should we focus on identity categories like gender or sexual orientation to break down the broad category of violence and understand it? These questions, we hope, will begin to address more central and specific issues as we work to unmask subtle forms of sexism, heterosexism, and racism and all of their interconnections that may limit our social change efforts despite our best intentions.

I raise these questions in the hopes that we can be open to taking into account lesbian specificity in domestic violence (Eaton, 1994; Ristock, 1994). As I write this chapter, *People* magazine has done a cover story on Olympic diver Greg Louganis, who talks about his abusive male lover; *OUT* magazine has done a story called "Murder at the Lizzie Borden Inn" about a lesbian, Andrea Martin, who stabbed her lover and is now using the battered woman syndrome as a defense strategy. Amanda Bearse, who plays the nonlesbian next door neighbor Marcy D'Arcy in the sitcom "Married . . . With Children," has publicly come out as a lesbian and revealed that she was physically abused in her lesbian relationship. Another female buddy film, *Boys on the Side,* with Whoopi Goldberg playing the lesbian, follows a familiar theme of lesbian impossibility. The based-on-a-true-story Australian film, *Heavenly Creatures,* shows two young girls, lovers, brutally kill one of their mothers as another example of our culture's appetite for the psycho-femme/killer dyke plot. Ready or not, we have been moved beyond the discussion of how to respond to relationship violence from within the "safety" of lesbian communities. I suggest that we look closely at the construction of lesbian abuse in our feminist theorizing and in our educational and social action to help us move beyond some of the subtle and not-so-subtle heterosexism that has made it, at times, difficult to do this work.

Notes

1. My interview research project has been made possible through grants provided by the Lesbian Health Fund of the American Association of Physicians for Human Rights and from the University of Manitoba/Social Sciences and Humanities Research Council of Canada.

2. The following comments are taken from the needs assessment, as written in our final report (Balan, Chorney, & Ristock, 1995). They come primarily from focus groups, interviews, and the training evaluation forms. The comments reflect common themes that were recorded by the project coordinators.

References

Alcoff, L., & Gray, L. (1993). Survivor discourse: Transgression or recuperation? *Signs: Journal of Women in Culture and Society, 18,* 260-290.

Balan, A., Chorney, R., & Ristock, J. L. (1995). *Training and education project for responding to abuse in lesbian relationships. Final report,* (Project No. 4887-07-93-011). Ottawa: Health Canada.

Carlson, B. E. (1992). Questioning the party line on family violence. *Affilia, 7*(2), 94-110.

Chesley, L. C. , MacAulay, D., & Ristock, J. L. (1992). *Abuse in lesbian relationships: A handbook of information and resources.* Toronto: Toronto Counselling Centre for Lesbians and Gays.

Chrystos. (1991). *Dream on.* Vancouver, BC: Press Gang.

Comstock, G. D. (1991). *Violence against lesbians and gay men.* New York: Columbia University Press.

Crenshaw, K. (1992). Whose story is it anyway? Feminist and antiracist appropriations of Anita Hill. In T. Morrison (Ed.), *Race-ing justice, en-gendering power* (pp. 402-441). New York: Pantheon.

Durbin, K. (1992, June). Psychofemmes. *Mirabella,* pp. 44-48.

Eaton, M. (1994). Abuse by any other name: Feminism, difference, and intralesbian violence. In M. Fineman & R. Mykitiuk (Eds.), *The public nature of private violence: The discovery of domestic abuse* (pp. 195-224). New York: Routledge.

Elliot, P. (Ed.). (1990). *Confronting lesbian battering.* St. Paul: Minnesota Coalition for Battered Women.

Faderman, L. (1988). *Odd girls and twilight lovers: A history of lesbian life in twentieth century America.* New York: Columbia University Press.

Flagg, F. (1987). *Fried green tomatoes at the Whistle Stop Cafe.* New York: McGraw-Hill.

Goldstein, R. (1992, April). Base instinct. *The Village Voice, 8*(14), 37-41.

Haines, M. (1992, May 24). Only female serial killer in the U.S. *Winnipeg Sun,* p. 24.

Hammond, N. (1989). Lesbian victims of relationship violence. *Women and Therapy, 8,* 89-105.

Hart, B. (1986). Lesbian battering: An examination. In K. Lobel (Ed.), *Naming the violence* (pp. 173-190). Seattle, WA: Seal.

Herek, G. M., & Berrill, K. T. (Eds.). (1992). *Hate crimes: Confronting violence against lesbians and gay men.* Newbury Park, CA: Sage.

Holloway, W. (1996). Gender and power in organizations. In B. Fawcett, B. Featherstone, J. Hearn, & C. Toft (Eds.), *Violence and gender relations: Theories and interventions* (pp. 72-81). London: Sage.

Irvine, J. (1990). Lesbian battering: The search for shelter. In P. Elliot (Ed.), *Confronting lesbian battering* (pp. 25-30). St. Paul: Minnesota Coalition for Battered Women.

Istar, A. (1986). The healing comes slowly. In K. Lobel (Ed.), *Naming the violence* (pp. 163-169). Seattle, WA: Seal.

Kaye/Kantrowitz, M. (1992). *The issue is power.* San Francisco: Aunt Lute Books.

Kelly, L. (1988). *Surviving sexual violence.* Minneapolis: University of Minnesota Press.

Koss, M. P., Goodman L. A., Browne, A., Fitzgerald, L., Puryear Ketia, G., & Russo, N. F. (1994). *No safe haven: Male violence against women at home, at work, and in the community.* Washington, DC: American Psychological Association.

Lie, G., & Gentlewarrier, S. (1991). Intimate violence in lesbian relationships: Discussion of survey findings and practice implications. *Journal of Social Service Research, 15,* 41-59.

Lobel, K. (Ed.). (1986). *Naming the violence.* Seattle, WA: Seal.

Lockhart, L. L., White, B. W., Causby, V., & Isaac, A. (1994). Letting out the secret: Violence in lesbian relationships. *Journal of Interpersonal Violence, 9,* 469-492.

MacKinnon, C. (1992). Sexuality. In H. Crowley & S. Himmelweit (Eds.), *Knowing women: Feminism and knowledge* (pp. 114-117). Cambridge, MA: Polity.

Renzetti, C. M. (1992). *Violent betrayal.* Newbury Park, CA: Sage.

Renzetti, C. M. (1995). Studying partner abuse in lesbian relationships: A case for the feminist participatory research model. In C. Tully (Ed.), *Lesbian social services: Research issues*. New York: Haworth.

Ristock, J. L. (1991). Beyond ideologies: Understanding abuse in lesbian relationships. *Canadian Women's Studies, 12,* 74-81.

Ristock, J. L. (1994). And justice for all? . . . The social context of legal responses to abuse in lesbian relationships. *Canadian Journal of Women and the Law, 7,* 415-430.

Ristock, J. L., & Pennell, J. (1996). *Community research as empowerment: Feminist links, postmodern interruptions*. Toronto: Oxford University Press.

Segal, L. (1992). Sensual uncertainty or why the clitoris is not enough. In H. Crowley & S. Himmelweit (Eds.), *Knowing women: Feminism and knowledge* (pp. 117-131). Cambridge, MA: Polity.

Vance, C. (1992). Social construction theory: Problems in the history of sexuality. In H. Crowley & S. Himmelweit (Eds.), *Knowing women: Feminism and knowledge* (pp. 132-146). Cambridge, MA: Polity.

Van Gelder, L. (1992). Attack of the killer lesbians. *Ms., 2,* 80-82.

Chapter

16

Comparable Worth

When Do Two Jobs Deserve the Same Pay?

Carolyn J. Aman
Paula England

> In an office I used to have before the lab moved to this hospital, we had windows and I would look outside and I would see a fellow out there mowing a lawn, raking leaves, and he was paid $300 to $500 more a month than I was. His job specifications did not require that he could read or write. They only required that he could push a lawn mower and rake leaves.
>
> *Hospital secretary, quoted in Willborn (1989, p. 1)*

The wage gap between women and men has decreased in the past 10 years, from a female-male earnings ratio of around 60% in the early 1980s to nearly 70% in 1991 (see Table 16.1). Yet, with women who hold full-time jobs

TABLE 16.1 Median Annual Earnings for Year-Round, Full-Time Workers, by Sex: 1951-1991

Year	*Earnings (1991 $)*		*Women's Median Earnings as a % of Males'*
	Women	*Men*	
1951	8,865	13,865	63.9
1955	10,146	15,866	63.9
1960	11,125	18,301	60.8
1965	12,137	20,238	60.0
1970	13,719	23,108	59.4
1975	13,948	23,714	58.8
1980	13,589	22,587	60.2
1985	14,520	22,486	64.6
1990	15,166	21,177	71.6
1991	15,090	21,601	69.9

SOURCE: U.S. Department of Labor, Women's Bureau (1994).
NOTE: Earnings have all been adjusted by the Consumer Price Index to reflect their buying power in 1991. Thus, changes over time can be interpreted as real changes in buying power.

making only 70% of what men do, the remaining gap is still large (Institute for Women's Policy Research, 1993). This gap cannot be explained by women having less education than men. As Table 16.2 shows, the distribution of women and men across all levels of education is similar (with slightly more men than women at both very low and very high educational levels), but men earn far more at each educational level than women. The sex gap in pay stems from many factors, only some of which are under the control of employers. Discrimination of various types by employers is among the factors causing the gap. Our focus here will be on one very subtle type of wage discrimination—that at issue in "comparable worth" (sometimes called "pay equity"). We begin by contrasting this form of discrimination with other better known types.

Legal Status of Types of Discrimination Affecting Pay

There are three types of sex discrimination that can affect the sex gap in pay: (a) discrimination in hiring or job placement, affecting which jobs

TABLE 16.2 Median Earnings of Full-Time, Year-Round Workers, by Sex and Education Completed: 1992

	Women		*Men*	
Years of School Completed	*Median Earnings ($)*	*% of Employed Women at This Education Level*	*Median Earnings ($)*	*% of Employed Men at This Education Level*
Less than 9th grade	12,176	2.4	16,980	3.9
9th to 12th grade (no diploma)	13,760	5.4	21,179	6.6
High school graduate	18,648	36.4	26,766	32.9
Some college (no degree)	21,987	19.4	31,413	18.0
Associate degree	24,849	8.7	32,349	7.2
Bachelor's degree or more	31,378	27.6	43,855	31.3

SOURCE: U.S. Bureau of the Census (1993).
NOTE: All figures pertain to employed persons 25 years of age or older.

women and men work in; (b) wage discrimination, in which women and men are paid differently even though they work in the same job; and (c) the distinct type of wage discrimination at issue in comparable worth, in which the sex of the typical worker in a job affects the pay employers set for all workers in the job. Federal legislation prohibits the first two types of discrimination. The third, comparable worth discrimination, perhaps because it is so subtle, remains legal in the United States.

The first type of discrimination, discrimination in hiring or job placement, affects the sex gap in pay whenever employers won't hire or promote women into better-paying jobs simply because of their sex. This type of discrimination is prohibited by Title VII of the 1964 Civil Rights Act, which forbids discrimination in hiring, benefits, and other personnel decisions, on the basis of sex, race, color, national origin, or religion, by employers with 15 or more employees (Kay, 1988). Executive Order 11246 (affirmative action), which affects organizations that sell goods or services to the federal government or get federal grants or aid, also has the goal of ensuring women and minorities the right to enter higher-paying positions if they have the qualifications. The executive order requires these employers to take proactive steps to recruit, hire, and promote qualified women and minorities (Kay, 1988).

The second type of discrimination, wage discrimination within a job, occurs when women and men are in the same job and are doing the same work, but do not receive the same pay. This is what people commonly call "lack of equal pay for equal work." The Equal Pay Act of 1963 made this illegal. It prohibits employers from paying men more than women (or vice versa) when they are doing the same work, unless the pay difference is because of differences between the individual men and women in question in their seniority, merit, quality or quantity of production, or some factor other than sex (Kay, 1988). Title VII of the Civil Rights Act of 1964 also prohibits this (among many other forms of) discrimination.

But this prohibition of wage discrimination *within* jobs can only have a limited effect on the overall sex gap in pay because women and men are often not in the same jobs. In the United States and most other nations, jobs show a substantial degree of sex segregation. Many occupations are predominantly female—for example, secretaries, child care workers, nurses, elementary school teachers, and dental hygienists. Other occupations are almost entirely male-segregated enclaves—for example, pilots, engineers, fire fighters, and unskilled laborers. Although segregation has decreased somewhat since about 1970 as more women have moved into male-dominated fields such as law, medicine, engineering, and management, it is still quite pervasive. An index of segregation shows that for each occupation to have the same sex composition as the labor force as a whole, over 60% of men and/or women would have to change occupations (Blau, 1988; England, 1992). If very detailed job categories are used, segregation is shown to be even more pervasive. Because of this extensive job segregation by sex, a large sex gap in pay can persist even when women receive equal pay for equal work in the same job, because men and women are rarely in the same jobs and predominantly male jobs generally pay more.

Federal legislation prohibiting lack of equal pay for equal work in the same job does not do anything about the inequity the woman quoted at the beginning of this chapter is complaining about—that as a medical secretary she earns much less than a groundskeeper. Although it would be illegal (under Title VII's prohibition of hiring and placement discrimination) for her employer not to let her compete for the groundskeeper job, once she has taken the job of medical secretary, no equal pay legislation requires the employer to pay her job as much as a predominantly male job—even if her job requires more education and skill. The secretary's complaint of discrimination is based on the idea that she is being paid less than the groundskeeper despite the fact that her work is more demanding in many ways. Her complaint embodies the third type of discrimination, the type at issue in comparable worth. Proponents of comparable worth argue that equal pay should be given to work of equal value (and unequal pay to work of unequal value). Failure to do this permits sex discrimination, because jobs often pay less not because of a difference in skill level or work conditions but simply because the jobs are filled by women.

In a number of court cases, plaintiffs have tried to get federal courts to treat this type of discrimination as a violation of Title VII of the Civil Rights Act since this law contains very general language about prohibiting sex discrimination in any of the terms of employment. To date, however, the federal appellate courts have not accepted this interpretation of the law, arguing that requiring comparable worth was not the intent of Congress. It is only where there is a "smoking gun" that the between-job pay inequity in comparable worth has been interpreted by the courts as a violation of Title VII (England, 1992). An example of a smoking gun would be a memo in which an employer explicitly stated that one job was being paid less than another because it was filled by women, and not for any other reason. By contrast, statistical proofs with no smoking gun are permitted in hiring-discrimination cases. Because employers are seldom stupid enough to write smoking-gun memos, in effect there is no legal redress for the sort of discrimination at issue in comparable worth.

The Subtlety of Comparable Worth Comparisons

The idea behind comparable worth is simple. It is that the pay level of a job should not be affected by the sex of those doing the work, but it may be affected by the demands of the job. Despite the simplicity of this principle, comparable worth discrimination is a very subtle form of sex discrimination that is invisible to most people. The subtlety and invisibility may be because people seldom make comparisons between the pay in "female" and "male" jobs.

A proportional definition of justice underlies the principle of comparable worth. According to proportional justice, a situation is just if the ratio of a person's (or group's) rewards to inputs is equal to the ratio for a "comparison other" (Adams, 1965). A *comparison other* refers to any person or group to whom the first person or group is compared. One theory in social psychology states that this conception underlies many judgments about what reward distributions are just (Adams, 1965). For example, many people believe that jobs requiring more education should pay more because, to qualify for these jobs, workers have to expend the effort and cost to obtain the education. The higher pay makes rewards proportional with the inputs of effort and cost that education requires. A similar argument is sometimes made for jobs that require more responsibility or effort or involve more danger.

If most people believe in "proportional justice," then why don't people notice that many predominantly female occupations pay much less than male occupations requiring a similar (or even smaller) amount of inputs such as education, training, or effort? And why don't they question such injustice? Researchers in social psychology suggest an explanation for this blind spot. A clue comes from their studies of the sorts of individuals, groups, and positions to which people usually compare their own situation. Similarity is the general principle that has been found to affect the selection of comparison others (Major, 1989). We tend to make comparisons between phenomenon that are similar. Thus, men and women generally compare themselves with others in the same job, or a job that is very similar—not only in terms of amount of education, effort, skill, or difficulty involved but in terms of the types of tasks done and perhaps the sex of those holding the job. Given extensive sex segregation, this means that women in predominantly female jobs will usually compare their pay to others in the same or a similar job that is also filled by women, and men in male jobs will compare their pay to that of others in the same job they hold or other male jobs. In addition, the similarity principle means that women are likely to compare themselves mostly to other women and men to other men. Again, this makes it less likely that the pay of women in mostly female jobs will ever be compared to that of men in mostly male jobs. In both these ways, the similarity principle mitigates against comparisons *between* male and female jobs. As a result, many employers, the public, and even workers themselves rarely draw the conclusion that lack of equal pay for jobs of comparable worth is unjust. Until relevant comparisons are made, comparable worth discrimination goes unnoticed. With this type of discrimination seldom noticed and not against the law, its prevalence is not surprising.

Prevalence of Violations of the Principle of Comparable Worth

The quote with which we opened, featuring the secretary paid much less than a groundskeeper whose job does not require literacy, is not an isolated example of comparable worth discrimination. When relevant comparisons *are* made between female and male occupations, female occupations are often shown to be relatively underpaid. Consider some further examples: Women workers for the city of San Jose discovered that secretaries, most of whom had high school degrees and some years of college, were generally earning less than workers in male jobs that required no more than an eighth-grade education, including men who washed cars for the city (Blum, 1991). Nurses (with their science- and math-intensive college degrees) sued the city of Denver because their jobs paid less than male jobs such as tree trimmer and sign painter (Blum, 1991). The California School Employees Association complained that the largely female job category of school librarian (often requiring a master's degree) paid less than custodians and groundskeepers, predominately male jobs requiring no more than a high school degree (Steinberg, 1990). In each of these cases, the workers in the largely female jobs had made the comparisons between male and female jobs and were shocked by the injustice of the pay differences.

But even a long list of examples does not tell us how widespread this type of discrimination really is. Researchers have used two types of studies, those using national data and job evaluation studies for a single employer, to determine the prevalence of comparable worth discrimination.

Studies using national data have shown that the sex composition of a job affects its wages. These analyses include all occupations, using data for a particular nation (most studies have been done for the United States). Of course, such studies must take into account the demands of jobs. If predominantly female jobs pay less than predominantly male jobs *because* women's jobs do not require as much skill, education, or endurance of difficult working conditions, then the pay difference would not be an instance of comparable worth discrimination. National studies investigate the effect of a job's sex composition on its wages through a statistical technique called multiple regression analysis that determines the extent to which each of many factors affects the pay level of jobs. The factors used to explain jobs' pay include requirements of the jobs for various skills, working conditions, and education. After ascertaining statistically how much the differences between occupations' pay levels are explained by differences on these factors, the analysis determines whether the sex composition of the occupation affects its pay over and above what can be explained by the factors mentioned above. Such studies virtually always find that predominantly female occupations pay less (relative to predominantly male occupations) than would be expected considering the demands of the jobs (England, 1992; Sorensen, 1989; Treiman & Hartmann, 1981).

Job evaluation studies differ from national studies in that they focus on jobs within one organization, such as a business or a government. These studies generally use the "point factor system." Jobs are assigned points based on "compensable factors." Compensable factors are characteristics of jobs that employers think should—and do—affect which jobs pay more than others. Most commonly, they relate to the skill, effort, responsibility, and working conditions of each job. The scores on compensable factors are weighted to reflect which compensable factors will count more in pay. For example, the mental effort required by a job may be rated as twice as important (and weighted twice as much) as the physical effort (Beuhring, 1989). Sometimes the weights are obtained from a statistical analysis of the existing pay system. This is accomplished by working backward from the existing pay and skill demands of jobs to determine the relative importance (weight) of each skill or factor. Other times, employers do not use data, but rather decide a priori which factors they want to weight more heavily. Then each job is given a total point score—the sum of its score on each factor times the weight for that factor.

Job evaluation studies commonly find that female jobs pay less than male jobs that were given the same number of points by the job evaluation, indicating a systematic pay bias against female jobs relative to male jobs (England, 1992). Table 16.3 provides an example of results from a job evaluation study done for state government jobs in the state of Washington. The state of Washington used the results of this study to correct (at least partially) such inequities. For selected job titles, the table shows how many points the job received on each of four factors and its total points. For each job, the table also shows the typical pay level in 1984 before adjustments; the pay in 1995, after comparable worth adjustments had been phased in and some across-the-board raises had been given; and whether the job is filled mostly by women or men. If you choose any pair of jobs with approximately the same number of points from the job evaluation, where one job is filled largely by women and the other by men, the male job invariably pays much more before the adjustments. After adjustments, male and female jobs with about the same points had more similar salaries than before, although these gaps were not always entirely closed. For example, a registered nurse's job had a total of 345 points compared to 175 points for an auto mechanic (Table 16.3). Even though registered nurses' jobs required greater knowledge and skills, mental demands, accountability, and more stressful working conditions, auto mechanics received higher annual salaries ($22,236) than registered nurses ($20,954). However, after the adjustments in 1995 registered nurses made $36,948, and auto mechanics made $29,772. In 1984, both

TABLE 16.3 Selected Results of the Washington State Comparable Worth Study: Job Evaluation Points and Pay Before (1984) and After (1995) Comparable Worth Adjustments

	Job Evaluation Points					*Usual Annual Salary ($) Before Adjustments (1984)*		*Usual Annual Salary ($) After Adjustments (1995)*	
Job Title	*Knowledge and Skills*	*Mental Demands*	*Accountability*	*Working Conditions*	*Total Points on Four Factors*	*Male-Dominated Jobs*	*Female-Dominated Jobs*	*Male-Dominated Jobs*	*Female-Dominated Jobs*
Warehouse worker	61	10	13	13	97	17,030		23,280	
Delivery truck driver	61	10	13	13	97	19,367		28,368	
Laundry worker	61	8	11	20	100		12,276		20,508
Telephone operator	80	13	15	10	118		11,770		20,736
Data entry operator	80	15	20	10	125		13,051		21,228
Intermediate clerk typist	92	17	23	0	132		12,161		21,996
Library technician	106	23	23	0	152		13,963		23,280
Licensed practical nurse	106	26	30	13	175		14,069		28,716
Auto mechanic	106	26	30	13	175	22,236		29,772	
Maintenance carpenter	122	30	30	15	197	22,970		30,468	
Secretary	122	35	40	0	197		14,867		23,556
Chemist	160	53	53	11	277	25,625		34,044	
Civil engineer	160	53	70	0	283	25,115		37,572	
Computer systems analyst	184	70	70	0	324	24,019		34,044	
Registered nurse	184	61	80	20	345		20,954		36,948
Librarian	212	80	61	0	353		21,969		32,400

SOURCE: Data provided by Helen Remick, University of Washington, Affirmative Action Office, 1992 and 1996.
NOTE: Annual salary is the midpoint of the range of pay for that position. Changes between 1984 and 1995 reflect comparable worth adjustments, which were phased in over 7 years, as well as across-the-board raises.

licensed practical nurses' jobs and auto mechanics' jobs had a total of 175 points; however, auto mechanics were paid $8,167 more than licensed practical nurses. After the comparable worth adjustments, the wage gap decreased. Auto mechanics were paid $29,772, which is $1,056 more than licensed practical nurses were paid ($28,716).

Implementing Comparable Worth Wage Policies

Job evaluation studies not only reveal comparable worth discrimination, they are also the primary method used to remedy the discrimination. Comparable worth wage policies are commonly implemented through the point-factor system that we just described. Unfortunately, gender bias can be incorporated into the very job evaluation systems being used to reduce inequity. A more detailed look at the point-factor system will demonstrate its usefulness to eliminate comparable worth bias as well as its ability to build gender bias into the system used to set job pay levels.

Using the point-factor system of job evaluation involves five basic steps that are usually performed by managers or outside consultants. (Other workers could be included in the evaluation process as well, but this is rarely the case.) In the first step, written descriptions of each job are assembled (Beatty & Beatty, 1984). The job descriptions include the actual tasks performed in each job, as well as the skills, effort, responsibilities, and working conditions associated with each job. The descriptions may also include time typically spent on various tasks. Bias can enter at this stage if the people describing the jobs do not include some of the skills demanded in women's jobs. For example, women's jobs commonly involve "emotional labor," which both benefits the organization and entails effort on the part of the worker (Hochschild, 1983). If emotional labor is overlooked in job descriptions, female jobs may be undervalued because no credit can be given for a skill that is not in the job descriptions.

Once a description of each job is written, the next step is to choose the compensable factors and rate each job on these factors. Again, bias can enter into evaluations at this step if the compensable factors that are selected are those more typical of male jobs than female jobs. For example, more female jobs than male jobs involve "people skills." If this type of skill is not counted as a compensable factor (and this is often the case), neither male nor female jobs will be compensated for this element. However, because female jobs require more of this type of skill, this omission will lower the points given to the average female job more than to the typical male job. Another type of bias enters this step if evaluators give women's jobs fewer points than they deserve on one or more factors. This would be a fairly overt form of bias in which an evaluator gives fewer points on a given factor to a female job than a male job, even though the two job descriptions read as if the jobs require an equal amount of the factor in question.

In the third step, evaluators decide how to weight each factor. Whether the weights are set by a statistical analysis of current pay practices or by a priori notions of which factors are more important, the result may be that factors emphasized in male jobs are given heavier weights. For example, responsibility for a budget (more common in jobs men hold) may be weighted more heavily than responsibility for the well-being of many clients or students (more common in jobs held by women). If so, this lowers the total points given to female jobs.

In the fourth step of the job evaluation process, the total points for each job are calculated based on the sum of points on each factor, multiplied by the appropriate weight. The final step of a job evaluation process uses the point scores for jobs to determine the pay. Often, a scattergram is drawn in which the total points assigned a job (on the horizontal axis) is plotted against its current wage. (Because the pay for a given job can vary within a band, often the midpoint of the band is used.) The plotted points tend to cluster around a line because there tends to be a positive relationship between the jobs' total points and their pay. Those jobs that fall above the best-fitting line, called the policy line or pay line, pay more for their number of points (have a higher pay to total point ratio) than those jobs falling below the line. When firms have not previously used job evaluation to set pay, and a job evaluation study is done, the usual finding is that female jobs fall under the pay line. This means that they pay less than male jobs receiving the same points from the evaluation. Of course, if the job evaluation has been biased against female jobs in any of the ways described above, then the job evaluation's estimate of how much the pay in female jobs should be raised to bring them to parity with male jobs evaluated as worth the same will be too small.

If employers are doing a job evaluation to identify and eradicate comparable worth discrimination (often, they have other reasons to use job evaluation), they may use the results to adjust wages. One way to make wages more equitable is to raise the wages of those jobs falling below the pay line. It is rare for employers to lower existing wages of workers although they may target jobs above the pay line for slower wage increases.

What Has Been Done and Can Be Done to Promote Comparable Worth

A variety of comparable worth bills has been introduced in the U.S. Congress since 1980 (Bureau of National Affairs, 1981; Paul, 1989). They range from comprehensive measures that would prohibit this sort of discrimination by any employers in the nation to more limited bills that would mandate a study of the pay system for federal government workers. None of the bills has survived to become law, however. None has even made it out of committees for a floor vote. Comparable worth discrimination will only become illegal for most employers if there is new legislation at the federal or state levels prohibiting it.

The one type of legislative action that has been successful at the state level is passage of bills that mandate comparable worth principles be used to set pay in state government jobs. Somewhat less than half of all states have done job evaluation studies and then implemented comparable worth pay adjustments where female jobs have been found underpaid due to discrimination (National Committee on Pay Equity, 1989; Sorensen, 1994). In virtually every state where such studies have been done, they have revealed systematic underpayment of female jobs. The job evaluation done by the state of Washington (see Table 16.3) is an example of such an effort. But because these adjustments only affect those who work for government agencies, they have had a limited effect on the overall sex gap in pay among workers in those states because most people work in the private sector (Blum, 1991; Lowe & Wittig, 1989). Not including Minnesota, which has mandated pay equity adjustments at the local level, over 90 counties, cities, and school districts have either implemented pay equity plans or made comparable worth adjustments (Cook, 1985, 1986; National Committee on Pay Equity, 1989). Many of these localities are in California (e.g., Long Beach, Los Angeles, San Jose, Santa Cruz), but cities as diverse as Colorado Springs, Spokane, Minneapolis, and Chicago have also implemented comparable worth policies (Cook, 1985, 1986; National Committee on Pay Equity, 1989).[1] Again, however, pay adjustments have affected only public sector workers.

In the private sector, any job evaluation studies focusing on comparable worth adjustments are voluntary at this point: No law requires comparable worth in wage setting in the United States. Many workplaces already use job evaluation studies in decisions about pay; between one half to two thirds of U.S. workers are in jobs where wages are affected by job evaluations

(Belcher, 1974; Schwab, 1984). Yet the job evaluations are seldom used to ensure equal pay for male and female jobs given the same number of points by a job evaluation. One way employers avoid equal pay is by doing a separate job evaluation study for each job group in the company. One common strategy is to compare clerical jobs only to other clerical jobs, managerial jobs only to other managerial jobs, and blue-collar jobs only with other blue-collar jobs. In this way, there is no comparison between male and female jobs (Treiman & Hartmann, 1981). Comparable worth proponents endorse such evaluations to eradicate gender bias in setting wages.

In contrast to the United States, comparable worth legislation has been enacted in half of the jurisdictions in Canada, a majority of which require that employers in both public and private sectors set the relative job pay levels in accordance with comparable worth standards (Gunderson, 1989).

Despite the lack of federal legislation making comparable worth discrimination illegal for all employers in the United States, awareness of the issue sometimes helps employee groups in women's jobs to push for wage increases. Unions representing workers in predominantly female jobs have used evidence of comparable worth discrimination in their negotiations with some employers (Lowe & Wittig, 1989). Knowledge of comparable worth discrimination among the women (and the few men) in predominantly female jobs can be a powerful force for political organizing; such action led to a strike in San Jose and a lawsuit in San Diego (Blum, 1991). Occasionally, employers voluntarily undertake job evaluation with the intention of setting pay equal for male- and female-dominated jobs of comparable worth.

The Pros and Cons of Comparable Worth

The basic argument for laws that would mandate comparable worth in wage setting is that it is simple justice. If the wages in women's jobs are low simply because the jobs are filled by women rather than because of greater demands in male jobs, this is discrimination. Such practices are as unfair as discrimination in hiring or unequal pay for equal work in the same job, both of which Congress decided to make illegal. Another argument in favor of comparable worth is that women are spending more of their lives in paid employment today than in past decades. This discrimination, then, affects more people now than in the past when fewer women were employed. Also, an increasing proportion of women are single mothers who provide the major or sole financial support for their children. The pay increases could thus bring many children out of poverty. Finally, if the bargaining power of husbands and wives is affected by their relative earnings, by raising women's pay, comparable worth would make marriages more egalitarian.

The most frequent argument against comparable worth is that wages should be set by the free market rather than by the government (Paul, 1989). Of course, proponents of comparable worth do not propose that the government should stipulate a wage that employers must pay for each job title. Rather, they argue for laws mandating that employers take steps to ensure that the relative wages they pay in various jobs are not systematically biased against predominantly female jobs. Otherwise, employers should be held legally accountable if plaintiffs can prove that such bias exists. But for some critics, even this is too much governmental regulation.

To put the issue in perspective, many current laws put certain limits on the decisions employers can make. This is true of minimum-wage laws, the Equal Pay Act that prohibits sex discrimination in wages among those doing the same job, and Title VII of the Civil Rights Act (which makes many forms of race and sex discrimination illegal). Thus, unless one opposes all these laws, the issue is not whether government should regulate employment relations but which kinds of regulation are warranted. We think comparable worth legislation is necessary because the pervasiveness of such discrimination has been well documented by research.

A related argument against comparable worth states that employers do not control what wage they pay a particular job. Instead, they have no choice but to pay "market wages"—the going rate in the overall labor market for a given job. Economists sometimes make this argument. According to the most orthodox version of neoclassical economic theory, wages are determined by supply and demand in a competitive labor market. Because employers are in competition with each other, they must pay at least the going rate in a given job or no one will work for them. In this view, employers cannot pay less than the going wage, and they will not pay more because they want to maximize profits.

This view of how labor markets work ignores discrimination, however, by claiming that market forces will eliminate discrimination in the long run. (The theory also does not say how long the long run is, and it may be very long.) But if there is discrimination of various types in the labor market, this discrimination will affect the market wages. The going rate in various jobs will be lower relative to skill levels in female jobs. According to national and job evaluation studies, the effect of occupational sex composition on wages suggests that discrimination *is* occurring and *is* affecting market wages. If discrimination has affected the wage many employers are willing to pay in an occupation because the workers are women, then the market wage itself embodies discrimination (England, 1992; Grune, 1984; Treiman & Hartmann, 1981).

Employers' different responses to shortages in male and female occupations provide further evidence that a gender-neutral picture of "supply and demand" is not the whole story. When there is a shortage of employees in a male occupation, the wage is often raised. But when it is a female occupation, often greater effort is expended to find a new source of cheap labor rather than raising pay. For example, U.S. hospitals have complained of a shortage of nurses for over two decades but have often imported foreign nurses instead of raising pay (Grune, 1984). In our view, when market wages embody discrimination, governmental regulation is needed to rid the market of such inequity.

Another argument against comparable worth states that it is the segregation of women in "women's jobs," not the lower payment of such jobs, that is the real problem. Our response to this is that discriminatory barriers that keep women out of "men's jobs" *and* the discriminatory pay in women's jobs at issue in comparable worth are *both* real problems and deserve legal remedies. If it is wrong for sex to affect whether one will be hired in a job, then it is also wrong for the sex of job incumbents to affect the pay offered in the job. Both arguments flow from a simple principle of nondiscrimination. One should not have to change jobs (with all the attendant costs of new training and possibly losing a pension or health benefits) to escape a discriminatory wage.

A final argument against comparable worth policies is that they will be too costly for employers. This is why many employers oppose comparable worth proposals. (Of course, employers and their lobbyists also opposed all existing antidiscrimination legislation, including the Equal Pay Act, but they have learned to live with it.) Opponents argue that the resulting costs will hurt both employers and the economy as a whole. That is, if employers pass on any increased labor costs to consumers by raising the prices of goods, this may cause inflation and make American products more expensive and less competitive in international markets. Opponents of comparable worth also maintain that governmental enforcement mechanisms would be expensive. One response to this complaint is simply to say that if comparable worth is a matter of justice, costs should be irrelevant (Williams & Kessler, 1984). Another response is that the costs are surprisingly low. In states that have implemented comparable worth wage adjustments for government workers, the costs have usually been somewhere in the range of 1% to 9% of the payroll budget (Sorensen, 1994).

Conclusion

There is strong evidence from national data and job evaluation studies that compared to jobs filled largely by men, jobs filled largely by women are systematically underpaid relative to their demands for skill, effort, responsibility, education, and difficult working conditions. This discrimination contributes to the sex gap in pay. It directly affects millions of women (and the fewer number of men in predominantly female jobs). It indirectly affects the spouses and children in the families of those discriminated against.

Yet the United States has no comprehensive legislation prohibiting this form of discrimination. Over 30 years ago, when the Equal Pay Act and the Civil Rights Act were passed, Congress outlawed two types of sex discrimination. Congress decided that sex should not affect pay differences among people doing the same work and that sex should not affect hiring decisions. Instead, qualifications should govern pay and hiring. Comparable worth policies would extend this simple principle of nondiscrimination to decisions employers make about the relative pay of different jobs. Pay differences among jobs could be based on factors measuring the demands of the job, applied consistently across all jobs, but the sex of those holding the job should not be a consideration. Unfortunately, however, this subtle but pervasive type of sex discrimination remains prevalent today.

Note

1. Updated information on the status of comparable worth in individual cities can be obtained from the National Committee on Pay Equity, 1201 16th Street, N.W., Suite 411, Washington, DC 20036.

References

Adams, J. S. (1965). Inequity in social exchange. In L. Berkowitz (Ed.), *Advances in experimental social psychology: Vol. 2* (pp. 267-299). New York: Academic Press.

Beatty, R. W., & Beatty, J. R. (1984). Some problems with contemporary job evaluation systems. In H. Remick (Ed.), *Comparable worth and wage discrimination* (pp. 59-78). Philadelphia: Temple University Press.

Belcher, C. W. (1974). *Compensation administration.* Englewood Cliffs, NJ: Prentice Hall.

Beuhring, T. (1989). Incorporating employee values in job evaluation. *Journal of Social Issues, 45,* 169-189.

Blau, F. (1988, December). *Occupational segregation by gender: A look at the 1980s.* Paper presented at the annual meetings of the American Economic Association, New York.

Blum, L. (1991). *Between feminism and labor: The significance of the comparable worth movement.* Berkeley: University of California Press.

Bureau of National Affairs. (1981). *The comparable worth issue.* Washington, DC: Author.

Cook, A. H. (1985). *Comparable worth: A case book of experiences in states and localities.* Manoa: University of Hawaii at Manoa, Industrial Relations Center.

Cook, A. H. (1986). *Comparable worth: A case book . . . 1986 supplement.* Manoa: University of Hawaii at Manoa, Industrial Relations Center.

England, P. (1992). *Comparable worth: Theories and evidence.* New York: Aldine de Gruyter.

Grune, J. A. (1984). Pay equity is a necessary remedy for wage discrimination. In U.S. Commission on Civil Rights (Ed.), *Comparable worth: Issue for the 80's: A consultation of the U.S. Commission on Civil Rights* (pp. 165-176). Washington, DC: U.S. Commission on Civil Rights.

Gunderson, M. (1989). Implementation of comparable worth in Canada. *Journal of Social Issues, 45,* 209-222.

Hochschild, A. R. (1983). *The managed heart: Commercialization of human feeling.* Berkeley: University of California Press.

Institute for Women's Policy Research. (1993). *The wage gap: Women's and men's earnings* (Briefing paper). Washington, DC: Author.

Kay, H. H. (1988). *Text, cases, and materials on sex-based discrimination* (3rd ed.). St. Paul, MN: West.

Lowe, R. H., & Wittig, M. A. (1989). Comparable worth: Individual, interpersonal, and structural considerations. *Journal of Social Issues, 45,* 223-246.

Major, B. (1989). Gender differences in comparisons and entitlement: Implications for comparable worth. *Journal of Social Issues, 45,* 99-115.

National Committee on Pay Equity. (1989). *Pay equity activity in the public sector, 1979-1989.* Washington, DC: Author.

Paul, E. F. (1989). *Equity and gender: The comparable worth debate.* New Brunswick, NJ: Transaction Books.

Schwab, D. P. (1984). Using job evaluation to obtain pay equity. In U.S. Commission on Civil Rights (Ed.), *Comparable worth: Issue for the 80's: A consultation of the U.S. Commission on Civil Rights* (pp. 83-92). Washington, DC: U.S. Commission on Civil Rights.

Sorensen, E. (1989). The wage effects of occupational sex composition: A review and new findings. In M. A. Hill & M. R. Killingsworth (Eds.), *Comparable worth: Analyses and evidence* (pp. 57-79). Ithaca, NY: Industrial and Labor Relations Press.

Sorensen, E. (1994). *Comparable worth: Is it a worthy policy?* Princeton, NJ: Princeton University Press.

Steinberg, R. (1990). Social construction of skill: Gender, power, and comparable worth. *Work and Occupations, 17,* 449-482.

Treiman, D. J., & Hartmann, H. I. (1981). *Women, work, and wages: Equal pay for jobs of equal value.* Washington, DC: National Academy Press.

U.S. Bureau of the Census. (1993). *Money income of households, families, and persons in the United States: 1992* (Current population reports, Series P-60, No. 184). Washington, DC: Government Printing Office.

U.S. Department of Labor, Women's Bureau. (1994). *1993 handbook on women workers: Trends and issues.* Washington, DC: Government Printing Office.

Willborn, S. L. (1989). *A secretary and a cook: Challenging women's wages in the courts of the United States and Great Britain.* Ithaca, NY: Industrial Labor Relations Press.

Williams, R. E., & Kessler, L. L. (1984). *A closer look at comparable worth: A study of the basic questions to be addressed in approaching pay equity.* Washington, DC: National Foundation for the Study of Equal Employment Policy.

Epilogue: The Mermaid

There's these three guys and they're out having a relaxing day fishing. Out of the blue, they catch a mermaid who begs to be set free in return for granting each of them a wish. One of the guys just doesn't believe it, and says: "OK, if you can really grant wishes, then double my IQ." The mermaid says: "Done." Suddenly, the guy starts reciting Shakespeare flawlessly and analyzing it with extreme insight.

The second guy is so amazed he says to the mermaid: "Triple my IQ." The mermaid says, "Done." The guy starts to spout all the mathematical solutions to problems that have been stumping all the scientists of varying fields, including physics and chemistry.

The last guy is so enthralled with the changes in his friends that he says to the mermaid: "Quintuple my IQ." The mermaid looks at him and says: "You know, I normally don't try to change people's minds when they make a wish, but I really wish you'd reconsider." The guy says: "Nope. I want you to increase my IQ times five, and if you don't do it, I won't set you free."

"Please," begs the mermaid, "You don't know what you're asking . . . it'll change your entire view on the universe . . . won't you ask for something else? . . . a million dollars, anything?" But no matter what the mermaid said, the guy insisted on having his IQ increased by five times its usual power. So the mermaid sighed and said, "Done."

And he became a woman.

Index

About the Contributors

Carolyn J. Aman is a Ph.D. candidate in sociology at the University of Arizona, where she also received a master's degree in sociology. Her research focuses on gender and labor markets and social psychology. Her dissertation uses an experimental study and statistical analyses to explore issues relating to comparable worth. In 1996 she received the Sally Hacker Dissertation Award from the Sex and Gender Section of the American Sociological Association.

Deborah Ware Balogh is Professor of Psychological Science and Coordinator of Teaching Assistant Development at Ball State University. Her area of teaching and research specialization is adult psychopathology, with concentrations in vulnerability to schizophrenia and personality disorders. In addition to her contributions in the psychopathology literature, she has coauthored—with Arno F. Wittig, David V. Perkins, and Bernard E. Whitley, Jr.—*The Ethics of Teaching: A Casebook,* a guide for instructors that offers suggestions for dealing with ethically problematic situations in the college classroom.

Nijole V. Benokraitis is Professor of Sociology in the Division of Criminology, Criminal Justice, and Social Policy at the University of Baltimore. She has published a number of articles and book chapters on such topics as institutional racism, displaced homemakers, sex discrimination, fathers in two-earner families, and family policy. She has published *Marriages and Families: Changes, Choices, and Constraints* (2nd ed.) and has coauthored, with Joe R. Feagin, *Affirmative Action and Equal Opportunity: Action, Inaction, and Reaction* (1978) and *Modern Sexism: Blatant, Subtle, and Covert Discrimination* (1995, 2nd ed.). She is currently working on the fourth edition of *Seeing Ourselves: Classic, Contemporary, and Cross-Cultural Readings in Sociology* (coedited with John Macionis, 1997). She has served as a consultant in the areas of sex and race discrimination to women's commissions, business groups, community colleges and universities, and programs of the federal government.

Regina F. Bento is Assistant Professor of Management at the Merrick School of Business, University of Baltimore. She received a Ph.D. in management from Massachusetts Institute of Technology and an M.D. degree, with a specialization in psychiatry, from the Federal University of Rio de Janeiro, Brazil. Her research has been published in a number of periodicals including the *Journal of Managerial Psychology, Human Resource Management,* and *Information and Management.* She has also published a chapter on incentive pay and organizational culture in *Performance Measurement, Evaluation and Incentives* (1992). She has served as a consultant for corporations, hospitals, and social service organizations. Her current research focuses on the barriers and opportunities for cooperation in the workplace in a variety of contexts including MIS experts and health care professions.

Judith E. Owen Blakemore is currently Associate Professor of Psychology and Department Chair in the Department of Psychological Sciences at Indiana University–Purdue University in Fort Wayne, Indiana. She received her Ph.D. in developmental psychology from Northern Illinois University. She has published several articles on gender role development, particularly on children's interactions with infants, in journals such as *Child Development, Developmental Psychology,* and *Sex Roles.* Her current research explores preschool children's attitudes about violations of gender-appropriate behavior. Her professional memberships include the Society for Research in Child Development, the American Psychological Association, the Society for the Psychological Study of Social Issues, and Sigma Xi.

Judith A. DiLorio is currently Assistant Vice Chancellor for Academic Affairs and Associate Professor of Sociology at Indiana University–Purdue University in Fort Wayne, Indiana. She received a Ph.D. in sociology from the Ohio State University and teaches courses in gender and sex inequality. She has served as Director of the Women's Studies Program at Indiana University–Purdue University and was instrumental in establishing a bachelor of arts in women's studies degree. She has published articles in the *Journal of Contemporary Ethnography, Journal of Peace and Change, Arena Review,* and several anthologies on the sociology of gender roles. Her current research interests focus on feminists in academic administration and changes in the division of domestic labor among U.S. households.

Paula England is Professor of Sociology at the University of Arizona. She has published numerous articles on gender and labor markets, drawing on sociological and economic theory and using quantitative analysis of national data. She is the author of two books, *Households, Employment, and Gender* (with George Farkas, 1986) and *Comparable Worth: Theories and Evidence* (1992), and editor of two anthologies, *Industries, Firms, and Jobs* (with George Farkas, 1988) and *Theory on Gender/Feminism on Theory* (1993). She has testified as an expert witness in a number of Title VII discrimination cases and in a hearing on comparable worth held by the U.S. Commission on Civil Rights.

David L. Fairchild is Professor of Philosophy, Chair of the Philosophy Department, and NCAA Athletics Compliance Coordinator at Indiana University–Purdue University at Fort Wayne, Indiana. He received a Ph.D. in philosophy from Northwestern University. The author of 35 articles and essays published in professional journals, his research interests are centered on ethical issues in sport, logic, and critical thinking. His sports research has been published in the *Journal of the Philosophy of Sport, Quest, Journal of Thought,* and the *Fédération Internationale Du Sport Universitaire.* He is past President of the Philosophic Society for the Study of Sport, served on the editorial review board for the journal, and is currently the society's archivist. His fifth book, *Living the Questions: A Philosopher's Introduction to Critical Thinking,* was published in 1996.

Joe R. Feagin is currently the Graduate Research Professor in Sociology at the University of Florida. For 30 years he has done extensive research on racial and gender discrimination issues, which is reflected in *Racial and Ethnic Relations* (5th ed., 1996), coauthored with Clairece Booher Feagin; *Living With Racism:*

The Black Middle Class Experience (1994), coauthored with Melvin Sikes; *White Racism: The Basics* (1995), coauthored with Hernán Vera; and *The Agony of Education: Black Students at White Colleges and Universities* (1996), coauthored with Hernán Vera and Nikitah Imani. An earlier book, *Ghetto Revolts* (1973), coauthored with Hernán Vera, was nominated for a Pulitzer Prize, and *Living With Racism* recently won the Gustavus Myers Center's Outstanding Human Rights Book Award. He has served as Scholar-in-Residence at the U.S. Commission on Civil Rights. He has also chaired the American Sociological Association's Section on Racial and Ethnic Minorities and is currently a national council member of that association.

Juanita M. Firestone is currently Associate Professor of Sociology at the University of Texas at San Antonio. She received a Ph.D. in sociology from the University of Texas at Austin. She has 10 years of experience in the sociology of gender and the military as well as survey research, quantitative analysis, and computer applications. She has numerous publications, including research on the voting behavior of women in Congress, sexual harassment in the military, and on Hispanic women in Texas. Her teaching and research specializations include gender issues, military sociology, public policy evaluation, social stratification, and research methods. She was Chair of the university's Faculty Senate and is past President and Program Chair of the Women's Caucus of the Southwestern Social Science Association.

Linda Stone Fish is Associate Professor of Family Therapy in the Department of Child and Family Studies at Syracuse University. She received a Ph.D. in marriage and family therapy from Purdue University. She has numerous publications in the areas of inhibited sexual desire, dual-earner families, family therapy theory, and feminist family therapy in such journals as the *Journal of Marital and Family Therapy, American Journal of Orthopsychiatry, Americana Journal of Family Therapy, Journal of Family Psychology,* and *Family Relations.* She has also coauthored a chapter on the Delphi technique, which will be published in *Family Therapy Research: A Handbook of Methods.* Her scholarly work is concentrated in the areas of relationship development and family therapy theory.

Lisa M. Frehill is Assistant Professor of Sociology at New Mexico State University. She received a Ph.D. in sociology (with a minor in systems engineering) from the University of Arizona. With a bachelor's degree in industrial engineering from GMI Engineering and Management Institute (formerly General Motors Institute) and 6 years of experience as an engineer at General Motors Corporation, she has a general research interest in women in male-dominated jobs. Her dissertation used national data sets to examine sex differences in deciding to major and persist in engineering on the undergraduate level. She is completing a project on the portrayals of women and minorities in introductory engineering textbooks. Other current research projects include an analysis of racial occupational segmentation in the late 1800s and early 1900s on the Great Plains.

Melissa Kesler Gilbert is currently on the faculty in women's studies at Portland State University in Oregon and is completing an interdisciplinary doctorate degree in sociology and women's history from Boston College. She has published articles and book chapters on feminist pedagogy and computer-assisted learning, women and retirement, discrimination against women in federal employment, and family-leave policies. Her oral history project on the women who founded the Boston Women's Health Book Collective (authors of the best-selling *Our Bodies, Ourselves*) was the basis of her video documentary, *Something From Inside Me: Esther Rome*. She has received a number of grants for her community-based learning projects, which promote the use of feminist oral history and documentary in the classroom. She also serves as a program consultant and evaluator for women's organizations, service agencies, and health care providers.

Richard J. Harris is Associate Professor of Sociology at the University of Texas at San Antonio. He received a Ph.D. in sociology and demography from Cornell University. He has over 16 years of experience in social demography, demographic techniques, and demography of aging, survey research, and quantitative analysis. He teaches courses in research methods, survey research, and demography. He was Secretary of the General Faculty and University Assembly and founder and coordinator of the Survey Research Laboratory. His research publications include studies on high school dropouts, school finance inequities in Texas, family and occupational changes in Texas, and the economic and social aspects of undocumented migration.

Beth Bonniwell Haslett is Professor of Communications at the University of Delaware. Her teaching and research interests include gender issues in organizations, organizational communication, and management. She is the author of *Communication: Strategic Action in Context,* and coauthor, with F. L. Geis and M. R. Carter, of *Organizational Women: Power and Paradox.* In addition, she has published over 20 articles and given over 50 presentations at national and international conferences. She consults with government and state agencies and businesses in both the private and public sectors on communication and organizational issues. She is currently finishing a book on children's communication and writing another book on organizational communication.

Mary E. Kite is Professor of Psychological Science at Ball State University. She earned a Ph.D. in Social Psychology from Purdue University. Her research interests include gender-associated stereotyping and prejudice. She has served as Chair of the Task Force for Multi-cultural Issues for Division Two of the American Psychological Association and is currently Associate Chair of the Teaching Awards Committee for that division. Reflecting her interest in girls' and women's achievement, she has mentored high school girls as part of a summer science project funded by the National Science Foundation.

Susan Lipman is an honors graduate of the University of Delaware with a double major in Communication and Women's Studies. She was awarded the Edmund S. Glenn Award at the University of Delaware for promoting and working on intercultural understanding. She currently manages a coffee house in Newark, Delaware, and plans to attend law school or graduate school in the future.

Ann Marshall is a Ph.D. candidate in the interdisciplinary Social Science Program at the Maxwell School of Citizenship and Public Affairs at Syracuse University. She received master's degrees in Sociology and in Political Science at the same institution. Her dissertation research is on local political organizing and participation in the National Women's Political Caucus.

Richard C. Monk is Professor of Criminal Justice at Coppin State College. He received a Ph.D. in Sociology from the University of Maryland and has been teaching sociology, criminology, and criminal justice for over 25 years. He has received research grants from the National Endowment for the Humanities and the Bureau of Criminal Justice Statistics. His many publications include the edited books *Taking Sides: Clashing Views on Controversial Issues in Race and Ethnicity* (2nd ed., 1996), *Clashing Views on Crime and Criminology* (4th ed., 1996), and *Structures of Knowing* (1986). He is coauthor, with Joel Henderson, of *Social Theories and Social Policy* (1996). He has served as coeditor of a special issue on police training and violence for the *Journal of Contemporary*

Criminal Justice (August, 1996) and a special issue on race, crime, and criminal justice for the same journal (1992).

Susan B. Murray is a Lecturer in Sociology at San Francisco State University. She received her doctorate from the University of California at Santa Cruz. Her areas of specialization include gender, feminist theory, child care, and violence against women. She has done fieldwork research while working with child care advocacy groups, union organizers, battered women's shelters, rape crisis centers, and other groups working for social justice. She writes that "sociology is my vocation. In my research my goal is to see the world as others see it and to bring these views into critical focus using sociological theory. In my teaching I bring these voices into the classroom and create opportunities for students to experience the places in society that have been obscured from their world view." She has published articles in the *NWSA Journal* and *Gender & Society* and is currently working on a book on child care work as a gendered occupation.

Janice L. Ristock is Associate Professor and Coordinator of the Women's Studies Program at the University of Manitoba. Her research includes abuse in lesbian relationships, feminist social service organizations, and conducting community-based research. She has recently published, with Joan Pennell, *Community Research as Empowerment: Feminist Links, Postmodern Interruptions* and is currently coediting, with Catherine Taylor, *Sexualities and Social Action: Inside the Academy and Out.*

Lynn Hecht Schafran is an attorney specializing in gender discrimination law and Director since 1981 of the National Judicial Education Program to Promote Equality for Women and Men in the Courts, a project of the NOW Legal Defense and Education Fund in cooperation with the National Association of Women Judges. She is a graduate of Smith College and the Columbia University School of Law. She is widely published on the subject of gender bias in the courts and the legal profession and is the author of *Promoting Gender Fairness Through Judicial Education: A Guide to the Issues and Resources.* Her awards include being named a Fellow of the American Bar Association and awarded the first Florence K. Murray Distinguished Service Award of the National Association of Women Judges, the Smith College Medal, the gold medal of the Foundation for Improvement of Justice, and the American Bar Association's Margaret Brent Women Lawyers of Achievement Award.

Yanick St. Jean is Assistant Professor in the Department of Sociology at the University of Nevada. She received a Ph.D. in Sociology from the University of Texas at Austin. She has published a chapter on American attitudes toward Haitians with AIDS in *Normative Social Action: Cross-National and Historical Approaches* (1996), a chapter on black women and sexism/racism in *Living With Sexism: Gendered Oppression in the Late 20th Century* (in press), and an article on sexism and racism in the *Journal of Comparative Family Studies.* She is presently coauthoring a book on the experiences of black women and their families.

Jo Young Switzer has been Vice President and Dean of Academic Affairs at Manchester College, Indiana, since 1993. She is also responsible for academic support services, athletics, the library, and academic computing. She received a doctorate in communication studies at the University of Kansas and has completed the Institute for Educational Management Program at Harvard University. She was a faculty member in the Department of Communication at Indiana University–Purdue University for 9 years. She also taught in the Department of Communication Studies at Manchester College prior to becoming academic dean. A national award-winning teacher, she has coauthored with Jeanne Tessier Barone a textbook, *Interviewing Art and Skill*, and has written several instructors' manuals for college textbooks. She has made numerous presentations on gender issues that affect colleges and universities and serves as a consultant on professional development opportunities for women.

Carolyn I. Wright earned a master's degree in marriage and family therapy, Department of Child and Family Studies, from Syracuse University. She is currently a Ph.D. candidate in the Marriage and Family Therapy Program at Syracuse University. In addition to her work as a medical family therapist, she is the coordinator and clinical supervisor of the Family Therapy Program at St. Joseph's Maternal Child Health Center, an outpatient medical clinic for low-income patients in Syracuse, New York. Her research interests include sexism in health care and the effect of sexism on poor women in particular.